The

PORTABLE

MBA

in

STRATEGY

The Portable MBA Series

The

PORTABLE

MBA

in

STRATEGY

SECOND EDITION

Edited by

Liam Fahey

and

Robert M. Randall

John Wiley & Sons, Inc.

New York • Chichester • Weinheim • Brisbane • Singapore • Toronto

We dedicate this book to our parents—

Michael C. and Veronica Fahey

and

Randolph C. and Ellen Moore Randall—

all of whom were crucially influential.

This book is printed on acid-free paper. ∞

Copyright © 2001 by John Wiley & Sons, Inc. All rights reserved.

Published simultaneously in Canada.

Library of Congress Cataloging-in-Publication Data:

The portable MBA in strategy / [edited by] Liam Fahey, Robert M. Randall. — 2nd ed.
    p. cm.
  Includes bibliographical references index.
  ISBN 0-471-19708-4 (cloth : alk. paper)
  1. Strategic planning. 2. Business planning. I. Fahey, Liam, 1951– II. Randall, Robert M., 1940–

HD30.28.P674 2001
658.4′012—dc21

00-033003

10 9 8 7 6 5 4 3 2 1

Preface

The intent and thrust of the second edition of *The Portable MBA in Strategy* is similar to that of the first edition: to bring the best in thought and practice in the field of strategic management (or business strategy) to the following audiences:

- Managers and others who have an MBA degree and are interested in staying abreast of the field of strategic management.
- Any person working in an organizational setting who is interested in learning about the scope, substance, and processes of strategic management.
- Students, at both the graduate and undergraduate levels, who need a compendium of material from the leading thinkers in the field. This book could serve as a primary or supplementary text in any course related to strategic management.

Although we have retained essentially the same structure for this edition of the book, it incorporates significant changes and improvements:

- Five new chapters extend the scope and coverage of developing and executing strategy.
- Extensive redesign of many chapters reflects current and emerging change in the theory and practice of managing strategy.
- In all chapters, the authors have added the latest analysis methods and modes of implementation, or current company illustrations of "best practice" for strategic management in the e-commerce era.

The contributors to this edition again constitute a select list of outstanding thought leaders. Seventeen contributors are leading professors at the most prestigious business schools in the United States and Europe. Five contributors are innovative consultants. Each contributor is an expert is his or her domain; each has extensive experience working with leading organizations, putting into practice the principles, precepts, and methodologies expounded in each chapter. The consulting work and publications by many of the contributors are internationally recognized. The "About the Authors" section at the end of the book lists their accomplishments in detail.

The Portable MBA in Strategy addresses the following four questions:

1. What is strategic management? What is it that managers do when they engage in strategic management? How and why is strategic management different from other types of management, such as financial management or human resources management? Why is strategic management so important?

2. What is strategy? How does one identify an organization's strategy? How do strategies differ from one organization to another? What are the key differences in strategy across organization levels; for example, corporate and business-unit strategies?

3. What should an organization do when it sets about formulating or changing its strategy? What kinds of analysis should it do? How should it analyze the environment? How should managers analyze their own organization? How can an organization go about identifying, developing, and assessing strategic alternatives? What kinds of analytical methodologies are available?

4. What is involved in implementing strategy? How can managers translate a strategy into action? How can the organization be better managed with a view to executing more efficient and effective strategy? How can strategy development and execution be more tightly linked?

PART ONE: STRATEGY: WINNING IN THE MARKETPLACE

The rationale for investing precious talent and resources to research, analyze, and develop a strategy—no matter how it is refined, communicated, and executed—is to enable an organization to thrive in its external marketplace, and most especially, in the world of customers and rivals. A strategy embodies a set of choices—investments in products, customer segments, and technologies; the functionality and style of offerings and the degree of service; and the selection of target markets and prices—that will enable an organization to profitably attract and sell to customers and then retain them. Without an effective strategy, an organization cannot sow the seeds for financial success in tomorrow's marketplace as well as today's. A strategy must define how an organization can expect to outwit, outmaneuver, and outperform rivals. Without a strategy, an organization will always be at the mercy of its rivals, forever reacting defensively to their initiatives.

Chapter 1 provides an introduction to managing strategy in the marketplace. Chapters 2 through 7 then address strategy from six distinct vantage points: (1) corporate strategy, (2) business unit strategy, (3) global strategy,

(4) small business strategy, (5) digital strategy, and (6) political strategy. Taken together, these chapters comprehensively illustrate the relevance and usefulness of strategy to any business. Obviously, the challenges specific to designing and executing strategy vary greatly across these vantage points.

Chapter 1, "Managing Marketplace Strategy," by Liam Fahey and Robert M. Randall, postulates that the strategy in every organization must aim to simultaneously lay the foundation for tomorrow's success while it strives to outmaneuver and outperform its rivals in today's competitive arena. To achieve this balanced goal, managers must take into account fundamental shifts in the competitive landscape that are common to almost all industries. This chapter briefly outlines three key elements of marketplace strategy—scope, posture, and goals—and shows how these elements can be woven into three distinctly different types of strategy—inventive, renovative, and incremental. It concludes by enumerating critical attributes of strategy.

Chapter 2, "Corporate Strategy: Managing a Set of Businesses," by H. Kurt Christensen, illustrates the choices that managers in multibusiness firms typically confront when they must choose between current and potential businesses: Which businesses should they invest in? Which ones should they withhold investment in or even divest? Which businesses should be divided and then developed and managed as entirely separate businesses? How can synergies be created and fostered across distinct business units or sectors? The chapter examines in some detail three ways a corporation can remodel its set of businesses: internal development, strategic alliances, and divestment.

In Chapter 3, "Business Unit Strategy: The Quest for Competitive Advantage," Anil K. Gupta proposes ways to improve strategy making at the level of an individual business unit in a multibusiness firm, lessons that apply equally well to a large single business organization. He addresses five interrelated tasks central to creating a business unit strategy: (1) setting business unit goals, (2) defining business unit scope, (3) defining the intended bases for competitive advantage, (4) designing the business unit's value chain system, and (5) managing the value chain. The chapter demonstrates how these tasks present a set of interrelated choices.

Chapter 4, "Competing across Locations: Enhancing Competitive Advantage through a Global Strategy," by Michael E. Porter, warns that corporate, business-unit, or small-business strategists are increasingly confronted by opportunities that are not constrained by geographic boundaries, by rivals in many geographic regions, and by customers and suppliers demanding international operations. Thus, any organization hoping to dominate or be a significant leader in a specific product area, or in an industry, must address the issues and challenges inherent in developing and executing a global strategy. Porter provides an analysis framework for understanding the competition between rivals in an international arena. He also explains the importance of location strategy: how companies should decide in what regions of individual countries to locate their home base or one or more operations of their business such as R&D, manufacturing, marketing, or sales.

Chapter 5, "Strategy for the Small Business," by Irene M. Duhaime, highlights the importance of strategy for small businesses with fewer than 500 employees, including start-up enterprises, family-owned businesses (which are often single-product organizations), or privately held companies. Although strategy presents some unique challenges in these organizational settings, small firms nonetheless must continue to grapple with the central strategy issues discussed in prior chapters: What business are they in and how might this change? How should they compete to attract, win, and retain customers? And, what goals should they pursue? This chapter explains how each of these choices is particular to, or different for, various types of small business, such as entrepreneurial start-ups and long-established family businesses.

In Chapter 6, "Digital Strategy," Jeffrey Sampler demonstrates how the Internet and the rapidly emerging electronic economy it has created challenge many of our fundamental ideas about strategy. He outlines the new principles for winning in the digital world. This chapter details how the tidal wave of e-business—through the discontinuous and pervasive change it brings in its wake—represents both a massive opportunity and critical threat to every organization. To affect winning strategies in an Internet-driven world, organizations will have to reexamine, just for starters, the nature and content of their assets, how they can nurture and speed up innovation (the sparkplug of new strategy), and how they can make decisions faster and more intelligently.

In Chapter 7, "Political Strategy: Managing the Political and Social Environment," John F. Mahon, Barbara Bigelow, and Liam Fahey address another fundamental reality of strategy. Devising and executing strategy would be far simpler if only organizations did not have to manage relationships with a broad array of competing external entities as diverse as channels and end-customers, industry and trade associations, governmental agencies and the courts, and social and community and labor groups. Thus, managing these relationships— what organizations now refer to as *political strategy*—presents innumerable threats and opportunities to which strategists at each organizational level must be intimately attuned. Regrettably, political strategy is frequently accorded little prominence in strategic management textbooks, so carefully heed this chapter's demonstration of how political strategy is increasingly critical to the success in the marketplace for corporations, business units, small businesses, and e-businesses.

PART TWO: STRATEGY INPUTS: ANALYZING THE EXTERNAL AND INTERNAL ENVIRONMENTS

All the elements of the changing strategy landscape noted in Chapter 1, as well as the key attributes of strategy described in Chapters 2 through 7, combine to suggest that developing, executing, and monitoring strategy requires a deep and profound understanding of an organization's external and internal environment. In too many organizations, this understanding is not relentlessly explicated, challenged, and refined. The four chapters in Part Two show readers what is involved in analyzing organizations' external and internal environments (and many of the connections between these environments) and demonstrate the direct linkage between such analysis and all facets of developing and executing strategy.

In Chapter 8, "Mapping the Business Landscape," David J. Collis and Pankaj Ghemawat illustrate the wisdom of probably the oldest precept in strategy analysis: Because opportunities and threats can only emerge from change, strategists must identify and evaluate the forces shaping and driving change in and around their competitive domain or industry. They show how to analyze any competitive domain or industry using two distinct but related analysis frameworks—the "five-forces" industry analysis framework and the value net framework. Such industry assessment is an essential constituent of the core environmental analysis for most firms.

Chapter 9, "Macroenvironmental Analysis: Understanding the Environment Outside the Industry," by V.K. Narayanan and Liam Fahey, illustrates how and why every industry—and every business—is shaped and propelled by change in its macroenvironment: the political, social, technological, economic, ecological, and institutional milieu. They show how to scan and monitor project change in each of these six domains within the macroenvironment and how to determine the implications of such change for the firm's strategy.

Chapter 10, "A Strategic Assessment of an Organization's Assets," by Liam Fahey, provides a framework for identifying and assessing all an organization's assets; that is, those resources that an organization possesses or can draw on to use for its economic gain. Key assets typically include financial capital, personnel, physical plant and equipment, knowledge and intellectual property, relationships with external entities, perceptions of external parties (e.g., customers, suppliers, financial institutions), and organizational attributes such as culture and decision-making systems. An inventory of the current stock of these assets, and an analysis of whether an organization is gaining or losing the ones it needs most, always serves as an essential input to strategy development and execution.

In Chapter 11, "Creating and Leveraging Core Competencies," C.K. Prahalad, along with Liam Fahey and Robert M. Randall, demonstrates why an understanding of assets is necessary but not sufficient. Any organization must transform its assets into competencies, that in turn, serve as the source of new business opportunities, and thus support a growth strategy for a multibusiness firm or corporation. This chapter illustrates what core competencies are, what is involved in developing and refining them, and how they can be leveraged to create new competitive space.

PART THREE: STRATEGY MAKING: IDENTIFYING AND EVALUATING STRATEGIC ALTERNATIVES

Most organizations find it extraordinarily difficult to consistently generate and develop strategy alternatives that offer the potential to promote success now and under future conditions. It's daunting to translate analysis of the external and internal environment into opportunities, that is, genuinely new (inventive) strategy alternatives or even extensions of their current strategy. To overcome this difficulty, organizations need to become familiar with the analysis frameworks necessary to develop and assess a range of strategy alternatives.

Chapter 12, "Identifying and Developing Strategy Alternatives," by Marjorie A. Lyles and Liam Fahey shows why identifying and crafting opportunities into genuine strategy alternatives requires considerable skill, creativity, and perseverance. This chapter offers various analytical methodologies to identify and refine strategy alternatives. It emphasizes differences in the approaches that should be adopted by firms depending on whether they seek to generate inventive, renovative, or incremental alternatives. The chapter also draws attention to organizational processes that have proved useful in generating alternatives as well as in preventing managers and other stakeholders from becoming too attached to outmoded strategies.

Chapter 13, "Evaluating Strategy Alternatives," by George S. Day, shows managers how to evaluate the strategy alternatives that their organization generates. Then the author explains the next step: how to rank and prioritize strategy alternatives. Typically, all alternatives cannot and should not be pursued. But which ones merit commitment of the organization's key resources—the attention of its best and brightest leaders? This unavoidable challenge has proven nettlesome in many organizations. And the stakes are high: the cost of bad choices may be the demise of the organization. This chapter details an established framework of analysis—a set of tests in the form of questions—that provides an organization with a systematic and comprehensive means of evaluating and testing strategy alternatives before managers commit to a specific strategic direction.

PART FOUR: MANAGING STRATEGIC CHANGE: LINKING STRATEGY AND ACTION

However elegant and grand their design, strategies that do not get executed cannot enhance organizational performance. Yet, as is evident in all the chapters in Parts One, Two, and Three, creating and executing change in any organization's marketplace strategy simply does not happen unless considerable change occurs within the organization. Setting the stage for implementation are change in the organization's mind-set, operating processes, structure, and decision-making processes. Managing strategic change—redefining how the organization seeks to win in the external marketplace—and managing the organization so that it can change are intimately interrelated.

In Chapter 14, "Strategic Change: How to Realign the Organization to Implement Strategy," Russell A. Eisenstat and Michael Beer tackle a challenge that has bedeviled many organizations' efforts to achieve strategic change—realigning the organization with the intended alteration in strategic direction. Seeking such alignment requires managers to continually diagnose whether the organization possesses the capabilities it needs to achieve its chosen strategy and to determine what must be done if it does not. This chapter lays out a systematic approach to achieving such alignment.

Chapter 15, "Strategic Change: Reconfiguring Operational Processes to Implement Strategy," by Ellen R. Hart, illustrates how and why strategic change increasingly involves reconfiguring the organization's core operating processes—how products are designed and developed, how products are manufactured, how products or services are delivered to customers. Reconfiguring the work is involved in each core process and interconnecting these processes, is central to delivering value to customers. This chapter provides a detailed methodology on how to do it.

In Chapter 16, "Strategic Change: Managing Strategy Making through Planning and Administrative Systems," John H. Grant and Nandini Rajagopalan specify how making and executing strategy should be coordinated throughout the organization using systems for planning and administration. Without coherency among planning processes and related administrative systems, an organization's units—business units, product groups, and functional departments—will push and pull it in conflicting directions. Thus, the role of planning and related administrative systems is to coordinate strategy development and execution. This chapter describes organizational processes designed to achieve integrated and coordinated strategy making.

In Chapter 17, "Strategic Change: Devising a Context-Sensitive Approach to Implementation," Julia Balogun and Veronica Hope-Hailey elaborate an integrated but contingent strategy implementation framework that emphasizes the role of managers as managers of change within and around their organization. They outline a set of interdependent design choices that managers responsible for executing strategy must always consider. Further, they demonstrate how each design choice is always contingent on both the marketplace context in which the intended strategy must win and key contextual features within the organization such as the diversity of its culture and its readiness for change.

In Chapter 18, "There Is No Universal Strategy Formula," Ian Wilson makes a persuasive case that managing strategic change requires that an organization's leaders eschew a simplistic approach to strategy making and instead find a balance between apparent opposites—focusing on the short run versus looking at the long run, achieving sales growth versus controlling costs, meeting market/customer needs versus beating the competition, seeking lower price versus offering higher quality, leading versus following the market, or holding to a strategic vision versus encouraging flexibility in tactical action. Harnessing such opposites with strategies that take a "both/and" approach to change instead of adopting strategies that allow only "either/or" choices can lead to higher quality thinking and action in strategy development and execution.

LIAM FAHEY
ROBERT M. RANDALL

June 2000

Acknowledgments

First and foremost, we want to acknowledge the efforts of the contributors—23 strategic management authorities based in leading universities and consulting firms in the United States and Europe—who worked patiently with us to prepare this second edition of *The Portable MBA in Strategy*. To make this book possible, the contributors distilled and shared their broad experience in applied strategic management and their many years of research. Studious readers will realize why many of the contributors have been honored by leading universities for their outstanding teaching skills.

In addition to the current John Wiley & Sons publishing team and the production team at Publications Development Company of Texas, headed by Nancy Land, we also want to acknowledge the contribution of a former Wiley editor, John Mahaney. In 1992, he invited us to recruit the best strategic thinkers in the world for the first edition of this book. It was a project that drew on our experience as the editors of the strategic management publication *Planning Review*. That first edition of *The Portable MBA in Strategy*, a *Fortune* magazine Book Club selection when it was published in 1994, has since then been translated into French, Chinese, and Portuguese.

All during the editing of this second edition, we were supported by friends from the strategic management editorial community who answered our questions and made suggestions. We appreciate their help.

And finally, by their willingness to share our moments of elation and frustration during the editing process, our family partners have demonstrated world-class patience and understanding, for which they deserve our heartfelt appreciation and worldwide acknowledgment. So, thank you, Pat and Deborah.

Babson Park, Massachusetts   LIAM FAHEY
E-mail: LFahey95@aol.com   ROBERT M. RANDALL
San Francisco, California
E-mail: Randall_Publishing@compuserve.com

Contents

PART ONE

STRATEGY: WINNING IN THE MARKETPLACE

MANAGING MARKETPLACE STRATEGY

1

Liam Fahey

Babson College and
Cranfield University

Robert M. Randall

Randall Publishing

One of the oldest adages in business strategy is "Winning in today's marketplace is never enough." If you've ever questioned its validity, consider the following:

- In the early 1990s, among the companies cited by academic researchers, consultants, and the business press as shining examples of astute strategic management were such leaders in their respective industries as 3M, Avon, Boeing, Coca-Cola, Compaq, CompUSA, Disney, General Motors, Heinz, Kodak, Kellogg, Motorola, Raytheon, Reebok, Sunbeam, Xerox, and Waste Management. Yet, through the late 1990s and into 2000, each company has battled vigorously but sometimes in vain to arrest declining sales growth, sagging profits, and stagnant or deteriorating market share.

- Business periodicals such as *Business Week, Fortune,* and *Forbes,* as well as the business sections in leading daily newspapers, perpetually chronicle the fall from grace of companies that only a few years earlier were launched with apparent unlimited optimism and attained early marketplace success. For example, AutoNation, launched in 1995, created a new model for selling previously owned cars. Its superstores looked like cafes, and contained computer kiosks and child-care centers to lure customers to immense lots; each offered as many as 1,000 late-model cars. Wall Street's projections propelled the firm's share price above $40 by early

1997. By late 1999, the share price had dropped below $10, sales were declining, and stores were being closed. Among the reasons for AutoNation's woes: the emergence of competition from the Internet, improvement in the services and prices offered by traditional dealers, and a leveling off in the prices of new cars. All these factors contributed to much slower sales than forecasted.

- The list of Japanese companies that seemed invisible in the previous decade, but have incurred major declines in their sales and profits in the past five years, reads like a who's who of world industry: Nissan, Honda, Sony, and Mitsubishi, are a few examples.

Every organization must simultaneously lay the foundation for tomorrow's success while it strives to outmaneuver its rivals in today's competitive arena. Accomplishing these two tasks is the prime directive of strategic management. This is so for at least three reasons:

1. The competitive landscape where strategy is put into action, or more broadly, what practitioners, consultants, and academics refer to as the environment in which an organization will earn tomorrow's success, is likely to be quite different from the environment it confronts today. Change comes in the form of new products, new technologies, new competitors, old competitors with new strategies, new regulations, and new ways of communicating (e.g., over the Internet). Xerox Corporation's struggle to adjust to the onslaught of digital technologies, the incessant product introduction of historic competitors such as Canon, the emergence of new competitors, and rapidly changing customer preferences, exemplify how difficult it can be for a large corporation to position itself for the future while producing satisfactory sales and financial performance results. Less precipitous change in the form of changing demographics, social values, and lifestyles, also affects most businesses.

2. To succeed in the environment of tomorrow, the organization itself must undergo significant and sometimes radical change. Rare indeed is the firm that over the past 10 years has not had to discard old ways of developing and marketing products, change core assumptions about how to win in the marketplace, or embark on the tortuous, but exciting process of modifying key elements of its historic culture. To mention only a few, Procter & Gamble, General Electric, IBM, and Allied Signal, as well as most of the companies noted earlier, have invested millions of dollars in change programs to create organizationwide cultures and mind-sets that they believe will enable competitive success in the anticipated new competitive conditions of the first decade of this millennium.

3. Adapting to and, in many cases, driving change in and around the marketplace while managing significant *internal* change places an extremely heavy burden on the leaders of any organization. Yet that is precisely the

dual task that confronts strategic managers. They must accomplish two complex activities simultaneously:

- Exploit the present while sowing the seeds for a new and very different future.
- Build bridges between change in the environment and change within their organizations.

This chapter provides an introduction to managing strategy in the marketplace. It begins by briefly noting key markers of change in the competitive environment that confront every organization. It then identifies the three distinct general characteristics of every strategy that organizations employ to win the competitive arena—scope, posture, and goals. Next, it delineates three distinct forms of strategy—inventive, renovative, and incremental. Classifications like this aren't arbitrary. They codify the language of strategy making and identify the range of choices available to an organization. Using them to make decisions requires the members of a leadership team to develop a shared language that promotes better communications and better insight. The final segment of the chapter enumerates strategy principles—each of which contributes to developing a shared understanding of what strategy is all about.

THE CHANGING STRATEGY LANDSCAPE

Any discussion of strategy must take into account the dominant changes in the business environment that serve as the backdrop for strategy development and execution at the dawn of the new millennium. The changes occurring in the first half of the 2000s represent fundamental shifts in the competitive landscape compared with the early 1990s. Although we highlight only a few critical environmental shifts, they nonetheless illustrate why any organization can't hope both to win today and also to sow the seeds of tomorrow's success if it does not understand how and why tomorrow's world may be radically different from yesterday's.

Product[1] Proliferation

New products, product line extensions, and model and style changes emerge with bewildering frequency. Customers thus confront ever-increasing choices in and around every product category. The purchaser of something as commonplace as a bicycle nowadays can choose from in excess of 2,000 varieties. Teenagers buying clothes face a range of products, options, and styles and critical decision paths that leave their parents totally bemused. Everyday consumer activities, such as shopping for a toaster, can become exercises in learning about emerging technologies—analog computer chips, home network wiring, and connectivity of appliances to personal computers and phones.

Convergence of Technologies

Technologies and the products that flow from them are becoming ever more interrelated and comingled. Advances in voice, data, and video technologies integrate the television set, cable and wireless communications, computers, home appliances, telephones, software, games, sports, and leisure. Historically unrelated technologies such as computers, robotics, and artificial intelligence are coming together to redefine manufacturing. And who would have thought that computers would soon be routinely talking to toasters and toasters loaded with microchips would be talking back! A mobile phone can now be used not only to make phone calls but to access the Internet, to check voice mail, to send e-mail messages, and even to obtain soft drinks from a vending machine.

Breakdown of Traditional Industry or Segment Boundaries

Partly as a consequence of product proliferation and converging technologies, demarcating industry boundaries, or segments of an industry, presents increasing difficulties. Where are the boundaries of the telecommunications industry? Even the long established and staid auto industry defies easy delineation: auto analysts now must decide whether to consider minivans, SUVs (sport-utility vehicles), electric cars, and many types of light trucks as separate industries or distinct segments. Demarcating the boundaries of many emerging industries such as robotics and biotechnology has become well-nigh impossible.

Global Competition

For the first time ever, we are now experiencing genuine global competition in many industries such as automobiles, computers, pharmaceuticals, and many types of capital equipment, with rivals from North America, Asia, and Europe, aggressively invading each other's "home" territories.[2] Canon and Kodak fight each other intensely for market share in almost every country on the face of the earth. Many traditional companies are just now beginning to face the demands of global customers. And the Internet allows even small firms—often firms that did not exist a few months ago—to sell their wares anywhere in the world.[3]

Shortening "Half-Shelf" Life of Knowledge

An obvious but often unheeded consequence of pervasive and discontinuous change is that knowledge about product evolution, technology change, competitors' strategies, customers' buying preferences, industry demarcation and governmental policies rapidly becomes obsolete. The advent of digital technology has caused firms across many industries to abandon the technologies that buttressed their manufacturing processes, to change the content of their products, and to alter their relationships with customers. Yesterday's facts become today's fallacies; today's certainties become tomorrow's ambiguities.

Interconnectedness of Participants

Firms increasingly manifest networks of relationships and alliances with all types of entities in and around an industry: rivals, suppliers, channels, end-customers, governmental agencies, and vendors of specific forms of knowledge, skills, personnel, and capital (e.g., consulting firms, advertising agencies, logistics providers, banks, and venture capital firms). IBM, Hewlett-Packard, Merck, Microsoft, Motorola, to name but a few examples, exemplify firms that capably manage networks of relationships with different types of partners—suppliers, channels, large end-customers, and so on—depending on the business unit or product sector. Even start-up firms now must connect in unique and valuable ways with sources of capital, labor, and management expertise; specialists in the latest technology developments; and of course distribution channels and end-customers.

Increasing Sophistication of All Participants

All the participants in and around an industry or an industry segment exhibit increasingly sophisticated business intelligence and efficiency of operations, as well as the capacity to establish relationships with other organizations, influence regulation, and manage diverse and often conflicting stakeholders. As firms upgrade their technologies, adapt and exploit e-business, develop new customer solutions, and reconfigure internal operations, the old ways of doing business in any industry or "competitive space" become less competitive.

Intermittent Winners and Losers

Increasingly, industries or product segments are no longer dominated for long periods by one or even a few winners.[4] In the tug-of-war rivalry in almost every product domain, some firms emerge as leaders for a time only to be replaced by those who introduce superior solutions. Despite dominating certain product categories for years, renowned market successes such as Proctor & Gamble (soaps and diapers), IBM (minicomputers and workstations), and Ford (Taurus) and Toyota (Camry) eventually suffered major downturns in sales and profits due to the actions of rivals. In notoriously fast-changing markets such as software, where rivals play the innovation game dexterously, leadership often changes dramatically in a matter of months with the emergence of distinctly new products, radical extensions of the core product, or sometimes, just the rumors that such a product will soon be launched.

Increasing Prevalence of Discontinuity

When all the preceding change drivers work in combination, the dominant feature of the competitive landscape is not just change but discontinuity. In other words, learn to expect radical breaks with prior trends and patterns. Top management often forgets that its own innovations—truly new products; new ways of manufacturing, delivering, and servicing products; new alignments with other players; new and exciting ways of exploiting the Internet—cause rivals and customers to alter their expectations and their decisions. Changes in governmental regulations—such as recent proposals to allow banks, insurance firms and security brokerages to compete in each other's domains—sometimes set off earthquakelike effects to be felt in related industries. No longer can the past, or even the present, be taken as a slow unfolding prologue to the future. The change marathon does not have an official start (some government interventions or acts of nature being exceptions to the rule). So heed this warning: The competitive race is not just continuous but exhibits many twists and turns, some of which will be difficult if not impossible to anticipate.

THE NEED FOR STRATEGIC MANAGEMENT

Change is thus both the reason for and purpose of strategy. Without change in the firm's environment, new business opportunities could not arise. The explosion of e-commerce over the Internet, for example, has given rise to many opportunities for firms in almost all industries including new products or services and new ways of reaching customers. By the same token, unless a strategy generates significant change in the firm's competitive context, such as products that are new to the marketplace, extensions of existing products or new ways of delivering value to customers, it quickly devolves into a "me-too" strategy. It's almost a truism to state that such a strategy can't generate any advantage over rivals.

Organizations therefore must commit themselves to managing and leading change, which requires that they understand it and transform it into opportunity. To cope with change, strategic management must address three interrelated tasks:

1. Managing strategy in the marketplace: designing, executing, and refining strategies that win in a changing marketplace. Strategy is the means by which the organization creates and leverages change in and around the marketplace that ultimately provides superior value (compared with that of rivals) for customers.

2. Managing the organization: continually reconfiguring the organization—how it thinks, how it operates. Without such internal change, the organization can't hope to hone its capacity to identify, adapt to, and leverage environmental change.

3. Practicing strategic management: continually enhancing the linkages or interface between strategy (what the organization does in the market-place) and organization (what takes place within the organization). Throughout this book, we learn that how these linkages are managed determines whether the organization wins today and positions itself for tomorrow.

MANAGING STRATEGY IN THE MARKETPLACE

For many years, torrid debate has marked attempts in both the academic and managerial literatures to define and delineate what strategy is and what it is not. Yet few would disagree that the ultimate purpose of strategy in any business context is to provide superior value to customers and to do so in a way that generates profitable growth over time. Strategy thus entails a purpose and a means for achieving that purpose. In deciding on purpose and means, managers must make choices. Indeed, throughout this book, strategy is a synonym for choices. The sum of these choices about where and how to commit an organization's resources determines whether the organization wins in the marketplace—whether it can get and keep customers and outperform rivals.

These choices are influenced by the organization's understanding of current and potential change and their capacity to anticipate, create, and leverage change. But what levers can organizations manipulate to make change work to their advantage? Once they learn to pull the right levers, how can they continue to improve their performance? How can they continuously exploit change for superior performance? Strategy creates or leverages change in three related ways:

1. *Scope.* Through the choice of products or solutions the firm offers and the customers it seeks to serve, an organization determines the scope of its strategy. For example, should AT&T purchase one or more cable-TV companies? Should Saturn add a midrange line of automobiles? Should a small U.S. industrial components manufacturer enter the European market? To think about scope, you ask questions about what you want to offer to what customers in what geographic regions.

2. *Posture.* How aggressively the firm competes in its chosen businesses or product-customer segments to attract, win, and retain customers establishes the posture of its strategy. For example, should a cable-TV company add new elements of service to its customers, such as electronic payment; or should it upgrade its equipment thereby making it more customer friendly; or should it lower prices? Should Saturn add more functionality and features such as fast acceleration, more attractive coffee-cup holders, higher miles per gallon? To think about posture, you ask "how will we differentiate our offering" questions.

3. *Goals.* The choice of what attainments a firm will pursue sets the goals of its strategy. For example, should AT&T try to be a participant in the cable-TV business in every geographic region? Should Saturn seek to aggressively penetrate the car rental market or selective foreign markets? To think about goals, you ask "what results do we want" questions.

Issues and choices involving scope, posture, and goals are recurring themes throughout this book. Because of their importance to any understanding of strategy, each is briefly discussed in the following subsections.

Business Scope

Central to any consideration of strategy are questions concerning business scope. Scope decisions compel an organization to recognize the limits of the options available to it. No organization can market an unlimited array of products or offer unlimited services. Even with the assistance of partners, most firms can't reach all potential customers. Indeed, few firms are able to compete or "be a player" in all product-customer segments of their industry. So by evaluating scope choices, an organization picks the playing field that works to its advantage, given its rivals.

Scope determination revolves around four questions:

1. What product (or product groups) does the organization want to provide to the marketplace and what customers, or more specifically, what customer needs, does it want to serve (product-market scope)?
2. What geographic regions does it want to reach with its product-market scope (geographic scope)?
3. What stakeholders[5] does it want to involve in shaping and executing its product-market scope (stakeholder scope)?
4. What assets, capabilities and technologies[6] does it possess or can it develop to serve its product-customer segments (organization scope)?

These four questions compel an organization to systematically and carefully assess what business it is in, where opportunities exist in the marketplace, and what capacity it has or can create to use these opportunities.[7] Product-market and geographic scope directly address marketplace strategy, that is, the products the firm wants to sell to which customers. Stakeholder and organization scope address the firm's capacity to develop and execute its marketplace strategy.

Product-Market Scope

Every organization continually confronts choices pertaining to product-market scope. It can add to or delete products; it can seek new customer needs; it can withdraw its offerings from specific customer groups. However, breadth and complexity of the relevant product-market scope issues and questions are distinctly different at the corporate or sector and business-unit levels, as shown in Table 1.1.

At the corporate level, a principal challenge is to identify the businesses in which the corporation can generate value-adding opportunities. What businesses can be developed and enhanced over time? Which businesses should be divested? What product or customer synergy can be extracted across existing

TABLE 1.1   Scope: Key Questions and Issues

Corporate Level

Business scope	What businesses is the firm in? What business does the firm want to be in?
Stakeholder scope	What stakeholders can the organization leverage to aid in attaining its goals?
Scope relatedness	How should the businesses in the organization be related to each other, if at all?
Means of changing scope	Internal development, acquisitions, alliances, divestment, aligning with/opposing stakeholders.
Strategic issues	In which business sectors should the business invest? Retain the current level of investment? Reduce investment or divest itself entirely?
Strategic challenges	How can the corporation add value to its individual businesses? What might be the basis of synergy between two or more businesses within the corporation?

Business-Unit Level

Product scope	What range of products does the firm want to offer to the marketplace?
Customer scope	What categories of customers does the organization want to serve? What customer needs does the firm want to satisfy?
Geographic scope	Within what geographic terrain does the organization want to offer its products to its chosen customers?
Vertical scope	What linkages does the organization have (and want to have) with suppliers and customers?
Stakeholder scope	What stakeholders can the organization leverage to aid in attaining its goals?
Means of changing scope	Adding/deleting products or customers, moving into/out of geographic regions, aligning with/opposing stakeholders.
Strategic issues	In what products should the organization invest? Retain at current levels? Divest itself? What relationships does the organization want to develop with stakeholders?
Strategic challenges	How can opportunities be identified and exploited? What is the best strategy to do so?

or potential businesses?[8] The difficulties inherent in this strategic task are well exemplified in the myriad major corporations in industrialized countries around the world that in the past few years have reported significantly lower performance results than anticipated. In the United States, examples are Exxon, Westinghouse, Quaker Oats, Du Pont;[9] in Europe—Siemens, ABB, Philips, Volvo; and in Japan—Sony, Matsushita, Mitsubishi, Nissan. Many of these firms have had to sell off once promising or "can't miss" businesses that they anticipated would be the future stars of their portfolios.

Corporate and Business Unity Scope at GE   The case of General Electric (GE), a multinational conglomerate, illustrates differences in the context and setting of corporate and business-unit scope issues and questions. Viewed from the perspective of the CEO or the board of directors, GE's *corporate scope* is assessed by continually posing the following types of questions about each of its more than 10 business areas (e.g., aerospace, lighting, aircraft engines, financial services).

- Which business areas confront the greatest opportunities in the form of potential new businesses (new products that would give rise to a new business for GE)?
- What emerging or potential opportunities might not be exploited, given the present configuration of business areas? How might business areas be realigned to pursue these opportunities?
- Which areas should be encouraged to develop new opportunities through the internal development of new products, based on their current knowledge, capabilities, and competencies?
- Which business areas can take existing products to new types of customers or to customers in new geographic regions?
- Which areas should receive minimal, if any, new funds for business development?
- Which areas should be managed with the intent of generating cash to invest elsewhere, perhaps in other areas, or in the development of new business areas?
- What new opportunities might be created by linking products, skills, and competencies from two or more business areas?
- What opportunities might be created by aligning with one or more other corporations?

Some of the same questions can be directed, with considerably more focus and specificity, to each of GE's business areas. Each area must consider which specialized businesses or business units it wants to grow, hold, or divest. The Financial Services area is an example:

- Which of its more than 20 business units or product groups should be extended through the introduction of new products or services and/or the acquisition of new other entities that would add new products and/or extend existing product lines?

- Which business units should emphasize expansion into new geographic markets?
- Which business units ought to be pruned or scaled back?
- Are there business units that should be divested?
- What opportunities could be pursued by combining the products, technologies, and competencies of two or more business units?

Geographic Scope

A geographic dimension is unavoidable in (product-market) scope determination: business-unit and corporate strategy must consider the regional, international, and global context of business. Dramatic improvements in information technology, telecommunications, and transportation allow information, goods, and services to be shipped around the world at a speed that was unimaginable a mere decade ago. The emergence of e-business over the past five years—in fact, all the consequences of the new capability to do business using the World Wide Web—greatly enhances the ability of any organization to quickly and simultaneously reach customers in many regions of the world. This new global reach requires every organization to reassess its portfolio of opportunities.

Geographic scope thus presents the following issues and questions:

- What national or regional markets represent opportunities for the firm's current and future products?
- What differences and similarities exist among customers across these national or regional boundaries?
- How can the firm's products be customized or adapted for each customer group?
- How can what is learned about customers, distribution channels, competitors, and the firm's success or failure in one geographic market be leveraged in others?

Stakeholder Scope

The increasingly networked nature of organizations means that issues of scope also apply to the interorganizational or political arena: the interaction between the organization and its external stakeholders such as industry and trade associations, community groups, governmental agencies, courts, the media, social activist groups, as well as industry participants such as distributors, end-customers, suppliers, and competitors. Success in dealing with stakeholders is frequently critical to success in the product or economic marketplace. For example, many computer, software, consumer electronic, and biotechnology companies have forged alliances with their product rivals, institutions specializing in technology development, large end-customers, social and community groups, and sometimes even governmental agencies to push their preferred technology standard, or to obtain favorable treatment from one or more governmental agencies.

Among the scope issues and questions involving critical stakeholders are the following:

- Which stakeholders can affect attainment of the organization's goals and how can they do so?
- What are the similarities and differences in the "stakes" or interests of these stakeholders?
- Which stakeholders can the organization align itself with to enhance goal attainment and how can it do so?

Organization Scope

As noted earlier, how well strategic managers guide and lead change within their own organization greatly affects success in marketplace strategy. As marketplace strategy changes over time, it requires managers to acquire additional assets such as new financial capital, personnel with new skills, and new types of knowledge. It also requires managers to extend and refine existing capabilities or competencies, and in many cases to develop new capabilities and competencies. For example, many firms are now honing new e-business capabilities. In part, due to the changes sweeping the strategic landscape noted earlier, managers increasingly confront whether their firm should perform specific functions or activities (e.g., using its own sales force or manufacturing facilities) or instead assign the work to a vendor or form an alliance with a company that specializes in performing the task. Such "outsourcing" and "make or buy" decisions lie at the heart of organization scope challenges. Thus, strategists always confront several key organization scope issues and questions:

- What stocks of assets do we require to develop and execute our current and desired marketplace strategy?
- What capabilities and competencies do we now possess and how can we leverage these to ensure success of our current and desired marketplace strategy?
- What new capabilities and competencies will be required?
- Which technologies will be required to create and sustain our current and desired capabilities and competencies?
- Which assets, capabilities, and technologies do we develop ourselves, outsource to others, or develop in conjunction with which potential partners?

Scope delineates the businesses or product-customer segments the organization is in or wants to be in. It does not, however, address or provide much guidance as to how to compete in the marketplace to attract, win, and retain customers—the substance and focus of competitive posture.

Competitive Posture

It is never enough to know where you want to compete (product-market and geographic scope); you must also know how to compete. Posture addresses how an organization differentiates itself from current and future competitors *as perceived and understood by customers*. Differentiation is the source of value (compared with the value provided by competitors) that customers obtain when they buy the firm's product or solution. Without some degree of differentiation, customers have no particular reason to purchase an organization's product offerings rather than those of its competitors. For example, unless customers perceive some unique or superior value associated with buying a computer from Dell, they will have no specific incentive or reason to buy from that company rather than from its competitors. But if Dell provides them with a compelling value proposition, such as low price, superb service, and customized products—it is more likely to lure customers away from powerful rivals such as Compaq. A critical purpose of strategy is to create—and to continue to enhance—some degree of differentiation.

But how does an organization develop a strategy that will enable it to create and sustain valuable differentiation, as perceived and understood by customers? Although not intended as an exhaustive listing, Table 1.2 indicates key modes of competition (or modes of differentiation) employed by organizations in any competitive context or industry.

The intensity of the pressures to attract, win, and retain customers in almost every industry or industry segment forces organizations into a never-ending race; they struggle continually to redefine and renew their posture. As detailed in Box 1.1, every firm in the personal computer business continually extends its product lines; upgrades its product features; builds additional functionality into the products; adds new service elements; promotes, advertises, and uses every form of customer interaction to advance its image and reputation; broadens the distribution base for its products; works to strengthen its relationships with dealers and users—all with the intent of enhancing the value delivered for the prices charged.

The ultimate power of the modes of competition resides in their combination. They can be integrated to form distinctly different postures recognizable by and attractive to important customers. Some firms such as Southwest Airlines successfully execute a no-frills posture: though it provides customers only essential functionality (the plane will get you from location A to location B), minimal features and services (no meals on board, limited seat assignments), and low price, it makes you feel good about riding on one of their airplanes. Southwest's wry TV ads tease customers, "You are now free to move about the country." At the other end of the spectrum are high-end postures

TABLE 1.2   Competitive Posture: Sample Key Dimensions

Product line width	Breadth of product line
Product features	Style Design "Bells and whistles" Size and shape
Product functionality	Performance Reliability Durability Speed Taste
Service	Technical assistance Product repair Hot lines Education about product use Warranties
Availability	Access via distribution channels Ability to purchase in bulk How quickly product can be obtained
Image and reputation	Brand name Image as a high-end product Reputation for quality of service
Selling and relationships	Sales force that can detail many products Close ties with distribution channels Historic dealings with large end-customers
Price	List price Discounted price Price-performance comparisons Price-value comparisons

associated with products such as Rolls Royce and Rolex. They emphasize a brand image of exclusiveness, a name that "makes a statement," and high price. The one-stop shopping posture employed by Amazon.com or Wal-Mart offers customers the functionality of being able to obtain all the products they require from one source: books, CD recordings, and videos in the case of Amazon.com and a vast array of household, food, and consumer goods in any Wal-Mart store.

Goals

The choices made in business scope and competitive posture are intended to achieve some purpose or goals.[10] By the same token, any choice of marketplace goals such as a commitment to double market share over a five-year time period, will affect choices in scope and posture. For example, Amazon.com

Box 1.1

Rivalry in the Personal Computer Business

Rivalry in the personal computer (PC) business is so intense, business journalists describe it as the PC wars. Diverse firms inhabit the "PC space": IBM, Dell, Compaq, Gateway, Hewlett-Packard, Toshiba, NEC, and many other small rivals.

The rivalry has multiple dimensions. Each of the generic modes of competition (see Table 1.2) provides insight into the nature and intensity of the rivalry.

Product Line Width   All competitors are continually expanding their product lines. New lines arrive in the market almost every month. Some firms announce as many as 30 or 40 new products in a year. Firms fight furiously to stay ahead of each other with the latest notebook, laptop, and desktop models.

Features and Functionality   This is a fierce battleground. Firms continue to proclaim new gains in "speeds and functions." Compaq, for example, has historically emphasized the performance capability of its products. Apple continues to push its user-friendly interface and graphics capabilities. Firms loudly proclaim in advertising and in trade shows how their products offer more functionality (e.g., greater memory) than rivals' specific products.

Service   This has become the focus of some rivals' attempts to achieve fundamental differentiation. Almost all firms offer a package of support services that includes an 800-number, installation support, and technical assistance. Direct distributors such as Dell and Gateway endeavor to use service features such as rapid response to customers' inquiries as a means of distinguishing the value they provide to customers from that of their more mainline rivals such as IBM, Compaq, and Toshiba.

Availability   Firms take radically different approaches to reach different customer segments. Dell and Gateway have always gone direct to customers; unlike IBM, Compaq, Toshiba, and others, they do not use distributors. IBM and Compaq are now endeavoring to develop some direct means of reaching customers without jeopardizing their long-standing relations with distribution channels.

Image and Reputation   All firms engage in extensive advertising, some of which is pointedly directed at rivals. Dell has used the following assertion in one of its advertisements: "The gateway to the hottest PC technology isn't Gateway."

Selling and Relationships   As noted, some firms such as Dell and Gateway sell directly to customers; others go through dealers. Dell, for example, tries to create an individualized relationship with each customer through information technology that tracks each customer's prior purchases.

Price   Although rivals continue to create and add value for customers through the preceding modes of competition, prices generally continue to decline.

became America's most popular site to buy books and records by choosing growth goals instead of profit goals.

Consideration of goals inevitably leads to two central questions:

1. What does the organization want to achieve in the marketplace?
2. What returns or rewards does it want to attain for its stakeholders—its stockholders, employees, suppliers, and the community at large?

Specific goals that organizations typically consider are noted in Table 1.3.

TABLE 1.3   Goals: Key Questions

What does the organization want to achieve in the marketplace?

Vision or intent	In the broad marketplace, where does the organization want to be 5, 10, or 15 years from now?
Businesses	What primary and secondary businesses does it want to get into, stay in, or get out of?
Position	What ranking does it want to attain in each of its businesses in terms of marketplace leadership?
Products	With regard to each product line: What market share does it want to strive for, over what time period? What type of new customers does it want to attract? Which competitors does it want to take share away from?
Differentiation	What type of differentiation does it want to establish?

What returns or rewards does the organization want to attain for its stakeholders?

Shareholders/owners	What level of shareholder wealth creation does it want to strive for? What returns (such as ROI) are sought on specific investments?
Employees	What quality of working experience does it want to provide for employees at all levels? What level of remuneration does it want to provide to all levels in the organization?
Government	How can the organization contribute to attainment of the goals of specific governmental agencies? What other contributions can the organization make to good government?
Customers	What degree of customer satisfaction and value does it want to provide its customers? How can the organization help its customers achieve their goals?
Society	In what ways does the organization want to demonstrate that it is a "good citizen"? Are there specific social projects to which it wants to make a monetary or other contribution?

Every organization has an explicit or implicit hierarchy of goals that involve some mixture of marketplace, finance, technology and other goals. At least four levels of goals need to be considered: (1) strategic intent/marketplace vision, (2) strategic thrusts and investment programs, (3) objectives, and (4) operating goals (see Figure 1.1).

Strategic Intent or Marketplace Vision

Strategic intent or marketplace vision refers to the long-run concept of what the organization wants to achieve in the marketplace in terms of products, customers, and technology. Amazon.com's intent or vision appears to be to give customers the opportunity to purchase a wide variety of consumer products from one source. Apple Computers' famous original intent and vision was to build a user-friendly computer that would put a computer in every home in the United States.

Many firms express their intent or vision in a "statement" similar to this: To be the leader in the provision of a specific product class to particular types of customers on a global scale. For some firms, the driving intent or vision embodies a goal of reshaping and reconfiguring an industry or some industry segment. Home Depot's vision or intent was to create a whole new shopping experience for customers interested in making home improvements and to enable customers to perform challenging do-it-yourself projects.

Strategic Thrusts and Investment Programs

These articulate the significant product and other investment commitments that the firm is undertaking or plans to undertake to realize its intent or vision

FIGURE 1.1   An organization's hierarchy of goals.

Strategic Intent/
Marketplace Vision

Strategic Thrusts/
Investment Programs

Objectives

Operating Goals

over three- to five-year (and sometimes considerably longer) periods. Companies typically make thrusts to bring new products to market, dramatically extend existing product lines, reach new customers, and dramatically change the modes of competition. Representative goals might include building a leading presence in the European or South East Asian marketplace, reorienting R&D so that it can develop products that surprise and delight customers instead of just enhancing current offerings, and/or fashioning a set of alliances that brings together two or three types of related technologies.

Objectives

These goals transform strategic thrusts into action programs. Objectives tend to specify results that embrace a time horizon of one to three years and represent the organization's broad targets or milestones. A business unit's strategic thrust to launch a radically new product line in the European market might be guided by these objectives: launch each new product line in every major European country within three years, attain 15 percent of the European market within three or four years, achieve average gross margins of 25 percent, and be represented in every major distribution channel in each major country.

Operating Goals

These are short-run targets (usually achievable within one year) that are measurable, specific, and detailed. They can be viewed as accomplishments that contribute to the attainment of objectives. These typical operating goals penetrate certain key accounts with a set number of months; attain a particular market share for each product in a specific geographic market; enhance customer satisfaction by some percentage (based on some scale of measurement such as customer surveys); or improve margins by a specific amount.

Goals make sense of the organization's actions. For a firm entering the European market for the first time, a decision to enter into a strategic alliance with multiple distributors may be motivated by the goal of achieving rapid market penetration to preempt anticipated moves by one or more competitors. The same decision for the same firm in another product sector in the U.S. marketplace might be motivated by the desire to move inventories of existing products before it launches a new replacement product line. Also, goals facilitate coordination of what otherwise might be disparate and conflicting market actions. Thus, when they are managed well, goals inspire organizational members and coordinate actions across departments and functional units so that all stakeholders can contribute to winning in the marketplace.

THREE DISTINCTIVE STRATEGY FORMS

Even a cursory review of the actual marketplace strategies pursued by organizations suggests that they can choose many distinct combinations of business scope, competitive posture, and driving goals. To highlight the extent of the possible differences and their implications, we briefly describe three distinct strategy forms: inventive strategy, renovative strategy, and incremental strategy. The three strategies and relationships among them are illustrated in Box 1.2, the case of Amazon.com.

Inventive Strategy

An inventive strategy revolves around new, "breakthrough" products or solutions such as Chrysler's minivan, Dell's customized, high-speed delivery, high-service Internet-based system for offering and delivering personal computers, and MTV's packaging of programming aimed at the "young generation." Inventive strategy creates a new "competitive space" or marketplace niche; it is a strategy that no other competitor is now successfully executing.

The novelty of the strategy that is the essence of its inventiveness is embodied in its scope, posture, and goals. The radically new product or solution characterizes scope: It is new to the market and creates a new customer need or functionality. Posture typically aims to transform how customers and others "see" the product or solution domain, how and why they buy it, and how they use it. Starbucks reinvented what it means to drink coffee, where one should drink it, and indeed to some extent how it should be consumed. It is no surprise therefore that the marketplace goals associated with an inventive strategy almost always center on creating a fundamentally new form or mode of value for customers. A truly inventive strategy is driven by a "strategic intent" or "marketplace vision" that aims to create and exploit an opportunity that does not exist, is not recognized, or is not dared by competitors in today's marketplace.

The following are highly visible and revealing examples of inventive strategy:

- Chrysler created the minivan. It represented a completely new automobile solution: a seven-seat "car" that did not look conventional but performed and maneuvered better than a van. It transformed customers' conception of what an automobile should look like and how it might be used. It aimed to tap into a widespread latent and as yet unserved need in the automobile market.
- CNN (Cable News Network) invented the notion of 24-hour TV news. It created an entirely new solution to the need for round-the-clock coverage of national and international news pertaining to public affairs, sports, entertainment, weather, and other news domains.
- The Internet has emerged as an escalating source of inventive businesses. Charles Schwab & Company totally redefined what it means to be a stock brokerage business: Online access allows even small investors to relentlessly buy and sell stocks. EBay invented the online auction as a way of bringing together buyers and sellers of an unimaginably wide array of products ranging from rare antique furniture and personal memorabilia to everyday consumer goods and even industrial components.

Box 1.2
Inventive, Renovative, and Incremental Strategies: Amazon.com

Founded in 1995, Amazon.com created a whole new way of marketing and selling books and records—a classic *invented strategy*. It transformed product-market and geographic scope by eliminating prior constraints on the volume and range of books a seller could carry and the breadth of customers it could reach. It transformed posture by creating new forms of functionality (customers can quickly search for specific types of books or books related to a particular title), new forms of service (Amazon encourages readers to "review" books as a way of recommending them to their peers and it remembers its customers' previous selections and offers them books on related subjects), new features (customers can learn more about books over the Internet than they could from most bookstore clerks), and price advantage (books are offered at lower prices than in a typical bookstore and customers receive their choices by low-cost overnight delivery, saving them the cost of a shopping trip). It established a truly remarkable initial intent or vision: to be a one-stop shopping location for any type of book.

However, Amazon.com could not be content to sit on its laurels. It continued to *renovate its strategy*. It began to sell CDs, videos, children's toys, consumer electronics, and a host of other consumer goods, even building supplies. It has also begun to run auctions of an increasingly wide variety of goods ranging from rare books to people's personal junk. It now runs what it calls a mall: a group of other stores referred to as zShops that Amazon.com refers customers to for products which it does not carry.

Collectively, these extensions of its marketplace scope aggregate to a continuation of its inventive strategy: to become the first e-business to serve as a genuine one-stop shopping venue for consumers, almost irrespective of the products they wish to purchase. Thus, the firm has elevated its strategic intent or vision from being (merely) a one-stop location for any book.

As Amazon.com penetrates more and more specific product-customer segments of the consumer market, the *incremental* aspects of its marketplace strategy become more and more important. It will have to continue to add items within each of its myriad product lines within each product category—books, toys, CDs, consumer electronics, building supplies, auctions, and so forth. It will conduct experiments to try modest service changes and then gauge customer reaction. It can augment and improve how it advertises and promotes the range and novelty of the books, records, and consumer products it carries to reach new customer segments or to obtain an ever increasing share of each customer's purchases.

A number of marketplace and organizational challenges always confront any team of executives as they embark on crafting and executing an inventive strategy. The following challenges exemplify the difficulties inherent in successfully launching and leading an inventive strategy intended to create a whole new market space or industry segment:

- Create a product or solution that is radically different from any currently available in the marketplace.
- The product or solution must provide distinctly superior functionality for customers. Users of the product or solution must find significant value in its use, compared with the products or solutions they currently use.
- The product or solution must offer a platform for continued development and innovation. Otherwise the strategy results in a product or solution that is nothing more than a one-hit wonder.
- The product or solution must appeal to a wide array of customers and must be amenable to being adapted or customized to different customers' tastes, preferences, and uses.

Yet despite these difficult marketplace and organizational hurdles, many organizations have been able to create and execute an inventive strategy. Start-up enterprises sometimes manifest classic examples of invented strategy. They bring a fundamentally new product or solution to the marketplace that ultimately meets the challenges outlined previously. Many of the e-business based new organizations noted in this chapter such as Amazon.com, eBay (auctioning collectibles over the Internet), and E°TRADE (inexpensive stock trading over the Internet), have crafted such powerfully successful inventive strategies that they are now spawning streams of dedicated and well-financed rivals. Many long-established, mainstream corporate organizations create and execute inventive strategies too, as illustrated in the Chrysler minivan example. In Japan and Sweden, many 500-year-old companies have survived by reinventing their strategy century after century.

An inventive strategy is necessary if the organization hopes to catapult itself "out of the pack" or into a position of "breakthrough" market leadership. The firm must create and exploit an opportunity that is new to the marketplace. It is no surprise therefore that an inventive strategy entails the most risk because it involves doing something that no other organization has done. By the same token, it possesses the possibility of greatest marketplace and financial returns.

Renovative Strategy

An inventive strategy requires an organization to think thoughts and take actions—undertake something fundamentally different, both strategically and operationally—than it has ever done previously. Given the high risk of failure, or at least of making painful mistakes when pioneering unknown territory, the efforts of established organizations to renovate their existing strategy (i.e., to change scope, posture, and goals in significant ways) are considerably more common than their attempts to implement inventive strategies. It also seems fair to suggest that the vast majority of new entrants to specific product markets manifest strategies (i.e., scope, posture, and goals) that are variants of their rivals rather than genuinely inventive strategies.

Several factors make it more likely that organizations will choose renovative strategy instead of inventive strategy. First, it is much easier, intellectually and organizationally, to extend and leverage an existing strategy. In the garment industry of the 1950s through 1970s, the name of the change game was, "raise or lower the hemline of dresses a few inches." When the degree of change is minimal, a firm does not have to imagine and create a totally new product or solution or devise radically new ways of delivering value to customers. Second, if the strategy has proven successful in generating both marketplace and financial returns, the natural inclination of senior executive teams is "to ride this core strategy for as long as we can." Third, there is considerably less personal and organizational risk associated with renovating an existing strategy, at least in the short run.

Renovative strategies manifest common attributes. Scope, posture, and goals are significantly modified rather than radically reinvented. Although such change may be extensive, the organization's current products or solutions serve as the initial platform for changing scope. Managers search vigorously for opportunities that they can pursue using their current strategy as the point of departure. Then they extend, improve, and adapt product lines. They actively pursue new customers. They take a more aggressive posture toward competitors. Posture may shift from an approach that offers little differentiation to one that seeks extensive customer intimacy or new forms of relationship with distinct customer groups. Goal change may be abrupt and substantial; for example, a business may endeavor to switch from being a follower to being a leader in introducing new products or adapting and extending existing products or to shift from taking a largely undifferentiated to a highly differentiated posture:

- Computer, software, and electronics firms continually renovate their strategy by introducing new products and extensions to existing product lines that enable customers to experience "new functionality" (i.e., do things they could not previously have done).
- Over the past 15 years, Marriott Hotels has continually renovated its strategy. To its original hotel chain, it has added resort complexes, a low-end hotel line called Fairfield Inns, and an extensive catering or food service business in institutions including universities, prisons, and governmental agencies.
- Increasingly, firms are moving beyond their original products to provide many types of services associated with the product class.
- After watching Charles Schwab and E°TRADE revolutionize how individuals and institutions trade stocks, Merrill Lynch launched a massive

commitment to renovate its strategy in the brokerage business through the use of the Internet. It wants to add a massive e-business component to its product offerings, and in the process reconfigure almost every facet of the firm's relationship and involvement with customers.

Any organization contemplating renovating its strategy needs to ask the following questions:

- How will the proposed product or solution be different from existing products or solutions and from those that others may be planning to introduce?
- What is the nature and extent of the opportunity that the product or solution is intended to create?
- In which ways will the product or solution create distinctive value for different categories of customers?
- How can the anticipated customer value be augmented and defended in the face of current and emerging competitors' current and potential strategies?

Renovative strategy allows many firms to create significant new opportunities in product, customer, technology, and competency domains that are familiar to them. As Marriott Hotels extends into low-end and high-end hotels, and new forms of food delivery and catering, the firm remains in the same business, broadly defined. It can continue to leverage its long-established assets such as a widely recognized brand name and distinctive competencies such as the ability to identify, acquire, and develop real estate.

Incremental Strategy

Incremental strategy typically occurs when an organization is unable to, or chooses not to renovate or reinvent its strategy. It involves only modest change with respect to scope, posture, and goals. The firm chooses to make only slight changes to the basic solution it offers, the customers it pursues, how it competes, and the goals it seeks to achieve. For many firms, it might best be described as "doing largely the same thing, only more of it, with slight differences in execution over time."

Firms tend to fall into or adopt an incremental strategy when they have a successful product or solution. If they have a proven "product winner," why would they want to tamper with it in any extensive way? Winners are gaining some degree of market share, margins are typically increasing, and rivals might even concede their victory in the particular product-market segment. The self-satisfying maxim, "if it ain't broke, don't fix it," begins to be the watchword heard throughout the organization. If stable conditions continue to make it the right strategy for the right industry at the right time, an incremental strategy can be rewarding. The firm's costs are low and its return on investment tends to be predictable. However, if management has misread the capacity of the market to change suddenly, this can be a very risky strategy. Companies that are fat and blissfully happy grazing in their own private pasture tend to attract wolfish competitors.

The following situations exemplify use of incremental strategy.

- A toothpaste manufacturer that over a number of years makes only minor changes to the physical product and modifies its marketing, promotion, and sales programs in modest ways, mostly in response to the initiatives of rivals.
- In the downtown areas of most major cities, luxury hotels compete directly against each other for high-end business customers. In many instances, they only incrementally change the hospitality package they offer customers: the amenities they provide; the services they offer; the advertising and promotions they engage in to attract customers; the relationships they try to develop and sustain with frequent customers; and the price they charge.
- The business school that offers the same degree programs for a decade or more, even though it makes annual changes to the curriculum in each program (e.g., adding and dropping individual courses, and adapting the material in each course), and continues to seek students from new corporate and other institutional customers.

Firms also find it easy to engage in incremental strategy when the competitive context or industry segment in which rivals combat each other manifests little disruptive change over some period of time. New products or solutions are not introduced; new customer needs or functionalities do not emerge; major channel disruptions do not occur; and, customers do not make radical new demands of their suppliers.

Incremental strategy has generated significant financial rewards for many firms for substantial periods. As measured by enhancing revenues and profit margins, these firms have not only stayed in business but have generated real value for customers and acceptable returns for shareholders, employees, and managers.

That is the good news. The bad news, however, is that the types of changes noted at the beginning of this chapter—product proliferation, convergence of technologies, breakdown of traditional industries, global competition, shortening life of knowledge advantages, interconnectedness, increasing sophistication of all participants, intermittent winners and losers, and increasing discontinuity—render incremental strategy less and less viable as a choice for firms wishing to emerge as dominant market leaders or even to make dramatic market share gains. As new entrants exploit inventive strategy and historic rivals renovate their strategies, any firm pursuing an incremental strategy literally places its survival in jeopardy. To compete in the hospitality business, even quaintly primitive bed-and-breakfast hotels in remote corners of the world now have interactive Web sites, 800-numbers, high-speed digital connectivity, and customized service capability.

Comments on the Strategy Forms

The most striking feature of the three strategy forms is the fundamental differences among them. Inventive and incremental strategies are simply not on the same scale with regard to scope and newness of the opportunity, or the risks and rewards they entail. Inventive strategy represents a venture into the unknown; the organization quite literally invents its own future. Incremental strategy embodies the commitment of a management team to continuously enhance what it is already doing in the marketplace.

In large part because of these differences, it should not surprise us to find an organization with a number of distinct products or solutions simultaneously pursuing each strategy mode. Many pharmaceutical, software, electronics, and chemical firms invest considerable amounts of time, expertise, and money to invent the drugs, applications, products, and compounds that will result in a new business—new not just for them but to the marketplace. Many firms such as Nokia, IBM, GE, and Microsoft now establish "strategic investment funds" or "venture funds" with the avowed purpose of inventing or creating "really new products" or breakthrough solutions.

At the same time, these firms try extensively, and in some instances dramatically, to renovate their strategies. They acquire related product lines, develop alliances with existing distribution channels to reach new categories of customers, shape agreements with rivals in foreign countries as a means to enter and penetrate these markets, and in many cases, establish long-term cooperative relationships with end-customers. Success in renovating strategies generates the funds required to invest in, create, launch, and lead one or more inventive strategies.

Over time, an inventive strategy evolves into a renovative strategy, and perhaps even into an incremental strategy. Home Depot has continued to renovate its marketplace strategy adding distinctly new product categories over time such as garden centers and developing special services for professionals such as small home construction companies. It has also extended its product offering by acquiring specialist companies such as National Blinds, a catalog company specializing in window coverings and wallpaper. Yet Home Depot continually modifies each product category, adapts and adjusts how it services customers (often running experiments that are unique to individual stores), and how it lays out products in stores to make them more amenable to "walking shoppers."

Eventually, inventive and renovative strategies often assume many traits of incremental strategy. As the online auction house eBay.com adds more and more product categories, it will have to concentrate considerable organizational effort on upgrading and enhancing how it attracts, wins, and retains customers. It will have little choice but to augment and improve how it services customers, and how it advertises and promotes the value it delivers to customers.

However, some firms just don't move from an inventive strategy to its renovation. They also seek ways to transform the inventive strategy into opportunities to create inventive extensions of it. Home Depot, for example, has honed the art of building, running, and leveraging its prototypical store (the essence of an incremental strategy) over 15 years. In the past few years, it has created new forms of stores: Expo Design Centers. These small stores (by comparison to its typical stores) specialize in higher priced products—a one-stop-shopping opportunity for major home or building renovations that also provide a dedicated project manager to oversee the entire renovation from beginning to end—thus further extending the inventive strategy.

KEEPING YOUR STRATEGY ON TARGET: THE RIGHT ATTRIBUTES AND KEY PRINCIPLES

Although inventive, renovative, and incremental strategies are fundamentally distinct in terms of their scope, posture, and goals, they are also characterized by common attributes. These attributes give rise to several strategy principles. Each principle contributes to developing a coherent understanding of what strategy is all about and what it takes to create and execute a winning marketplace strategy.

First, strategy cannot be a single decision, action or event. Irrespective of whether it is inventive, renovative, or incremental, *strategy is always manifest in a series of decisions, actions, and events* pertaining to scope, posture, and goals. Ford's strategy with regard to its popular Taurus product line is reflected in the range of the product line it manufactures, the segments of customers it targets, how it decides to distribute to and service these customers, what type of image and reputation it wants to develop for the product line, and how it decides to price each model within the product line.

No strategy can produce exciting marketplace results (sales, market share, brand recognition) and economic returns (margins, cash flow, profits) unless it creates and takes advantage of an opportunity. And, opportunities, as noted earlier, ultimately exist in the customer marketplace. Thus, *creating opportunity resides at the heart of inventive, renovative, and incremental strategy.* An inventive strategy endeavors to establish an opportunity by offering customer solutions such as a form of transportation (the minivan) or a way of providing electronic news (CNN) that is entirely new to the marketplace. Even an incremental strategy must commit to extending the firm's opportunity space through continually, albeit in most cases slowly, adapting the product, seeking new customers, and modifying posture.

However, *opportunities can't occur without creating or exploiting change* both in the external environment and within the organization. Opportunities do not fall like manna from heaven. In both an inventive and renovative strategy, the organization changes the competitive marketplace in a significant way by introducing a new solution or dramatically extending existing product lines, as exemplified by Amazon.com (see Box 1.2).

Recognizing that strategy is always about creating and exploiting change implies that *strategy content (scope, posture, and goals) is always conditional* on current and anticipated marketplace change (and on circumstances within the organization). The specifics of any strategy's scope, posture, and goals must take into account the customer needs that are being created or served, the potential reactions of competitors, the emergence of new technologies, and potential changes in governmental regulations. Thus, no matter how well conceived and executed, a strategy that is inappropriate for the prevailing marketplace conditions simply can't succeed. When the first VCRs were introduced, they were not a hit with consumers. The inventive strategy failed in part because the technology of the TV set did not allow for easy use of VCRs, consumers were not yet educated in the use of VCRs, and the early models proved far too expensive for most of the customers who wished to purchase them. So even a breakthrough product can flop if the strategy for getting customers to learn to want the innovation isn't well conceived. There is not one right strategy for all competitive conditions, or all phases of an organization's evolution.

Although it may be implicit in the preceding observations, *strategy content must be continually enhanced and adapted.* Stated differently, strategy scope, posture, and goals can never be allowed to become stagnant. This is true no matter how successful the strategy. Every successful automobile model (e.g., VW's trend-setting and unique Beetle, Toyota's Camry, Honda's Accord, Ford's Taurus), eventually loses consumer appeal and market share, and is either replaced or radically restyled. As soon as the firm stops amending and augmenting scope, posture, and goals, the strategy becomes a sitting duck for rivals.

But strategy must be amended not just for its own sake but to attract, win, and retain customers. Perceived *opportunities are realized when they translate into superior value for customers.* When strategy does not create or add value for customers, there can be only one result: new products do not gain a toehold in the market; changes in posture do not deliver expected gains in market share; and ultimately, companies go out of business.

To create and realize opportunities *demands an obsession with the future,* rather than a preoccupation with the past, or even the present. Creating and leveraging the change that provides the opportunity for either an inventive or renovative strategy almost always means the organization willingly risks moving into a future where the past and even the present offer little guidance. At the start of the millennium, a host of e-businesses are crafting strategies and changing their business model based on their analysis of scenarios of a discontinuity just months away.

An emphasis on the future means that an organization must be dedicated to understanding how and why the future might evolve: What new products serving what customer needs might be available? How might competitors be-have differently? What new technologies might evolve? How might the econ-omy be different? These questions go to the heart of sowing the seeds of tomorrow's success, as opposed to just winning today. Thus, *to enjoy continued strategy success, an organization must commit itself to outwitting rivals:* to outsmarting or outthinking them. Outwitting requires that an organization do many things before its rivals:

- Anticipate key marketplace changes and the relationships among them.
- See how change gives rise to opportunity.
- Determine how to realize specific opportunities.
- Learn about customers' needs from rivals' actions; and craft responses to new entrants' strategies.

A few cutting-edge companies have used scenario learning to give their management team the experience of "living in" various possible futures with operating conditions, customer values, resources, competition, governmental restrictions, and other variables that would be distinctly different from those they manage today. Using the scenario methodology, they may be able to outwit their rivals by learning how to adapt to discontinuities before they actu-ally occur.

Outwitting rivals is necessary but never sufficient. Strategy always re-quires action in the marketplace: introduce products, pursue new customers, modify each posture component, and announce changes in goals. *Success in each strategy form requires that the organization outmaneuver rivals.* For ex-ample, get new products to the market before rivals do; imbue products with features that add superior value for customers; lock up rapidly growing cus-tomers either through contracts or more intimate relationships; involve cus-tomers in product development and modification.

Finally, strategy is always about achieving goals, that is, results. An inven-tive strategy that brings an innovative new product or solution to the market that customers are not interested in purchasing (the problem with the initial introduction of VCRs) will be a failure in terms of attracting, winning, and re-taining customers. Keep in mind also that outperforming rivals demands more than gaining market share and enhancing financial measures such as margins, profits, and shareholder value. An inventive strategy outperforms rivals by suc-cessfully creating a whole new market space or segment. A renovative strategy may outperform rivals by transforming a whole segment of an industry by being the first to launch a new product line. *Strategy must always be assessed along multiple dimensions as to whether it outperforms rivals.*

SUMMARY

Designing and executing strategies to win in the marketplace is a never-ending challenge. Given the persistent and increasingly discontinuous change in and around the marketplace, strategists can't depend on simple recipes or algorithms. They must be committed to anticipating and understanding such change in the external marketplace as well as within their own organization, and must recognize the connection between them.

NOTES

1. Product includes all forms of services, not just physical products.
2. Global competition is discussed in detail in Chapter 4.
3. This point is developed further in Chapter 5.
4. The examples cited in the bullet list at the beginning of this chapter attest to the difficulty of retaining market leadership in any market space.
5. The analysis of stakeholders is treated extensively in Chapter 7.
6. Assets are the exclusive focus of Chapter 10, and Chapter 11 addresses the topic of capabilities and competencies.
7. In a sense, these issues serve as the focus of this book.
8. These and many related questions are addressed in detailed in Chapter 2.
9. These are in addition to the many firms noted at the beginning of this chapter.
10. The argument here is that strategy is about both means and ends. Means are meaningless without some understanding of goals, and vice versa. Some authors equate strategy with means and thus keep goals distinct from any consideration of strategy.

CORPORATE STRATEGY: MANAGING A SET OF BUSINESSES

2

H. Kurt Christensen
Georgia State University

Each of the firms in the following examples has made a change in corporate strategy. For the most part, such moves are not opportunistic; they are elements of explicitly formulated strategies. An explicit strategy spells out how the corporation will use its assets and capabilities to build and maintain the competitive advantages that favorably influence its customers' purchase decisions. Such a strategy sets the general direction for the corporation; but over time, management must decide if it makes sense to maintain the course or to alter its strategy in the face of changes in its environment:

- Vodafone Group Plc, Britain's largest wireless phone company, acquired AirTouch Communications of San Francisco to expand its global reach. The combined company then sought Mannesmann of Germany to complete its pan-European mobile network. In the United States, its network is not complete, but it is comparable to that of its larger competitors.

- U.S. retailer, Sears, Roebuck & Co. has been scaling back its specialty store activities. It has recently sold its Parts America chain and other auto parts operations, and has also sold an 81 percent stake in its HomeLife chain of furniture stores.

- RealNetworks, Inc. has popularized the use of real-time audio and video on the World Wide Web. It sold Microsoft a nonvoting 10 percent stake for $30 million, and licensed its "streaming" technology to Microsoft for an additional $30 million. Microsoft will bundle RealNetworks' software with its Internet Explorer. Microsoft does not need to divert its attention to a peripheral-to-them technology, and RealNetworks receives funds for improving its software and accumulating enough customers to become the industry standard for sending audio and video over the Internet.

- McDonald's has purchased three nonhamburger businesses: Chipotle Grill, a chain of burrito and taco bars in Colorado; Aroma, a chain of 23 coffee shops in London; and Donato's Pizza, a chain of pizza restaurants in the Columbus, Ohio, area. A decision to expand one of those businesses geographically would enable McDonald's to leverage competencies in real estate, restaurant operations, marketing, and its global supply infrastructure.

In large, complex corporations, strategy formulation occurs at both the business and corporate levels. Dividing diverse corporations into business units is necessary for strategic planning to be meaningful. Business-level planning determines the boundaries of the business and decides how the business should compete in its chosen product-market. At the corporate level, central management selects the businesses that offer the most opportunity for the corporation. And central management affects the competitiveness of its business units by determining which resources and capabilities will be leveraged across the corporation's businesses. A critical question for central management is: What can the XYZ business do because it is part of ABC Corporation that it could not do if it were outside the corporation?

The focus of this chapter is corporate strategy.[1] First, we outline the domain and key components of corporate strategy to provide a context for considering the logic of corporate diversification, which is discussed next. Why does diversification have the potential to create economic value? Yet why does it so frequently destroy value instead? Third, we explore the product-market, geographic, and vertical dimensions of a corporation's scope. Fourth, we look at the concept of relatedness—how the business units in the corporation will be related to each other—and the different ways that relatedness can be created. Finally we consider the methods that can be used to change a corporation's scope.

THE DOMAIN OF CORPORATE STRATEGY

Corporate strategy concerns itself with three important issues that corporate executives must address:

1. *The corporation's scope.* In what mix of businesses should it participate?
2. *The relatedness of its parts.* On what basis should the business units in the corporation be related to each other?
3. *The methods for managing scope and relatedness.* What particular methods—acquisition, internal development, strategic alliances, or divestment—should be employed in making specific changes in the corporation's scope and relatedness?

In determining the corporation's scope, central management must consider each of the three scope dimensions: product-market, geographic, and vertical. Product-market scope addresses what product-markets the corporation should participate in. Two contrasting examples: Intel's product-market scope has historically been tightly focused on personal computer chips, while General Electric has 12 businesses operating in very different product-markets. Geographic scope establishes where the corporation should operate. Until recently, few retailers ventured far from their home country, but Carrefour has entered the Americas, and Wal-Mart is moving aggressively into Europe. Vertical scope considers which stages in the vertical chain a company should participate in. General Motors has largely exited the parts manufacturing business, reducing its vertical scope, while McKesson HBOC serves customers throughout the healthcare chain, from pharmaceutical companies to managed care and retail organizations. These scope dimensions need to be analyzed separately because each has a different underlying rationale.

In determining relatedness, central management must decide whether it seeks relatedness based on a single, externally perceived, competitive advantage across its businesses. This type of relatedness has provided significant benefit to some companies; for example, Hewlett-Packard has gained a reputation for technically *au courant* products with value-adding features. However, such a strategy is viable only as long as the market rewards the particular competitive advantage that serves as the basis for relatedness. In addition, companies can eventually outgrow this strategy. In fact, Hewlett-Packard has broadened its scope in the printer business to include both the mass market and its historical focus, the value-added-features segment.

Relatedness is often based on shared *resources* and/or the ability to transfer specific *capabilities* from one unit to another. A shared resource can relate to everything from a brand name to a machine or a distribution system, and a transferred capability can be in general management or within one of the functional areas, such as marketing. Such resources contribute to the creation of something customers want, are hard or impossible to imitate, don't depreciate quickly, and permit their value to be captured by the firm possessing them.

Changing Scope

Corporations expanding their scope may do it by internal development, acquisition, or strategic alliances. The preferred method depends on a corporation's current resources and capabilities and how they fit with what is needed to succeed in a particular market. Each method poses significant, but different, organizational challenges:

- *In internal development.* Organizing a start-up, and then overcoming the internal impediments to leveraging resources and capabilities across organizational units.
- *In an acquisition or merger.* Assessing candidates without complete information, and then achieving successful integration after the deal closes.
- *In a strategic alliance.* Managing a partnership, and then renegotiating changes as partners' needs and objectives change.

Corporations reduce their scope when they perceive that a line business no longer fits their future strategy. Their next objective: How can we maximize the return from this divestment? In doing so, they choose from the following five methods of divesting: sale as a going business, leveraged buyout (LBO), spin-off, harvest, or liquidation.

The scope changes of major corporations are important news items in the press, as are comments by external parties about a company's current or intended scope. For example, AT&T's agreement to purchase McCaw Cellular Communications received much media attention because of AT&T's ability to help McCaw expand its cellular network nationwide. Its more recent decisions to buy TCI's cable business and MediaOne signal AT&T's determination to be a key player in the U.S. local telephone market, using cable lines for that purpose. Scope decisions (and their attendant explicit or implicit decisions about relatedness) tend to be central management's most expensive, most visible, and potentially farthest reaching decisions. They represent a major way in which central management can create economic value.

Relatedness and Scope

Scope and relatedness decisions can profoundly affect the economics of a corporation's businesses. A firm that acquires or internally develops only businesses that leverage its marketing channel will enjoy significant scope economies. With more products available for amortizing fixed costs, the firm will have a more efficient channel than will competitors who have narrower product lines. And, other factors being equal, each business in the firm will have lower marketing and distribution costs than it would have as a stand-alone company. Most of Procter & Gamble's and Lever Brothers' businesses are related in this way.

This efficiency generates discretionary funds that can be allocated to value-creating activities like product development, enhanced promotion, lower prices, or higher returns for shareholders. Thus, related diversification, based on product development, manufacturing, or marketing can significantly affect the economics of the corporation's businesses.

On the other hand, a firm that follows a conglomerate strategy does not strive for such operating synergies across businesses. Rather, it seeks to create only financial and managerial synergies across its units. If central management is lean and manages wisely, the businesses in a conglomerate can have the flexibility of a stand-alone unit while enjoying the financial resources and general management support often not available to their stand-alone competitors. With the exception of previously undermanaged units, however, the value added at the corporate level by a conglomerate is more modest than is possible with related diversification.

Scope decisions are also important because of their impact on central management's responsibilities. They define the domain of central management's accountability. When a merger or acquisition poses cultural risks in integration, it is central management's role to manage these risks acceptably.

Where potential synergies exist across businesses, central management must assume the responsibility for seeing that they are created.

Corporate management's collective track record in making scope changes has been poor, but is improving. Even though diversification has been occurring on a large scale since the 1950s, far too little has been learned from the many mistakes that have been made. Researchers have studied corporate diversification extensively, and most have concluded that diversification has produced far less value than its proponents have predicted (despite a few big successes). Most firms that diversify do not create economic value; more often they destroy it. Typically, value is destroyed because the underlying reasoning for the diversification doesn't make sense.

THE LOGIC OF CORPORATE DIVERSIFICATION

Most of the justifications for diversification provided by corporate executives and reported in the business press can be clustered into the following list of five reasons. The logic for the first four reasons is flawed. For each, both the rationale and the flaw are considered:

1. *To take advantage of what the buyer perceives to be an exceptional market opportunity.* Typically, this opportunity is characterized in terms of an extremely high market-growth rate. As the argument goes, rapidly growing markets provide an exceptional opportunity because new entrants are less likely to evoke retaliation by existing competitors. Consequently, a determined player has a greater chance of becoming the dominant, and most profitable, player.[2]

   The flaw. A successful acquisition can be expected only when there will be a fit between the market opportunity created by the deal and the firm's resources and capabilities. Every buyer should ask: "What does our company bring to the opportunity? Can we do anything in that marketplace that others can't do as well or can't do better?" Both IBM and Kodak entered the copier industry. IBM eventually withdrew, but Kodak has remained a player. Kodak could leverage its in-depth knowledge of imaging technology, a critical area in which IBM was at a relative disadvantage. Kodak continues to leverage this technology in its strategic alliance with Danka of Japan. Kodak performs the research, development, and manufacturing, while Danka carries out all marketing, sales, and facilities management activities.

2. *To remedy low growth potential in current product-markets.* Firms in mature markets often can't achieve their growth goals without diversifying into one or more new businesses.

   The flaw. An early diagnosis of the limits of opportunity in an existing business may be a shrewd management judgment,[3] but recognizing the absence of opportunity in an existing business does not confer the capability to succeed in a new one. In fact, the mind-set necessary to run a mature business successfully is profoundly different from the mind-set necessary for success in a rapidly growing business. R.J. Reynolds diversified because of diminished opportunity in its core tobacco business. The company made several problematic acquisitions in the 1970s, and its foray into the foods business in the 1980s wasn't a triumph either. In both instances, shareholders would have been better off if the money spent on diversification had been distributed to them instead.

3. *To create a more stable earnings stream.* Wall Street hates surprises and likes predictability. Companies with more stable earnings over time have slightly lower costs of capital, and, other things being equal, they generate a slightly higher risk-adjusted rate of return. Despite the theoretical correctness of the argument, such efforts typically fail.

   The flaw. Diversification undertaken for this reason has very modest upside potential, and the downside risk can be considerable. Businesses whose earnings streams are inversely correlated—one is cascading at the precise time the other is trickling—tend to be both difficult to find and fundamentally different—requiring very different capabilities and management practices. The likelihood of serious management mistakes is therefore high. Acquisition costs for such a business can also be high, relative to the increased shareholder value possible from reduced earnings variability. Few individuals would place a bet with a small upside and a large downside, yet executives diversifying solely to smooth an earnings stream are doing precisely that.

   For these reasons, institutional investors (and some individual investors) strongly prefer to manage the earnings variability *of their own portfolio* by changing their mix of holdings, not by having management seek to do this by diversifying.[4] EMI diversified out of the music business and into the electronics and medical equipment businesses in part to smooth its very volatile earnings stream from the music business. It experienced some success in these industries, but it eventually returned to its roots as an entertainment company and gave up its attempt to be strong in technology-based product businesses.

4. *To save the individual investors among shareholders a double taxation of their dividends by reinvesting corporate profits in new businesses.* Given the reality of double taxation—the taxing of corporate profits and also investor income—it is theoretically possible for a corporation to diversify and give its individual shareholders an advantage. However, that outcome is not very likely.

   The flaw. In most instances, the costs of entry and of learning how to run the new business significantly exceed the tax benefit.

   As noted, none of the preceding four frequently stated reasons should be the impetus for diversification.[5] The fifth reason is the only valid reason.

5. *To exploit synergies across businesses or between a business and its corporate parent.* Synergies are the additive benefits gained because units operate within the same corporation.[6] Synergies may increase revenues or

reduce costs (or both), by sharing resources or transferring capabilities from one unit to another. Diversification that fosters genuine synergies can create economic value.

Nevertheless, synergistic benefits from diversification are predicted far more frequently than synergy is actually achieved.[7] Sometimes, the alleged synergies do not exist because the underlying rationale is flawed. A common error is to overestimate revenue-generating synergies by a substantial margin. During the 1980s, a number of financial services firms expanded their product offerings, expecting that one-stop shopping would be a competitive advantage because it would dramatically increase the flow of customers. Overall, these hopes were not realized. Led by CEO James Robinson, American Express, for example, learned this lesson the expensive way. (For a similar initiative in the late 1990s, see the discussion of Citigroup in Box 2.1.)

Another common error is to overestimate the extent to which relationships can be leveraged. Advertising firms that diversified into management consulting have found that cross-selling is much more difficult than anticipated because a relationship with executives in one department of a client company is generally not leverageable into another department or into the executive suite. Most of these acquisitions have subsequently been divested.

Three factors have led to systematic overestimation of synergy. First, synergy must be understood in terms of *net positive synergy*. In practice, many situations capable of generating some positive synergy cannot overcome the negative synergies that are incurred at the same time. In an acquisition, these can include:

- The control premium (the amount by which the price the buyer pays exceeds the market value of the firm prior to the offer).
- Traceable cash flows associated with the deal (fees to investment bankers, lawyers, and accountants).
- The allocation of corporate expenses to the acquired unit.
- Negative synergies with other parts of the business.
- The cost of mistakes made in learning how to oversee or manage the new business.

Second, many advocates of diversification have seriously overestimated the extent of management synergy. Long discredited is the argument that management is generic and transportable across all markets and industries, and that it can be applied without acquiring industry knowledge and without paying considerable attention to the substance of the business. Although there *are* management skills and practices that can be applied in a wide variety of businesses and settings, few, if any, are applicable in all settings. Attention to the industry context and to the substance of the business is necessary in virtually all cases. Consequently, although managerial synergy exists in some situations, it is less pervasive and has a more modest impact on performance than many had believed.

Box 2.1

Citibank plus Travelers equals CitiGroup

On April 6, 1998, Travelers Group Inc. and Citicorp announced an $83 billion merger between their two companies. CitiGroup would offer traditional banking, consumer finance, and credit card services (mainly through Citicorp's Citibank unit); property-casualty and life insurance (through Travelers' insurance units); and investment banking, retail brokerage, and asset management (through Travelers' Salomon Smith Barney unit). The two companies' 1997 revenues totaled $48.7 billion, with operating earnings of $7.5 billion.

For this merger to create value, customers must desire one-stop shopping for financial services. CitiGroup co-chairman John Reed said, "The customer doesn't want to shop from place to place and be sold time and time again." They will see CitiGroup, not as a conglomerate, but as "a company providing a broad range of services," according to Reed. He continued, "Now we have the opportunity to serve customers, especially in the United States, with convenient, efficient access to all the expertise and the full range of value-added products and services they need, a capability unmatched by anyone, anywhere." Travelers had previously enjoyed some successes in cross-selling, in particular selling a range of Travelers insurance products to Primerica Financial Services customers. Nevertheless, it is not clear how many customers want most or all of their services from one provider.

The Citibank brand name is also highly regarded outside the United States. To the degree that Travelers products can be sold through Citibank offices, the potential synergies are considerable. Yet it is not clear how many non-U.S. consumers will want one-stop shopping. As a practical matter, cross-selling outside the United States will proceed one step at a time.

In addition to revenue-generating synergies, cost savings are also important to the merger's success. CitiGroup co-chairman Sanford Weill and his colleagues have a reputation for eliminating redundant or otherwise unnecessary expenses. CitiGroup is on target to reduce annual expenses in 1999 by $2 billion, with further reductions expected in 2000. These cost savings alone will go a long way toward justifying the premium for Citibank reflected in the exchange ratio of the two companies' shares.

Third, it is easy to underestimate the administrative challenges in achieving potential synergies. Achieving synergies across businesses can be deterred by strategy, operating policy, and cultural differences. In practice, a new corporate parent usually finds it difficult to exercise the right mix of flexibility and firmness in creating synergies with a newly acquired unit.

Net positive synergies can provide a valid motivation to diversify, but considerable care must be exercised to determine:

- The extent of the positive synergies.
- The negative synergies that can't be avoided.
- The net effect.

Only when the net synergy is positive can diversification create economic value.

DIMENSIONS OF CORPORATE SCOPE

Central management most profoundly impacts the corporation through the scope changes it formulates and implements. How it relates the corporation's businesses to each other, how it manages entry into new businesses and divests an existing business, and how it facilitates or hinders the development of cross-business synergies will directly affect corporate performance.[8] Because of the importance of the major kinds of scope decision, each needs to be considered in detail.

Product-Market Scope

Whether it thinks about it consciously or not, every corporate management chooses to participate in a particular product market or set of product markets. In some instances, a sound logic guides the choices; in others, the choices appear more haphazard and opportunistic. Companies seeking to make the best choices about which markets to participate in must address two issues:

1. Should they diversify around only one or more than one resource or capability?
2. What specific resource and capability choices should serve as the basis for diversification?[9]

When firms diversify on the basis of a single resource or capability associated with their core business, they are limiting their choices.[10] Several pharmaceutical firms have diversified around a research capability tightly focused on a limited number of therapeutic categories. For another example, Corning Corporation diversified around a core competence in glass technology. Firms such as GE that diversify on the basis of different commonalities or links between different pairs of units are less focused . Least focused of all are conglomerates such as Loews, which diversify with little or no regard to product-market commonalities. In conglomerate diversification, only financial and/or managerial synergies are sought. Both the highest potential for value creation and the greatest organizational challenges reside with related diversification, with the reverse true for conglomerate diversification.[11,12]

Related Diversification

Firms can diversify on the basis of common product technology, manufacturing technology, marketing channels, customer needs, related needs of a particular customer group, or some combination of these elements. For example, 3M has built its strategy around its capability in adhesive chemistry. Leveraging that capability has taken the company into a wide array of businesses, including Post-It Notes™, sandpaper, copying machines (toner must adhere to paper in making a copy), floppy and optical storage disks (coating adheres to disks), coated papers, Scotch™ adhesive tape, and video, correction, and box-sealing tapes.[13] In contrast, Procter & Gamble (P&G) has built its strategy around marketing capability through the grocery and over-the-counter drug channels. Leveraging that capability, P&G participates in a wide array of businesses including laundry detergent, disposable diapers, bathroom tissue, cake mixes, toothpaste, cosmetics, cough medicines, and other in-home remedies. P&G's businesses have different product and manufacturing technologies, but share the same marketing channels; 3M's businesses share adhesive product technology but reach different customers through several marketing channels.

A successful choice of product-market scope will take into account a company's existing capabilities, its ability to maintain and enhance them over time, the value-creating potential that its capabilities have in its chosen markets, and its effectiveness in implementation.

Geographic Scope

The second dimension of the corporation's scope, its geographic scope, charts the geographic boundaries of the markets the corporation serves. Businesses choose to deliver goods and services to local, regional, national, international, or global markets.[14] In many product and service businesses, the economics of national or international scope are so compelling that local or regional competitors are few or nonexistent. However, local or regional markets can be viable when:

- Products are perishable (e.g., sushi).
- Transportation costs are a substantial portion of total product costs—typically when the product is inexpensive and bulky (e.g., unfilled metal cans) or heavy (e.g., gravel).
- Customer needs and wants differ significantly across regions or locales (e.g., barbecue sauce taste preferences vary considerably across regions of the United States).
- There are few economies of scale (e.g., a fine-cuisine restaurant).

For a growing number of businesses, serving a market that crosses national borders is essential for survival. When they choose to serve foreign markets, business leaders make several important decisions.

Selection of Served Countries

A key decision is what particular countries to serve (and in what order an expansion will serve them). In making this decision, they must consider the attractiveness of each national market. A critical aspect is the level of country-specific risks—expropriation, onerous legislation, or political or economic instability. A company's other commitments and interests in the region also influence this decision. (Does the company already operate, or plan to establish operations, in nearby countries?)

Strategy Variation

Central management needs to decide how much strategy variation to have across countries or regions. Firms follow a global strategy when they employ essentially the same strategy in each country where they operate; keeping local adaptation to a minimum. At the other end of the spectrum, firms follow a multidomestic strategy when their subsidiaries in each country formulate and implement their own strategies. Most firms avoid both extremes by seeking to capture as many economies of global strategies as they can without being insensitive to differences in customer needs and preferences across countries. Global competition in many industries has become sufficiently intense that most companies seek as global a strategy as customer needs permit.[15] Coca-Cola has been able to follow a global strategy because the association it seeks to create in consumers' minds, having a Coca-Cola and a good time, has universal appeal. Philips N.V., the Netherlands-based multinational, had for many years successfully operated with a multidomestic strategy but has moved in recent years toward regional and global strategies. A multidomestic strategy has become an unaffordable luxury in industries that are globalizing and becoming increasingly competitive.

Functional Activities

Executives need to consider which functional activities to carry out in foreign markets. Companies can:

- Export on an order-by-order basis (lowest commitment).
- Warehouse and market in the host country.
- Manufacture, warehouse, and market there.
- Do each of the preceding and perform research and development there (highest commitment).

The order of activities indicates increasing commitment to the host country. Some companies move through the sequence one step at a time.[16]

Ownership Form

Central management needs to consider what ownership form to employ. This means assessing the relative benefits of a wholly-owned subsidiary, an equity joint venture (typically with a local partner), a licensee, franchisee, or local agent. A wholly-owned subsidiary is easier to manage, but many firms opt for a local partner (even where not legally required) because of the partner's market knowledge and ability to relate to the host country government. In many industries, the perception of "foreignness" in a wholly-owned subsidiary can be a barrier to business success.

Licensing, franchising, and using a local agent offers relatively low-risk, low-return options. When considering licensing, management must assess the likelihood that a licensee will eventually become a direct competitor. When hiring a local agent, management must anticipate whether he or she has sufficient incentive to build the business to its potential in the region. In franchising, management must assure itself that the franchisee can manage the business (and make any needed local adaptations) in a manner consistent with the corporate strategy.

Reporting Relationship

Corporate management must determine the *reporting relationship*—how the foreign units will be managed. Will the head of the business in the host country have a primary reporting relationship to a regional business-unit head, to a worldwide business-unit head, or to a country manager? With a global strategy, the primary reporting relationship will almost always be to a worldwide business head. Regardless of the primary reporting relationship, there is a need to coordinate action across all other dimensions. Central management needs to determine the form that coordination will take.

These issues—selection of served countries, strategy variation, functional activities, ownership form, and reporting relationship—need thoughtful consideration early in the process of determining geographic scope. The decisions arrived at need to be internally logical and consistent with the corporation's product-market scope.

Vertical Scope

For this third dimension of scope, companies make decisions about the stages in the vertical chain (from raw material to consumed product) in which they will participate. Not every chain has the same number of stages, and some stages can have important subdivisions. Typical stages include raw materials extraction, raw materials processing, component manufacture, product assembly (manufacture), distribution, and consumption. (See Figure 2.1.)

A decision to become more highly integrated has important implications.[17] First, it increases the size of the "bet" (capital investment) that a company is placing on that vertical chain's end-use market. Second, when a company integrates backward (closer to the raw material source), it is frequently entering a more capital-intensive business that needs to be managed differently from its core business. When a company integrates forward (closer to its customers), the marketing task becomes different enough to cause

FIGURE 2.1   A typical vertical chain.

Raw Materials Extraction	Raw Materials Processing	Component Manufacture	Product Assembly	Distribution	Consumption
Iron ore mined	Steel ingots formed; rolled into sheets	Automobile fender formed	Automobile assembled	Automobile dealer sells car	Buyer uses car

difficulty for companies that are very capable in their core business. When Texas Instruments integrated forward into the watch business, it was successful for a while but eventually found itself at a disadvantage because it had an inadequate understanding of the jewelry and consumer marketing aspects of the product. It eventually withdrew from the watch business.

Motivated in part by Japanese companies' success with low levels of vertical integration, some U.S. companies are rethinking whether all their present vertical integration is necessary or desirable. Very few businesses have a technological imperative for integration. In most cases, integration is not needed to ensure a regular supply of materials or to reduce production costs, despite the rhetoric to the contrary. Carefully drawn long-term contracts can, in most instances, provide the control- or supply-assurance benefits of ownership without ownership's costs and administrative complexity.

Vertical integration may be appropriate to prevent market foreclosure (being shut out of a market). For example, if a company's competitors seek to purchase supplier or customer organizations, vertical integration may be warranted to avoid the risk of heavy dependency on an organization that is both a supplier and a competitor. This has been a factor motivating mergers in the nexus of network TV, cable TV, and entertainment programming, such as Disney's acquisition of ABC. Vertical integration may also be warranted where sharing confidential information across units is necessary to accomplish systemic innovation.[18]

Executives considering vertical integration should be attentive to potential negative synergies. During the past two decades, one factor contributing to General Motors' modest return on investment has been its relatively heavy integration into component manufacturing, where its per-hour labor costs are almost twice those of independently owned component manufacturers. This was a motivating factor in the spin-off of its parts unit into an independent company, Delphi Automotive Systems.[19]

When an integrated firm's vertically integrated units can't serve its competitors, they won't have the same economies of scale as an independent contractor. For this reason, most airlines that formerly had catering operations have sold them and now buy food at a lower cost from vendors that serve many clients.

Combining the Scope Dimensions

We have discussed each scope dimension separately because each has a different focus, set of issues, and set of considerations appropriate for resolving the issues. However, there are two important relationships among product-market, geographic, and vertical scope:

1. Product-market scope and geographic scope decisions should be made in the context of a specific industry because its geographic boundaries are strongly influenced by its economics. Where industry economics favor globalization, a decision to enter a particular industry (a product-market decision) largely determines the geographic scope decision. For example, it is hard to be a strong player in the copier industry without a global geographic scope.

2. Substantial breadth in any dimension adds to the complexity of the corporation and, consequently, to the management challenge of operating it. Because of the difficulty of managing a high level of complexity, corporations with a very broad product-market scope tend not to have a high vertical integration, and highly integrated corporations (like Exxon or Texaco) tend not to have a very broad product-market scope.

DETERMINING SCOPE AND RELATEDNESS

Arguably, the major influence on a corporation's scope is its concept of relatedness: On what basis does it seek to have its business units related to each other? Implicit in any relatedness decision is that central management must build and maintain one or more resources or capabilities. As noted earlier, 3M's businesses are related by adhesive chemistry technology. Because this technology is critical to corporate success, 3M's executives need to be certain that this activity is state-of-the-art and capable of serving as its growth engine. Much executive time needs to be expended to see that the needed linkages and synergies across units are in fact developed. Where businesses in a corporation are related on the basis of one of several resources or capabilities (linked diversification) rather than on the basis of a single resource or capability, central management's task is significantly more complex.

Creating value at the corporate level is not easy. Placing a formerly independent company into a multibusiness corporation (or creating a new business from the bottom up) can unleash negative synergies. Even where considerable autonomy is granted to an acquired unit, central management still must make final decisions on major investments, ensure legal compliance, and see that accounting systems are sufficiently compatible for corporate financial statements to be meaningful. The newly acquired unit will be assigned its portion of corporate overhead. Unless the acquisition has the potential for creating substantial positive synergies, economic value will not be created by the acquisition. The principle is the same for new businesses that are developed internally: On balance, does the company's involvement in this business create net positive synergy?

IDENTIFYING OPPORTUNITIES THAT CREATE VALUE

How can executives identify acquisition and self-development opportunities that are likely to create sufficient economic value for their company? These evaluative questions can help:

- How attractive is the industry (or industry segment)?
- Can important resources or capabilities be leveraged?
- Are costs of transactions (with suppliers or customers) high and likely to remain so?
- Can the buyer capture enough of the value it seeks to create?
- Can the initiative be implemented effectively?

Each of these questions is considered in turn.[20, 21]

How Attractive Is the Industry (or Industry Segment)?

Attractive industries have these characteristics:

- *Their customers have differing needs and wants.* When customers' needs and wants are heterogeneous, companies can often differentiate their products in ways that better meet the needs of one or more market segments. On the other hand, when customers view an industry's products or services as commodities that cannot be meaningfully differentiated, competition centers around price, leading to thin margins and modest earnings at best.
- *They are growing at least moderately.* In growing industries, a new entrant's initiatives (or an acquired business' expansion plans) are less likely to prompt competitors' retaliation—the norm in low- to zero-growth industries.
- *Their owners do not perennially generate low average returns on investment.* Perennially low returns are caused by some combination of low entry barriers, high exit barriers, high supplier or customer bargaining power, many substitutes, and aggressive rivalry among direct competitors.[22] Two unattractive industries are airlines (where seasonal excess capacity is chronic) and steel (where competitors owned by foreign governments are more interested in creating jobs and foreign exchange than

profits). On the other hand, the pharmaceutical industry has been attractive for many years because the large number of therapeutic categories for which drugs can be developed moderates head-to-head competition, and because third-party payers have historically not been particularly price-sensitive.

Where customer needs are heterogeneous and products can be differentiated, the profitability across different industry segments (or strategic groups) can vary considerably.[23] In one study, the range of earnings *within* an industry was *six times* that across industries.[24] Consequently, a company's acquisition target or new business (internal development) market can be much more attractive than the industry as a whole. When the disparity is large, however, the corporation should satisfy itself that the factors that make the segment so much more attractive are likely to continue. In the minicomputer industry, once-attractive segments that made hardware targeted to specific industries (such as banking) have effectively been replaced by "generic" hardware in combination with industry-specific software. In response to these developments, IBM reduced its five minicomputer hardware lines to one and then had to compete head-to-head with very aggressive, low-price competitors.

For initiatives that pass this hurdle, attention should turn to the corporation's ability to take advantage of the opportunity: What does it bring to the table?

Can Important Resources or Capabilities Be Leveraged?

A corporation can be viewed as a combination of resources and capabilities. Its resources, which enable it to operate and provide value for its customers, are its people, funds, physical assets, external reputation (including corporate and brand names), and intellectual property (e.g., patents). Company executives adjust the mix of resources (by hiring people, buying machinery, raising capital, and training people) and then apply those resources to create capabilities that support customer-perceived competitive advantages.

The first step in identifying a firm's capabilities is to ask these questions: "What do we do particularly well?" and "Is what we do well important in creating and maintaining the customer-perceived competitive advantages that motivate people to buy our products rather than a competitor's?" To make this judgment, consider a capability's functional breadth, product-market breadth, imitability, and leverageability.

Functional Breadth

Some capabilities—for example, a product development capability—cross functional lines. Some management capabilities (such as managing decentralized units with the right mix of freedom and control) and financial capabilities (efficient working capital management) also cross functional lines. These capabilities may exist across a wide range of organizations.

Although cross-functional capabilities can be important, at least some of a company's most important capabilities reside within one or more of its line functions—R&D, manufacturing, and marketing. However, the capability often does not encompass the entire functional area. For instance, is a company's capability really R&D, or is it limited to a particular technology or field of science? Is its capability really manufacturing, or is it defined further by material and process technology (small batch, large batch, or mass production)? Is its capability marketing, or is it really advertising or direct sales or market segmentation?

Product-Market Breadth

Marketing capabilities in particular need to be examined to determine their product-market breadth. Marketing to consumers is very different from marketing to business customers, and marketing durable goods is very different from marketing items consumed directly. Even within these categories, customers' needs and purchase criteria may vary in ways that require different marketing approaches.

One can easily overestimate the product-market breadth of a company's capabilities. When Heublein purchased Hamm's Beer, it expected to be able to leverage its alcoholic beverage marketing capabilities, only to discover that beer drinkers had different motivations from drinkers of hard liquor. So Heublein's alcoholic beverage marketing capability did not transfer successfully.

Imitability

When other things are equal, capabilities that are hard to imitate create competitive advantages which, in turn, create economic value. Philip Morris purchased Miller Brewing to leverage its capabilities in marketing low-cost, mass-produced, disposable consumer goods.[25] It was very successful initially, but became less so when Anheuser-Busch began imitating Miller's marketing capabilities. This step was easy for Anheuser-Busch; it simply hired outstanding marketers with consumer product experience. On the other hand, Crown Cork & Seal developed a capability for outstanding customer service in the metal container industry, and for more than 30 years its service capability was not imitated successfully.

The capabilities hardest to imitate are those where competitors lack (and cannot get) critical information, where the time lags in imitation are very long, and where socially complex processes are involved.[26] Product development processes, for example, can require several functional areas to work together under moderate-to-heavy time constraints. In the mid-1980s, Japanese auto manufacturers were able to develop a new model almost two years faster than their American counterparts. American companies are catching up now, but their effort required far-reaching changes in the management of complex organizational processes.[27]

Leverageability

Leverage is the advantage gained from using an existing resource or capability in a new market, or to improve performance in a market currently served. Leverage can create substantial economic value. In considering the leverageability of resources or capabilities, their operating leverage and capacity are important factors. When fixed costs are a large percentage of total costs, operating leverage is high, and amortizing those costs over a larger output can reduce average unit cost significantly.[28]

Intangibles, such as a brand name, can be leveraged, too. For example, when using an established brand name in a new, related product area (where the brand name has relevant meaning for customers), the constraint is the need for some additional investment in advertising and promotion. (On the other hand, leveraging it into a new geographic area may necessitate a higher investment to get the name known.)

A major responsibility of corporate executives is to see that cross-business synergies are identified and exploited. Leveraging of resources and capabilities is the major source of these synergies. The next step in identifying value-creating opportunities is to consider transaction costs.

Are Costs of Transactions[29] (with Suppliers or Customers) High and Likely to Remain So?

Much business activity involves a market transaction—hiring employees, purchasing raw materials and components, hiring an advertising agency, and selling products or services through a distributor or franchisee, to name a few. There are some powerful incentives for conducting such transactions efficiently:

- Revenue generation is tightly coupled to meeting customer needs.
- Administrative coordination problems are reduced because organizations are smaller.

Two organizations in difficulty just a few years ago, General Motors and IBM, provide negative illustrations of economic efficiency. Both of these corporations lost a clear customer focus, had significant administrative coordination problems (in new product development and other areas). At IBM, CEO Lou Gerstner has exercised personal leadership to make the company more customer-focused and reduce the barriers to coordination.

However, in some circumstances, market transactions are far less efficient because transaction costs are high. Whenever transaction costs are high, there is an important information deficiency, such as in the following three instances:

1. When developing major, systemic innovations, the need for confidentiality may make timely progress difficult or impossible. Because information can prudently flow more freely within a single organization, expanding the scope of the corporation to include both units can substantially reduce transaction costs.

2. When one party to a market transaction is much better informed than the other and can't be trusted to be fully honest about sharing that information edge, and when there is only a small number of suppliers (or customers, as the case may be), it makes sense to expand the corporation's scope to include both units in the transaction.

3. When a transaction involves a task of extreme complexity, or when there are so many scenarios about the future that the time and cost to develop a contract for a market transaction would be excessive, placing both units into the same organization and making the decisions sequentially as time passes will be more efficient.[30]

For corporate executives, one major implication of an analysis of transaction costs is that it reveals the situations where vertical integration is typically *not* needed. This view suggests that vertical integration usually isn't required to ensure a regular source of supply or to ensure quality: Contracts, if carefully drawn, usually can provide both.

Can the Buyer Capture Enough of the Acquisition's Value It Seeks to Create?

Many diversification initiatives have not met their proponents' expectations for a variety of reasons. In some circumstances, the associated costs cancel out the anticipated benefits. In the case of self-development, how many new business initiatives fail before one succeeds? In the case of an acquisition, can the buyer capture enough of the value it intends to create?

Acquisition costs tend to be high. First, there is a *control premium,* the amount by which the price the buyer pays exceeds the market value before acquisition. Historically, in acquisitions of public companies, this has been approximately 40 percent. In the mid-1980s, it exceeded 60 percent! The control premium represents the present value of the amount of performance improvements that the buyer gives to the seller in return for the privilege of control. Second, boards of directors of selling companies are legally required to act as *fiduciaries* for the shareholders, usually selling to the party that makes the highest offer. In many instances where there are competing bids, an auction is held. Often, an overeager buyer suffers the winner's curse, or the penalty for overpaying. (In acquiring privately held companies, much less information is publicly available, and competing bids—and, consequently, the winners' curse—are less likely.)

To create net positive synergy, there must be sufficient economic value to cover the net present value of the control premium; deal-related fees to investment bankers, lawyers, and accountants; any additional costs associated with the new corporate parent; any negative synergies. If the value created does not exceed this minimum level, then, on balance, value has been destroyed.

Can the Initiative Be Implemented Effectively?

The greater the intended synergies among new and existing units, the more interaction there needs to be across these units. Units have structures, processes, and cultures, and they may or may not be compatible.[31] Implementation can be difficult when a company positioned in a mature business purchases a company in a rapidly growing segment of the same industry, with the expectation of swift knowledge transfer.

The logic of effectively managing mature units is very different from the one that is most effective for rapidly expanding units. For mature units, revenues and costs can be predicted more accurately, financial performance is an effective measure of unit performance, a larger portion of communication between units can be in written form (memos and plans), and effective controls can substantially improve performance. In a rapidly growing unit, on the other hand, an effective, expeditious product development process is more important than adherence to budget; organization structure and processes are less developed; and some controls (e.g., time clocks) can have negative effects. A new acquirer must ensure that the financial statements of the acquired unit can meaningfully be combined with those of the parent, but most other types of corporate support should be withheld. Many of the other elements of the mature parent company's system may destroy value in the growing, acquired unit. Before making any other organizational changes, management must consider why the unit was purchased and whether the unit's present arrangements provide better fit with a rapid growth environment. This approach requires a different mind-set on the part of those corporate staff members who see uniformity as an end in itself.

Frequently not asked is the opposite question: "Are there features of *the organization of the acquired unit* that we should emulate if we are trying to reposition ourselves into the growing segments of the market?" Acquirers seem to be much more effective at imposing their processes and culture on the acquiree than the reverse, regardless of the initial motivation for the acquisition.

To summarize, in determining whether particular scope changes are likely to create economic value, careful consideration needs to be given to:

- The attractiveness of the industry (or industry segment).
- Whether important capabilities or competitive advantages can be leveraged from existing to newly acquired businesses (or the reverse).
- Whether, in the case of vertical integration, factors are at work that make an arm's-length market transaction a less attractive alternative.

TABLE 2.1   Identifying Value-Creating Opportunities

1. What are our unique *resources?*

    Consider brand names, corporate name, proprietary manufacturing technology, patents, and other intellectual property.

2. What are our distinctive *capabilities?* What do we do particularly well?

    For capabilities *within a single function*, like R&D or marketing, consider the functional and product-market breadth. For example, "Marketing inexpensive products to consumers through the drug and discount channels" is a much more useful and accurate definition than "Marketing."

    Identify capabilities that *cross functional lines* and specify what makes each distinctive. For example, a product development process might be distinctive because, relative to competitors, it is speedier, involves less redesign, or is better targeted to customer needs.

3. What other companies (if they were fully informed) would want to merge with us, acquire us, or enter into a strategic alliance with us to get this benefit?

4. Into what product markets can these resources or capabilities be leveraged?

    In each market, can our firm create competitive advantages?

    Are these advantages easily imitated by others?

    Have unattractive industry segments been avoided?

5. What *complementary* resources or capabilities are needed?

    To take advantage of this opportunity, what resources do we need that we don't have now?

    What things do we need to be able to do that we don't do now?

6. Is this initiative likely to generate a satisfactory *return?*

7. Can the organization *implement* this initiative effectively?

- Whether the buyer can retain enough of the value created so that the upside potential is sufficient to make the downside risk a prudent one to bear.
- Whether the intended scope change can be implemented effectively.

Most diversifying moves have failed because of deficiencies one or more of these areas. Creating economic value through diversification is challenging because the corporation has to do many things well to succeed. Table 2.1 provides a summary of the questions to consider in identifying value-creating opportunities.

METHODS OF CHANGING SCOPE: EXPANSION AND CONTRACTION

A company might want to change its scope for one or more of the following reasons:

- Changes in its customer and competitive environments may make its present strategy less attractive.
- Output from its R&D lab may have promising applications outside its present businesses.
- Customers may want a wider range of product offerings.
- The company may have "missed" a major technical development.
- Shareholders may have grown impatient with efforts to create shareholder value in noncore businesses and may want divestment.

Each of these situations, as well as many others, calls for a change in a corporation's scope.

Although many circumstances can motivate a change in corporate scope, only limited methods are available for expanding or contracting scope. If scope expansion is desired, it can be done by internal development, acquisition, or some sort of strategic alliance (e.g., licensing, franchising, equity joint venture). Each of these options is considered here.

Internal Development

When a company develops a new business internally, it essentially builds it "from nothing": it develops the product or service, establishes the facilities, runs the operations, and does the marketing. In many instances, this sequence is an alternative to acquisition of an ongoing business.

Several factors affect the ease and desirability of internal new business development. First, how closely related is the new business to one or more of the company's existing businesses? The more closely related it is in product technology, process (manufacturing) technology, and product-market and customer target, the easier it is to develop the new business internally. The less closely related it is, the greater the number of complementary resources and capabilities necessary to bring the new business into operation.

If the primary relationship with the current business is in product-technology, the corporation can be propelled into very different product markets. Building on its capability in glass technology, Corning Glass Works has at various times been in the businesses of housewares, electronic components, television tubes, fiber-optic cables, medical instruments, laboratory glassware, industrial materials, and ophthalmic products (eyeglass blanks). Despite the company's core capability in glass technology, Corning has entered businesses employing different manufacturing technologies, customer types (business versus consumer), marketing channels, competitive advantages, and customer purchase criteria. Companies defining themselves in terms of a core technological capability need to consider carefully whether they can develop the complementary capabilities (in manufacturing and marketing) necessary for success in each of the product markets to which their technology takes them.

The reverse can occur where an organization's core capability is in marketing. Allegiance Corporation's hospital supply unit, for example, provides one-stop shopping for a wide array of products, including latex gloves, bandages, hospital beds, medical instrumentation, and medical devices. The products Allegiance offers have many different technologies and manufacturing processes.

Internal development has some disadvantages. First, it tends to be slow. In each area where new capabilities are needed, people need to be identified, hired, and given time to become productive in their new organizational setting. Second, although research is not conclusive, internal development seems to be not particularly profitable. A careful study found that internally developed new businesses generated returns that were moderate at best.[32] Because of these limitations, acquisition is a frequently used method for diversifying into new businesses.

Acquisition

Acquisitions have at least three advantages:

1. They are faster to accomplish than internal development, because the company acquired is typically "up and running."
2. Compared with internal development, more information is available to the prospective buyer to evaluate the move. In addition to the information the candidate provides to the prospective buyer, audited financial statements and filings to government agencies are available for publicly traded corporations; suppliers, customers, and even competitors can also be contacted for information (often through a third party).
3. A certain percentage of internally developed new businesses fail. By acquiring a going concern, the buyer does not need to pay for any of the failures along the way.

Acquisitions are not without their disadvantages:

1. An acquirer never has as much information about the target as it would like (especially in an unfriendly transaction), and it frequently gets some unexpected bad news after the deal closes.
2. Acquisitions can be expensive: As noted, a control premium of 40 percent is not uncommon for a publicly traded company. In practical terms, that means the first 40 percent increase in shareholder value created by the new owners goes to the sellers. (The control premium is usually paid at closing, in which case the sellers receive it whether or not the new owners are actually able to add value.[33])
3. Integration into the new parent can be difficult, sometimes destroying more value than the acquisition was expected to create.

An acquisition alternative worthy of consideration is the strategic alliance.

Strategic Alliances

A strategic alliance is any formal, interorganizational, collaborative relationship. In alliances, a firm seeks to receive the benefit of another company or business without owning it. A strategic alliance can take many forms, including: a long-term supply or marketing agreement, joint R&D, joint manufacturing or, in an equity joint venture, the creation of a new legal entity for specified purposes.

One or more of the following motives drives most joint ventures:

- Minimizing costs.
- Improving a firm's competitive position.
- Transferring organizational knowledge.

Merck and Johnson & Johnson, for example, created an equity joint venture to market pharmaceutical products that have moved from prescription to over-the-counter status. Merck gets its over-the-counter products marketed for a lower cost, and Johnson & Johnson is able to leverage its consumer products marketing capability over a wider range of products. An equity joint venture between Toyota and General Motors (GM) to build cars in the United States has provided GM with knowledge of more cost-effective and higher quality manufacturing processes, as well as with the opportunity to sell a car produced by the joint venture for a lower price. For its part, Toyota has received some U.S. manufacturing plant capacity more quickly than it could have built facilities.

Of all the anticipated knowledge-related benefits from strategic alliances, the hardest to transfer are an organization's complex routines, such as those used in an effective product development process.[34] Frequently, replicating the organization through the creation of a new entity—typically, an equity joint venture—is the only effective way to transfer those routines.

Parties considering strategic alliances need to ask: "What am I giving up, and what am I receiving in return? Is this in my short-run best interest? Is this in my long-run interest? Am I tutoring a new competitor (especially one that could unfavorably alter industry structure)?" The potential benefits of strategic alliances are often readily apparent, while the potential downside is less so. Because the potential downside is so great, organizations should choose partners in strategic alliances with great care. For each potential partner, these characteristics should be determined:

- Motivation to participate.
- Potential conflicts of interest.
- Preferred duration for the alliance.
- Level of integrity.

In microcomputer software, Microsoft had a joint venture with IBM to develop OS/2 at the same time it was devoting considerable energy and attention to developing its Windows desktop operating system, a direct competitor. Microsoft's success with Windows has negatively impacted sales of OS/2.

In many strategic alliances, the major item of value that changes hands is information. In such arrangements, it is important to make certain that the information that motivated entry into the venture is being received. The requisite number of people in the organization must either have it relayed to them or must be, for a time, assigned to the venture. Many American companies in joint ventures with Japanese companies complain that they spend too much time training the Japanese managers transferred in and out so frequently by their Japanese partners. What the Japanese partners are doing in these instances is ensuring that the information desired from the venture is acquired by many persons in their organization. American venture partners have not always been so effective in gathering information.

When thoughtfully designed and implemented and when partner motives are compatible, strategic alliances can be a great mutual boon to companies. But when these qualities are not present, such alliances can fail—or fail to accomplish one party's objectives and leave that party worse off than if it had not entered into the alliance. It may have tutored or strengthened a competitor, and if the alliance was intended to create a critically important capability or competitive advantage, the company has lost valuable time in attempting to make the alliance work.

When potential strategic alliances are analyzed with insufficient care and are implemented ineffectively, companies find that they often yield more heartbreak than help. Yet, with thoughtful analysis and implementation, strategic alliances have great potential to build capabilities or competitive advantages that can genuinely make a difference in the increasingly competitive business environment.

Thus, in expanding corporate scope, internal development, acquisition, and strategic alliances possess different strengths and challenges. The remaining task is to consider reductions in the corporation's scope.

Divestment

A corporation might have several reasons for wanting to remove one or more units from its portfolio:

- It may be correcting a past error in which it made a problematic acquisition. Xerox's purchase of Crum & Forster (a financial services firm) in the mid-1980s was greeted skeptically in the financial markets, so it was no surprise to many when Xerox announced its intention to divest it several years later.
- Changes in the competitive environment may no longer justify retaining a particular unit in the corporation. When the ready-to-eat cereal market grew more competitive, Ralston Purina divested its cereal business

because it felt it lacked a large enough market share to be a strong player.

- A corporation may divest a unit that it acquired reluctantly. For example, some businesses in the rapid-growth stage may integrate backward because suppliers do not exist or will not (or cannot) expand capacity rapidly enough to meet the businesses' needs. Later, when a market exists and has become more competitive, divestment may make sense.

- A corporation in financial difficulty (or seeking to work down a high level of debt) may divest a unit because of its marketability. Such a unit is typically a proven strong performer. TWA's sale of its routes to London is an example.

Companies can use different methods to accomplish a divestment. Because a company's goal is to exit from the business in as timely a fashion as is feasible, the objective is simply stated: Use the method that realizes the highest return.

In many instances, the most profitable divestment method to the seller is a *sale of the business* to another company in the same industry. Where there are operating synergies with other businesses of the buyer, the seller may be able to capture (through a high price) the economic value of a significant portion of the synergies the buyer can create. Unless the sale is explicitly structured otherwise, the seller receives the total proceeds at closing, and these funds can immediately be used for other corporate purposes or for distribution to shareholders.

In a *leveraged buyout* (LBO), the unit is sold to a group of managers in partnership with an investment firm in a highly leveraged transaction.[35] Sales to an LBO group can be very attractive to the sellers. However, the buyers may be astute negotiators, and it is not atypical for the selling company to hold some debt or equity in connection with the transaction. LBOs are not appropriate for rapid-growth businesses because they require too much investment to build the business. LBOs work best in mature markets, which can generate the cash flow needed to service the high level of debt. Because LBOs tend to be fully priced, a substantial portion of the debt service comes from funds generated by improved efficiency and the subsequent increases in cash flow. As a result, an undermanaged unit in a mature industry can make a particularly attractive LBO candidate.

When a unit is capable of functioning on a stand-alone basis, a *spin-off* may make sense. A spin-off typically does not generate revenue for the divesting corporation.[36] Rather, the capital stock of a division or subsidiary of a corporation is transferred to the stockholders of the parent corporation. A major consideration in designing a spin-off is to ensure that the unit is a viable entity on a stand-alone basis. Where the resources (e.g., plant, warehouse, or sales force) shared with another unit of the parent are significant, contractual arrangements for continued sharing or for the transfer of sufficient resources to the spin-off are critical. Further, the parent may need to make a cash infusion so that the spin-off's balance sheet is healthy enough for the unit to exist viably on its own. Esmark did this a decade ago when it successfully spun off its Swift meat unit.

A fourth divestment method is a *harvest* of the business. As with other divestment methods, the parent makes a final decision to exit from the business. Unlike the other alternatives, it continues to operate the business because in its judgment the net present value of continuing to operate the business for a specified time significantly exceeds the value available through sale or liquidation. Almost all investments are curtailed, R&D spending is drastically reduced and eventually eliminated, and all expenditures are scrutinized carefully. As sales volume declines, capacity is reduced until all assets are eventually liquidated. Harvesting is most likely when the parent company, with its inside knowledge of the business, has a more optimistic view of a declining business's prospects over the next few years than outsiders do.

A *liquidation of assets* is the least profitable avenue of all, because assets are worth much less than a going business. Liquidation is considered seriously only when no buyer is forthcoming, when the business lacks stand-alone capability, and when harvesting is not justified. When Control Data exited from the supercomputer business, it had to liquidate because, despite the investment made in the business over the years, the unit did not have a competitive product and had no value as a going concern.

SUMMARY

Corporate strategy addresses three questions:

1. What should the product-market, vertical, and geographic scope of a corporation be?
2. How should the units in the corporation be related to each other?
3. Where scope changes are needed, what method(s) should be used to bring current scope into alignment with desired scope?

Many corporations have been criticized by the capital markets for making what outsiders felt were inappropriate scope decisions. In the increasingly competitive markets of the 2000s, more attention needs to be paid to relatedness, or how the businesses in the corporate fold are linked to each other. When other things are equal, businesses that leverage important capabilities or competitive advantages will perform more strongly than their peers. The alternative methods of changing scope have profound implications for a company's present and future performance. They are equally deserving of corporate management's attention because, through these decisions, a company seeks to accomplish the strategic intentions embodied in its desired relatedness and scope.

NOTES

1. For a discussion of business unit strategy, see Chapter 3.

2. Boston Consulting Group, *Perspectives on Experience* (1968).

3. When the judgment is flawed or unduly pessimistic, it can be a substantial management misjudgment. Sometimes, it diverts management's attention from alternative ways in which it could meet the same needs of existing customers. The problems in the core business may continue to deepen at the same time the company is adding little to the business it diversifies into. Sears, Roebuck & Co., for example, diversified into financial services, to which it added little, while failing to address its retail business problems, and discount and specialty retailing continued to eat away at its market share.

4. However, the owner of a single-business firm—with most or all of his or her assets tied up in the firm—might wish to diversify to reduce exposure to a single business. Even in this case, purchasing debt or equity securities in other firms or mutual funds should be considered.

5. In addition to these stated reasons, three unstated reasons have motivated diversification. Some CEOs have diversified to satisfy ego needs, such as the desire to face a new challenge, to leave a large imprint on corporate history, or to have acquisition-related stories to share with other CEOs. Second, many executives find it more fun to manage a growing organization than a flat or shrinking one. A third unstated reason has been the increase of the CEO's personal wealth, where corporate size has too heavy a weighting in top executives' compensation. See Alfred Rappaport, *Creating Shareholder Value: The New Standard for Corporate Performance* (New York: Free Press, 1986).

6. Charles W. Hofer and Dan Schendel, *Strategy Formulation: Analytical Concepts* (St. Paul, MN: West, 1978).

7. This is discussed in H. Kurt Christensen, *Note on Synergy* (unpublished paper).

8. These are examples at the corporate level of strategic leadership, discussed in Chapter 1.

9. This question is the central theme of Chapters 10 and 11.

10. Richard P. Rumelt, *Strategy, Structure and Economic Performance* (Cambridge, MA: Harvard University Press, 1974).

11. H.K. Christensen and C.A. Montgomery, "Corporate Economic Performance: Diversification Strategy versus Market Structure," *Strategic Management Journal* (1981), 2:327–343.

12. R. Grant, "On 'Dominant Logic,' Relatedness and the Link between Diversity and Performance," *Strategic Management Journal* (1988), 9:639–642.

13. Readers are referred to Chapter 8 for a more detailed discussion of technology as a source of 3M's competencies.

14. Global strategy is the focus of Chapter 4.

15. The creation of trading blocs in Europe, North America, and elsewhere argues for more coordination across national boundaries than the multidomestic strategy implies.

16.   For a discussion of the step-by-step approach of Japanese firms to the European marketplace, see Achim A. Stoehr, "Japanese Positioning for Post-1992 Europe," in Liam Fahey, *Winning in the New Europe: Taking Advantage of the Single Market* (Englewood Cliffs, NJ: Prentice-Hall, 1992).

17.   For a related discussion of the analysis of vertical integration, see Chapter 8.

18.   In some adversarial situations, partial integration may make sense to gain cost (and other) information that will provide leverage in bargaining and will create an implied threat that a company will integrate fully if price or performance becomes unsatisfactory. Backward integration of canned-product companies into can manufacturing is one example.

19.   It will take longer than originally intended for these benefits to be realized, since labor union negotiations have successfully extended the period of GM-level pay and benefits.

20.   This discussion utilizes the terminology of product-market scope. However, the same questions can be made appropriate for assessing geographic scope decisions simply by substituting "national market" or "regional market" for "industry," "industry segment," or "product-market."

21.   Michael E. Porter, "From Competitive Advantage to Corporate Strategy," *Harvard Business Review* (1987), 65(3):43–59.

22.   See Michael E. Porter, *Competitive Strategy: Techniques for Analyzing Industries and Competition* (New York: Free Press, 1980), Chap. 1.

23.   For explanations of variation in profitability across and within industries, see Chapter 8.

24.   Richard P. Rumelt, "How Much Does Industry Matter?" *Strategic Management Journal* (1991), 12(3):167–185.

25.   "The Seven-Up Division of Philip Morris," Harvard Business School Case (1985), p. 5.

26.   Margaret A. Peteraf, "The Cornerstones of Competitive Advantage: A Resource-Based View," *Strategic Management Journal* (1993), 14:179–191.

27.   Kim Clark and Takahira Fujimoto, *Product Development Performance* (Boston: Harvard Business School, 1991).

28.   Birger Wernerfelt, "From Critical Resources to Corporate Strategy," *Journal of General Management* (1989), 14(3):4–12.

29.   A transaction is an economic exchange in which one party gives up something in return for something else. The items exchanged can be products, services, or funds. Transaction costs are the costs associated with making a particular transaction. They can range from relatively low (as when a company orders standard office supplies from a catalog) to relatively high (as in a merger with a high control premium). Organizations make most of their transactions externally—in markets. But, when organizations make "something they can buy," that transaction occurs internally within the organizational hierarchy. For a given transaction, lower transaction costs will usually occur in a market, but in some instances these costs are lower in a hierarchy.

30.   Oliver E. Williamson, *Markets and Hierarchies: Analysis and Antitrust Implications* (New York: Free Press, 1975).

31.   Chapters 16 and 17 cover in detail the role of structure and decision processes in shaping and executing strategy.

32. E. Ralph Biggadike, "The Risky Business of Diversification," *Harvard Business Review* (1979), 57(3):103–111.

33. The exception is when there is an earn-out provision and the final price depends in part on earnings in the years after the acquisition closes. This is more common in acquisitions of a privately held firm.

34. The manner in which routines embodying knowledge constitute a central element in an organization's culture is noted in Chapter 17.

35. An entire company can be involved in an LBO, but in the context of divestment, LBOs occur at the unit level.

36. However, when a spin-off is combined with an initial public offering (IPO) for the newly spun-off unit, there can be a cash return to the divesting parent.

BUSINESS UNIT STRATEGY: THE QUEST FOR COMPETITIVE ADVANTAGE

3

Anil K. Gupta
University of Maryland

This chapter addresses the challenge of strategy creation at the "business unit" level. We use the term *business unit* broadly to include single-business companies operating independently as well as a division, a subsidiary, or a profit center within the multibusiness corporation.

There is a fundamental difference between strategic concerns at the corporate versus the business unit level. While corporate strategy, within a multibusiness corporate setting, deals with broad issues such as what businesses to be in and how to exploit synergies across businesses, business unit strategy deals with how to compete successfully within a given industry.[1]

The challenge of creating (or re-creating) a business unit's strategy can be broken down into five interrelated subtasks:

1. *Setting Business Unit Goals.* What financial and nonfinancial targets will drive the business unit's strategic direction over the coming future?

2. *Defining Business Unit Scope.* What are the boundaries of the product-market arena—its "sandbox"—in which the business unit will play?

3. *Defining the Intended Bases for Competitive Advantage.* Why should targeted customers prefer buying from you rather than from your competitors?

4. *Designing the Value Chain System.* How will the business unit create and sustain competitive superiority along the intended bases of competitive advantage?

5. *Managing the Value Chain.* How will the business unit manage its own value chain activities as well as the integration of these activities with the value chains of customers, suppliers, and other business partners?

The process of developing answers to these questions must be both creative and analytical. The need for analysis is obvious; managers must have fresh and accurate data about markets, competitors, and customer needs if they are to make appropriate long- and short-term decisions. However, the imperative for creativity derives from the following observations:

- *Major Discontinuities in the External Environment.* The external environment of the firm is constantly changing—sometimes incrementally and, at other times, in a quantum and discontinuous fashion.[2] Changes in the external environment almost always require that the business must invent at least some new rules of the game. From the perspective of a financial services firm such as Merrill Lynch, the aging of the population represents an ongoing incremental change whereas the emergence of Internet trading represents a radical discontinuous change.

- *Proactive Reshaping of the Industry Structure.* Changes in the external environment do not always originate from external forces. Firms, large and small, can often proactively reshape the external environment. Reshaping the industry proactively is always an act of creation and changes the rules of the game. Sun Microsystems recently announced that it will begin to offer application software, such as word-processing programs, over the Internet. Unlike the historical approach to application software, these programs need not be purchased for installation on the personal computer (PC); instead, they can be rented from Web servers on an as-needed basis. Sun's move is aimed squarely at undercutting the power of the Windows operating system, the core product of Microsoft, a much larger competitor. Despite its market dominance, Microsoft has been forced to follow suit and has announced that it too will embrace the renting of application programs over Web servers.

- *Need to Break out of the Competitive Pack.* In the absence of collusion, it is a given that competitors inevitably will find themselves pursuing conflicting goals. In the PC industry, at least three of the major players (Compaq, Dell, and Hewlett-Packard) have at various times declared their intention to be the market share leader in the industry. In such a situation, continuing to play by the old rules leaves the firm highly vulnerable to preemption by the more innovative competitors.

SETTING BUSINESS UNIT GOALS

As the old saying goes, "If you don't know where to go, any road will take you there." Thus, the establishment of goals is the first step in developing a coherent business strategy.

The setting of business unit goals should be driven by three considerations: a balanced focus on both short- as well as long-term measures of performance, a recognition of the business unit's role in the corporate portfolio, and a bias in favor of goals that stretch the capabilities of the business unit.

Short-Term versus Long-Term Measures of Performance

We take for granted that the ultimate goal of every business is to maximize return to shareholders. It is critical to remember, however, that maximizing return to shareholders is not synonymous with maximizing short-term profitability (profit margins, return on capital employed, etc.). At any point in time, the market value of a company (or business unit) represents the net present value of all expected future earnings over the short as well as the long term. Thus, any efforts directed at short-term profitability must be assessed not only for their impact on current income but also for their impact on the firm's ability to generate future income.

A direct implication of the preceding arguments is that the maximization of next year's or even the next five years' earnings would rarely be the ideal goal for all businesses in a corporation. At the same time, the needs of ongoing feedback and managerial control require that business unit performance be assessed at least annually. The solution to this dilemma lies in adopting a balanced multidimensional approach to the setting of business unit goals and to the measurement and assessment of business unit performance. The most extensive recent work in this area has been done by Kaplan and Norton[3] who suggest that businesses should be assigned goals and measured from four perspectives:

1. *Financial* (profit margins, return on assets, cash flow).
2. *Customer* (market share, customer satisfaction index).
3. *Internal Business* (employee retention, cycle time reduction).
4. *Innovation and Learning* (percent sales from new products).

Measured by these criteria, business unit goals would almost always differ across business units and would be a function of industry trends, the nature of competition, the business unit's historical performance, and managerial aggressiveness and ambition, as well as propensity for taking risks.

A Recognition of the Business Unit's Role in the Corporate Portfolio

Some business units operate fairly autonomously whereas others have a high degree of interdependence with other business units. Considered in the context of interdependence and the resulting synergy, optimizing the performance of the entire corporation will generally not be synonymous with optimizing the performance of every business unit in isolation. In such a context, the setting of business unit goals must take into account the business unit's role as one component in an interconnected system.

Consider, for example, the Lexus and the Corolla product lines of Toyota. In a company such as Toyota, *product* innovations typically originate in the luxury division and then migrate to the mass-market division. In contrast, *process* innovations typically originate in the mass-market division and then flow up to the luxury division. In this context, it would be highly appropriate if the goals of the two divisions also include explicit responsibility for innovation and transfer of product or process know-how as the case may be.

A Bias for Stretch

Complacence is the enemy of creativity and innovation. Thus, it is essential that, in setting business unit goals, corporate executives should encourage and demand the setting of *stretch goals—*goals that cannot be achieved by continuing to play by the historical rules. As Jack Welch, the celebrated chief executive of General Electric has observed, "If you know how to get there, it's not a stretch target."[4] Of course, in setting stretch goals, it is important to remember that, while the path toward the realization of the goals may not be clear at the outset, the goals themselves must remain within the bounds of potential feasibility. Beyond a certain threshold, when the goals begin to appear completely unrealistic and unachievable, they rapidly start to lose their motivational value and effectiveness.

DEFINING BUSINESS-UNIT SCOPE

Business unit scope refers to the boundaries of the product-market arena—the "sandbox" where the business unit will "play." Even when the overall industrial sector is clearly defined, every business unit has considerable choice regarding the boundaries of its own product-market domain within the broad arena.

The three dimensions of business unit scope are customer segment scope, geographic scope, and product and service scope.[5] Consider the case of General Electric's Lighting Division. Customer segment scope refers to issues such as whether GE Lighting should focus on lighting for the home, for offices, for factories, for automobiles, for highways, and so forth. Geographic scope refers to the question of which country markets GE Lighting should target. Finally, product and service scope refers to the range of products and services GE Lighting should offer to its targeted customers.

Defining the scope of a business unit requires paying attention to strategic imperatives as well as managerial choices. We use the term *strategic imperative* to refer to those scope decisions dictated largely by the industry context, a reality that leaves little room for managerial discretion. For example, given potentially huge economies of scale in both R&D and production in the semiconductor industry, it would be highly imprudent for a chip manufacturer to define its geographic scope as anything other than global. On the other hand, there is always room for managerial discretion. For example, for much of its history, Dell Computer defined its target customers as corporations, government agencies, and educational institutions; it is only in the latter half of the 1990s that Dell broadened its customer scope to also include individual home-based customers.

Strategic Imperatives as Drivers of Business Unit Scope

Suppose the letters "A" and "B" refer to two adjacent product-market arenas: two customer segments (e.g., industrial and individual customers), or two geographic markets (e.g., France and Germany), or two product lines (e.g., automobile tires and truck tires). How should a manager decide whether it is a strategic imperative (a must) for the business unit to compete in both arenas if it chooses to compete in any one of them? The answer to this question rests on the answer to another question: What is the size of the competitive advantage that a well-managed player who competes in both A and B will derive relative to a well-managed player who competes in just A or just B? The larger the magnitude of such advantage, the stronger is the strategic imperative for the business unit to play in both arenas rather than in just one of them. The size of this advantage, in turn, depends on the magnitude of both demand-side and supply-side synergies between arenas A and B.

Demand-side synergies refer to the benefits that customers might derive from a single source of supply. These benefits can range from almost none to very large. For example, consider a company such as Caterpillar. Even if it could, it is doubtful that Caterpillar would perceive any benefits from buying both steel and computers from the same supplier. Within Caterpillar, steel and computers are purchased at different times, with differing degrees of frequency, by different purchasing departments using very different purchasing criteria; thus, steel and computers have almost no demand-side synergies. However, Caterpillar may perceive significantly higher benefits from purchasing computer hardware, software, and related services from a single source; thus, hardware, software, and related services may be said to have very high demand-side synergies. In contrast, *supply-side synergies* refer to improved designs or cost efficiencies that a supplier can realize on account of playing in both arenas. Here too, the synergies can range from almost none (e.g., when Xerox sold photocopiers as well as insurance services) to very large (e.g., Amazon.com's move into the retailing of other products besides books).

For a compelling example of the power of both demand- and supply-side synergies, consider what happened when Microsoft created an integrated Microsoft Office package in the early 1990s. Prior to this move, the dominant word-processing program (WordPerfect), the dominant spreadsheet program (Lotus 1–2-3), the dominant database program (dBase), and the dominant presentation graphics program (Harvard Graphics) were supplied by different companies. Microsoft's integrated bundle of programs was not only more user-friendly for the customer (demand-side synergies such as a common interface and easier data portability) but also more efficient to develop (supply-side synergies due to partial commonality in software code). Microsoft's resulting dominance in office application software illustrates the power of recognizing strategic imperatives ahead of competitors.

The Exercise of Managerial Discretion

In those contexts where the strategic imperatives to play in two or more contiguous arenas are weak or nonexistent, the business unit nonetheless must determine whether it should play in only arena A, only arena B, both arenas, or none of them. Given the absence of a strategic imperative to compete simultaneously in both arenas, the answer to this question should be derived separately for each arena.

For each arena, four considerations should drive the decision to play or not to play in the particular arena: market size and growth rate, size of competitive advantage, springboard value, and cost of entry. An arena becomes increasingly more attractive when (1) its size and growth rate are larger, (2) the business unit would be able to create and sustain a significant competitive advantage, (3) the arena would be an excellent springboard for potential entry into other attractive market segments, and (4) the potential cost of entry would be lower than these potential benefits. Dell Corporation's decision to go beyond the institutional market and also target home-based customers had these primary drivers for its change in business scope: a much higher growth in the home customer segment compared with the largely saturated institutional customer segment, and the emergence of Internet retailing, which significantly reduces Dell's cost of serving this traditionally lower margin segment.

Box 3.1 summarizes Dell Computer's business scope. As this box illustrates, a comprehensive definition of business unit scope requires paying explicit attention to all three dimensions: customer segment scope, geographic scope, and product and service scope. Dell started its life in the early 1980s as an assembler of desktop PCs for small businesses. As is obvious from Box 3.1, the company's business scope expanded dramatically over the 20 years.

DEFINING THE INTENDED BASIS FOR COMPETITIVE ADVANTAGE

A central component of any business unit strategy is clarity about why customers should prefer to buy goods and services from you rather than from your competitors. Addressing this question requires paying attention to the following five core ideas:

1. *Always Think of Competitive Advantage in Relative Terms.* Competitive advantage can only be defined in relative, rather than absolute, terms. Even

---

Box 3.1

Dell Computer's Business Scope—Circa 1997

Customer Segment Scope

Large enterprises (> 18,000 employees)
Large corporate accounts (2,000–18,000 employees)
Preferred accounts (400–2,000 employees)
Small- to medium-sized businesses (2–400 employees)
Federal government agencies
State and local government agencies
Educational institutions
Home office/small office customers

Geographic Scope

Worldwide (every continent but not yet every country)

Product and Service Scope

Product Lines
Dell Dimension (high-end desktops)
Dell OptiPlex (network-ready desktops)
Dell Inspiron (high-end notebooks)
Dell Latitude (network-ready notebooks)
Dell PowerEdge (network servers)

Services
DellWare (one-stop shopping service for thousands of hardware and software products)
Dell Asset Management (financing and leasing services)
Dell Premier Pages (online interfaces with key corporate accounts)

Abstracted from V.K. Rangan and M. Bell, "Dell Online," Harvard Business School Case 9-598-116, 1998.

---

products or services that are unique in their industry must compete with other alternatives from other industries that are available to customers.

2. *Be Explicit about Competitive Advantages as Well as Disadvantages.* Customer buying decisions are based on an aggregated evaluation of your product and service bundle vis-à-vis that of competitors. What matters is your net competitive advantage, that is, the balance between your relative advantages and disadvantages rather than just your competitive advantages.

3. *Strive for Multiple Sources of Competitive Advantage.* Competitive advantage must be thought of as existing in layers, like an onion's skin. That is, a company's offerings can be better than competitors' along many different dimensions—price, delivery time, quality, technology, and esthetics, to name a few. The more layers that contribute to competitive advantage, the more sustainable would be the business unit's dominance of its market.

4. *Align the Two Faces of Competitive Advantage—What the Business Unit Does Onstage and Its Capabilities Backstage.* Onstage advantage in terms of customer buying criteria cannot be sustained without backstage advantage in terms of required resources and competencies.

5. *Expect the Terms of Competition to Shift over Time.* The relevant grounds for competitive advantage can and often do change, sometimes dramatically, over time.

Always Think of Competitive Advantage in Relative Terms

It is tempting for managers to define the basis for their business' competitive advantage in absolute terms such as excellent products, excellent service, and great prices. These statements, however, obscure an important issue: What matters in the marketplace is not how good the company's products, services, and prices are but whether any or all of them are perceived as superior to those of competitors.

To see how relative competitive advantage can work in a market, consider a 10-year survey on new car reliability published by *Consumer Reports* magazine in April 1991. According to this survey, in 1980, on average, General Motors' cars had 110 problems per 100 new cars compared with about 43 problems per 100 cars for the "worst" of the three major Japanese suppliers (Toyota, Nissan, and Honda). By 1990, the figures for General Motors were down to 40 problems per 100 cars. However, the Japanese companies were now at about 17 problems per 100 cars. Obviously, GM had made remarkable improvement in the reliability of its cars during the decade of the 1980s. However, the data also suggest that, on a relative basis, in 1990, GM was still at a competitive disadvantage. As the company has realized to its disappointment, when the customer compares one supplier with another, what counts is relative superiority and not absolute performance.

Be Explicit about Competitive Advantages as Well as Disadvantages

It is virtually impossible for any business, no matter how well managed, to be superior to all competitors on every customer buying criterion. Otherwise, such a player's market share would have to be 100 percent, something that's not true even for Microsoft's operating system for PCs. At any point in time, every business must be seen as having a relative competitive advantage along some attributes, a relative competitive disadvantage along some other attributes, and competitive parity along the remaining attributes. And, this realization must be explicit in the minds of the company's senior managers.

There are two critical reasons why every company must be explicit and specific not only about its competitive advantages but also about its competitive disadvantages and competitive parities:

1. When deciding whose products and services to buy, the customer always evaluates the entire bundle of attributes. Thus, the customer weighs your company's relative advantages against your relative disadvantages. Alternatively stated, your company's net competitive advantage rests on the balance between the advantages and the disadvantages. Thus, ignoring or feigning blindness to your competitive disadvantages runs the serious risk of grossly overestimating the impact that your competitive advantages are likely to have on your market share and profit performance.

2. Explicit surfacing of competitive disadvantages is an essential first step in figuring out whether such disadvantage can be eliminated either through internal transformation or through the outsourcing of the particular activity to a more competent external supplier. For any company, as for any manager, there is nothing worse than "unconscious incompetence."

Strive for Multiple Sources of Competitive Advantage

Every business should strive for multiple sources (rather than just one source) of competitive advantage. For many years, strategy theory postulated that businesses should strive to compete on the basis of either low cost or differentiation. However, the notion that every business must choose between either "differentiation" or "cost leadership" simplifies the reality facing most companies too grossly to be of much practical value.

Take the case of two highly successful product lines within Daimler-Chrysler—the upmarket Mercedes-Benz and the mass market Neon. We would argue that passionate cost control (not cost reduction, per se) is just as critical for Mercedes-Benz as it is for Neon. It is true that Mercedes-Benz' target customers are much less price sensitive than those of Neon. However, it would be a mistake to conclude that customers' lack of price sensitivity should, in any manner, affect this division's passion for cost control. Suppose that Daimler-Chrysler engineers can figure out how to reduce the cost of a Mercedes E300 by 4 percent without reducing its performance or diminishing customer-perceived features in any way. Because this product line's customers are not very price sensitive, the next step may not be to reduce the prices by 4 percent. Instead, the decision may be to invest part or all of the cost savings in improved features or higher performance. Since Mercedes customers are performance rather than price sensitive, it is even conceivable that these improvements may lead to an increase in the final price. Thus, passionate cost control in the case of the Mercedes-Benz product line may well be one of the drivers behind improved performance and higher, rather than lower, prices.

In contrast, in the case of Chrysler Neon, given the high price sensitivity of its target customers, it is likely that a 4 percent cost reduction might lead to a decision to reduce the prices by a like amount. However, despite this passion for cost control and lower prices for this unit, it would be unwise to suggest that lower prices should constitute the only basis for competitive advantage. While the Neon customer may not care much about leather seats or high acceleration, he or she may place very high importance on other differentiable attributes such as reliability, legroom, safety, and fuel efficiency.

There is always more than one way to differentiate any product, even if it apparently is a commodity product such as steel (where the differentiation may be along attributes such as consistency of product quality and short delivery times). Further, not all types of differentiation necessarily increase the cost structure (as in the case of Swatch watches with their wide variety of strap and dial designs). Thus, within the bounds of the prices that the target customer would pay, the more numerous the types of differentiation advantage that a business unit can create, the more sustainable would be its dominance of the market.

Box 3.2 lists the multiple points of potential competitive advantage for a typical product along the entire purchase and consumption cycle from the time

---

Box 3.2

Discovering Opportunities for Creation of Competitive Advantage

Analyze the whole customer purchase and consumption cycle:

- How does the customer realize the need for a purchase?
- How does the customer define his/her needs?
- How does the customer identify alternatives?
- How does the customer choose the vendor?
- How does the customer place the order?
- How does the customer pay for the order?
- How does the customer follow up on inquiries?
- How are the goods and services delivered?
- How are the delivered goods stored?
- How are the delivered products and services used?
- How are the delivered goods maintained and upgraded?
- How does the customer decide when to replace the goods and services?
- How does the customer dispose of the old goods?

that the customer recognizes the need for a purchase to the time that he/she needs to get rid of the obsolete product or packaging.

Align the Two Faces of Competitive Advantage—What the Business Unit Does Onstage and Its Capabilities Backstage

To use the analogy of a theater, it is critical to think of competitive advantage and disadvantage at two levels of reality—onstage and backstage. Onstage advantage refers to competitive advantage in terms of customer buying criteria. In the competitive battle between Coke and Pepsi, onstage advantage or disadvantage would refer to relative positions on attributes such as price, image, taste, and availability. In contrast, backstage advantage refers to competitive advantage at the level of the underlying resources and competencies that drive the creation of onstage advantages or disadvantages. In the contest between Coke and Pepsi, backstage advantage would refer to relative positions on attributes such as cost structure, advertising efficiency, advertising skills, and strength of bottling infrastructure. In our experience, companies often make the mistake of launching competitive attacks on their rivals without first analyzing and ensuring that an alignment exists between onstage and backstage advantage.

In the absence of backstage advantage, launching an attack on a rival almost always proves disastrous for the attacker. Let us examine this point in greater detail by looking once again at the cola wars. Suppose this is 1975 and you are managing Pepsi's soft drinks business. You trail Coke in major distribution channels (supermarkets, vending machines, and fast-food outlets). You would like to steal some share away from Coke in the supermarket channel. How do you do it? Should you, for example, cut prices or increase dealer margins or increase ad spending or some combination of these moves? In answering this question, it is important to remember that each of these onstage moves will invite retaliation from Coke. The backstage driver of each of these moves is cost structure. If Coke's cost structure is lower than Pepsi's, then you can bet that, in the ensuing war of moves and countermoves, Coke will have an inherent advantage over Pepsi in cutting prices, increasing ad spending, and increasing dealer margins. Thus, any attempt by Pepsi to use any of these moves to wrest market share away from Coke is almost certain to backfire. The result might well be both lower market share as well as lower profit margins.

So, what should Pepsi do? Let us say that market research indicates that, in blind taste tests, consumers prefer the sweeter taste of Pepsi over that of Coke. Armed with this knowledge, perhaps the wisest move might be to launch a Pepsi taste-test challenge against Coke. In most other industries (e.g., cars or consumer electronics), a competitor would almost always imitate and neutralize your product advantages feature by feature. However, in the soda business, for the hard core of consumers, taste preferences tend to be very rigidly held. Thus, any attempt by Coke to sweeten its formula to retain the swing consumers runs a high risk of alienating the core base of loyal consumers. In other words, a taste-test challenge by Pepsi is likely to leave Coke frozen in retaliating against Pepsi in kind and with equal vigor, speed, and effectiveness.

Suppose Pepsi does launch a taste-test challenge and starts to steal market share away from Coke. If you were managing Coke and were largely frozen out of the option of fiddling with your product attributes, what would you do? Note that Coke's backstage advantage lies in a lower cost structure. Thus, you would retaliate against Pepsi not on the product front but on other fronts such as lower prices, higher ad spending, and/or higher dealer margins; on these other fronts, a backstage advantage on cost structure does matter.

Competitive battles should be seen not as one-shot skirmishes but as a dynamic multiround game of moves and countermoves. A smart company would be wise to follow another piece of advice from GE's Jack Welch: "If you don't have a competitive advantage, don't compete." The idea behind these words is consistent with that of the famous Chinese military adviser, Sun Tzu: "You must already have a win before you launch the attack."

Expect the Terms of Competition to Shift over Time

There are at least two reasons for this shift:

1. *Change in Customer Priorities and Buying Behavior.* Customers' priorities change over time for a variety of reasons—recession, availability of substitutes, changes in the customer's product or process technology, and so forth. Prior to the emergence of the quartz watch, timekeeping quality was a primary differentiating factor. However, once the quartz watch became ubiquitous, the cheapest quartz watch kept better time than the most expensive mechanical watch. Thus, the differentiating factor switched from timekeeping quality to features (such as a sports stopwatch and watch plus calculator) and design (e.g., unusual or traditional dial faces). The industrial valves sold by companies such as Fisher Controls, Masoneilan, and Neles Controls provide another example. As the buyers of these companies have become increasingly global, the ability to offer a globally coordinated supply of valves has become an important differentiating factor in addition to product features, quality, service, and prices.

2. *Achievement of Competitive Parity.* Even if customer priorities remain unchanged, competitive dynamics themselves often result in changing the relevant bases for competitive advantage. Take the case of Honda automobiles. The superior reliability of Honda cars was a major, though not the only, factor behind the emergence of Honda Accord as the best selling

car in the United States during the late 1980s. However, the obviousness of reliability as a key success factor also implied that this was one of the areas where the weaker competitors pushed the hardest to improve their own performance. As the reliability gap between Honda and its competitors diminished to a marginal level, reliability has become a standard attribute of cars in this class. Customers can now assume that several, if not all, competitors are highly reliable. This achievement of competitive parity has shifted the battle to other variables such as styling. When Honda's styling was viewed by its target customers as "dated," it suffered a loss in market share even though the reliability of its cars has apparently remained superb. In any industry, key success factors will invariably change over time, if for no other reason than the achievement of competitive parity along the key success factors of yesterday.

Box 3.3 summarizes Dell Computer's competitive advantages as of 1997. As can be seen from this box, Dell succeeded in building multiple bases of superiority over its competitors. In large measure, these advantages in terms of customer buying criteria have derived from Dell's backstage superiority in managing the supply chain. We discuss the details of how Dell has designed and managed its supply chain in the following section.

Box 3.3

Dell Computer's Competitive Advantages—Circa 1997

Backstage Advantages (In terms of Internal Resources and Capabilities)	**Onstage Advantages** (In terms of Customer Buying Criteria)
Superior supply chain management (see Box 3.4 for details) Superior ability to forecast market demand	Lower cost of ownership First mover in bringing leading-edge component technology to the customer (on average, components in Dell's PCs were 60 days newer than in IBM or Compaq PCs) Higher degree of product and service customization to specific customer segments Lower failure rate out of the box More efficient and convenient purchasing process for experienced PC users

Abstracted from V.K. Rangan and M. Bell, "Dell Online," Harvard Business School Case 9-598-116, 1998.

DESIGNING THE VALUE CHAIN SYSTEM

The concept of value chain originates from the work of Michael Porter[6] and refers to the set of interrelated activities all the way from the upstream to the downstream that a business unit carries out by itself and in concert with its suppliers, customers, and other business partners. The design and management of the value chain system has a direct and determining impact on the creation of customer value, the magnitude of competitive advantage, and the creation of shareholder value. In the absence of clarity regarding the design of the value chain system, other statements regarding business strategy are little more than a set of hopes, wishes, and dreams and thus highly incomplete.

There are two main components of the design of the value chain system for any business unit:

1. *Design of the Value Chain Architecture.* What is the design of the basic value-creation system through which inputs will be converted into outputs?
2. *Internalization versus Outsourcing.* Within the context of the value chain architecture, which activities will the business unit execute itself and which other activities it will outsource to suppliers, other business partners, or even customers?

Design of the Value Chain Architecture

The conversion of raw inputs into higher value added outputs always involves a whole network of value chain activities that are connected to each other through serial and/or parallel links. We use the term *architecture* to refer to the design of this network. There is always more than one way to design the architecture of a value chain. For example:

- U.S. Steel and Nucor Steel have historically adopted very different value chain architectures for producing sheet steel for, say, home appliances (e.g., refrigerator doors). U.S. Steel starts with iron ore, and then by utilizing the traditional integrated steel mill technology, converts it into solid steel ingots, which are then reheated and rolled into steel sheets. In contrast, Nucor starts with a more expensive raw material, scrap steel, and then by utilizing a combination of minimill and compact strip process technologies, converts the scrap into sheet steel in one continuous process. For much of its 30-year history as a steel maker, Nucor's total costs have been less than the variable costs of U.S. Steel. Not surprisingly, Nucor is now close to overtaking U.S. Steel as America's largest steel producer.
- The traditional furniture manufacturer assembles the entire furniture (e.g., a sofa, a dining table, or a bookcase) in the factory and then ships the items to retail stores. Given the bulkiness of the items, storage and

shipping costs tend to be high. Thus, most retail stores keep only a few display pieces in stock and the furniture is generally produced and shipped within a few weeks after the placement of a customer order. The ensuing logistics and cost considerations also imply that, around the world, the furniture industry is largely local in terms of both production and consumption.

In contrast, IKEA has chosen to design its furniture in such a way that the furniture components can be flat-packed in a compact cardboard box and are relatively easy to self-assemble by the customer. Such a design approach allows IKEA to radically reduce the cost of long-distance shipping and storage. The net result is that IKEA can manufacture in Poland or Thailand where labor and raw material costs are low and sell in markets as far apart as Milan or Washington, D.C. This unique value chain architecture allows IKEA to enjoy a significantly lower cost structure because it can optimize the choice of sourcing and production locations, lower storage and shipping costs, and no assembly costs (this activity has simply been "outsourced" to the customer). In addition, IKEA's customers can take their new furniture home with them when they purchase it instead of waiting months for delivery.

Box 3.4 compares the value chain architecture pioneered by Dell in the PC industry with that of its major rivals. As this box illustrates, to differentiate itself from its rivals—IBM, Compaq, and Hewlett-Packard—Dell has chosen to adopt a radically different value chain architecture. When Dell made its decision, its competitors bought components from the suppliers, assembled the PCs in their factories, and shipped the finished PCs to retail stores or resellers for sale and delivery to customers. In contrast, Dell has utilized toll-free telephone lines (and now the Internet) to sell directly to end-customers without using any third-party intermediaries. The PC is custom-produced after an order has been received and is shipped directly from the factory to the customer's location. In addition, Dell has designed an integrated supply chain linking its suppliers very closely to its assembly factories and the order-intake system. As recounted by Michael Dell, the company's founder and CEO: "We tell our suppliers exactly what our daily production requirements are. So it's not 'Well, every two weeks deliver 5,000 to this warehouse, and we'll put them on the shelf, and then we'll take them off the shelf.' It's 'Tomorrow morning, we need 8,562, and deliver them to door number seven by 7 A.M.'"[7] The net result is that Dell's average inventory levels are a fraction of the figures for its competitors. Box 3.4 also summarizes the multiple types of competitive advantages that Dell is able to create on the basis of its dramatically superior value chain architecture. As a consequence, Dell has been consistently and enormously profitable and has steadily increased its market shares in an otherwise brutally competitive commoditylike industry.

As the Nucor, IKEA, and Dell examples point out, alternative value chain architectures are rarely equivalent in terms of their ability to create customer

---

Box 3.4

Dell Computer's Value Chain Architecture—Circa 1997

Dell's "Direct" Model
(Build-to-order pull-through system, just-in-time materials, continuous manufacturing flow, and direct shipment)

Suppliers → Dell → Customers

Competitors' "Indirect" Model
(Build-to-stock system)

Suppliers → PC Manufacturer → Retailer/Reseller → Customer

Advantages Created by Dell's Direct Model

Elimination of transaction costs associated with retailers and resellers.

On average, 7–13 days of inventory versus 60–100 days in the typical indirect model.

Six percent lower cost of components (because component prices fall continually and Dell's PC components are, on average, 60 days newer).

First mover advantage in offering leading-edge component technologies.

Direct contacts with customers and, thus, superior understanding of customer needs and also superior ability to forecast demand.

Build-to-order manufacturing and, thus, superior ability to customize hardware and software configurations for each customer.

No need to discount or take back unsold inventory in the retail/reseller pipeline.

Converts average sale into cash in less than 24 hours (versus 35 days for Compaq).

Abstracted from V.K. Rangan and M. Bell, "Dell Online," Harvard Business School Case 9-598-116, 1998.

---

value, competitive advantage, and shareholder value. Also, once a company has adopted a particular value chain architecture, it may incur substantial costs in switching from the current to a new architecture. Thus, it is crucial to make a wise choice of value chain architecture with an eye toward competitive implications not only for today but also for tomorrow. In broad terms, the following three criteria should govern the choice of architecture:

1. Will this architecture allow us to market, sell, and provide the intended products and services to the target customers in the most effective and efficient manner?

2. Will this architecture allow us flexibility to scale up, scale down, expand or contract the product and service bundle and, if needed, switch to a superior value chain architecture?

3. Assuming "yes" answers to the preceding two questions, will this value chain architecture be difficult for competitors to imitate and neutralize?

These criteria may often be in conflict and thereby force the company to make difficult trade-offs. Also, new technologies (e.g., the Internet) often permit the design of new and radically superior value chain architectures (e.g., print-on-demand publishing vs. the traditional model). Thus, the company must always be alert to potentially radical innovations. As the competition to date between Barnes & Noble and Amazon.com points out, the cost of delay in switching over to a radically superior value chain architecture can often be very large.

Internalization versus Outsourcing

Allowing for some exceptions, the guiding principle for decisions regarding internalization versus outsourcing should be that the business unit itself should not do any activity that other firms (its "business partners") can do more effectively and efficiently. For example, a company may compete in the market for notebook computers. Suppose that, compared with other firms, this company is relatively weak in flat panel display technologies. If the company decides to make its own flat panel displays, then it controls a larger set of activities internally but, at the same time, risks downgrading the quality and performance of its overall product and service bundle. The alternative, going outside for displays, adds to the company's competitive advantage in the eyes of the customer but, at the same time, increases the company's dependence on external partners. Alternatively stated, the question of internalization versus outsourcing requires the company to make trade-offs between the size of the total payoffs and the company's share of the total payoffs.

No universal guidelines exist for how broadly or how narrowly the company should rely on partners. The optimal solution depends primarily on the specifics of the particular situation and a comparison between the capabilities of the business unit and those of potential business partners. Take, for example, the PC notebook manufacturer discussed earlier. Assume that the core capabilities needed to dominate the flat panel display market are product technology (design) and process technology (manufacture). If the company is weak in both product and process technologies, the optimal solution may be to purchase such displays from the best external supplier. However, what if the company is a leader in product technology but weak in process technology? The company may then be better off keeping the design activity in-house while giving a product design license to an external subcontractor who would produce the displays exclusively for this company. Alternatively, what if the business unit is weak in product design but a leader in process technology? In such a scenario, the best option may be to seek a product design license from an external partner but retain the manufacture of the displays inside the business unit.

Answering the question of internalization versus outsourcing correctly requires an extremely fine-grained analysis of the company's dominating skills (its "core competencies") as well as its relative weaknesses. The power of such analysis and of following through on the conclusions from it is illustrated well by Marriott Corporation. During the late 1970s, Marriott concluded that, in the lodging business, its dominating competencies were in hospitality management (its ability at managing people and operations) rather than in real estate management. Yet, bulk of the company's asset investment was in real estate. This discovery led to a fundamental shift in the company's approach to the allocation of its resources. As one element of its strategy, the company began to sell the real estate to investor syndicates while retaining a long-term (typically, 75-year) contract for the management of the hotels. As the other element of its strategy, the company began an aggressive program of reinvesting the capital generated by the real estate sale for the development of new hotel properties. After appropriate development, these new properties would similarly be sold to external investors, with Marriott retaining a long-term management contract. From 1975 to 1985, the pursuit of this strategy not only boosted Marriott's return on capital dramatically (from less than 10% to over 20%), but it also catapulted Marriott from a newcomer in the lodging business to the market share leader in full-service lodging in the United States.

Relying on other companies to perform essential activities at which they are superior may strengthen the overall bundle of products, services, and prices being offered to the customer; however, this strategy is not entirely risk-free. At least three types of risks are associated with relying on external partners:

1. *The Risk of Nonperformance.* A partner may fail to live up to its obligations either because its capabilities decline (either the quality of its product or service, or its advantage over other suppliers) or because its priorities no longer include serving a particular business unit. A business unit can guard against this risk in several ways. It could develop alternative suppliers so that there are always multiple options and no one supplier becomes too powerful. It could maintain a credible threat of eliminating dependence on the supplier by performing at least a portion of the activity in-house through "partial integration." Or, it could become a part-owner in the supplier by buying an equity stake so that the business unit is able to monitor and shape the supplier's policies regularly and directly.

2. *The Risk of Disproportionate Value Expropriation.* This is the risk that the partners may skim most of the profits generated by the value chain system while leaving your business unit only marginally profitable. It seems that IBM's PC business unit fell into this trap when it decided to rely on Microsoft to provide the operating system and on Intel to provide

the microprocessor. IBM left for itself the task of designing, assembling, and marketing the PC. Given that IBM did not have a superior operating system and microprocessor of its own, its decision to rely on Microsoft and Intel was brilliant in terms of creating a stronger value chain system. However, unfortunately for IBM, over time, the operating system and the microprocessor have become more complex and higher value-adding activities that Microsoft and Intel control almost as a monopoly. In contrast, the emergence of clone manufacturers has made the task of designing, assembling, and marketing the PCs more and more commoditylike. The net result has been that Microsoft and Intel, not IBM, largely control the value chain system enabling these suppliers to skim the bulk of the profits from IBM's PC business. In fact, in the PC industry, the operative words are no longer "IBM standard" but the "Wintel" standard (for MS Windows and Intel).

There are three approaches that a business unit can use to guard against the risk of profit skimming by its partners in a value chain system. One, it can retain some critical nonsubstitutable activities. Two, it can keep upgrading its competencies in these critical activities so that its dominant superiority prevents a decline in partners' dependence on the business unit. Three, it can acquire an equity stake in the business partners early in the game before they become too powerful. IBM failed to take advantage of any of these three ways to protect its PC business. First, its own activities (design, assembly, and marketing) became less critical and more easily substitutable over time. Second, Microsoft and Intel kept upgrading their own dominance of the activities initially "assigned" to them by IBM. And third, IBM made the judgmental error of forgoing the option of acquiring and retaining an equity stake in both Microsoft and Intel.

3. *The Risk of Elimination.* This is the risk that business partners will squeeze out your business unit altogether. This risk is basically an extreme version of the risk of "value expropriation" discussed earlier. The basic safeguards against this risk are the same. The business unit should select and manage its own internal value chain activities in such a manner that these activities remain critical, superior, nonsubstitutable, and unimitable; alternatively, the business unit should attempt to acquire an equity stake in the business partners early in the game.

MANAGING THE VALUE CHAIN

Having designed an optimal value chain system, the business unit must provide three key elements for the effective management of the value chain:

1. Excellence in the management of individual activities.
2. Excellence in internal integration across activities.

3. Excellence in the integration of the company's value chain with the value chains of suppliers, customers, and other business partners.

Managing Individual Value Chain Activities

Every business is a collection of activities. For example, a partial list of activities that make up Dell's PC business might look something like the following:

- Hiring, training, development, and retention of people.
- Marketing research.
- Product design.
- Sourcing of raw materials and externally produced components.
- Manufacture of internally produced components.
- Assembly of PCs.
- Marketing and sales of PCs.
- After-sales service.
- Physical distribution of PCs.
- Management of working capital.
- Management of capital structure.

In managing each of these value chain activities, the main goals should be: maximization of resulting customer value, minimization of resulting cost structure, and minimization of required asset investment. The achievement of these goals requires, first of all, a good analysis of the "drivers" of customer value, cost structure, and asset investment associated with the particular activity. Consider, for example, Procter & Gamble's disposable diaper business. Suppose we want to understand the drivers of the cost structure in this business. The analysis would begin by first identifying the exact breakdown of the cost structure into its principal components. The next step would be to take each of these cost components and to determine why the cost is what it is, what keeps it from being higher and, how it could be lowered. Suppose fluff pulp, one of the key ingredients in a diaper, costs \$.006 per diaper. Analysis might lead P&G to identify four main drivers of this cost. First, product design determines the quantity and quality of fluff pulp needed per diaper. Second, economies of scale exist in the purchasing of fluff pulp. Third, the timing of purchase decisions affects the market price for fluff pulp paid by P&G. And fourth, the choice of production technology and learning curve effects jointly determine the yield rate, the percentage of defective diapers that have to be destroyed before final packaging and shipment. Similarly, one could identify the drivers of the cost for each of the other items. It is only by managing each of these drivers in competitively superior ways that the diaper business can hope to achieve a competitively lower cost.

In managing the drivers of customer value, cost structure, and asset investment, numerous trade-off decisions need to be made. For example, although decreasing the amount of fluff pulp per diaper may reduce the cost structure, it may also make the diaper less absorbent thereby reducing the delivered customer value. Fundamental decisions about the business unit's intended bases for competitive advantage should generally serve as the guiding principles in making these trade-off decisions.

Managing Internal Integration across Activities

By integration across activities, we mean integration across activities such as product design, process design, manufacturing operations, marketing and sales, customer service, and distribution.

To understand how internal integration can affect the total strength of a business unit's value chain, consider the following hypothetical example. AIRCON and COOLAIR are the two leading manufacturers of air conditioners. Both companies are absolutely and equally dedicated to customer satisfaction and to the notion that "the customer is king." Suppose that, in the first year of introducing a completely new model, 1 percent of the customers of each company call in to the service center with some complaints regarding the product. Given their commitment to customer satisfaction, in each company, the customer service center acts courteously and promptly to resolve the customers' problems. At AIRCON, data regarding customer complaints are communicated routinely to the product design, manufacturing, and shipping departments. In sharp contrast, at COOLAIR, such internal integration does not exist and nothing more is done besides satisfying the customer and writing off the cost of the service center as a necessary expense. The likely outcome will be that, over time, AIRCON will become more knowledgeable about the factors that cause customer problems in the first place and will take actions to prevent these problems at the source. Consequently, over time, AIRCON is likely to gain a competitive edge over COOLAIR on both counts: "delivered quality" and "the cost of delivering this quality."

There are at least three important ways in which internal integration can strengthen any company's value chain: (1) improving the quality of delivered products and services and lowering the costs of doing this, as illustrated in the AIRCON/COOLAIR example; (2) slashing the "delivery cycle time" from customer order to customer delivery or from raw material input to customer delivery; (3) reducing the "development cycle time" from product conceptualization to product commercialization.

All three benefits are important. The value of higher quality and lower costs is obvious. Shorter delivery cycle times have a significant enabling effect on the lowering of inventory costs, on the customization of products, and on responsiveness to shifts in customer preferences. Finally, shorter development cycle times generally lead to an increase in the rate of new product development while reducing the risk of market failure because of shorter time lags between the collection of initial market data and the launching of the new product.

External Integration of the Value Chain

External integration refers to the integration of the company's value chain with the value chains of suppliers, other business partners, and customers. Like internal integration, tighter external integration has the potential to increase delivered value while simultaneously reducing costs. For example, take the case of a company that makes semiconductor chips and boards for industrial markets worldwide. Suppose that one of the company's business units is charged with the mission to develop a market for the company's products in the automotive industry. One such product might be integrated circuit boards for antilock braking systems (ABS). In this case, several important benefits might result from tighter communication between the brake system design team of the auto manufacturer and the ABS electronics design team of the semiconductor company: a shorter design cycle, a more customized design, and a less costly design. If the semiconductor manufacturer is located in the United States and the auto manufacturer in Germany, for the needed external integration of the value chains to occur, it may be necessary for the semiconductor manufacturer to establish an ABS design center in close physical proximity to the auto manufacturer's design center in Germany.

More effective communication is a fundamental requirement for tighter integration of the company's value chain with the value chains of its business partners. Such tighter communication can be achieved in a variety of ways: electronic links, face-to-face interaction, and physical proximity to name a few.

Box 3.5 illustrates the numerous ways in which Dell Computer has strived to optimize the management of its value chain. As shown earlier, Dell has historically enjoyed a huge advantage over its rivals based on a superior value chain architecture. However, it is only a matter of time before competitors switch over to the Dell approach and neutralize its architecture-driven advantage. When that happens, the battle will shift from who has a better value chain architecture to who can manage the value chain better. It would appear that, through its relentless optimization efforts, Dell is well prepared for this eventuality.

SUMMARY

This chapter has outlined the logic that should drive the creation of strategy at the business unit level—that is, a division or other type of profit center inside a multibusiness company as well as single-business companies operating independently. Business unit strategy deals primarily with how the business unit should compete within its broadly defined industry.

The five key elements to the design of business unit strategy are:

1. Setting business unit goals.
2. Defining the product-market scope of the business unit.

Box 3.5

Ongoing Optimization of Value Chain Activities at Dell Computer: Illustrative Examples from the 1990s

Sourcing

Reduced number of suppliers from 204 in 1992 to 47 by 1997.

Persuaded suppliers to warehouse bulk of their components within 15 minutes from Dell's plants.

Manufacturing

A new plant built in 1997 was based on a cell-based production system, which is considerably more efficient than the traditional assembly line production system in use at Dell's earlier plants.

Mid-1990s: Reduced the average number of human touches to the hard disk drive from 30 to 15 thereby cutting the rate of rejected hard disk drives by 40 percent and the overall failure rate for Dell's PCs by 20 percent.

Logistics

In 1997, stopped accepting delivery of monitors from the Sony factory in Mexico to its own factory in Texas. Instead, monitors were to be picked up by the transportation company from the Sony factory for direct delivery to the customer. This change by itself resulted in estimated savings of $30/unit at over 6 million units/year.

Marketing and Selling

In July 1996, launched online store www.dell.com to enable customers to engage in self-service configuration, order placement, follow-up on order status, and tech support 24 hours a day and at dramatically reduced costs for Dell. Even when customers completed only part of the purchase or tech support process over the Internet and had to be assisted by a human being over the telephone, Dell realized significant cost-savings in these Web-initiated encounters.

Abstracted from V.K. Rangan and M. Bell, "Dell Online," Harvard Business School Case 9-598-116, 1998.

---

3. Defining the intended bases for competitive advantage.
4. Designing a value chain system for the business unit.
5. Managing the value chain.

Box 3.6 summarizes the key questions that need to be addressed in crafting and managing each of these elements.

Box 3.6

Defining Business Unit Strategy: Key Questions

Setting Business Unit Goals

What financial goals (e.g., return on assets) do we wish to pursue?

What market position and customer satisfaction goals (e.g., market share) do we wish to pursue?

What internal business goals (e.g., employee retention, cycle time reduction) do we wish to pursue?

What innovation and learning goals (e.g., percent of sales from new products) do we wish to pursue?

Defining the Scope of the Business Unit

Which customer segments do we want to target?

What will be the geographic scope of our market presence?

What product and service bundle will we bring to our targeted customers?

Defining the Intended Bases for Competitive Advantage

Along which dimensions do we intend to become and remain superior to competitors?

Along which dimensions will we accept the possibility of being at par with competitors? Why?

Along which dimensions will we accept the possibility of being at a disadvantage with respect to competitors? Why?

Designing the Value Chain System

What is the basic design of the value chain architecture that we will embrace and implement?

Which customer-relevant activities should we perform ourselves?

Which customer-relevant activities should we source from business partners (including the option of forming alliances or joint ventures with them)?

How will we reduce/eliminate the risks of nonperformance, value expropriation, and elimination by our business partners?

Do we have the resources and capabilities to implement such a value constellation?

If implemented as designed, will this value constellation succeed in creating the desired customer value, competitive advantage, and shareholder value?

Managing the Value Chain

For each activity in our value chain, what are the drivers of customer value, cost structure, and asset investment?

How will we manage each value, cost, and asset driver for competitive superiority?

How will we ensure high integration across the value chain activities including those performed by our business partners?

NOTES

1. As discussed in Chapter 2, strategic management at the level of a multi-business corporation falls within the realm of what is generally termed *corporate strategy*.

2. Many of the key changes evident in the external environment are described in Chapters 8 and 9.

3. Robert S. Kaplan and David P. Norton, "The Balanced Scorecard—Measures that Drive Performance," *Harvard Business Review* (January/February 1992): 71–79.

4. General Electric, *1993 Annual Report*, p. 5.

5. Stakeholder scope, as noted in Chapter 1, and discussed in more detail in Chapter 7, adds the notion of a business unit's political strategy to the three elements of competitive or marketplace strategy noted here.

6. Michael E. Porter, *Competitive Advantage* (New York: Free Press, 1985).

7. Joan Magretta, "The Power of Virtual Integration: An Interview with Dell Computer's Michael Dell," *Harvard Business Review* (March/April 1998): 75.

COMPETING ACROSS LOCATIONS: ENHANCING COMPETITIVE ADVANTAGE THROUGH A GLOBAL STRATEGY

4

Michael E. Porter
Harvard University

One of the most powerful forces affecting companies since World War II has been the globalization of competition. We have seen transport and communication costs fall, the flow of information and technology across borders increase, national infrastructures grow more similar, and trade and investment barriers ease. The result has been marked growth in international trade and investment. In an ever-widening range of industries, a global, as opposed to a domestic, strategy is a necessity.

Unsurprisingly, as the globalization of competition has become more apparent, research and corporate practice in international strategy have taken on greater prominence. Thinking about international strategy has focused by and large on the power of the multinational company to create competitive advantage through globalness. A global strategy involving operations among many countries has been seen as a powerful means of reaping economies of scale, assimilating and responding to international market needs, and efficiently assembling resources such as capital, labor, raw materials, and technology from around the world. Authors as diverse as Ohmae, Reich, and Bartlett and

This article draws on an earlier article, "Global Competition and the Localization of Competitive Advantage," written with Rebecca E. Wayland, published in *Proceedings of the Integral Strategy Collegium,* Graduate School of Business, Indiana University, (Greenwich, CT: JAI Press, 1995). I have also benefited from research by Herman Cristerna and joint work with Michael Enright, of the University of Hong Kong, and Örjan Sölvell and Ivo Zander, both of Stockholm School of Economics. I am also grateful for the helpful comments offered by David Collis and Hans Thorelli.

Ghoshal see the global firm as transcending national boundaries. The national identity of a corporation must be replaced, in this view, by a strategic paradigm that knows no borders.

When considering the globalization of competition, however, one must confront an apparent paradox: Although companies do indeed compete globally and inputs such as raw materials, capital, and scientific knowledge now move freely around the world, strong evidence shows that location continues to play a crucial role in competitive advantage. First, striking differences persist in the economic performance of nations and of states and cities within nations. Second, in a wide variety of industries, the world's leading competitors are all based in one or two countries; this tendency is especially marked if industry is defined narrowly in terms meaningful for setting strategy and if industries are excluded in which government policy heavily distorts competition. This geographic concentration of competitive advantage appears not only in established industries such as automobiles and machine tools but also in new industries such as software, biotechnology, and advanced materials. Third, global companies have indeed dispersed activities to many countries, but they continue to concentrate in one location a critical mass of their most important activities for competing in each of their major product lines or businesses. Interestingly, however, these "home bases," as I call them, are not all located in the home country or even in the same country.

This chapter aims to reconcile these seemingly divergent perspectives into a framework for understanding the nature of international competition and the shift from domestic to global strategy in particular businesses. In creating competitive advantage, global strategy must integrate the roles of both location and a global network of activities. To bring the framework to life, I employ extended examples drawn from three premier global competitors: the Novo-Nordisk Group, based in Denmark; Hewlett-Packard, based in the United States; and Honda, based in Japan (see Box 4.1). The chapter concludes by examining how its framework can be employed to develop a concrete global strategy for a particular business.

While the discussion here is framed in terms of global competition, the principles can be applied much more generally. The same framework applies in examining competition across locations at any level—cities, states, regions, or even groups of neighboring countries. The same thought process can be used by a local competitor seeking to compete nationally or by a national competitor seeking to compete regionally.

A GENERAL FRAMEWORK FOR GLOBAL STRATEGY

Most issues in competitive strategy are the same for domestic and global companies; in both cases, success is a function of the attractiveness of the industries in which the firm competes and of the firm's relative position in those industries.[1] The firm's performance within the industry depends on its

Box 4.1

Case Studies of Three Global Corporations: Novo-Nordisk Group (Denmark), Honda (Japan), and Hewlett-Packard (United States)

To look at global strategy in practice, we examined the international activities of three prototypical global corporations headquartered in Europe, Japan, and the United States, respectively. For each of these successful international leaders, we profiled their international operations and probed deeply into the international configuration and coordination of their activities.

Novo-Nordisk Group ("Novo"), headquartered in Denmark, is the world's leading exporter of insulin and industrial enzymes. Novo generates 96 percent of its revenues outside its home country and has strong positions in Europe, the United States, and Japan.° Twenty-seven percent of its employees are based outside Denmark and 19 percent of its total assets are located outside Europe. Novo has seven R&D locations and nine production sites outside Denmark. The company distributes its products in 100 countries and has its own marketing subsidiaries in 43 countries. Novo sources animal pancreases, a key raw material for insulin, in more than 20 countries. It also sources its capital from around the world, funding 83 percent of its short-term debt and 54 percent of its long-term debt in currencies other than the Danish kroner. The company is listed on the London and New York stock exchanges.

Honda, headquartered in Japan, is one of the world's leading producers of automobiles and is the world leader in motorcycles.°° Honda generates 61 percent of its revenues outside Japan and holds particularly strong market positions in Asia and North America.† Twenty-two percent of its employees and 39 percent of its total assets are based outside Japan. The company maintains production and assembly facilities in 39 countries and distributes its automobiles and motorcycles in 150 countries. Inputs and capital are sourced worldwide; the company is listed on the Tokyo and New York stock exchanges.

Hewlett-Packard (HP), headquartered in the United States, is the world's largest and most diversified manufacturer of electronic measurement and testing equipment as well as a leader in other products such as printers, medical instruments, and computers. HP generates 54 percent of its revenues outside the United States.† Thirty-eight percent of HP's 93,000 employees and 50 percent of its total assets are based outside the United States. HP operates 600 sales and support offices and distributorships in 110 countries. It is listed on the London, Paris, Tokyo, Frankfurt, Stuttgart, Switzerland, and Pacific stock exchanges.

Globalization has led each of these firms to spread their activities around the world. Hewlett-Packard's locational philosophy is instructive. HP locates low-skilled manufacturing activities with high direct labor content in low-cost areas, at an estimated savings of 40 to 75 percent compared with U.S. locations. Some component assembly and manufacturing for personal computers (PCs) is conducted in Singapore, and electronic component manufacturing is

(Continued)

Box 4.1 *(Continued)*

conducted in Malaysia. Hewlett-Packard also locates some medium-skilled activities in lower-cost countries. Some product and process engineering activities (such as manufacturing cost reduction programs) are conducted at the PC manufacturing facilities in Singapore, process engineering for some new electronic component products has been transferred to the manufacturing plant in Malaysia, and some software coding and maintenance has been subcontracted to countries such as India, China, Eastern Europe, and the former Soviet Union, where college-educated programmers are available at 40 to 60 percent lower cost than in the United States.

° Information on Novo is based on M.J. Enright, "Novo Industri," Case 9-389-148 (Boston: Harvard Business School, 1989) and field research.
°° The profiles of Honda and Hewlett-Packard in this chapter are based on M.E. Porter and R.E. Wayland, "Global Competition and the Localization of Competitive Advantage," *Proceedings of the Integral Strategy Collegium*, Graduate School of Business, Indiana University, JAI Press, Greenwich, CT, 1995.
† Figures are taken from recent annual reports and other corporate filings.

---

competitive advantages (or disadvantages) vis-à-vis its rivals. Competitive advantage is manifested either in lower costs than those of rivals or in the ability to differentiate and command a premium price that exceeds the extra cost of differentiating. Some competitive advantages arise because of differences in operational effectiveness, but the most sustainable advantages come from occupying a unique competitive position. Both domestic and global companies must understand the structure of their industry, identify their sources of competitive advantage, and analyze competitors.

"Global" strategy, then, refers to the special issues that arise when firms compete across nations. The need for a global strategy depends on the nature of international competition in a particular industry. There is not a single pattern of international competition, but many. Not all industries require a global strategy. The types of international competition in industries can be arrayed along a spectrum. At one end are multidomestic industries, present in many countries (even every country) but industries in which competition takes place on a country-by-country basis with little or no linkage. Examples include most types of retailing, metal fabrication, construction, and many services. Indeed, numerous industries are regional within nations or even local. At the other end of the spectrum are truly global industries, in which competition in different countries is linked because a firm's position in a given country significantly affects its position elsewhere. Prominent examples are commercial aircraft, consumer electronics, and many types of industrial machinery.

In multidomestic industries, there is no need for a global strategy. Here, the international strategy should be a series of distinct domestic strategies. Country operating units should be given wide latitude and autonomy. In global industries, however, firms must create integrated strategies involving all countries simultaneously. Just because a firm is multinational, therefore, does not mean that it has or should have a global strategy. The essential question in global strategy is this: When and how is the international whole more than the sum of the domestic parts?

To understand the underpinnings of competitive advantage and what a global strategy might contribute, it is necessary to disaggregate what a firm does into its value chain (see Figure 4.1).[2] A firm competing in a particular business performs an array of discrete but interrelated economic activities; for example, it assembles products, its salespeople make sales visits, it processes orders, it recruits and trains staff, and it purchases inputs. All activities normally involve some procedures or routines, human resources, physical assets, enabling technologies, and the creation and use of information. A firm's "strengths," "competencies," "capabilities," and "resources"—common phrases in discussions of strategy—can best be understood in terms of the particular activities to which they apply.

The value chain groups a firm's activities into several categories, distinguishing between those directly involved in producing, marketing, delivering, and supporting a product or service; those that create, source, and improve inputs and technology; and those that perform overarching functions such as raising capital or overall decision making. Within each of these categories

FIGURE 4.1 Competitive advantage and activities.

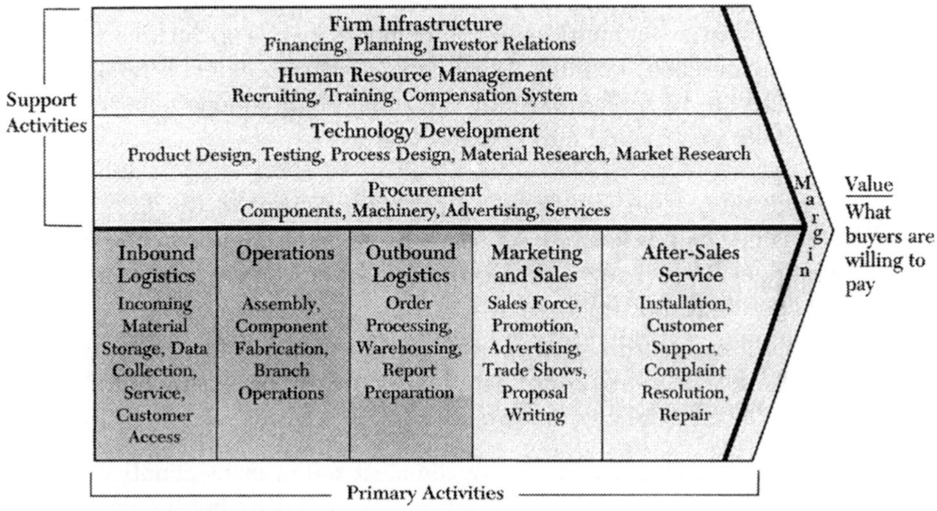

• Companies are collections of discrete activities, in which competitive advantage resides.

appears an array of discrete activities or economic/organizational processes, at the level of field repair, inbound materials receiving and storage, billing, and reviewing and rewarding employees. The particular activities performed depend at least partly on the business.

Activities form the basic foundation of competitive advantage in either cost or differentiation. As noted, competitive advantage results when a firm can perform the required activities at a collectively lower cost than rivals or can perform some activities in unique ways that create nonprice buyer value and support a premium price. Creating buyer value depends, in turn, on how a firm influences the activities of its channels and end-users.

Competitive advantage in activities can arise from both operational effectiveness and strategy. Operational effectiveness refers to performing given or similar activities at the state of best practice. This includes the use of the most cost-effective purchased inputs, managerial practices, and the like. Part of the need for a global strategy is to enhance operational effectiveness through such things as global sourcing and transfer of knowledge.

A firm's strategy defines its particular configuration of activities and how they fit together. Different strategic positions involve tailoring activities to produce particular product/service varieties, to address the special needs of particular customer groups, or to access most efficiently certain types of customers. Broadly targeted competitors seek to gain advantages by sharing activities across an array of industry segments. Narrowly targeted competitors (which I term *focusers*) seek advantage by tailoring activities to the needs of one (or a few) particular segment(s). Global strategy also bears on strategic positioning by affecting the trade-offs underlying a position or the ability to tailor activities to it.

The value chain provides the basic tool to highlight the strategy issues unique to a global strategy. Both domestic firms and global firms have value chains. The domestic (or multidomestic) company performs all the activities in the home (or in each) country. What distinguishes a global strategy, however, is the latitude to spread parts of the value chain among countries. The basic choices can be grouped into two areas:

1. *Configuration.* Configuration focuses on where each of the activities in a firm's value chain is located; for example, assembly can be in one country, and product R&D in another. Moreover, a given activity can occur in one location or be dispersed to many.

2. *Coordination.* Coordination focuses on the nature and extent to which dispersed activities are coordinated in a network or remain autonomous, that is, tailored to local circumstances.

Any firm that competes internationally must sell in many countries. Some activities, such as many of those involved in sales and distribution, necessarily are tied to the customer's location. A firm seeking to sell in a country must either establish its own marketing and sales and physical distributions activities there or rely on others (e.g., distributors or joint venture partners). Other activities in the value chain, however, can be uncoupled from the customer, giving the international firm discretion over the number and location of such activities. In multidomestic strategy, the company performs the entire value chain in each country, and each country subsidiary has near or complete autonomy to tailor the activities to the country. In a global strategy, the company selectively locates activities in different countries and coordinates among them to harness and extend the competitive advantage of the network.

Configuration

The international configuration of a firm's activities creates competitive advantage through the choice of where to locate each activity and the number of sites. One motivation for locating an activity is comparative advantage in performing the activity, such as, for example, a location with the most cost-effective pool of raw materials or people. Some multinational software firms locate software debugging and program maintenance activities in India, for example, to access low-cost but good-quality programmers. Because the location with comparative advantage varies by activity, the global firm has the potential to gain the benefits of arbitraging comparative advantages across locations.

A second and less understood motivation for the choice of location is competitive or productivity advantage. Here, as will be discussed further, activities or groups of activities are located in the countries with the most attractive environments for innovation and productivity growth.

Choice of location includes deciding not only where to locate but how many sites to maintain. The firm might concentrate an activity in one location to serve the world or disperse the activity to several or many locations. By concentrating an activity, firms may gain economies of scale or may progress rapidly down the learning curve. Concentrating a group of linked activities in one location may also allow a firm to better coordinate among them. Dispersing activities to a number of locations, in contrast, may be justified by the need to minimize transportation and storage costs, hedge against the risks of a single activity site, tailor activities sensitive to local market differences, facilitate learning about country and market conditions that can be transmitted to headquarters, or respond to local government pressure or incentives to locate in a country in order to sell or produce there.

The global firm should disperse only those activities necessary to obtain these benefits, and no more. Both efficiency and the ease of innovation are enhanced, other things being equal, if as many activities as possible are colocated. This minimizes coordination and transhipment costs. Sometimes, a firm must disperse one activity to a country to gain the ability (or permission from local government) to concentrate other activities elsewhere. Establishing local assembly plants in a variety of countries, for example, may allow a company to import scale-sensitive components into each of the countries and thus to concentrate production of the scale-sensitive components elsewhere.

The particular activities to be dispersed should be those incurring the least sacrifice in terms of economies of scale or learning and requiring the least close coordination with other activities.

Coordination

A global strategy can also contribute to competitive advantage by coordinating activities across locations. Coordinating methods, technology, and output decisions across dispersed activities contributes potential competitive advantages. These include the ability to respond to shifting comparative advantages (e.g., raw materials prices or exchange rates); to share learning among countries; to reinforce the corporate brand reputation for mobile buyers who encounter the firm in different places (e.g., McDonald's or Coca-Cola); to differentiate with or more efficiently serve multinational buyers who simultaneously deal with several of the firm's country units; to bargain more effectively with governments by using the carrot and stick of expanding or contracting local operations; or to respond more cost-effectively to competitive threats by choosing the location at which to do battle. Some of these benefits relate to operational effectiveness, while others reinforce a company's unique position. Successful coordination is important to gaining the benefits of dispersing activities. These potential advantages of coordination are weighed against the benefits of allowing each dispersed unit to act autonomously and tailor its activities to local circumstances. An international strategy involving high levels of autonomy for dispersed units is favored where local needs and conditions vary, all customers are local, or few economies of scale are present. In practice, the balance between coordination and autonomy varies by activity.

Several forms of coordination across locations are possible, including setting common standards, exchanging information, and allocating responsibility among sites. Coordination that involves allocating responsibilities across countries, such as assigning to different locations worldwide responsibility for producing particular models, can unleash economies of scale. Coordination involving information exchange reaps the benefits of worldwide learning. Coordination, then, can allow a firm to realize the advantages of dispersing its activities; conversely, the failure to coordinate activities can lessen those advantages. A central issue in coordination is how and where information, technology, and other knowledge gained from disparate locations becomes integrated into and reflected in products, processes, and other activities. The home base performs these essential functions.

Coordination across geographically dispersed locations involves daunting organization challenges, among them those of language and cultural differences and of aligning individual manager's and subsidiary's incentives with those of the global enterprise as a whole. Some forms of coordination, such as allocating responsibilities for component production to different locations, require less ongoing interchange than others.

PATTERNS OF GLOBAL STRATEGY

Some competitive advantages of a global strategy arise from location; others arise from the overall global network and the way it is managed. Every global strategy normally begins with some kind of advantage in location, reflected in the company's competitive position. This advantage allows the firm to penetrate international markets and to overcome the inherent disadvantages of competing in another country. Without some asymmetry among firms based in different countries, competition will remain multidomestic.

The initial location-based advantages are extended and supplemented through a global network. The advantages of other locations can also be tapped by dispersing activities.

Global competition has not one but many patterns, depending on the particular activities concentrated or dispersed, the location of various activities, and how activities are coordinated. In multidomestic industries, industry structure favors a highly dispersed configuration in which each country contains virtually the entire value chain. In such industries, strong benefits follow from allowing country units nearly full strategic autonomy. Competition in an industry globalizes when the competitive advantages of a global network are substantial enough to overcome the local focus and local knowledge of domestic or country-centered competitors.

Global strategy thus takes many forms. The particular global strategy utilized by McDonald's in the fast-food industry differs a good deal from that of Intel in the microprocessor industry or Boeing in commercial aircraft. Figure 4.2, which sketches Citibank's global strategy in retail banking, illustrates this. As in many service businesses, Citibank disperses many activities, including branch operations, marketing, and even many forms of processing. Active coordination occurs on image, branch design, and service standards, however, and local autonomy is narrowly drawn.

Firms can play a major role in shaping the benefits and costs of a global versus a domestic strategy. Firms can redefine competition through strategic innovations that increase the advantages of a global strategy or that reduce its disadvantages. Becton Dickinson, for example, created worldwide demand for disposable syringes as an alternative to reusable glass syringes. Partly by being the first mover, Becton Dickinson emerged as the world leader. Other firms have triggered globalization by pioneering new approaches to competing that increased economies of scale or by inventing product designs or production processes that reduced the cost of tailoring products to differing country needs. Many global industry leaders have emerged because they were early to perceive and act on these levers. Theodore Levitt's 1983 work on the globalization of markets is typically seen as arguing the merits of world products.[3] Yet often unrecognized is the essay's more important emphasis on the ability of the firm to create world products by pioneering new approaches to segmentation and marketing rather than by passively responding to preexisting needs.

FIGURE 4.2 Citicorp: Global strategy in retail banking.

Concentrated	Dispersed

Common brand name
Product development
Software development
Global information
  infrastructure
Credit card clearing system
Human resource training
  program development
	Branch and ATM
	  networks
	Telebanking centers
	Advertising and promotions

Coordinated	Decentralized

Consistent corporate image
Consistent branch office
  design
Consistent service delivery
	Adaptation to local
	  language and business
	  customs
	Regulatory compliance

Location and Global Competition

The globalization of competition allows firms to gain competitive advantages independent of location by coordinating activities across a wide range of countries. Globalization has not eliminated the importance of location in competition, however. In hundreds of industries that have been studied, including services and newly emerging fields such as software, advanced materials, and biotechnology, the world leaders are typically headquartered in just a few countries and sometimes in only one country.[4] The three case studies companies presented in Box 4.1 all fit this rule. Honda is not the only Japanese success story in the automotive and motorcycle industries: Nine of the world's automobile companies and the four dominant global motorcycle companies are all based in Japan. Similarly, Hewlett-Packard is not the only successful U.S. firm in its industries: U.S. firms are preeminent in workstations, PCs, medical instruments, and test and instrumentation equipment. Two Denmark-based companies, merged into Novo-Nordisk only in 1989, now dominate in insulin exports. Novo-Nordisk is also a world leader in industrial enzymes, a field in which other Danish firms compete as well.

The geographic concentration of leading firms within nations demonstrates the importance of location to competition even more clearly. The United States presents a particularly interesting example. Despite free trade among the states, a common language and laws, and great similarities across states along many dimensions, successful competitors in particular businesses are far from evenly distributed. Publishing has a heavy concentration in New York City; movies and television production, in Hollywood; office furniture, in western Michigan; pharmaceuticals, in Philadelphia and New Jersey; hosiery and home furnishings, in North Carolina; artificial hips and joints, in Indiana. Countless other examples could be added. A similar pattern of geographic concentration can be found, in varying degrees, in every advanced nation.[5]

A close look at the configuration and coordination of activities in global companies, including Novo-Nordisk, Hewlett-Packard, and Honda, also reveals the strong influence of location. Accounts emphasizing the widespread geographic dispersion of activities by multinationals can be misleading. Company diversification often means extensive foreign activities, but these may span many entirely different product areas. In a given business, activities are far less dispersed.

A more important distinction in assessing geographic dispersion is that between the types of activity located in different countries. International firms tend to concentrate their most sophisticated activities in a single country—often, though less so over time, in their home country. Novo-Nordisk markets its insulin products around the world and sources some inputs globally, but it conducts the most strategically important activities in the value chain—all production and core product and process R&D—in Denmark. Honda has extensive worldwide manufacturing and distribution, but Japan remains the home base for strategy, design, and the production of Honda's most sophisticated components, including all core engine research. Hewlett-Packard's operations encompass more than sixteen thousand product lines sold around the world, yet it concentrates worldwide responsibility (HP refers to this as "worldwide re") for each product line, including core manufacturing, R&D, and decision making, in one particular location.

Additional evidence comes from Asea Brown Boveri (ABB), often cited as the prototype of a company with no national identity.[6] ABB has multiple operations located throughout the world, but it bases global responsibility for establishing business strategy, selecting product development priorities, and allocating production among countries in each product line in a particular geographic location. Leadership for power transformers is based in Germany; electric drives in Finland; and process automation in the United States. Moreover, multinationals seem to be relocating headquarters of particular businesses from one nation to another with increasing frequency.

Comparative Advantage versus Competitive Advantage

The apparent paradox between the globalization of competition and a strong national or even local role in competitive advantage can be resolved by recognizing that the paradigm that governs the competition among locations has shifted from comparative advantage to the broader notion of competitive advantage.

Comparative advantage due to lower factor costs (e.g., labor, raw materials, capital, infrastructure) or size still exists, but it no longer confers competitive advantage in most industries nor supports high wages. Globalization now allows firms to match comparative advantages by sourcing inputs such as raw materials, capital, and even generic scientific knowledge from anywhere and to disperse selective activities overseas to take advantage of low-cost labor or capital. The global firm must do these things to attain operational effectiveness. Failure to disperse activities to access comparative advantages will lead to a competitive disadvantage, but doing so yields the firm no advantage.

Similarly, the size of the home market is far less important than the ability to penetrate the much larger world market. Moreover, advancing technology has given firms the capacity to reduce, nullify, or circumvent many weaknesses in comparative advantage. Japanese firms, for example, have prospered in many industries, despite the high local costs of energy and land, by pioneering energy-saving and space-saving innovations such as lean production. New technology also diminishes economies of scale,[7] while vertical integration now gives way to greater outsourcing to specialized suppliers.

The competitive advantage of locations arises not from the availability of low-cost inputs or size per se, but from superior productivity in using inputs: Basic inputs create competitive disadvantages, not advantages. The enduring advantages of a location come from providing an environment in which firms can operate productively and continuously innovate and upgrade their ways of competing to more sophisticated levels, thereby allowing rising productivity. Innovation refers not only to technology in the narrow sense but also to ways of marketing, product positioning, and providing service. The most dynamic and innovative companies in such locations can outpace their rivals elsewhere, even entrenched competitors enjoying low-cost factors or economies of scale in older methods of operating. In productivity competition, firms spread activities globally to source inputs and access markets, but competitive advantage arises from innovation and productivity growth heavily localized at the firm's home base for a particular product line: the location of its strategy development, core product and process R&D, and a critical mass of the firm's sophisticated production (or service provision).[8] At the home base reside the essential skills and technology; it is the integration site for inputs and information sourced from global activities; and the most productive jobs are located there. The location of a firm's owners or of its corporate headquarters becomes far less significant than the location of the home-based activities for each strategically distinct business.[9]

The Competitive Advantage of Locations

The competitive advantages of a location lie in the quality of the environment it provides for achieving high and rising levels of productivity in a particular field. While we tend to think of the sources of competitive advantage as primarily arising within a company, a company's potential for advantage and many of the necessary inputs reside in its proximate environment. Only this can explain why so many successful companies in particular fields emerge in the same country and even in the same region within a country.[10]

My research has highlighted four aspects of a national (and state or local) environment that define the context for growth and innovation and productivity: factor (input) conditions; the context for strategy and rivalry; demand conditions; and related and supporting industries. These four areas, which I collectively term the "diamond," help explain why companies based in particular locations can achieve consistent innovation and upgrading in particular fields (see Figure 4.3).

Factor (Input) Conditions

Factors of production are the basic inputs to competition; they include land, labor, capital, physical infrastructure, commercial or administrative infrastructure, natural resources, and scientific knowledge. The notion of comparative advantage normally refers to the cost and availability of inputs. General purpose inputs, such as sound roads and ports or a cadre of college-educated employees, are necessary to avoid a competitive disadvantage, but they are no longer sufficient for gaining a locational advantage.

FIGURE 4.3 **The "Diamond": Sources of locational competitive advantage.**

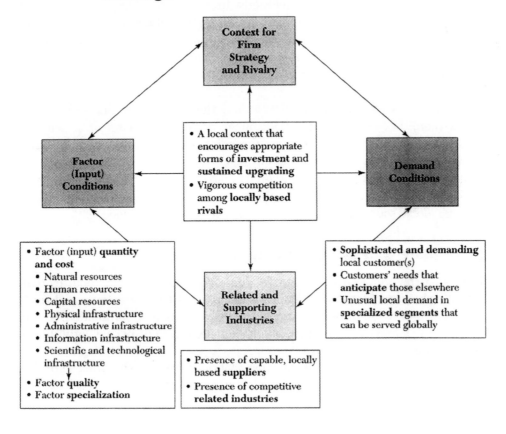

The advantages of a location for productivity competition arise instead from high-quality inputs—especially specialized inputs such as pools of skills, applied technology, physical infrastructure, regulatory regimes, legal processes, information, and sources of capital tailored to the needs of particular industries. In the United States, preeminence in software rests on a unique concentration of highly trained programmers and other computer science professionals, unparalleled research programs in computer-related disciplines, an efficient body of rules governing software licensing and use, and well-developed and expert sources of risk capital for software firms (many American venture capital firms specialize in software). Hewlett-Packard benefits from some of these advantages in its computer-related businesses. Nations and regions do not inherit the most important factors of production for sophisticated competition; they must create them. This, in turn, depends on the local presence and quality of specialized institutions in education, training, research, data collection, and other areas. Such institutions become a potent source of locational advantage.

More paradoxical as a locational advantage is the role of selective disadvantages in basic inputs, such as high costs of land or local raw material shortages. These can lead to competitive advantages because they trigger innovation and/or stimulate the development of specialized institutions. In Holland, for example, a poor climate and land shortages have led to innovations in such areas as greenhouse cultivation methods, breeding technology, and handling techniques for cut flowers, a product for which the Dutch hold more than 60 percent of world exports. Conversely, in locations with abundant labor, cheap debt capital, and bountiful natural resources firms tend to use these resources less productively, raising their vulnerability to more productive competitors based elsewhere.

The pools of specialized inputs, and the institutions that create and renew them, become an external advantage or collective asset of a location. This public good builds up over time through cumulative investment by many firms, institutions, and government entities. The presence of the external advantage obviates the need for individual companies to bear the internal costs. While a company may be able to gain access to some of the locational assets through global sourcing, many are hard to access from a distance.

Coordinate and Integrate Dispersed Activities

Unlocking the competitive advantage from dispersed activities requires that activities be coordinated globally. Coordination ensures consistency and reinforcement across countries, to enhance differentiation. Coordination is also necessary to allow learning and technology gained from dispersed activities to be integrated at the home base.[11]

The particular advantages of coordination in its various forms were described earlier. All three of our example companies exhibit these benefits, but

Novo-Nordisk's case is particularly interesting. In raw material procurement, Novo-Nordisk's sourcing is dispersed to 20 countries, but coordinated centrally to take advantage of price and currency shifts. In marketing, all subsidiaries, agents, and distributors use consistent promotional materials, and Novo-Nordisk trains them in consistent selling approaches. Novo-Nordisk works hard to ensure a common image worldwide and reinforces it with periodic sponsorship of physicians' conferences on diabetes in Denmark.[12]

Coordinating across disparate country locations, however, raises formidable organizational challenges. Language, culture, and distance work against communication and common ways of thinking.[13] Country subsidiaries have a natural tendency to want autonomy, and to extensively tailor their activities to local circumstances. Successful global competitors overcome these challenges in a variety of ways. First, they establish clear positioning and a well-understood concept for global strategy. Second, subsidiary managers recognize the overall global position as a difficult-to-match source of advantage in their particular country; Thus, they are careful to tailor local activities in ways that do not undermine the global strategy.[14] Third, information and accounting systems are made consistent worldwide, right down to part numbers and client codes, facilitating operational coordination, appropriate trade-offs, and the exchange of information comparisons across locations. Fourth, the company makes active efforts to encourage personal relationships and the exchange of learning among subsidiary managers, both to foster mutual understanding and to give coordination a human face. Finally, any company that seeks a global strategy must put in place an incentive system that weights overall contribution to the company in addition to subsidiary performance.[15]

Preserve National Identity in Business Units

A firm's national identity in a particular business is not something to overcome, as some observers have suggested, but something to preserve. Competitive advantage in a business often arises from distinctive attributes of a firm's home environment; location places an imprint on the firm and shapes its method of competing. Foreign customers value national identity and culture, and the company characteristics they connote. Most Americans, for example, appreciate German cars because German manufacture has come to be synonymous with high standards of design, performance, and craftsmanship, not because German car companies have become "American" or "global."

When accessing foreign markets, a firm must adapt—in the sense that it must tailor its product to local needs and show sensitivity to local business practices. Yet the company should not lose its distinctive positioning and identity, which should, indeed, be nurtured and inculcated in foreign subsidiaries. At Honda, for example, managers hired to run international subsidiaries train for two years at the Japanese headquarters before assuming their responsibilities.

Use Alliances as Enabling Devices for Globalization, but Not as Strategy

Once a company understands how to configure its global network in a business, alliances with firms based elsewhere can be a means of more effectively or more rapidly achieving the desired configuration. Alliances are a means to build a network of dispersed activities not an end, and can make activities outside the home base more effective. Market access can often be enhanced by a local partner. The ability to sources inputs or to tap advanced skills and technologies in a new location may require a partner's well-established presence. Alliances, however, can blur a company's positioning and get in the way of a consistent positioning in every market. They complicate coordination and can slow innovation.

The best alliances are highly selective: They focus on particular activities and on obtaining a particular competitive benefit. Novo-Nordisk, for example, formed joint ventures with a variety of firms to gain access to particular national markets. Broad alliances, covering many activities and markets, tend to stunt a company's own development. They inhibit or relieve the sense of urgency about building the brand or developing the firm's own products. The best alliances are often transitional devices, assisting a firm to build on its strengths and to learn. In the long run, the partners may go their separate ways or upgrade the alliance to a full merger. A firm cannot rely on a partner for assets crucial to its competitive advantage.[16]

BUSINESS EXTENSION IN INDUSTRIES AND SEGMENTS WITH LOCATION ADVANTAGES

A location's competitive advantages provide a means for identifying the industries in which a firm can gain a unique competitive advantage vis-à-vis rivals based elsewhere, as well as those industry segments where the home-base environment provides the greatest benefits. New business development should concentrate in these areas.

The new paradigm of productivity competition raises cautions about extensive vertical integration. Vertical integration consumes resources and creates inflexibilities, and should be restricted to activities tightly connected to the overall strategy. Elsewhere, a company may be better served by developing strong relationships with local suppliers of specialized machinery and inputs.

Diversification should proceed along cluster lines. By diversifying, companies will better leverage not only their own internal assets but also the unique assets of location to which they have special access, such as suppliers, research centers, and skill pools. HP's diversification from measurement and test equipment into information systems and medical instruments has followed these principles, in each case involving a field in which the United States has unique strengths. Novo-Nordisk's move from insulin to industrial enzymes also followed cluster lines, as did Honda's diversification from motorcycles to automobiles. Innovations often originate at the interstices between industries and clusters, when related technologies and skills are combined. To get its start in automobiles, Honda drew on its small-engine technology expertise, nurtured in motorcycle manufacture. It combined this with assets in the Japanese automobile cluster, including a strong supplier base and demand conditions encouraging compact designs and energy efficiency.

Upgrade the Home Bases

An important part of a firm's competitive advantage in a business resides in the local environment where that business is based, not merely within the firm itself. Without a fundamentally healthy home base, a business's capacity for productivity growth and rapid innovation will diminish. The firm will be unable to assemble the resources, skills, technologies, and information most essential to competitive advantage. While dispersing sophisticated production or outsourcing critical components and machinery can often offset home base weaknesses and improve performance in the short run, the firm's ability to innovate over the long run will be threatened.

External competitive advantages add new and often unfamiliar dimensions to a company's strategic agenda. Firms should support specialized training programs and should promote university research in areas relevant to their particular business. Local suppliers should be nurtured and upgraded (depending heavily on distant suppliers nullifies a potential competitive advantage). Firms must guide and pressure local infrastructure providers to meet their needs and ensure that government regulations enhance productivity. Industry associations can play an important role in sponsoring training programs, research on standards and enabling technologies, and the collection of market information. Few companies see their local environment as a vital competitive resource. In the United States, many companies take their suppliers for granted and see education and training as the responsibility of government.

The example of Novo illustrates how global leaders take an active role in upgrading their home environment. Before the merger of Nordisk and Novo, Nordisk established the Nordic Insulin Fund (in 1926) to support insulin research projects in Scandinavia and the Steno Memorial Hospital (in 1932) as a center for research and treatment of diabetes. Novo founded the Hvidore Diabetes Hospital soon after and later (in 1957) founded the Hagedoorn Research Institute to conduct basic research on diabetes. The Novo Research Institute was created (in 1964) to investigate the causes and origins of diabetes. Today, the Steno Diabetes Center and Hvidore Diabetes Hospital treat 6,000 diabetes patients and conduct 25,000 diabetes consultations each year. Novo-Nordisk also sponsors international conferences on diabetes in Denmark, bringing together local experts and specialists from around the world.[17]

The history of the Danish insulin industry illustrates the power of active local rivalry to motivate continual innovation. The companies recognized one of the risks of their merger as the possibility that, while achieving some efficiencies, it would undermine dynamism. The parent company hopes to addresses this and other risks by keeping the two operations separate. The broader principle, however, remains: The presence of local rivals creates advantages. Seeking to eliminate local competition, under most circumstances, is a misguided effort.

Relocate the Home Base if Necessary

If the vitality of a firm's home base for a particular business deteriorates because of lagging customer sophistication, a requirement for new types of suppliers, ineffective local institutions, or for other reasons, the first response should be to upgrade at home. If such efforts are exhausted without success, however, a firm may need to shift its home base to a more favorable location. This is perhaps the ultimate manifestation of global competition.

Shifts of home bases from country to country occur with increasing frequency in multinational companies. As global competition exposes companies to the world's best rivals and nullifies traditional comparative advantages in access to capital, raw materials, and labor, the penalty of an unfavorable home diamond increases. Yet, the decision to relocate a home base must be approached reluctantly, because it entails becoming accepted as a true insider in a new location and a new culture.

Firms rarely shift an entire company's home base. Instead, they relocate the home base of particular product lines or business segments. One common catalyst (and enabler) of such shifts is acquisition of a foreign firm already established in a more vibrant location. Such acquisitions provide the critical mass for new home bases, which, over time, gain increasing worldwide responsibility in particular segments or businesses. Nestlé, for example, has relocated the world headquarters for its confectionery business to England, associating it with the acquired Rowntree MacIntosh company. England, with its sweet-toothed consumers, sophisticated retailers, advanced advertising agencies, and highly competitive media companies, constitutes a more dynamic environment for competing in mass-market candy than Switzerland. Similarly, Nestlé has moved its headquarters for bottled water to France, the most competitive location in that industry.

Although each of our example companies, Novo-Nordisk, Hewlett-Packard, and Honda, continues to enjoy a strong home diamond in its principal businesses, not all firms are so fortunate. The Canadian manufacturer Northern Telecom, for example, has relocated the home base for its digital central-office switching equipment from Canada to the United States.[18] Northern Telecom manufactured and installed the first local digital switch, the DMS-10, in the United States in 1977. The subsequent AT&T divestiture and mandate for equal access reconfigured the U.S. diamond for telecommunications service and equipment and led Northern Telecom to expand its U.S. operations dramatically. By 1991, the company had relocated its world headquarters for central-office switching to the United States. It now conducts all R&D activities for this product line in the United States, with a workforce of more than one thousand employees. Virtually all of the company's central-office switching manufacturing is also conducted in North Carolina.

The rationale behind Northern Telecom's move to the United States can be seen in the strength of the U.S. telecommunications equipment diamond. Compared to Canada, the United States presents a unique array of highly specialized factors, including sophisticated software engineering and world-class university research programs in computer science and telecommunications. American buyers and end-users are among the most sophisticated in the world, and the existence of 20 to 25 major independent U.S. switch buyers leads to intense competition that encourages Northern Telecom's customers to continuously upgrade their central-office switching capabilities. American firms in integrated circuit manufacturing and systems-level software design provide strong capabilities in related industries. The openness of the U.S. market to foreign rivals further intensifies the local rivalry within the U.S. market. (In telecommunications equipment, governments have tended to protect local markets and support monopoly suppliers.)

Hyundai's shift of its home base in personal computers from Korea to Silicon Valley, when it discovered that it simply could not "keep up" from a Korean location, provides another interesting example.[19] With all competitors sourcing low-cost parts internationally, crucial competitive imperatives were the rapid introduction of new models that met evolving customer needs and the ability to successfully access evolving distribution channels. In these areas, the United States was far ahead of other locations. Traditionally, foreign direct investment (FDI) has been seen as exploiting home base advantages. Wesson employs statistical evidence that confirms the prevalence of home bases seeking FDI to access the sophisticated advantages of other locations, even to the extent of relocating the firm's home base elsewhere.

COMPETING GLOBALLY FROM A DEVELOPING COUNTRY

Developing countries have become a growing part of the international economy, and many firms based in developing countries are exporters. The platform of a developing country, however, raises specific issues for the move to a global strategy.

The basic challenge is to shift from comparative advantage to competitive advantage. Most firms based in developing countries have internationalized through exports of resource or labor-intensive commodities or via original equipment manufacturer (OEM) agreements with multinationals that rest on resource labor costs. Such exports have been primarily directed to advanced economies. Opportunities to expand into other developing markets, including neighboring countries, have been limited by similarities in factor conditions and circumscribed by protectionist government policies.

Moving beyond the traditional modes of internationalization requires that firms based in developing countries create distinctive strategies. Without their own product or service varieties, production methods, or reputations, they find it difficult to penetrate foreign markets. At the same time, firms must extend their value chains to include international distribution, marketing, sourcing, and ultimately production. The best opportunities for true international strategies emanating from developing countries often lie within the region and with other like economies. While exports to advanced economies based on comparative advantage can continue, firms must take advantage of the opening of neighboring markets to build regional networks. The challenge becomes one of building distinctive product varieties and production methods while gaining knowledge and control of international marketing and distribution. Over time, the firm must build innovative capacity sufficient to enter more and more advanced markets based on competitive rather than comparative advantage.

INTEGRATING LOCATION AND GLOBAL COMPETITION

Since the 1950s, globalization has exerted an ever-increasing influence on competitive strategy. Aggregate statistics confirm the popular view that firms have become increasingly global in their sales and operations. The traditional role of comparative advantage has been superseded, and it is tempting to conclude that many corporations now transcend national boundaries.

Deeper investigation reveals, however, a striking localization of competitive advantage. This apparent paradox can be explained by recognizing the new paradigm of international competition, which makes productivity and innovation paramount. Firms must harness the comparative advantages from many locations to avoid a disadvantage. Firms' advantages over others, however, often lie in their locations' competitive advantage for raising productivity. This paradigm must guide a new generation of thinking about global strategy that integrates localization and globalization in wholly new ways.

Localization was once seen as a necessary evil to be balanced against the compelling benefits of a global strategy. Instead, the home base location should be seen as the root of competitive advantage. Global strategies can extend this advantage through dispersing activities to source comparative advantages, access markets, or tap particular skills or technologies. To play this role, however, dispersed activities must be coordinated. This new synthesis, which recognizes the complex role of location in competitive advantage, will drive competition in the coming decades.

NOTES

1. See M.E. Porter, *Competitive Strategy: Techniques for Analyzing Industries and Competitors* (New York: Free Press, 1980).

2. See M.E. Porter, *Competitive Advantage: Creating and Sustaining Superior Performance* (New York: Free Press, 1985).

3. See Theodore Levitt, "Globalization of Markets," *Harvard Business Review* (1983), 61(3):92–102.

4. See, for example, M.E. Porter, "Competition in Global Industries: A Conceptual Framework," in *Competition in Global Industries,* M.E. Porter (Ed.) (Boston: Harvard Business School Press, 1986); G.T. Crocombe, J.M. Enright, and M.E. Porter, *Upgrading New Zealand's Competitive Advantage* (Auckland, New Zealand: Oxford University Press, 1991); and O. Solvell, I. Zander, and M.E. Porter, *Advantage Sweden* (Stockholm, Sweden: Norstedts, 1991).

5. See also M.J. Enright, "The Determinants of Geographic Concentration in Industry," Harvard Business School Working Paper 93–052, 1993; and M.J. Enright, "Organization and Coordination in Geographically Concentrated Industries," in *Coordination and Information: Historical Perspectives on the Organization of Enterprise* (Chicago: University of Chicago Press/NBER, 1994).

6. See H. Cristeina, "The Role of Home-Based Advantages in Global Expansion: Five Case Studies" (Unpublished MBA research report, Harvard Business School, May 1993).

7. See, for example, R. Jaikumar and D.M. Upton, "The Coordination of Global Manufacturing," in *Globalization, Technology and Competition: The Fusion of Computers and Telecommunications in the 1990s,* S.P. Bradley, J.A. Hausman, and R.L. Nolan (Eds.) (Boston: Harvard Business School Press, 1993).

8. This group of activities, which varies in composition from industry to industry, will be termed home-based activities or core activities.

9. See also M.C. Porter, *The Competitive Advantage of Nations* (New York: Free Press, 1990).

10. Thomas confirms this result in pharmaceuticals, where firms facing local rivals (and strict product approval regulation) are the most innovative. See L.G. Thomas, "Spare the Rod and Spoil the Industry: Vigorous Regulation and Vigorous Competition Promote International Competitive Advantage," Emory University Working Paper, 1993.

11. Some observers have cited collaboration rather than competition as an important basis of competitiveness, referring most often to Japan and to the industrial districts of Italy. This view confuses vertical collaboration with buyers, suppliers, and local institutions, which diamond theory stresses, with horizontal collaboration among competitors. Horizontal collaboration is rare in successful Japanese and Italian industries (*keiretsu,* for example, do not contain direct competitors).

12. See, for example, M.E. Porter and C. van der Linde, "Green and Competitive: Ending the Stalemate," *Harvard Business Review* (September/October 1995), 73:120–134.

13. See also B. Kogut, "Country Capabilities and the Permeability of Borders," *Strategic Management Journal* (Summer 1991), 33–47; and R.B. Reich, "Who Is Us?" *Harvard Business Review* (1990), 68(1):53–64.

14. Honda's movement toward greater local content relates its establishment of new product-line home bases.

15. For a useful discussion of other organizational issues in global companies, see C.A. Bartlett and S. Ghoshal, *Managing across Borders: The Transnational Solution* (Boston: Harvard Business School Press, 1989).

16. For further discussion see M.E. Porter and M.B. Fuller, "Coalitions and Global Strategy," in *Competition in Global Industries,* ed. M.E. Porter (Boston: Harvard Business School Press, 1986); and M.E. Porter and P. Ghemawat, "Patterns of International Coalition Activity," in *Competition in Global Industries,* M.E. Porter (Ed.) (Boston: Harvard Business School Press, 1986).

17. M.J. Enright, "Novo Industri," Case 9–389–148 (Boston: Harvard Business School, 1989).

18. The Northern Telecom case is discussed in T. Wesson, "The Determinants of Foreign Direct Investment in U.S. Manufacturing Industries" (Unpublished doctoral dissertation, Harvard Business School, 1993).

19. Wesson, "The Determinants of Foreign Direct Investment in U.S. Manufacturing Industries" (Unpublished doctoral dissertation, Harvard Business School, 1993).

5 STRATEGY FOR THE SMALL BUSINESS

Irene M. Duhaime
Georgia State University

The previous four chapters all discuss strategy in the context of larger firms; that is, long-established corporations and the business units within them. Yet, many of these business entities began as small enterprises. Just 20 years ago, Home Depot consisted of only one retail outlet. Technology giant Hewlett-Packard started in a garage. The powerful Microsoft Corporation had its genesis in humble circumstances in the mid-1970s. Whether or not small businesses grow into well-known behemoths, they differ from their larger competitors in ways that have important implications for their strategies as well as for their management processes. To help small business managers maximize the success of their business enterprises, this chapter highlights aspects of strategic management and strategic tools that are especially relevant for them.

PUTTING SMALL BUSINESSES IN CONTEXT

The world economy depends on small business. In the United States alone, there are more than 23 million firms with fewer than 500 employees. They provide the majority of U.S. private employment accounting for 53 percent of the nonfarm workforce, and they generated virtually all net new jobs during the first half of the 1990s.[1] They produce 51 percent of the private gross domestic product in the United States.[2] Small firms make a crucial contribution to technology and innovation. In the twentieth century, small U.S. firms pioneered the development of the airplane, the optical scanner, the personal computer, soft contact lenses, the zipper, and e-commerce on the World Wide Web.[3]

Sometimes whole new industries have been established through the innovations of entrepreneurial start-up firms. In other cases, entrepreneurial firms transform existing industries. Nike is an excellent example of how entrepreneurial start-up firms can redraw traditional boundaries around companies and industries. In the 1970s, Converse All Stars typified the athletic shoe or sneaker industry; customers' only choices were black or white shoes, in low- or high-top styles. Nike reinvented this industry through its emphasis on product performance, style, and celebrity marketing coupled with its decision to outsource manufacturing of nearly all its shoes to foreign companies.[4] However, by disregarding the implications of the industry reaction it triggers, Nike can find itself at the mercy of new market conditions, even though it initiated them.

The term "small business" covers a wide spectrum of organizations, ranging from the many small businesses with only a handful of employees reporting directly to the owner, to others that have hundreds of employees and have a formal reporting structure for managing those employees. In this chapter, we focus on organizations with up to 500 employees, adopting the commonly accepted definition of small businesses used by the U.S. Small Business Administration (SBA). We also call attention to the special concerns of small businesses that are family owned and those that are entrepreneurial start-ups.

What's Different about Small Businesses?

Strategy merits separate consideration in the case of small businesses for several reasons pertaining to vulnerabilities and advantages over larger rivals. First, small businesses have little room for error in the strategy choices they make: the products or solutions they choose to offer; how they choose to compete; the goals they strive to attain. Indeed, many start-ups or new entrepreneurial ventures fail precisely because their initial choices do not result in a product that enough customers want. And, those small firms that initially succeed, often discover that they do not have the resources to weather a sudden downturn in their marketplace performance. Small businesses are in some ways more vulnerable to discontinuities in the business environment than large corporations, which are better able to shift resources internally to meet challenges. Second, they are more vulnerable than larger enterprises to the moves of rivals, customers, and suppliers. They do not have the "power" in negotiating with other entities that often accrues to larger firms, in part due to their size and scale. Third, small businesses are often especially vulnerable to dependence on a single product, or a single retail outlet, or a small set of customers, or customers in one geographic region.

Yet, small firms also possess (or perhaps, more precisely, should possess) advantages over their larger rivals. Because of their closeness to a small set of customers, small firms should be able to observe change in and around their customer base faster and more insightfully than their larger, bureaucratic rivals. Hence, in part because of their small size, they should be more flexible in their mind-set and be attuned to the need to shift key elements of their culture's guiding values, implicit beliefs and strong operating norms. The difficulties of large companies in making such shifts have been well documented. The family owners and the key top managers in a small firm often know and can talk to most employees over a short time period; what they learn from such conversations can change their outlook. With such mind-set flexibility, small firms should (and often do) manifest distinctive marketplace agility: the ability to instantly respond to emerging marketplace change. Such agility is often noted as the hallmark of successful start-up enterprises.

And yet, existing small businesses share at least one commonality with larger corporate entities: they often fall prey to newly arrived small rivals. Though many industry transformations result from product and technology advances initiated by small businesses, such changes tend to originate with entrepreneurial start-ups rather than small businesses already operating in those industries. To safeguard their survival and success through the shifts in their competitive landscapes over time, small businesses must recognize various change agents—new competitors, changing customer preferences, technology developments, and changes in governmental policies—and devise strategies and strategic processes to contend with them. In this respect, small businesses are no different than any other form of organizational entity.

Rapid Change Management

As discussed in Chapter 1, anticipating and managing change is the central concern and focus of strategic management. It may be a truism, but most small businesses face a competitive landscape characterized by rapid change. Managing change in marketplace strategy and within the organization constitutes perhaps an even greater challenge for small businesses. For all the reasons noted earlier, small businesses must be ever vigilant in detecting and anticipating change in and around their competitive milieu.

Consider the case of FurnitureCo, our fictitious name for a real company (see Box 5.1). FurnitureCo confronts a vast array of rivals producing many different designs, types, and styles of kitchen and dining room chairs and tables. Every year, rivals introduce new designs with great fanfare generated through retail promotions, modest advertising, and extensive showroom hoopla. Key retail chains continuously change their buying criteria in an effort to anticipate and guide customers' purchasing preferences. New technologies affecting both the design and manufacture of furniture are a yearly feature of trade and industry shows. Thus, each year, FurnitureCo must make many subtle changes in the styling of its two product lines and introduce new items in each line.

Strategy's Importance for Small Businesses

For the reasons already noted—vulnerability to marketplace change, paucity of resources—strategy is critical to a small business like FurnitureCo. As illustrated in this chapter, the analysis and thought processes associated with

---

Box 5.1

A Small Furniture Company

A small family-owned firm (FurnitureCo) manufactures two broad product lines: dining room and kitchen chairs and tables. Two generations of the founding family now constitute the management team. The firm has been in business for more than 20 years and has less than 100 employees. Sales are concentrated in a relatively small geographic area. The firm faces extensive competition from many other small furniture manufacturers and larger rivals that produce considerably broader product lines. It continually adapts and modifies its product lines based on input from its distribution channels and modest market research with its end-customers. It has one manufacturing plant. Although the firm has not had a loss-making quarter for a number of years, its quarterly profits tend to oscillate with demand spurred by new home building and some seasonal influences.

---

strategy enable small businesses not only to develop strategies to compete effectively, but to continually reassess those strategies against the changing environment. Without such strategic thinking, a small business is more likely to be the victim of, than a survivor of, the industry transformations that typify the contemporary competitive landscape.

Without a strategy that indicates which product lines to emphasize (and which not to get involved in), FurnitureCo might skip and switch from one product line to another, or more likely might attempt to dabble in many product types. This would greatly reduce its ability to develop a marketplace reputation with key distribution channels as a reliable and quality supplier of standard furniture lines. A concern with strategy causes the owners/managers of any small business to address explicitly the key choices it must make, and to monitor the results of those choices.

The Need for Internal Strategy Processes

Small businesses also need an effective internal strategy development process. By making efforts to identify and map strategic alternatives, managers of small businesses can capitalize on two critical attributes already noted: mind-set flexibility and marketplace agility. (Whether the small business managers anticipate which *specific* changes actually occur is less important than that they develop the habit of monitoring change and considering possible responses.) That habit will enable managers of small businesses to recognize change early and use their flexibility to "turn on a dime" to make strategic choices for the new environments.

Strategy's Challenge for Small Businesses

Most managers or owners of small businesses give little attention to strategic management. Strategic thinking and planning should be forced onto the small firm's agenda by setting aside a day for it on a regular basis. (How often such planning needs to be done depends on the particular business the firm is in, how volatile its industry is, how quickly its external and competitive environments are changing, and similar factors.) Consultants can assist with advance preparation for the strategy day and with facilitating the day's discussions to keep the focus on strategic, not operational, issues.

Consider the case of CoolCoil (see Box 5.2). A series of simple one-day meetings enables the management team to take periodic time-outs to review both strategic and operating issues. By doing so, managers and other employees can address issues in a level of detail that is simply not possible on a day-to-day basis.

Box 5.2

Planning at CoolCoil

CoolCoil is a small manufacturer of customized cooling coils, located in the southeastern region of the United States. With 145 employees, the company provides services to large oil exploration operations in the Gulf of Mexico. When new drilling mechanisms triggered a resurgence of oil exploration in the Gulf in the early 1990s, CoolCoil's sales began to increase significantly. Focusing on the growing operations, management began to lose sight of how to position the firm within the industry and the local market. CoolCoil's owners realized that they needed a strategic plan to ensure *profitable* growth. They engaged a business consultant to assist a team of top managers in developing a strategic plan for the company. The team met monthly at an off-site location. To foster widespread participation in the plan's development, team members had specific assignments to gather recommendations throughout the company.

CoolCoil had been experiencing some serious problems: shipping delays, high overtime costs, high training costs, and high supervision costs. Through the strategic planning process, the company was able to identify the root of these problems: the firm's inability to retain employees in the face of a tight local labor market. Based on the strategic plan, CoolCoil hired a human resource manager who initiated a program to target non-college-bound high school students who could advance from entry level to the machine shop. By adding a human resource manager and executing a recruitment strategy of visiting local high schools and attending job fairs, CoolCoil decreased turnover and significantly reduced employee turnover costs. These changes also positioned CoolCoil favorably against competition that faced higher wages or the turnover problems that CoolCoil had successfully addressed.

The Internet and Small Business Strategy

Few "forces of change" have so dramatically shifted the competitive context of small businesses, for both good and ill, as the World Wide Web. Commerce on the Internet, or e-commerce, with all the technological innovation it represents, now affects most small and large firms directly and through its impact on their competitors, channels, end-customers, suppliers, and marketplace dynamics. The good news is that the World Wide Web confers a lot of advantages on small firms. Let us look briefly at some of the critical implications of the Internet for the strategies of small businesses.

First, and foremost, the Internet opens up amazing marketplace opportunities for existing or potential small businesses. Publications such as *Business 2.0, Industry Standard,* and *Fast Company* regale readers in almost every issue with the stories of dot-com start-ups that successfully pioneer a new niche market. Any individual or small group can create a Web site and rapidly go into business over the Internet.

Second, the Internet grants small firms stunning and rapid access to the marketplace, enabling rates of sales growth that were unimaginable a mere few years ago. By selling over the Internet, even small firms today can be global in scope, or at a minimum, selling to customers in countries well beyond the borders of their home base. Many small hotels in leading tourist destinations now find that the Internet may account for up to 50 percent of their inquiries from prospective foreign customers. Because of the low cost of introducing their offerings over the Internet, small companies can achieve inexpensive and rapid penetration of global markets, until now a strategy that only large companies could afford.

Third, because the Internet makes it easy for small specialized firms to collaborate over networks to deliver low-cost, high-value services to customers anywhere, they can now compete directly against much larger, established enterprises. Information and communications technologies now make it more convenient, effective, and less expensive to collaborate with other entities than was the norm in the former traditional economy. In many instances, it no longer makes strategic sense to try to own all the necessary assets associated with a small business. Indeed, small firms focused on being the best at what they do have a potential competitive advantage over large organizations that are vertically integrated. It is not surprising therefore to find that small businesses are emerging as specialists in every phase of the activity or value chain—product design, product development, logistics, operations, marketing, sales, and service—that resides at the heart of any industry or product sector.[5]

Fourth, the Internet facilitates the emergence and growth of small firms in large part because increasingly it allows a set of individuals to develop and foster a business without committing large chunks of scarce resources to physical assets—what many now refer to as "bricks and mortar." The Internet places a heavy premium on intangible assets: knowledge, image and reputation, relationships, and organizational acumen.[6] For example, a small Internet-based, start-up firm devoted to helping couples plan their wedding, requires relatively little physical plant. But it can develop extensive knowledge of the "wedding process," develop a strong brand name for assisting in wedding plans, and establish critical relationships with participants in that process—florists, musicians, photographers, and so forth. By creating a virtual shopping mall, the Internet allows small firms to sell high-value services that originate in their intellectual property without having to invest assets in physical facilities.

Finally, the Internet should play to the inherent advantages of small business noted earlier: flexibility and agility. The Internet is ideally suited to allowing any small business to gather extensive data on customers, to monitor changes in its competitive environment, and to quickly adapt its product offerings.

STRATEGY CHOICE ISSUES

Chapter 1 introduces the major strategic choices which every firm faces: (1) the products the firm offers and the customers it seeks to serve, also known as the "scope" or "corporate strategy" choice; (2) how the firm competes, also known as the "posture" or "business strategy" choice; and (3) the goals the firm wishes to pursue, known as the "goal" or "aspiration" choice. This chapter focuses on how each of these choices is particular to or different for small, entrepreneurial and family businesses.

Corporate Strategy: What Business Is the Small Firm In?

The most elemental question to be addressed at the corporate strategy level is *what business or mix of businesses* the firm should compete in.[7] Will the small business compete in a single business or will it service a variety of businesses? FurnitureCo, for example, might want to address the following questions:

- Should it expand to manufacture and sell products outside its historic chair and table product lines?
- Should it add one or more new chair and/or table product lines?
- Should it divest its chair or table lines and concentrate only on one of its historic products?
- Should it begin to market and sell furniture products of one or more other small manufacturers?

Continually asking these and related questions compels FurnitureCo's managers to address which products they ought to produce and which customer segments they might pursue.

Asking these types of questions may be even more important for Internet-based small businesses. Because the Internet allows a small business to customize its solution or product offering, often to the level of individual customers, and not just customer segments, the small business owner or manager may be lured into going after every available customer. Some small Internet start-ups have tried to serve all customers who visit their Web site or who respond to their promotion and advertising; in doing so, they lose their product and customer focus.

Even for single-product firms, however, it pays to periodically and systematically reexamine the basic corporate strategy questions: What business(es) should we be in? What is the appropriate scale and scope of our enterprise? At the point the firm considers expanding beyond its base business by adding new product lines and/or going after new segments of customers, it should give *careful attention* to the other important corporate strategy questions:

- How should those businesses be related?
- How should those businesses (and the relationships among them) be managed?

FurnitureCo might examine how other prospective furniture product lines might be related to its existing chair and table lines:

- Would they use the same raw materials and other inputs?
- Would they use similar manufacturing processes and technologies?
- Would they require similar or different technical skills in the workforce?
- Would they be sold through the same distribution channels?

By explicitly addressing these issues and openly wrestling with the implications of their answers in implementing the strategic choices they make, managers of expanding small businesses can avoid the lack of focus that has crippled many larger diversified firms.

In family businesses, diversification into additional lines of business sometimes happens fairly early in the life cycle of the original business; each new limb of the family tree may develop or be given a semi-autonomous new branch of the family business. Despite informal family lines of communication (or, perhaps, *because* of them!), if the next generation's businesses are to be *legally* related to the family business, it is important to explicitly address whether those family businesses will be related in a *business* sense, and how to best manage the family of businesses (recognizing that "best" may have conflicting answers from a family perspective and from a business perspective).

What Markets and Customers Will the Firm Serve?

The second basic question to be addressed in forming a small firm's strategy is that of *what markets and customers* the firm will serve. For most businesses, a firm must decide the geographic scope of its markets. In some businesses, the products or services might be offered to a broad array of customer types ranging from individual consumers to industrial customers. For small businesses, it is especially important to consciously make these market scope choices because the small business's limited resources can be quickly exhausted by attempting to serve too broad a geographic scope or too broad a range of customer types.

FurnitureCo had to make explicit market and customer choices:

- It would concentrate on a certain style of furniture.
- It would focus exclusively on kitchen and dining room furniture.
- It would sell to a number of specialist furniture outlets and allow them to choose the geographic regions in which they would retail these product lines.

Choosing which markets/customers to serve means also deciding which *not* to serve. FurnitureCo decided not to produce more than two styles of each product line and not to manufacture furniture other than kitchen and dining room tables and chairs. Choosing which markets/customers not to serve is often a difficult decision for entrepreneurial start-up firms that initially see every new customer as an opportunity. An entrepreneurial firm must often refuse new undertakings to avoid expending resources (and entrepreneurial energy) needed for the growth strategies of its chosen business(es). For example, a deliberately chosen sequence of geographic (or customer group) rollouts provides a stronger base for lasting high growth than attempts to serve every eager customer.

Despite the generic nature of many of the questions previously noted, we should not ignore that in many small businesses, only one or a few managers are available to consider these issues, make choices, and execute the subsequent game plan (see Box 5.3). And sometimes, these choices may lead managers quickly into dealing with new distribution channels and customers, and often in new geographic regions.

The choices that a small business makes about corporate strategy and scope have implications for implementing the firm's strategies. As discussed later in this chapter, choices about the firm's organizational form and financial structure, its management or organizational structure, and the delegation of authority and responsibility must support and be consistent with its corporate strategy and business scope decisions.

Stakeholders

The products or services a firm chooses to offer and the customer groups and geographic segments it chooses to serve determine who the firm's stakeholders are. As noted in Chapter 7, stakeholders include industry and trade associations, community groups, governmental agencies, the courts, the media, social activist groups, and industry participants such as distributors, end-customers, suppliers, and competitors, in addition to firm-specific stakeholders such as the employees and the owners or shareholders.

Box 5.3

How Does Your Business Grow?

In the summer of 1995, designer Dary Rees had a problem. Her two-year-old, Miami-based home accessories and tableware business was starting to stagnate. Revenues were a seemingly healthy $2 million, and some forty-five hundred outlets across the country, including Nordstrom and Neiman Marcus, were carrying her merchandise. But she was running short of new stores to approach, and her products seemed to be losing their cachet. "I realized that if I wanted the business to keep growing," says Rees, "I'd have to go global."

So, passport in her purse, she was off. First stop, the National Association of Women Business Owners (an organization that assists women entrepreneurs), which signed Rees up for a trade mission to Amsterdam and London sponsored by the U.S. Commerce Department.

Today, Rees generates about 30 percent of her company's $3 million in sales from exports. And she already works through as many as twelve separate foreign distributors in France, the Netherlands, Singapore, and the United Kingdom, among others. Her goal is to generate $3 million in sales by the end of next year from her overseas business alone.

Knowing if or when a small business should look toward the export market can be tricky and a bit daunting, but before the process even begins, the budding exporter should be absolutely sure it's on solid ground at home. Then comes the vital task of picking suitable overseas markets. There are four simple but crucial questions that must be answered:

Is there a need or desire for your product outside the United States?

Does anyone in the company have exporting expertise?

Do you have the financing and time needed to adequately prepare to enter another market?

Do you have a thorough understanding of the marketplace you want to enter?

Source. First appeared in *Working Woman,* May 1997. Written by Kerry Hannon. Reprinted with permission of MacDonald Communications Corporation (www .workingwoman.com).

As in the case of any firm's political strategy[8] (that is, managing relationships with external stakeholders), a small firm needs to ask the following questions:

- Who are our current key stakeholders?
- How and why is each stakeholder important to our strategy?
- What is the nature of our relationship with each stakeholder?
- In which ways is the relationship not proving satisfactory?
- How can or should the relationship be improved?
- As we contemplate amending our strategy, with which new stakeholders will we need to develop a relationship?

Ever mindful of its need to use limited resources wisely, the small firm must actively nurture its relationships with its *existing* stakeholders. Indeed, managing stakeholder relationships may be even more critical for small firms than for larger ones because of the need to acquire resources cheaply and to leverage them wisely. Many start-up e-commerce firms develop intensive working relationships with experts in relevant technologies. FurnitureCo devotes considerable time and attention to managing its relationships with key suppliers and distribution channels. Senior managers visit each key supplier at least once every two months. They provide suppliers with tickets to sporting events. They invite senior managers of suppliers to visit their manufacturing location so that they can see for themselves how their products are integrated into the manufacturing process. These visits also serve as the source of new ideas for collaboration between the businesses.

Although efforts to cultivate a broader set of customers, suppliers, or distributors can pay off in reduced dependency, establishing new relationships carries initial costs. In deciding when and how to invest resources in broadening its set of stakeholders, a small firm should be influenced by internal factors such as its ownership objectives and growth aspirations, as well as by external factors such as the competitive environment it faces. A small Internet-based firm that wants to grow quickly may need to develop tight working relationships with venture capitalists and other sources of investment capital. A small family-owned firm that plans rapid growth may need to foster an intimate working relationship with one or more banks.

Acting individually, small businesses have less leverage on external stakeholders (e.g., trade and community organizations, government agencies, social activist groups, the media) than do their larger competitors. Collective action with other small businesses or with their larger counterparts may be necessary to gain the attention of those stakeholders. Thus, small firms frequently join many local business and trade associations with a view to influencing governmental agencies, social action groups, and local community and other interest groups.

Strong personal relationships with stakeholders typically characterize small firms, and this characteristic can be an important strength of such firms. The small firm's size generally limits the number of parties the firm must deal with, which facilitates personal relationships with customers, suppliers, distributors, and employees. Such personal relationships can create loyalty that large firms can only envy. Personal relationships build advantage in other ways as well. Such relationships afford close and personal knowledge of the customer that enables the small firm to provide custom products and superior service, even to anticipate the needs of those customers before they would be able to articulate them to a larger competitive provider. These close relationships are sometimes the basis of cooperative ventures that leverage the small firm's limited resources; for example, joint ventures with suppliers can lead to technological developments that provide competitive advantage for the small firm as well as its suppliers.

Business Strategy

Once the small business has chosen what business or businesses to compete in, it can focus on business strategy decisions. As important as choices about business scope are to a small business's success, equally critical are the firm's decisions about *how to compete,* or what competitive posture it will take in each business.

FurnitureCo can serve as a useful reminder to any small business of the importance of paying attention to the details of each mode of competition in any firm's posture (product line width, functionality, features, service, availability, image and reputation, selling and relationships, and price). FurnitureCo chose to build its image and reputation around a focused product portfolio—two product lines. It emphasized two elements of functionality: chairs that were comfortable to sit in and tables that were easy to clean. It constantly adapted features such as design and styling, sometimes shipping specific styles to particular channels. It developed a set of services for channels including repairs and stocking. It carefully nurtured an image of long-lasting durable furniture that was comfortable yet stylish. As noted, it invested significant management time in fostering relationships with channels (and suppliers). And, in part due to the value perceived by both channels and end-customers along each of these modes of competition, FurnitureCo's prices were typically higher than many other rivals, and it rarely offered discounts to move its products into or out of its distribution channels.

Every small business also has many options within and across these modes of competition; thus, busy managers, who are caught up in the details of day-to-day operations, may not detect that their competitive posture is inconsistent and thus is sending mixed signals to the marketplace. However, by carefully paying attention to what is happening with its channels and end-customers, a small business can leverage its inherent marketplace agility by adapting its posture as circumstances warrant.

The competitive posture of small businesses (how the firm seeks to attract, win, and retain customers) is especially closely connected to the enterprise's functional strategies—marketing, manufacturing, R&D, human resources and finance, and others. Thus, managers in any small firm must continually ask themselves:

- How does each functional area positively and negatively affect the firm's current competitive posture?
- How might each functional area constrain future competitive posture moves?
- What changes might be warranted for each functional area?
- In which ways do the functional areas conflict with each other or support and reinforce each other?

Often, the answers to these questions allow a small firm to refocus its posture or to commit additional resources to an already successful posture.

CoolCoil (see Box 5.2), by assessing and modifying its human resources policies, was able to alleviate detrimental operating and personnel issues, and thus concentrate its efforts on winning emerging marketplace opportunities.

Small e-commerce firms often require an innovative financial strategy to attract sufficient capital for funding the extensive marketing and promotion programs they need to build "share of mind" in customers. And innovative human resource policies are necessary to attract the kind of talent that will commit to a start-up enterprise despite low initial salaries, but with the (often unfulfilled) promise of significant returns at some future date. Without such talent, small start-up firms are not able to develop products or solutions to take to the marketplace or design postures that will win and retain customers.

MAKING STRATEGY CHOICES

In making the strategy choices discussed earlier, small firms can use many of the analytical tools available to larger enterprises.

SWOT

SWOT analysis (assessment of a firm's strengths, weaknesses, opportunities, and threats) is often the first tool used for deciding which battles to fight as well as how to wage those competitive battles. In using this tool, small firms need to be sensitive to a number of issues, and to remember that strengths, weaknesses, opportunities, and threats are highly interlinked.

Strengths and weaknesses should always be determined with respect to rivals, and not to one's own history. Thus, FurnitureCo might judge that by upgrading its manufacturing plant, it had significantly added to its manufacturing strength. Yet if a rival, even another small firm, has begun to use superior manufacturing technology and more efficient plant design, FurnitureCo's investment may still mean that its manufacturing prowess is a weakness compared with that of this particular rival.

However, both current and emerging or potential rivals need to be taken into account. Some small businesses only focus on current rivals, thus missing the threats inherent in the emergence of new rivals. For many small businesses, the real threat to their future success may reside in newly emerging e-businesses rather than new entrants in the traditional business.

A small firm assessing its opportunities and threats should pay close attention to the fragmentation of competitors in its chosen business/service as well as to the patterns of segmentation of market demand for those products/services. Highly fragmented industries that can't easily be dominated by large competitors may be more attractive to small businesses.

Any small business should concentrate considerable attention on the following questions:

- How can we translate our strengths into value for customers?
- How do our weaknesses inhibit us from generating value for our current and potential customers?
- What current and potential customer needs might represent opportunities for our firm?
- How might we reach new customers with our existing product offerings?

Sector Analysis

Small firms can also use the competitive landscape analysis or industry analysis detailed in Chapter 8 to refine their understanding of current and emerging opportunities and threats. In particular, industry sectors in which there is high segmentation of market demand can be desirable for small businesses. Such conditions permit small businesses to specialize in serving the needs of small pockets or segments of that demand and avoid head-to-head competition with the largest and strongest competitors in its industry. The furniture industry is a classic example of many small firms serving local and regional needs and tastes. By staying close to its vendors, channels, and end-customers, FurnitureCo is able to continually adapt the style and features of its two product lines, and thus partially avoid comparisons with the offerings of many larger rivals.

In choosing the pocket or niche of the industry it will specialize in, the small business should search for potential sources of advantage in segments it is considering. For example, in industries where family businesses or privately held firms are in the minority, these firms may gain an advantage over publicly held competitors that need to meet quarterly financial expectations of institutional investors. This need may limit the ability of publicly held companies to make long-term investments.

Most small businesses (either family businesses or entrepreneurial start-up businesses) find that focus or niche strategies capitalize on their strengths and offer the best opportunities for success. It is important for small businesses formulating strategy to recognize that often your most direct competitors are others like you. As a result, small businesses should avoid marketing strategies that focus solely on *why us (small firms) instead of the big guy.* Instead, your market strategy should center on *why us instead of others (small firms) like us.* As manager of a small business, you must remember that the target market that values what you have to offer will be looking at other companies like you as competitors for serving their needs.

Small businesses should continually ask themselves the following questions:

- What is the market segment that we can serve?
- What makes that segment attractive for our organization?
- How can we leverage our strengths to win in that segment?
- How do we protect ourselves from current and potential rivals?

Value Chain

Value chain analysis helps small businesses, family businesses, and entrepreneurial start-up companies to identify, assess, and refine their specific strengths, weaknesses, opportunities, and threats.[9] Entrepreneurial start-up businesses should perform value chain analysis to assess the costs and value added at each stage of the business.

Small firms in many traditional businesses are now confronted by fundamental shifts in the value chains of their industries. Although as noted earlier, these industry shifts can be the source of enormous opportunities for small firms, they may also constitute dramatic threats when they are not anticipated. Many start-up Internet-based small businesses aim to reshape some activity in the overall value chain; thus, existing small firms face competition from every direction.

A small firm assessing its strengths and weaknesses must be realistic as it views its resources and the implications of those resources for its ability to compete. Limited financial resources typically characterize small firms; most do not generate large amounts of excess cash flow, thus it is difficult to self-finance new ventures or significant expansions of the existing business. Entrepreneurs with high growth aspirations for their start-up firms often find themselves struggling to keep up with their businesses' financial demands. Torn between their need for additional financing and their desire to retain control of the business and autonomy in their decision making, they divert their attention from operating the business to make presentations for financing. Some helpful tips to assist small business owners in the resource acquisition process are offered in Box 5.4.

In assessing a small firm's strengths and weaknesses, it is important to recognize that although its size can limit the resources it has to accomplish its objectives, the small firm has a great deal of flexibility in the use of those resources. This flexibility can confer financial, physical, and human resource advantages. For example, in a small company every employee "does what needs to be done," assuming responsibility for the success of the business by doing any new task as the need arises. This natural cross-training that occurs in a small firm as its employees assume and learn a broad cross section of the functions necessary for the firm's success can be a significant competitive advantage. However, many small firms undermine the inherent advantage in having their employees learn a broad array of functions because top management is unwilling or unable to share real authority and responsibility. As a result, key employees become frustrated and cannot enjoy real satisfaction in the use of their expanded capabilities. Just as those more knowledgeable employees can be a valuable source of competitive advantage for the small firm that employs them, they are valuable to other firms, including the small firm's competitors, as well. A very real challenge, then, for the small firm wishing to gain competitive advantage from the flexibility of its small size, is to learn to delegate real authority from top management in order to retain valuable key employees. Only then

---

Box 5.4

Asking the Right Questions When Looking for Funding for Your Business

There are a number of questions which entrepreneurs and small business owners should address as they seek resources for their businesses. Here are a few of the most important:

1. How much capital do you need to launch your business or to take it to the next stage of growth? Make a detailed estimate of the financial needs of the business.

2. What are your personal trade-offs—how much control of your company you want to keep, how much financial risk you want to personally assume, and how much growth you want the business to achieve, how quickly?

3. What is you company's stage of development (start-up, expansion, etc.)? How does that match with the objectives of potential sources such as personal savings, friends and family, banks and other lenders, "angels" and other private investors, venture capital funds, corporate venture investors, and buyers of public offerings?

4. What aspects of your product or service are of most interest to those who might invest resources in your business? In preparing your business presentation, focus on the audience's interest rather than your own. What matters to them? What questions will they ask? Anticipate their concerns and be prepared with answers.

5. What do you plan to do with the resources you are seeking? Match the expected impact on your business with the objectives of potential sources of those resources.

6. What is the best case scenario that might result from your use of the resources? Worst case scenario? Have a contingency plan for how you will deal with those outcomes if they occur.

---

will the small firm's natural cross-training translate into the management depth it needs to expand and grow.

A small firm should continually ask itself the following questions:

- What are the key activities in the value chain associated with our business?
- What costs are associated with each activity?
- What customer benefits accrue from each activity?
- How can we integrate the activities to add further value for customers?
- How can we manage our human and other resources to maximize the value we can create for customers?

STRATEGY IMPLEMENTATION ISSUES

Small firms confront distinct implementation and organization issues as they develop, refine, and implement their strategy. We briefly address three key issues: organizational form, organizational structure, and organizational processes.

Organizational Form

Most small businesses face the ongoing strategic choice of what organizational *form* to use. For example, firms may choose to organize themselves as sole proprietorships, partnerships, corporations, limited partnerships, or limited liability companies. Each organizational form offers benefits to firms, and each has different tax, legal, and administrative implications, as illustrated in Table 5.1.

TABLE 5.1   Comparison of Various Business Forms

	Control	Liability	Taxation	Administrative Obligations
Sole proprietorship	Owner has complete control	Unlimited personal liability	Not a separate taxable entity	Only those generic to businesses
Partnership	Partners share control	Joint and several unlimited personal liability	Not a separate taxable entity	Only those generic to businesses
Corporation	Control distributed among shareholders, directors, and officers	Limited personal liability	Separate taxable entity unless subchapter selection	Some additional
Limited partnership	General partners control, limited partners do not	General partners: joint and several unlimited personal liability; limited partners: limited personal liability	Not a separate entity	Some additional
Limited liability company	Members share control or appoint managers	Limited personal liability	Not a separate entity if properly structured	Some additional

Source. William D. Bygrave, *The Portable MBA in Entrepreneurship* (New York: John Wiley & Sons, Inc., 1997), 296.

Periodic examination of the firm's choice of organizational form is advisable to ensure that the form in use best serves the firm's needs and objectives. It is also important to reassess the appropriateness of the organization's form whenever the firm undertakes other strategic decisions, such as expansion into new lines of business or major financing efforts. FurnitureCo will have to consider adopting a more corporate form as the firm's revenues grow and the need for professional managers outside the founding family becomes more apparent.

Organizational Structure

Our definition of structure includes any mechanisms that facilitate the formulation and implementation of strategy and the overall coordination of the business, such as hierarchical reporting relationships, standard operating procedures, and organizational culture, or widely shared norms and values.[10]

Small businesses with few employees tend to have simple hierarchical relationships, often with all employees reporting directly to the firm's president. As the firm grows, however, the president delegates responsibilities for various functions (finance, marketing, manufacturing, R&D) to others promoted or hired to manage those functions. A small business moving from a simple organizational hierarchy to a functional hierarchy must face decisions about when (and in what order) the functional areas will be delegated to others. Managers must be selected and new working relationships developed, while maintaining attention to the business's operations. Responsibilities and reporting relationships must be consistent with the firm's strategy and support the firm's strategy implementation.

Although hierarchy and standard operating procedures can be helpful in implementing company strategies, and necessarily gain importance as firms grow, it is often organizational culture that is most important in strategy implementation for small businesses, entrepreneurial start-up firms, and even mid-size (or larger) family businesses. Often, a firm's culture reflects both the myths and the realities related to the founder or key leaders of the firm. Stories about the firm's founding, early challenges that were overcome to successfully launch the firm, or employees' extraordinary efforts can provide inspirational models for new strategy initiatives.

Organizational Processes

In many small businesses, strategic decisions emerge over time, often from a sequence of operating decisions rather than from a formal strategic decision process. In entrepreneurial start-up companies, strategic decisions emerge as functional issues such as marketing, manufacturing, and human resources in turn come to the forefront and are critical to the next stage of the companies' development and success. In family businesses, strategic decisions emerge as

---

Box 5.5

Defining a Business Plan

A *good definition:* A business plan is a document that convincingly demonstrates the ability of your business to sell enough of its product or service to make a satisfactory profit and be attractive to potential backers.

A *better definition:* A business plan is a *selling document* that conveys the excitement and promise of your business to any potential backers or stakeholders.

Source. William D. Bygrave, *The Portable MBA in Entrepreneurship* (New York: John Wiley & Sons, Inc., 1997), 122.

---

family relationships interact with business issues; major strategic decisions tend to occur in family businesses as much in connection with transfers of those businesses across generations as in response to industry events.

To manage these issues, small businesses need a budgeting system integrated with the business plans, with a management control process for review of results and correction of the firm's course. In addition to the benefits that firms of all sizes derive from time spent on strategic thinking, described earlier in this chapter, it is particularly important for small and entrepreneurial start-up businesses to develop a written business plan, and to communicate with their

---

Box 5.6

Eight Reasons for Writing a Business Plan

1. To sell yourself on the business.
2. To obtain bank financing.
3. To obtain investment funds.
4. To arrange strategic alliances.
5. To obtain large contracts.
6. To attract key employees.
7. To complete mergers and acquisitions.
8. To motivate and focus your management team.

Source. Adapted from William D. Bygrave, *The Portable MBA in Entrepreneurship* (New York: John Wiley & Sons, Inc., 1997), 122–124.

Box 5.7

What Should the Business Plan Cover?

1. Cover page.
2. Table of contents.
3. Executive summary.
4. The company.
5. The market.
6. The product/service.
7. Sales and promotion.
8. Finances.
9. Appendix.

Source. Adapted from William D. Bygrave, *The Portable MBA in Entrepreneurship* (New York: John Wiley & Sons, Inc., 1997), 128–129.

---

stakeholders about a variety of objectives (see Boxes 5.5 and 5.6 on page 127). Although the basic outline of a written business plan can be the same (see Box 5.7) regardless of which stakeholder the plan is directed to, recognizing differences in stakeholders' interests and adapting the presentation of the plan to those interests, will enhance the company's likelihood of success (see Table 5.2).

TABLE 5.2 Business Plan Targeting Summary

Stakeholder	Issues to Emphasize	Issues to Deemphasize	Length (No. of Pages)
Banker	Cash flow, assets, solid growth	Fast growth, hot market	10–20
Investor	Fast growth, Potential large market, Management team	Assets	20–40
Strategic partner	Synergy, proprietary products	Sales force, assets	20–40
Large customer	Stability, service	Fast growth, hot markets	20–40
Key employees	Security, opportunity	Technology	20–40
Merger and acquisition specialists	Past accomplishments	Future outlook	20–40

Source. William D. Bygrave, *The Portable MBA in Entrepreneurship* (New York: John Wiley & Sons, Inc., 1997), 146.

SUMMARY

Strategy is just as relevant for any small business as it is for the world's largest and most renowned corporations. Any small business with a strategy that is inappropriate for the competitive environment it faces cannot expect to survive, much less flourish. Thus, the owner/manager or the management team in any start-up enterprise or family-owned firm not only must develop a marketplace strategy but must continually assess that strategy as events in the competitive environment unfold.

REFERENCES

Birley, S., ed. 1998. *Entrepreneurship*. Hants, England: Dartmouth Publishing.

Bork, D. 1993. *Family Business, Risky Business*. Aspen, CO: Bork Institute for Family Business.

Bull, I., H. Thomas, and G. Willard, eds. 1995. *Entrepreneurship: Perspectives on Theory Building*. Oxford, England: Elsevier Science.

Bygrave, W.D., ed. 1997. *The Portable MBA in Entrepreneurship*. New York: Wiley.

Covin, J.G., and D.P. Slevin. 1989. "Strategic Management of Small Firms in Hostile and Benign Environments," *Strategic Management Journal*, 75–87.

Danco, L. 1995. *Beyond Survival: A Business Owner's Guide for Success*. Cleveland, OH: Center for Family Business, University Press.

Fritz, R. 1997. *Wars of Succession: The Blessings, Curses and Lessons that Family-Owned Firms Offer Anyone in Business*. Santa Monica, CA: Merritt.

Gartner, W. 1985. "A Conceptual Framework for Describing the Phenomenon of New Venture Creation," *Academy of Management Review*, 696–706.

Katz, J.A., ed. 1997. *Advances in Entrepreneurship, Firm Emergence, and Growth*. London, England: JAI Press.

Kets de Vries, M.F.R. 1996. *Family Business: Human Dilemmas in the Family Firm*. London, England: International Thomson Business Press.

Lasher, William R. *Strategic Thinking for Smaller Businesses and Divisions*. Malden, MA: Blackwell.

Le Van, G. 1999. *The Survival Guide for Business Families*. New York: Routledge.

Neubauer, F., and A.G. Lank. 1998. *The Family Business, It's Governance for Sustainability*. New York: Routledge.

Sahlman, W.A., and H.H. Stevenson. 1992. *The Entrepreneurial Venture*. Boston: Harvard Business School Publications.

Small Business Administration. 1997. *The Facts about Small Business, 1997* (September). Washington, DC: Small Business Administration Office of Advocacy.

Shepherd, D.A., and M. Shanley. 1998. *New Venture Strategy: Timing, Environmental Uncertainty, and Performance*. Thousand Oaks, CA: Sage.

Timmons, J.A. 1994. *New Venture Creation: Entrepreneurship for the 21st Century*. Boston: Irwin.

Vesper, K.H., ed. 1990. *New Venture Strategies.* Englewood Cliffs, NJ: Prentice-Hall.
Williams, E.E., and J.R. Thompson. 1998. *Entrepreneurship and Productivity.* Lanham, MD: University Press of America.

NOTES

1. *The Facts about Small Business, 1997* (Washington, DC: Small Business Administration Office of Advocacy, September 1997). This report is prepared periodically (September 1997 is the latest available as this book goes to press). It and other materials of interest to small businesses are available at this Web site: http://www.sba.gov.

2. Ibid.

3. Ibid.

4. L.J. Bourgeois III, I.M. Duhaime, and J.L. Stimpert, *Strategic Management: Concepts for Managers,* 2nd ed. (Fort Worth, TX: Dryden Press, 1999).

5. The value chain was addressed in some detail in Chapter 3.

6. The importance of intangible assets, and the differences between tangible and intangible assets, are treated in some detail in Chapter 10.

7. This question is the focus of the discussion of corporate strategy in Chapter 2.

8. Political strategy is discussed in detail in Chapter 7.

9. Value chain analysis and its role as an input to strategy making are discussed in detail in Chapters 3 and 4.

10. Bourgeois et al. *Strategic Management: Concepts for Managers,* p. 260.

6 DIGITAL STRATEGY

Jeffrey L. Sampler
London Business School

The Internet and the burgeoning electronic economy it has created have challenged many of our fundamental ideas about business and organizations. This chapter first explores the strategic implications of this new technology by examining the changing nature of industry definition, business strategy, and firm organization. Such changes in strategic thinking also alter our fundamental understanding of the nature of competition and the planning process. We focus on six major implications of the new realities of e-commerce: redefinition of industry structure, power shift to the consumer, instant globalization, new business models, nature of the planning process, and changes in reward policies due to this new environment.

One of the most important questions facing every company in the world today is, what will be our "dot-com" strategy? How will we compete through electronic channels over the World Wide Web? And traditional companies that are moving onto the Web and adding ".com" to their corporate or business unit name must also ask, what about channel conflict with existing distribution and sales networks and the potential for cannibalization? These questions are often asked with anxiety, because companies founded before the era of web-based competition know that if solutions are not forthcoming, the strategic high ground and potential market dominance they now occupy will be lost to Internet start-up companies.

Indeed, it seems that the start-ups are winning this battle. Almost all the well-known Internet companies didn't exist a few years ago—Amazon.com, eBay, and Yahoo!, to name a few. And thousands more start-ups are competing with traditional corporate business units in almost every conceivable market.

131

Tracking the meteoric rise of Internet start-ups' IPO stocks has become a regular part of the evening TV business news coverage. The amazing valuations of these companies have created billionaires out of their founders—Jeff Bezos of Amazon, and Jerry Yang, of Yahoo! are now listed on the Forbes 400 annual list of the richest people in America. Many web-based start-ups have grown from concept to experimentation to capability to multibillion-dollar valuations seemingly overnight; never before has so much wealth been created so fast.

The most successful Internet companies have received such massive media attention that their business practices have become legendary. Many new magazines chronicle the escapades of the digital revolution—*Wired, Industry Standard, Business 2.0, Red Herring,* and *Fast Company,* to name but a few. But what do the tactical maneuvers and strategic innovations that the web-based companies have pioneered mean to the nature of strategic thinking? And what are the implications for managers engaged in strategy planning and implementation?

CHANGES IN STRATEGY THINKING

Pace

Almost every manager in every industry feels that the competitive business environment is steadily becoming more complex. This complexity is occurring for two primary reasons: (1) information technology and its globalization of competition are causing increasingly unpredictable environments, and (2) discontinuous change is occurring more quickly, which makes continuous adaptation even more difficult. How has strategic thinking dealt with this shift?

Historically, the dominant perspective in the strategy discipline throughout much of the 1970s and early 1980s was the Industrial Organization (IO) economic concept that is most associated with the work of Porter and others.[1] Strategic planning in the IO school of strategy was concerned primarily with industry structure, because this was considered to be the primary determinant of firm profitability. Thus, many strategic planning methods consisted of analyzing industry forces to determine the attractiveness of an industry and how to influence the structure of the industry, and ultimately, profits.[2]

However, strategic thinking based on such industry analysis has come under some criticism in recent years because it assumes more or less static environments. Critics point out that a snapshot of an industry—that is, an analytical study—is not an adequate means for formulating strategy in a dynamic environment.[3] Preparing an in-depth, systemwide analysis of the competitive environment, and then implementing a strategy based on that analysis, assumes that the environment is not changing in crucial respects more quickly than you can develop and implement the strategy. But few, if any, industries are exempt from discontinuity today. Nonetheless, traditional IO strategic thinking assumes that industry trends can be reliably extrapolated, and this supposition is also the basis for many strategic analysis tools, including competitor analysis, strategic groups, Profit Impact of Market Share (PIMS), and diversification typologies (such as the famous classification of business units into dogs, stars, cash cows, and question marks). Because the increasing rate of change has put increasing pressure on firms to react more quickly, time is often seen as a source of competitive advantage.[4] But merely doing the same things faster is not an adequate answer.

The rapid-paced digital operating environment requires all observers of the Internet Age to address one cosmic question: How can we compete in unpredictable, chaotic times? Current thinking includes hypercompetition,[5] disruptive technologies,[6] strategy as revolution,[7] strategy as real options,[8] competing on the edge,[9] and surfing the edge of chaos.[10] The common theme seems to be how to reinvent the firm, expect the unexpected, and compete when the future is not forecastable. The Internet has been a driving force in this destabilization. As a result, new paradigms, such as chaos theory and increasing returns to scale, are emerging as part of the language of current strategic thinking.

Strategic Assets

An alternative view to the IO model of strategy is the resource-based view of strategy. This perspective, which has been increasing in popularity over the past decade, suggests that the fundamental source of competitive advantage lies not in industry structure, but instead, in a firm's internal resources. That is, the firm's special capabilities and competencies are the principal drivers of firm profitability and strategic advantage.[11] Resources are said to confer competitive advantage to the extent that the resources must be difficult to create, buy, substitute, or imitate.[12] Moreover, recently much research in the resource school of strategic thinking has shifted from focusing on tangible assets as a source of advantage to intangible assets, which includes knowledge,[13] core competencies,[14] learning,[15] and "invisible assets" such as brand image or corporate culture.[16]

Competitive advantage results when firms that accumulate and utilize complex resources, especially intangible ones, are able to execute more complex strategies and thereby sustain competitive advantage over competing firms lacking such capabilities.[17] Prahalad and Hamel (1990) summarize much of this thinking by noting that the logic underlying many of these ideas involves "the collective learning in the organization, especially with how to coordinate diverse production skills and integrate multiple streams of technology."[18]

Such an increasing importance and focus on intangible assets has had several ripple effects in managerial practice. First, we have seen a greater emphasis on knowledge management as firms seek to harness and leverage their intellectual assets. Technology has assisted this in the form of products such as Lotus Notes and intranets. Moreover, the reality that the key strategic advantage of many firms is primarily knowledge-based has important implications for financial instruments, such as the balance sheet. How should companies capture, represent, and value these intangible assets that are the drivers of innovation and profits? Present day balance sheets reflect the sources of value for the Industrial Age—land and plant and equipment. They are not well designed to reflect value for the Information Age. The key sources of value in the electronic economy—intellectual property and specialized capabilities—do not appear on traditional balance sheets. Thus, one of the major challenges to firms and the financial community is to develop a new set of financial instruments that reflect intangible assets as well as tangible ones. Without this, managers will have difficulty in managing key assets of their companies.

Return on Assets

One of the fundamental tenets of traditional economic thinking has been decreasing or diminishing returns to scale. The logic was that as a company grew, it eventually encountered limitations, such as less fertile land for farming or less skilled workers for manufacturing, which in turn led to price equilibrium and limitations on market share. This may have been true for the industrial economy, but it is quite often less true in the Information Age. Since the 1980s, many information companies succeeded beyond all expectations because their strategy was based on the principle of increasing returns to scale.[19] Increasing returns occur because of positive feedback and network effects; for example, a telephone network is more useful, and thus more valuable, if more people are using it. The same logic holds true for a Visa card, the Windows operating system, an Intel chip, or an Internet portal.

Stating this in terms of tactics for the digital economy is simple. A company that can quickly convince a large number of users to accept its product or service will often win control of the market, and its early lead will continue to escalate because of increasing returns to scale. There is a strong first mover advantage. The Internet start-ups of today have learned the lesson of both the first mover advantage and the importance of setting standards by analyzing the success of Intel and Microsoft in the 1980s. Both were comparatively small firms in the early 1980s, but less than 10 years later they controlled a major share of the profits of the PC industry. Inspired by such success models, many firms have sought first mover advantage and the opportunity to establish standards, even if it meant giving their product or service away or paying customers to use it, to gain large numbers of users quickly. However, has strategy really become as simple as that? Just send out freebie software over the Internet?

In fact, a strategy of increasing returns to scale and being a standard setter only works if switching costs keep users from moving from one product to another. These costs could be contractual, but are often more implicit, such as the opportunity costs of learning. Once customers invest the time and effort to master a particular device or software application, they are loathe to repeat the process to switch to a product with the same function. So time invested in learning to use a software program or customizing it would seem to be a significant barrier to switching. But in a world of customer-friendly software, standards can be emulated or made compatible in new products. For example,

Microsoft's Internet Explorer allowed users to import Netscape bookmarks, which greatly reduced switching costs. Thus, compatibility or emulation of standards decreases the effects of increasing returns to scale.

Moreover, the benefits of having been the standard setter and of having grown rapidly due to increasing returns to scale can be negated by a competitor introducing new technologies and new standards—if the competitor can create a larger community of users (or perhaps a community that is more valuable to belong to), an unlikely scenario in many cases. For example, Linux, a free operating system maintained by a worldwide network of users, is now challenging the dominance of the Windows operating system in personal computers, which has more than an 80 percent market share. As a rule of thumb, the power of standard setting is limited by the rate of adoption of the product and the product life cycle (when new standards get introduced).

Even though increasing returns to scale is an incredibly potent strategy within the information economy, it works better in some cases than others. For example, it is most powerful in situations of high adoption rates, long product life cycles, limited compatibility, or limited ability to emulate standards. Incorporating the principles of increasing returns to scale into an overall strategic plan, rather than replacing strategy with a call for "experimentation—full speed ahead" or "just give the product away" is the more correct advice for many companies.

Role of Technology

The role of technology in organizations has altered dramatically in the past 30 years. If we turn back the clock to the 1950s and 1960s, we see that originally information technology (IT) played only a supporting role. Often the main IT applications were payroll and other such number-crunching exercises, and only for corporate giants. It was in those early days that an IBM executive estimated that the size of the global mainframe computer market was six!

If we fast-forward to the 1980s, we see not only dramatic improvement in the power of computers, but also a fundamental change in their role in the organization. Computers were starting to be used as a strategic weapon. The IT success stories of this era were American Airlines' SABRE reservation system, American Hospital Supply's ASAP order entry system, and Frito-Lay's handheld computers. These systems supported the development of new strategies. The primary logic guiding the relationship between business strategy and IT strategy was that the IT strategy should be aligned with the business strategy. In other words, the business strategy was developed first, and the IT strategy was developed to support it.

In today's environment, information technology plays a disruptive role.[20] It is powerful because it enables new strategies to be possible—no matter whether IT serves an operational or strategic function. The possibilities of new technology must often be considered first or in conjunction with the business strategy. Making decisions about the potential of new technologies is often a huge challenge for most long-established organizations because of the low level of technological awareness in many boardrooms. Moreover, innovative electronic commerce strategies require speedy creative thinking and the vision to meld the evolving capabilities of technology with organizational capabilities through rapid experimentation in the marketplace. Thus, strategic planning is changing not only in terms of form, but also process, to include the changing nature and impact of technology on the firm.

Innovation

Moreover, because consumers now have access to globally networked IT (the Internet), they have the potential to take a very different role—that of technology innovator. In previous generations of IT, the individual consumer was the recipient of technology innovations that played out at the corporate level, and their role was that of the adopter of innovation. In the Internet world, individuals often are the instigators or sources of innovation. Signs of this are everywhere, such as in online games, like Doom and Quake, where individuals add significant features to the game. As more evidence, two key trends are worth noting. First, many individuals have a more sophisticated PC at home than at the office. Second, even though business-to-business Internet commerce dominates business-to-consumer e-commerce revenue many times over, we see most of the innovations in design and business models occurring at the consumer level. These ideas are later adopted in the business-to-business area. So in many markets, consumers are driving innovation, and large organizations are then adopting innovations from individuals. The Internet has enabled a total reversal of the traditional innovation process.

Nature of Decision Making

The latest strategic thinking stresses the importance of flexibility and planning in an unpredictable environment. One area in which this strategy transition will be most visible is the decision-making process within many firms. In the past, decision making in many firms has been highly analytical. Before having a product, much analysis of the opportunity occurs, and from this a single best answer emerges. Indeed, much of the IO economics concepts of industry analysis were predicated on such logic—analyze an industry, look for opportunities within the industry, and act accordingly. In today's competitive environment, in the time that it takes to see an opportunity and then react to it by developing a new strategy, the opportunity has often disappeared, either because other firms have already reacted or the market has moved on.

Because of being beaten to market by Internet start-ups that can make speedier decisions, some traditional companies are shifting from an analytical decision making to an experimental process. In a world that is seldom predictable, firms must find a way to hedge risk and have the ability to adapt to an evolving future much more rapidly and flexibly. But what does experimentation really mean from a planning perspective?

First, the strategy experimentation process is different from scenario planning. Scenario planning prepares managers for macroenvironmental and market discontinuities that may occur several years ahead. But in e-commerce, several such discontinuities may take place in a matter of weeks or months. Scenario planning helps a firm mentally analyze different options, but seldom actually involves the commitment of resources or people to developing the new skills that may be needed. Experimentation involves having competing and complementary businesses running simultaneously. The challenge to the organization is then to understand which experiment is the most successful, and how to shift resources to that experiment as it becomes more important to the firm. At the same time, faltering projects must be shut down. However, this is an ongoing and dynamic process, not an event that occurs periodically.

The necessity of rapid experimentation not only changes the nature and process of planning, but also changes its speed and number of iterations. Some firms conduct many thousands of market experiments a year and other firms have learned to reinvent their business model in just a few days. One innovative consulting firm uses the following experimentation process steps, conducted iteratively: diagnose the competitive landscape, sketch market and operating scenarios for the near term, create a new vision for strategy, launch and rapidly refine experiments with customers, and quickly scale up the most successful initiatives. Such a process puts great challenges on senior management to integrate fragmented and potentially divergent organizations.

IMPLICATIONS OF RECENT CHANGES IN STRATEGIC THINKING

All of the preceding changes in our thinking about strategy have many implications for our fundamental understanding of competition, strategy, and the planning process. This section focuses on six major implications:

1. Redefinition of industry structure.
2. Power shift to the consumer.
3. Instant globalization.
4. New business models.
5. Nature of the planning process.
6. Changes in reward policies due to this new environment.

Redefining Industry Structure

Strategic planning had its roots in Industrial Organization (IO) economics and the structure-conduct-performance model.[21] Empirical studies have accounted for such an industry effect, with between 17 percent and 20 percent of financial performance variance being explained by industry characteristics.[22] However, this leaves much of financial performance unexplained by industry effects.

Research has suggested that redefining industry boundaries in terms of inputs (resources) rather than products (outputs), may lead to a potential way of reframing industry analysis. In particular, information may be the appropriate resource for redefining many industry boundaries.

If we view information as a significant resource of the firm, then the many recent advances in information technology have caused a dramatic increase in the amount of this resource and the ease with which it can be managed. Previously, according to traditional economic thinking, information was viewed as a cost—either as an activity to support operations or as the necessary accounting and documentation to support the business. However, Internet technologies represent a fundamental shift in the ability to capture, manipulate, store, and transfer information. Information exchanges over the Internet and intranets can now be viewed as a source of value creation, not a cost. For example, airline computer reservation systems, such as SABRE, not only support the transaction of booking seats, but have created an entire new source of value because they allow airlines to manage dynamic pricing for seats based on current and historical load factors (McKenney, 1995). This information revolutionized the airline industry and established a new performance metric—revenue per seat. The value is derived from the systems' ability to capture and analyze information that before would have disappeared with the event.

Information technology allows information to be separated from the transaction that generated the information. As a consequence, industry boundaries will be redefined every time a new firm gains access to the data generated by a firm in the industry.[23] The rise of the importance of information, coupled with improvements in IT to leverage this information, has caused a fundamental shift in our understanding and conceptualization of the competitive landscape facing many firms.

Power Shift to the Consumer

The Internet is fundamentally altering industry configurations and the balance of power among producers, intermediaries, and consumers. If this does not sound possible, a little tour through history might make you less skeptical. Are you old enough to remember Main Street—that humble row of shops operated by neighborly proprietors who knew your kids by name and catered to your every need? All that is gone now, replaced decades ago by look-alike shopping malls with Sears at one end, JCPenny at the other, and a row of specialty shops in between. Then, when you weren't looking, those suburban malls started down the long road toward retail irrelevance. "Category killers" like Toys R Us, Home Depot, and Staples slowly crushed many of the specialty retailers that once made the malls work. And Wal-Mart displaced Sears as America's biggest retailer.

As the retailing model changed, the impact on producers was enormous. With each shift, the balance of power tilted toward the retailers—largely because of the use of mainframe computers, scanner data, and EDI. For the first time, the retailer knew more than the producer about what was being sold. The implications of this technology revolution, which also facilitated retail consolidation, were profound. Most of the bargaining power is in the hands of Wal-Mart when it orders a million television sets from Philips. In the grocery business, it doesn't matter if you're Procter & Gamble or Unilever, you're still going to have to pay the big supermarkets for shelf space if you want to launch a new product. Mutual fund companies gave up a big chunk of their profits to be listed in Schwab's *OneSource* catalog of funds. The effects of retailing consolidation rippled back along the entire supply chain. Big producers gobbled up smaller competitors as it became nearly impossible for the number three or four seller in a product category to win shelf space.

The Internet's impact will be similarly far-reaching and will cause a power shift away from producers and retailers toward consumers.[24] Only this time it will not be a ripple that slowly builds over time. Instead, it will be a tidal wave—because the Internet is going to empower consumers like nothing else ever has. Armed with perfect information and zero search costs, consumers are going to weed out mediocrity, hype, and inefficiency with a vengeance. Examples of this are already apparent in many industries. In the automobile industry, already more than 20 percent of car buyers shop online before showing up at a dealership, and have already decided what car they will buy and the price they will pay before setting foot in the dealer showroom. New infomediaries, such as Autobytel, that aid consumers in sifting through this data, are already having a major impact. Autobytel is already responsible for more than $550 million of automobile sales every month!

As we begin to see the next major trend in retail, early signals of how it may unfold are apparent. The critical technology trend is that many consumers have sophisticated computers that are networked globally. Just as business has made extensive use of IT in the last generation of retail, IT is now shifting to the consumer. Currently, we see this in the form of the Internet, but in the future this may take many forms as low-cost access devices and satellite communication technology dramatically change the landscape of consumer technology. However, even today the Internet is beginning to radically alter the model of how goods are purchased. And the good news for consumers (and the potentially bad news for business/producers that depended on consumer ignorance) is that consumers have enormous new powers.

In previous generations of technology, the main locus of technology impact was either in production or distribution, but now IT is aiding consumption. And the consumer is the beneficiary of this shift in the focus of IT. This power plays out not only in lower prices, but also in potential bargaining power. For example, assume that I get bad customer service at a store. How many people can I tell? What does the large corporation have to fear from me, the individual consumer? What happens, however, when each consumer has a global broadcast channel because of the Internet? The tables have turned and the balance of power has been shifted. If you think this is not possible, ask Intel what happens when a math professor discovers an error in the math co-processor of the Pentium II chip and posts this information on the Internet. Hundreds of millions of dollars were spent in correcting this error.

But retailers and wholesalers have substantial new power too. They can identify and track customers more easily than ever before, and as a result they can customize their offerings for their best customers. Because of IT they can provide more customers with specialized or even personalized service at a lower cost. The result: highly profitable customized service.

Instant Globalization

In addition to the explosion of internetworked firms that the Internet has facilitated, there is an additional fundamental implication—the reach of each firm has been dramatically altered. In today's world, Internet start-up companies are global from their first day of business. We are witnessing business history—a new type of company that is "born global," a birthright provided by the Internet. To further clarify the significance of this, it is important to realize that these firms achieve this with very few people, often less than one hundred. Contrast this with the many studies of global corporations during the 1980s, such as the transnational corporation.[25] These works describe a similar process where firms dominate one country and then roll out their operations and products to different parts of the world. These firms have enormous investments in resources and people, and the process of globalization takes years if not decades. Today, because of the Internet, we see the rise of virtual global corporations.

The meteoric growth of the Internet and the rise of companies participating in e-commerce through the Internet are redefining the frequency and reach of interorganizational systems. The rise of vertical portals, such as Chemdex for suppliers and purchasers of chemicals, is shifting the basis of relationships, pricing, and power across the industry value chain. In addition to these specialized portals, we see the rise of global business superportals, such as Global Online. Global Online claims to be the world's first international e-commerce portal. It boasts connections across 200 countries, 18 languages, 29 currencies, 81 auction sites, 36,000 trade and product forums, 250,000 URLs of merchant and service provider links, and 15 million global business information links. The scale and complexity of such a network would not have been possible without the Internet as a platform for low-cost global connectivity.

New Business Models

The changing value of assets (intangible assets such as intellectual property can be sold without a big investment in tangible assets), increasing returns to scale, and low-cost globally networked technology have resulted in new business models being possible through the recombination and leverage of assets.

For examples, today on the Internet we see many new types of businesses—search engines, portals, vertical portals, and global auctions, to name just a few.

For existing firms, these new business models have several implications. First, if a firm produces a time-sensitive product (such as airline seats, hotel rooms, long-distance phone service, TV ads), then the likelihood that auctions or reverse auctions (such as Priceline) will develop. This may be seen as a method of disposing of unused or excess capacity at anything above marginal costs, which may be seen as an addition to existing revenue streams. However, firms in this situation also have the challenge of being forced to develop new segmentation schemes or establishing different value propositions to avoid the cannibalization of existing revenue streams. For most companies with large customer bases and revenue, this is a potentially high-risk experiment. Customers may drastically change their usage patterns to get the benefit of low prices.

Also, existing firms, unlike their start-up rivals, must decide whether to coordinate these new channel business ventures with existing businesses or treat them separately. There are ongoing examples of both models—Citibank and Wells Fargo have coordinated their Internet and traditional services, while BancOne has spun off its Internet banking channel into a separate business, WingSpan. It is unclear which will be the successful strategy, but the dilemma is clear. If a company keeps the Internet venture inside, will it be crushed by the existing business? Similarly, if a company separates its Internet activity, then it has at least two major challenges: (1) How can it leverage its existing business customer and skill base? and (2) How can it behave like a true start-up and move at the speed of its web-based rivals? Solving these issues will be one of the greatest managerial challenges for companies in the early twenty-first century.

Nature of the Planning Process

The pace of competition, magnitude of advances in technology, and location of innovation are leading to two changes to the planning process of many firms: (1) frequency of the planning cycle; (2) shifting roles and responsibilities within the planning process.

The three- to five-year planning cycles that were standard for large corporations in the 1980s and early 1990s are inadequate for many firms. Even annual planning cycles won't keep up with the current pace of change for businesses that have web-based rivals. One high-tech firm has even gone so far as to have "quarterly annual planning meetings." They use this phase to capture the frequency as well as the depth of the issues covered. However, the necessity of a shorter planning cycle must be balanced against the resources and time that it takes for meetings and to prepare and assimilate documents generated during the planning process. Eventually, all of a firm's time could be spent planning, rather than doing. Thus, simply doing more of the same in the planning process is not a solution—the roles and responsibilities of people in the process must also change.

One way to counter the frequency of the planning cycle demanded by a turbulent environment is to give more autonomy and decision-making responsibility to people throughout the organization. This allows lower-level managers to make adjustments to the initial strategy. In this world, a strategy consists of an intended direction and a definition of the latitude that managers will have in deviating from that plan. The need for such changes is even more compelling, because innovation is occurring outside the large firm context. Under such conditions, the line managers who directly interact with the consumer are most likely to be initially aware of these innovations and can suggest the best ways for responding to and adapting them. Thus, the strategy process is ongoing, with responsibility shared throughout the organization. Also, senior management must realize that their job will not be to develop "the right answer" to every problem or "the perfect strategy" for every market or even the "perfect product" for a set of customers. Instead senior management's role will be to chart a direction, set the range of latitude in deviating from this direction, and then coordinate, integrate, and periodically reset the strategic direction based on the adaptations executed by managers throughout the organization.

Changes in Reward Policies

The rapid and potentially disruptive effects of technology have increased the unpredictability of the future business environment. To compensate, many organizations modified their decision-making style. Consultants frequently advise traditional companies to adopt a strategy-making process that is flexible, evolving, and experimental, but is it really so easy to do? Traditional firms must adopt a fundamental change to meet these new requirements—changes in how we reward people.

In many firms, project managers whose projects stumble—products late to market, budget overruns—are often punished and blamed for these errors. In some cases, this may be correct, in others not. The implicit assumption behind this behavior is that managers are operating under conditions of relative certainty and predictability—the strategic plan has solved the "big" questions, and now it is merely a matter of execution. Implicitly, managers are being evaluated under the assumption that theirs is a job of stewardship, not entrepreneurship.

However, if a rapidly changing environment changes the job of project manager into one of innovation and experimentation, then the reward policy must also change. People shouldn't be punished or blamed if well-calculated plans go awry in unpredictable situations. Organizations must have the courage and maturity to separate the outcome from the process, and evaluate each independently. If this transition does not occur, many strategic experiments will fail. And who will then innovate and take chances after seeing their colleagues punished for such behavior? This is not to suggest that mistakes or sloppy management should be tolerated throughout the organization. Instead we propose that top management encourage rigorous examination of the areas of uncertainty in the firm's competitive environments and nurture a culture that rewards managers for creative innovation, skillful experimentation, and rapid rollout of product or service.

SUMMARY

Do all of these changes mean that strategy is totally different in the digital world? Taken individually, no; however, taken collectively, the implications are extreme. Some old ideas still hold, but those concepts are playing out much faster. The same driving skills that one needs to navigate freeways are inadequate for a Formula 1 driver; they must be refined and modified. This is the same challenge for companies. How to take these base skills and upgrade them to fit a new game with similar, but different requirements for success.

Also, it seems fitting to close this chapter with a warning. By the time you read it, many of these ideas may be out of date. In this world for active managers and students of management, there is no substitute for thinking. There is no magic silver bullet or magic phrase around which to invent strategy. However, I hope a few of the building blocks and implications mentioned in this chapter will be useful foundations for creating new strategies.

NOTES

1. R.E. Caves and M.E. Porter, "From Entry Barriers to Mobility Barriers: Conjectural Decisions and Contrived Deterrence to New Competition," *Quarterly Journal of Economics* (1997), 19: 241–261; and M.E. Porter, *Competitive Strategy* (New York, Free Press, 1980).

2. See Chapter 8 for a detailed discussion of Porter's Five Forces analysis framework.

3. R.A. Bettis and M.A. Hitt, "The New Competitive Landscape," *Strategic Management Journal* (1995), 16: 7–19.

4. G. Stalk and T.M. Hout, *Competing against Time* (New York: Free Press, 1990).

5. R. D'Aveni, *Hypercompetition: Managing the Dynamics of Strategic Maneuvering* (New York: Free Press, 1994).

6. C.M. Christensen, *The Innovator's Dilemma* (Boston: Harvard Business School Press, 1997).

7. G. Hamel, "Strategy as Revolution," *Harvard Business Review* (1996), 74(4): 69–82.

8. L. Trigeorgis, *Real Options: Managerial Flexibility and Strategic Resource Allocation* (Boston: MIT Press, 1996).

9. S.L. Brown and K.M. Eisenhardt, *Competing on the Edge* (Boston: Harvard Business School Press, 1998).

10. R.T. Pascale, "Surfing the Edge of Chaos," *Sloan Management Review* (1999), 40(3): 83–94.

11. J.B. Barney, "Strategic Factor Markets: Expectations, Luck, and Business Strategy," *Management Science* (1986), 32:1231–1241; C.K. Prahalad and G. Hamel, "The Core Competence of the Corporation," *Harvard Business Review* (May/June 1990): 79–91; and B. Wernerfelt, "A Resource-Based View of the Firm," *Strategic Management Journal* (1984), 5: 171–180.

12. J.B. Barney, "Firm Resources and Sustained Competitive Advantage," *Journal of Management* (1991), 17:99–120; S.A. Lippman and R. Rumelt, "Uncertain Imitability: An Analysis of Interfirm Differences in Efficiency under Competition," *Bell Journal of Economics* (1982), 13:418–438; and M. Peteraf, "The Cornerstones of Competitive Advantage: A Resource-Based View," *Strategic Management Journal* (1993), 14: 179–192.

13. S.G. Winter, "Knowledge and Competence as Strategic Assets," in *The Competitive Challenge.* D. Teece (Ed.) (Cambridge, MA: Ballinger, 1987): 159–184.

14. C.K. Prahalad and G. Hamel, "The Core Competence of the Corporation," *Harvard Business Review* (May/June 1990): 79–91.

15. P.M. Senge, *The Fifth Discipline* (New York: Doubleday, 1990).

16. H. Itami, *Mobilizing Invisible Assets* (Cambridge, MA: Harvard Business School Press, 1987).

17. S. Hart and C. Banbury, "How Strategy-Making Processes Can Make a Difference," *Strategic Management Journal* (1994), 15: 251–269.

18. C.K. Prahalad and G. Hamel, "The Core Competence of the Corporation," *Harvard Business Review* (May/June 1990): 79–91.

19. W.B. Arthur, "Increasing Returns and the New World of Business," *Harvard Business Review* (July/August 1996): 100–109.

20. C.M. Christensen, *The Innovator's Dilemma* (Boston: Harvard Business School Press, 1997).

21. J.S. Bain, *Barriers to New Competition* (Cambridge, MA: Harvard University Press, 1956); and E. Mason, "Price and Production Policies of Large-Scale Enterprise," *American Economic Review* (1939), 29: 61–74.

22. A.M. McGahan and M.E. Porter, "How Much Does Industry Matter, Really?" *Strategic Management Journal* (1997 Summer Special Issue), 18: 15–30; T.C. Powell, "How Much Does Industry Really Matter? An Alternative Empirical Test," *Strategic Management Journal* (1996), 17(4): 323–334; R.P. Rumelt, "How Much Does Industry Matter?" *Strategic Management Journal* (1991), 12(3): 167–185; R. Schmalensee, "Do Markets Differ Much?" *American Economic Review* (1985), 75(3): 341–35; and B. Wernerfelt and C.A. Montgomery, "Tobin's q and the Importance of Focus in Firm Performance," *American Economic Review* (1988), 78(1): 246–250.

23. J.L. Sampler, "Redefining Industry Structure for the Information Age," *Strategic Management Journal* (1998), 19: 343–355.

24. G. Hamel and J.L. Sampler, "The E-Corporation," *Fortune* (December 7, 1998): 80–92.

25. C.A. Bartlett and S. Ghoshal, *Managing across Borders: The Transnational Solution,* 2nd ed. (Boston: Harvard Business School Press, 1998).

POLITICAL STRATEGY: MANAGING THE POLITICAL AND SOCIAL ENVIRONMENT

7

John F. Mahon
Boston University

Barbara Bigelow
Clark University

Liam Fahey
Babson College and
Cranfield University

CORPORATE POLITICAL STRATEGY[1]

The following three cases represent three very different management issues—a crisis of confidence in a product suspected of being contaminated, a confrontation over allegations of monopolistic practices, and a newly available market opportunity. Each case must be managed in the political arena, and each requires executives to devise and implement political strategies to achieve a desirable resolution:

- *Case 1.* In early June 1999, Coca-Cola found itself in the midst of an international health scare that threatened its long-established brand image. The firm was informed that a number of children were treated at a hospital in northern Belgium for symptoms including headaches, stomachaches, dizziness, and nausea after drinking Coke at their school. The children told hospital officials that the Coke had smelled different than normal and caused a burning sensation on the tongue. A few days after the incident, Coca-Cola recalled 2.5 million bottles of Coke in Belgium. The Belgian government, however, then banned the sales of all beverages of the Coca-Cola company for an indefinite period. After a quick internal inquiry, Coca-Cola announced that production problems at two of its plants, Antwerp, Belgium, and Dunkirk, France, caused the contamination that probably led to the illnesses. As a consequence, France ordered the closure of the Dunkirk bottling plant; Belgium and Luxembourg banned all Coca-Cola products; Germany banned Coca-Cola products produced at the Dunkirk plant; and the Netherlands banned Coca-Cola products shipped through Belgium.

Coca-Cola's relations with governmental officials in a number of European countries and in the European Union had already been strained as a result of its proposed acquisitions of leading European brands in soft drinks and snack products. With newspaper headlines such as "200 Poisoned by Coca-Cola" and "Alarm across Europe for Coca-Cola Products" appearing throughout Europe, it's not surprising that surveys taken at the time revealed that many European consumers were suddenly reluctant to buy Coca-Cola drinks, at least in the near future. Recognizing that customer apprehension in Europe was widespread and that as a result its brand image could be tarnished worldwide, Coca-Cola apologized to Belgian consumers in full-page newspaper advertisements and announced that it would reimburse the medical expenses of any individual who had fallen ill as a result of consuming its products. Within a week of the initial incident, Belgium and French authorities partially lifted the ban on Coca-Cola products. A week later, Coca-Cola won approval from the Belgian Government to resume sales of all its products.

- *Case 2.* Throughout 1999, Microsoft, the world's largest software producer, engaged in an antitrust lawsuit with the United States government. Some observers in the print and electronic media argued strongly that Microsoft—the maker of Windows, the ubiquitous personal computer operating system—"bungled" the public relations aspects of its entanglement with the U.S. government. According to critics, the firm did not recognize that the case was as much about the public perceptions of the issues involved in the case as it was about the law. Microsoft concedes that it "has been clobbered" on the publicity front. Indeed, some observers believe that the public relations aspect of the case may be more important than any legal outcome.

- *Case 3.* In late 1999, Congress approved and President Clinton signed the satellite Television Home Viewers Act, which for the first time enabled satellite TV companies to compete with cable television providers by allowing them to carry local TV stations. Historically, satellite subscribers also required a traditional television antenna or cable service to receive local news, sports, and weather. Now for the first time, satellite TV companies were in a position to aggressively pursue market share of homes using a satellite dish rather than cable for basic and extended television programming.

This chapter explains what political strategies are, how they can be used to successfully navigate through the complex political and social environment that an organization operates in, and what methodology has proved effective for devising strategies. Keep in mind that political strategies aren't just for crisis management, such as the Coca-Cola case. Corporations also use political strategies to preempt or defend themselves against "attack" by other entities (the Microsoft case) or to help create new economic opportunities (the satellite TV case). Corporations also need political strategies for guiding day-to-day operations so that decisions taken to enhance short-term economic gains don't someday embroil the organization in costly legal battles or antagonize the public and its representatives.

Previous chapters have illustrated how strategic management can effectively direct the design and execution of strategies that anticipate, cope with, and leverage change. However, the conventional views of business strategy, as outlined in Chapters 2 through 6, address change in and around the economic or product marketplace, and would be insufficient in dealing with the issues raised by the Coca-Cola, Microsoft, and satellite TV cases. However, as the cases in this chapter all show, political strategy also can be critical to the success of organizations' product-market or economic strategies. In this chapter, we provide managers with a methodology for coping with continuous change in the social and political environment.

Three related theses undergird this chapter. First, as illustrated in both the Coca-Cola and Microsoft cases, changes in the political and social environment can provoke transformative changes in the competitive opportunities of organizations. Thus, organizations need to understand intimately the political and social milieu in which they operate. Second, organizations increasingly recognize the need to develop strategies that explicitly address their involvement in the political and social realm—their political strategy. Thus firms need to monitor changes in their political environmental and select management teams to define suitable strategies. Third, organizations not only react to their political and social environment but can be instrumental in shaping it. Thus, firms need to make their political strategy a key part of their overall strategy to shape and influence the external environment (or context) within which they do business.

The scope and sequence of this chapter are:

- We define political strategy, placing particular emphasis on the term *political.*
- We identify and discuss the three principal integrating elements and foci of political strategy: (1) issues, (2) stakeholders, and (3) arenas.
- We detail the types of political strategies and explain how an organization can shape and influence the political and social environment.
- We illustrate the linkage of political strategy to business or economic strategy.

WHAT IS CORPORATE POLITICAL STRATEGY?

Political strategy is the set of actions and tactics an organization undertakes in the political, regulatory, judicial, or social domain to secure a position of advantage and influence over other actors in the process. The organization's political activities entail identifying which issues it wants to pursue, who its opponents and allies are, and in which arena it wants to act. An organization has a political strategy when it defines a set of political actions, such as those noted in Table 7.1, to achieve some specific purpose.

Organizations can take a broad range of political actions. These vary from activities that extend over a very long period and cost significant amounts of money (e.g., lobbying or mounting a public relations program to improve the organization's image in the community) to those that are ad hoc, short-term, and low-cost (such as a gift to a local charity or the temporary assignment of an employee to a charitable organization to assist in a specific project).

Organizations execute political strategy within the political system, a constantly changing theater whose actors include governments and their agents, the public and its representatives, and the media and other influencers of public opinion.

The three cases illustrate how corporations attempt to execute political strategy in multiple arenas. Coca-Cola fights desperately to retain its positive position in the realm of public perceptions, to placate European Commission regulatory authorities, and to satisfy specific national regulatory bodies. Microsoft wages a battle in the "court of public opinion" while it tries to fend off the U.S. Department of Justice in the courts. Satellite TV companies vigorously lobbied congressional committees to change the existing regulations at the same time they vociferously promoted the benefits of a more "level playing field" with cable providers to consumers. Political strategy, therefore, can be executed in *formal* governmental arenas as well as in more *informal* arenas. Formal governmental arenas include elections and the legislative, regulatory, executive, and judicial systems. Informal arenas include public opinion, media actions, informal relationships with external groups, and local, state, and regional community-based activities.

Organizations seek to gain positions of permanent or temporary advantage through political strategy. For example, one firm may take another to court to protect its patents. The intended position of advantage may be an injunction from the court stipulating that the other firm cannot use the patent or that it must withdraw one segment of its product line from the marketplace. The distinctions between temporary and permanent advantage are subtle and easily lost. For example, when a legislative or regulatory action is involved, an organization needs the influence and support at the time of the vote itself, not before or after. That is the "temporary" advantage. But because political and regulatory actions, especially in the formal arena, set the rules of the game, the results of the vote may be long-lived and significant for the organization.

TABLE 7.1   Examples of an Organization's Political Actions

Action Category	Illustrative Action
Narrowly Focused Activities	
Lobbying	A finance officer meets with Senator _____ to discuss tax impacts on the organization as a result of political campaign contributions.
Letter writing and correspondence	CEO pens letter to Representative _____ on a specific issue of interest.
Speakers' bureaus	The public relations (PR) department provides a managerial speaker for local toastmasters club.
Charitable contributions	A donation of $100 is made to the United Way Fund.
Arbitration and mediation	Labor and management agree to binding arbitration on some contract issues.
Crisis management	A fire occurs in a local plant: the fire department is immediately contacted; subsequent calls are made to the local media and the plant's next shift of workers.
Broadly Focused Activities	
Advocacy advertising	The organization runs an advertisement expressing an opinion on the federal legislation on weapons control.
Image programs	The organization's slogan is prominently displayed in an intense media campaign.
Public relations and public affairs	The PR department launches a new campaign to deal with recent bad press.
Community relations	The R&D unit sponsors year-round community liaison activities (softball and bowling teams, fund-raising events).
Testifying before congressional committees	Legal counsel testifies before House Labor Committees regarding potential changes in labor laws.
Political risk analysis	The organization is preparing to enter a Third World country and seeks to assess the projected safety of its personnel and the security of its invested capital.

ELEMENTS AND FOCI OF POLITICAL STRATEGY

Political strategy requires an organization to identify those issues it wishes to pursue, the stakeholders involved in each issue, and the arenas in which it wishes to act. The Coca-Cola case noted at the beginning of this chapter and the case of

Box 7.1

Mattel: Planned Takeover of Hasbro

On January 24, 1996, Mattel, the world's largest toy maker, made a public offer to buy Hasbro, the second largest toy manufacturer, based in Providence, Rhode Island. The proposed combination with sales of $5.9 billion would account for approximately 40 percent of the $16 billion U.S. toy market and 61 percent of the doll business. It would have first or second position in every toy category worldwide. However, Hasbro management resisted the offer, and the media quickly dramatized the story by pitting "Barbie" (a popular Mattel toy) against "G.I. Joe" (a popular Hasbro toy). Mattel offered $5.2 billion to purchase Hasbro. The offer represented a 73 percent premium over what Hasbro shares were worth on January 24, 1996. From a financial perspective, Mattel believed that its offer should be irresistible to Hasbro managers, shareholders, and the worldwide toy industry.

Hasbro's executive team decided to resist Mattel's offer. They downplayed the financial or economic aspects of the offer and choose instead to fight this hostile takeover in the political and legal arena—not in the market arena. The battle lines were drawn—Mattel seeing it as an economic and market-based issue and Hasbro defining it as an issue with political, legal, and social impacts. Hasbro convinced the attorneys general of Rhode Island and Connecticut to seek corporate records as they were both concerned that serious antitrust issues were raised by this combination. With the support of Hasbro, the Rhode Island Congressional Delegation asked the Federal Trade Commission and the Justice Department to look into this proposal, and European antitrust regulators even began to express concern. Yet, in its efforts to remain independent, the most telling and influential weapons that Hasbro used in this battle were the Rhode Island state legislature and its governor as allies. In less than a week, the legislature had repealed a key state law that allowed owners of 10 percent or more of a company's stock to call a special meeting of shareholders, and the Governor signed it. The new law allowed only a company's board of directors or individuals authorized by the company to call a special meeting.

The day after the Governor signed the legislation, Mattel withdrew its offer. An analyst at Smith Barney observed that "Hasbro was victorious in keeping its independence, and the company's political clout was clearly highlighted in the fight. Even if the deal were to turn friendly, Hasbro would have a hard time returning the antitrust warheads it launched back to their silos" (Davis, 1996: 1a). In a letter to Hasbro, Mattel's chairman wrote, "You elected to take drastic steps, both politically and through the media to greatly increase the difficulty of achieving a merger in a timely manner. Unfortunately, your 'scorched earth' campaign has created an intolerable climate" (Reidy and Shao, 1996: 28).

From a strictly financial standpoint, Hasbro's shareholders may have been ill served by the firm's actions. Yet the community of Rhode Island benefited from Hasbro's actions because Hasbro is one of the largest employers in the state; it

---

> **Box 7.1**   *(Continued)*
>
> had recently contributed significant funds to build the Hasbro Children's Hospital in the Providence area; and its executives have contributed to several causes and charities in the state. These concerns are even more significant because Mattel let it be known that it would probably close Hasbro's facilities in Rhode Island if the merger succeeded.
>
> ———————
>
> Paul Davis, "No. 1 Mattel Drops Bid to Take Over No. 2 Hasbro." *Providence Journal-Bulletin*, February 3, 1996, p. A1.
> Charles Reidy and Michael Shao, "Mattel Gives Up Bid for Hasbro: 'Scorched Earth' Response Cited." *Boston Globe*, February 3, 1996, p. 28.

---

the attempted merger of two large toy companies, Mattel and Hasbro (see Box 7.1), illustrate each of these key elements of political strategy.

Issues

Issues serve as the primary organizing focus in political rivalry. In general terms, issues constitute the points of contention or conflict between an organization and other economic, social, or public policy entities. They involve situations in which the answers to "What should be done?" "Who is responsible?" and "How can this be prevented in the future?" are seen differently by different groups in society, each of which may have a different stake in the outcome. These situations are typically characterized by disagreements over facts (Does Microsoft have monopoly power in some of its product-markets?), values (Is genetic research morally correct?), and policies (How should we prevent contamination of consumer products in the future?).

The nature, scope, and characteristics of issues are best illustrated with examples:

- *Is atomic power generation safe?* Consider the history of nuclear power in the United States. The nuclear power industry has been embattled by opponents for the past 25 years. The opponents to nuclear power have adopted the tactic of questioning the safety and security of the power source. In its initial responses, the industry promoted the cost and political advantages: they proclaimed that nuclear power was cheaper than oil in the long run and that nuclear power could free the United States from dependence on foreign oil. However, these arguments weren't very compelling when oil was cheap and plentiful. The safety issue was definitely not the industry's first choice of topics to debate. The industry lost valuable time and momentum by not addressing the specific concerns of security and safety from the start.

- *Is a merger anticompetitive?* Seeking to gain the advantages of consolidation in the toy industry, Mattel simply viewed its takeover of Hasbro as a financial issue. Mattel argued that a merger would be good for both firms, the industry, and consumers. Hasbro, on the other hand, saw the takeover as an affront to its history, integrity, and future. It quickly raised concerns about the consequences of the takeover for employees in its home base of Rhode Island. It then "played the antitrust card" claiming that the combination of the two firms would violate the most basic tenets of long-standing antitrust law. By rapidly promoting political and legal forces to buttress its point of view, Hasbro compelled Mattel to withdraw its takeover offer.

- *What are the full consequences of product contamination?* European governmental agencies and consumers quickly determined that the possible contamination of one batch of Coca-Cola drinks in Belgium was a major public health and safety issue. Coca-Cola, on the other hand, saw it not just as a safety and health issue but as a major threat to its relationship with consumers, channels, governmental agencies, and competitors.

Issues like these can arise in many ways, but they are always fueled and ignited by change. First, as illustrated in the nuclear industry and Mattel-Hasbro cases, issues often arise for organizations as a consequence of different preferences of other groups in society with regard to the proposed change. Second, issues can arise out of broad societal trends and patterns that are outside the control of one organization. Consider, for example, these demographic trends in the United States today: increases in the total number of ethnic minorities; increase in the average age of the population; reduction in the number of unskilled jobs; and growth in the number of one-parent homes. Some issues that could emerge from these trends are: increased demands by ethnic minorities for representation within organizations; demands for increased benefits for the elderly, or for corporate support for care of employees' dependents (employees' parents, domestic partners, daycare for their children). Finally, as Coca-Cola and Mattel discovered, organizations can create issues for themselves as a consequence of their own actions.

To manage issues, we suggest that managers start by classifying them into four generic types: (1) universal, (2) advocacy, (3) selective, and (4) technical.[2] Here's how this classification system also helps managers learn to predict when an issue is likely to arise, what stakeholders are first involved, and the likely arena of solution.

Universal issues affect large numbers of people. Exposure to these issues is direct and personal, and personal impact is viewed as serious and imminent. Universal issues arise spontaneously in conversations. The general view is that the government is responsible for their resolution. Examples include inflation, unemployment, energy crises, and hazardous wastes. The current debate in the Clinton administration over the reform of healthcare in this country has sparked intense and widespread public debate—it is a universal issue.

Advocacy issues affect a smaller number of people than universal issues and stand lower on the list of public concerns. Usually introduced and promoted by those claiming to represent the public interest, they tend to be potential rather than actual problems. They do not emerge spontaneously in conversation, but, once raised, they cause people to react favorably to the need for action and solutions. The general view is, "Someone ought to do something about this"; the "someone" is unspecified. Consumer issues and improved healthcare access for the poor are examples of advocacy issues.

Selective issues are the focus of interest groups. They rarely arise spontaneously in conversation; when they are mentioned, usually only those directly affected express an interest or opinion. The problems and solutions are unique and affect only certain identifiable groups. Moreover, the costs of dealing with them are to be passed on to society at large. These issues generate great intensity, commitment, and activism among those most likely to benefit. Corporate dependent care is a selective issue. Those favoring it wish to have corporate and nonprofit organizations provide facilities for such care and absorb some of the costs involved.

Finally, technical issues are of absolutely no interest to the general public; people are content to leave them in the hands of the experts until a larger problem arises. Only persons with technical expertise would ordinarily discuss them. Examples include the application of general legislation or regulation to specific cases, the selection of the appropriate statistical method to analyze data, the use of morbidity and mortality statistics in healthcare and insurance.

Whether some issues should be treated as universal, advocacy, or selective is often a matter of intense debate. Opponents treat gay rights as a selective issue ("Gay rights should not be forced on the public"); proponents see it as a universal issue ("Gay rights are like any other civil rights").

These four categories (universal, advocacy, selective, technical) also determine the appropriate pathways for managing issues, the patterns that issues will follow, the role of the media, and the leaders who will fight for the issue. Universal issues have numerous champions, and the arena of action is generally a legislature, the higher courts, or the voting booth. Advocates of action will argue that government should do something about the problem or issue, but the costs in fact, are often passed on to the private sector. The media have intense interest in such issues because they have high public visibility and are newsworthy. Advocacy issues, in comparison, are articulated by specific groups who face a challenge in persuading the media of the newsworthiness of the issues while simultaneously seeking an appropriate arena for their resolution. Selective issues are championed by specific groups who are directly affected (working parents or people with certain disabilities or "orphan diseases"). They face enormous hurdles in obtaining media interest or in gaining access to any specific arena. Technical issues are ordinarily so complex that both the general public and the media are uninterested in them.

All of these specific types of issues provide different challenges in terms of arena selection, media interest, and the enlistment of general public support.

The Evolution of Issues

Issues emerge, take shape, and are resolved via many different evolutionary paths. Some issues may come and go very quickly while others (such as abortion and healthcare) may linger on for decades. To aid managers in their understanding of how issues evolve, the "traditional" or public policy-oriented view of issues and their life cycles was developed, as shown in Box 7.2.

A more inclusive view of issue life cycles developed by the authors incorporates the stages included in the traditional model, but focuses attention on earlier stages in an issue's evolution, before it became public. These are the stages in the authors' model:

- *Emergence.* Stakeholders first become aware of a development or change in the environment. Some examples: Mattel announces its takeover offer for Hasbro; a story about Coke causing illness in children breaks in the Belgian print and electronic media. Issues at this stage are ill defined and poorly understood.

- *Interpretation.* Stakeholders begin to interpret and make sense out of an issue. Because values often provide the basis for these interpretations, and because different stakeholders have different and often conflicting values, an issue may be interpreted in several ways. Hasbro's senior managers and

---

Box 7.2

Conventional/Traditional Issues Life Cycle Model

The traditional or public issues life cycle consists of five stages through which an issue develops and evolves. Gestation begins when a gap develops between a firm's actual performance and the public's expectation of that performance (Stage 1). This gap can be either real or perceived. The alcohol industry continues to deal with the issue of drunk driving and the causality (or lack thereof) of their products in drunk driving and accidents—a difference in the "facts." As the gap between the alcohol industry's claims and society's perceptions and expectations widens over time, more groups and individuals become involved, and the risk increases that the issue will become politicized (Stage 2). The shift in public sentiment over the effectiveness of the healthcare system is also illustrative of Stages 1 and 2. If the issue remains unresolved (that is, the gap is not narrowed by organizational or societal action), a legislative or regulatory phase can occur, where the issue enters a specific political or regulatory body for discussion and resolution (Stage 3). As the issue is resolved, it is often followed by a period of litigation as the interested parties test out the scope of the legislative or regulatory solution (Stage 4). Finally, after public policy has prevailed, or the public has exercised its choice through media or community pressure to which the organization acquiesces, there occurs an institutionalization of the matter by the organizations affected (Stage 5).

employees viewed the issue quite differently from those employed by Mattel; Belgian and European governmental officials were publicly reluctant to accept Coca-Cola's initial explanation of what caused the contamination and thus asked for further data gathering and analysis.

The third and fourth stages are similar to those described in the traditional model.

- *Positioning.* Stakeholders begin to take positions, and the issue becomes increasingly public and visible. At this stage, stakeholders often engage in political tactics such as coalition formation or constituency building. Hasbro quickly moved to provoke the attorney general of Rhode Island and Connecticut, the congressional delegation of Rhode Island, the Justice Department, and European regulatory authorities to take actions that would be manifestly visible in a variety of arenas; after two weeks of intense negative publicity, Coca-Cola brought its CEO to Brussels to meet with the appropriate governmental authorities, to issue a public apology, and to launch a series of newspaper advertisements accepting responsibility for the product contamination and demonstrating its commitment to regaining the public's trust and confidence.

- *Resolution.* The issue is resolved in some arena, whether formal or informal. (The traditional model assumes that resolution occurs in governmental arenas.) Mattel withdrew its takeover offer before the issue could be resolved in the judicial, regulatory, or legislative arenas; Belgian and other governments lifted their ban on the sale of Coca-Cola's products, and the issue then moved to both a formal arena—the media—and an informal arena—the court of public perceptions—as Coca-Cola tried to win back the public's confidence and trust.

Compared with the traditional model, this approach places more emphasis on the early stages of the life cycle of an issue. A business can best influence the outcome of an issue when it first emerges (e.g., by introducing new facts) or when it is first interpreted by the media (e.g., by linking the businesses' interpretation with widely held societal values). An organization does not need to wait until the issue has become public and positions of various stakeholders have solidified.

Stakeholders

Issues are shaped and driven by the actions of stakeholders, the people and groups who have an interest in the outcome of an issue. The activities listed in Table 7.1 necessarily involve stakeholders. In broad terms, stakeholders may be defined as "any group or individual who can affect or is affected by the achievement of the organization's purpose." For example, stakeholders include entities from outside an industry: public interest groups, environmental and consumer advocacy groups, local community groups, industry and trade associations, and a dizzying array of governmental agencies and organizations. But a key group of stakeholders are the industry insiders: suppliers, distributors, customers, and competitors. The relevant set of stakeholders, and whether they are the firm's political opponents or its allies with regard to any particular issue or set of related issues, varies from one issue to another. Table 7.2 lists typical questions that arise in an analysis of stakeholders to provide input for political strategy development and execution.

Stakeholders assume importance in the development and execution of political strategy to the extent they have power or influence over the outcome of one or more issues and how motivated they are to use that power. Some stakeholders have a direct economic influence on the organization. For example, customers hold a stake in the delivery of high-quality goods at reasonable prices, institutional investors are concerned with the security of their investment and their rate of return, and communities are concerned about the security of local jobs. After the Belgium accident, Coca-Cola developed a greater appreciation of the stake consumers hold in the quality and trustworthiness of its products. Some stakeholders have a noneconomic stake in the organization. Environmental groups often adopt an issue when they consider an organization's actions inimical to a healthy environment, and consumer advocacy groups might be concerned with the safety of an organization's products.

When it wanted to fight the merger with Mattel, Hasbro moved quickly to create a set of stakeholders that would support its rejection of Mattel's takeover offer. It convinced Rhode Island's congressional delegation that a significant number of jobs would be lost in the state if Mattel were successful in its takeover bid. It persuaded Rhode Island's state legislature and governor to quickly change key provisions in shareholder law.

How much impact a stakeholder has on the organization and its political and economic goals depends largely on the stakeholder's willingness to act. For example, the intensity with which a stakeholder holds a position or point of

TABLE 7.2   Critical Stakeholder Analysis Questions

1. What is the issue or set of issues?
2. Who are the relevant stakeholders?
3. What is the stake of each stakeholder and with what intensity is that stake held?
4. What claims, demands, and counterdemands result from each stake?
5. What differences and similarities exist across these stakes and/or stakeholders?
6. How can these stakeholders affect these issues?
7. How can these stakeholders affect the organization's interests?
8. What can the organization do to influence these stakeholders?
9. How can these stakes and stakeholders be prioritized?
10. What *should* the organization do?
11. What *can* the organization do?

view can make up for a lack of political power. Sometimes, however, this intensity can jeopardize the position the stakeholders advocate. For example, in both the gay rights movement and the prolife movement, we have examples of intense stakeholders on both sides of the issue. However, abortion clinic bombings and the recent murder of a physician who performed abortions (and the implication that the prolife organization allegedly verbally supported the bombings and the murder) have raised concerns over the reasonableness of the prolife movement.

Irrespective of the source of a stake, it causes stakeholders to place demands or claims on the organization. An industry or trade association, for example, often asks its members to support its efforts to change a specific piece of legislation. Consumer groups demand that businesses provide safer products. Shareholders frequently insist that the firm commit to generating higher financial returns for them. Most political strategy is focused on managing stakeholder demands and claims.

Assessing Threats and Opportunities for Cooperation

It is important for organizations to assess both the stakeholders' potential to cooperate and the threat they pose. Among other things, these assessments indicate how each major stakeholder could affect the organization's interests. It is crucial to note that opportunities to cooperate can vary dramatically between the political and product marketplaces and from one issue to another. For example, within the soft drink industry, product competitiveness is very high because manufacturers and bottlers are competing for market share. Yet, proposals for recycling or repackaging of soda bottles and cans can lead to cooperation across industry lines to achieve a political solution acceptable to all of the players in the industry.

Relationships among Stakeholders

There are two final observations concerning stakeholders. First, the relationships between and among stakeholders evolve over time and with reference to specific issues and problems. It is not uncommon to find within an industry two competitors who are strong allies with regard to one issue and fierce antagonists with regard to another. Thus, as one issue is resolved and another arises, today's enemies can easily be tomorrow's friends. Mattel and Hasbro could easily become staunch allies in seeking the need for governmental assistance to stifle the threat of counterfeit products.

Second, stakeholders constitute an intricate interconnected web of relationships in a constant state of flux. How the organization chooses to interact with one stakeholder may dramatically affect its relationship with others. A key task in political strategy, therefore, is the assessment of how the organization's actions or position on a given issue can affect relationships with other stakeholders on this issue and *on all other issues currently being dealt with by the organization.* Organizations that do not recognize this simultaneity of issues and stakeholder relationships are likely to commit grave errors.

Arenas

Arenas are the public and private forums where political strategy is played out. As noted, they may be either formal or informal. The more formal arenas include legislatures and political bodies (international, national, regional, state, local); judicial arenas (at all levels, including formal negotiations, mediations, and arbitrations); and regulatory arenas (at all levels). In designing and executing political strategy, organizations need to be aware of the significant differences between formal and informal arenas. The formal arenas are first and foremost public institutions. They are part of the formal governmental process and carry with them many forms of authority. They are capable of making and enforcing laws and regulations. Each type of formal arena has its own particular operating procedures, sets of rules, and norms. For example, in a court at any level, there are clearly defined judicial procedures: precedents have been set that affect decisions and the ways that attorneys can argue specific situations.

By contrast, action and discussion within the informal arenas can occur outside the glare of publicity and public hearings. The participants themselves determine the rules of the engagement and what, if any, enforcement of the outcomes will occur. The ability to influence the "rules of engagement" allows for greater flexibility to seek and find solutions. In contrast to formal arenas, there are no clearly defined routes of access: it is up to the parties involved, working toward satisfying their mutual interests, to determine how this shall take place. The National Coal Policy Project, for example, had no formal mechanisms or procedures for meeting. The participants made them up as they went along.

The discussion of strategy types later in this chapter shows how difficult it is to separate arenas from issues and stakeholders. Stakeholders typically have some measure of choice in arena selection. Selection of an arena by organizations and their stakeholders is central to the evolution of political rivalry and, in many instances, critically affects the outcome. Many of the examples offered in this chapter demonstrate the skill of stakeholders in selecting arenas that most favor their interests and avoiding arenas in which their interests may be more difficult to advance or defend. For example, U.S. airlines are well aware that no matter where in the world their planes are involved in an injurious or fatal accident, they will face litigation in U.S. courts. Litigants file their claims in U.S. courts because they tend to be far more generous in awarding settlements to dependents and survivors.

Though lobbyists for U.S. corporations inveigh against the numbers and costs of class action suits brought against them by environmental groups and plaintiffs' attorneys, more often firms have used the courts against their rivals or for their own political and economic advantage. Manville, a firm that once made products containing asbestos, filed for bankruptcy so it could treat victims of asbestosis as creditors in bankruptcy court and not as litigants in civil trials. Public interest groups exercise the same type of care in arena selection as do business organizations. The success that environmental groups have had in stalling the implementation of the North American Free Trade Agreement (NAFTA) by filing in court for environmental impact statements is yet another example of this tactic.

TYPES OF POLITICAL STRATEGY

Several strategy options are available to organizations as they seek to manage issues, stakeholders, and arenas (see Table 7.3). In discussing these options, it is important to recall that issues, stakeholders, and arenas interact with one another in every unfolding issue (see Box 7.3 for an example of this interplay in the case of Royal Dutch Shell). Most organizations deal with multiple issues

TABLE 7.3 Critical Political Strategy Analysis Questions

Issues

What issues currently confront the organization?
At what stage of the issues life cycle is each issue?
What issues are likely to emerge in the near future?
What issues should the organization create and/or champion?
What types of issues are they (universal, advocacy, selective, or technical)?
What stake does/will the organization have in each issue?
What stake does/will each stakeholder hold in each issue?
What alternatives are available to the organization to manage the issue?

Stakeholders

What stakeholders are currently involved in each issue?
What stakeholders are likely to emerge regarding each issue?
What are the stakeholders' demands and claims?
What impact are these stakeholders likely to have on the organization?
What is the organization's current and/or future base of power and influence with regard to each issue?
What alternatives are available to the organization in its dealings with stakeholders?

Arenas

In which arenas is each current issue?
Can the arena of current issues be changed?
In which arena will each future issue emerge?
What alternatives are available to the organization in selection and operation within arenas?

Box 7.3

Royal Dutch Shell: Disposal of an Oil Platform

In February 1995, Royal Dutch Shell's British subsidiary (40 percent U.K.-owned and 60 percent Dutch-owned) received permission from the United Kingdom's Department of Trade and Industry and the Minister of the Environment, and from the Oslo-Paris Commission, the European organization that governs sea disposals), to sink the obsolete oil platform Brent Spar in the deep portion of the North Sea. Over 30 different studies Shell commissioned over a four-year period to study deep-sea disposal reached the same conclusion—deep sea disposal was both economical and safe for the environment. Shell also had complied with all relevant regulations and no European government objected to the proposed plan. The sinking of the Brent Spar platform in the deepest reaches of the North Sea was viewed as a test case: the decommissioning of oil platforms would increase in the next few years as oil reserves dried up. Shell saw this decision as a routine, internal choice with regard to its operations; it had also been careful to involve all external organizations from which it needed approval to carry out the decision.

Shell's plans were delayed, however, when Greenpeace activists climbed aboard the platform to protest the dumping plans. Greenpeace, an organization dedicated to environmental causes, claimed that the platform contained over 130 tons of radioactive and toxic materials that would irreparably harm the marine environment. The organization began plotting its campaign in February when the British government announced that it would allow sea disposal of platforms.

Greenpeace's occupation of Brent Spar took Shell by surprise. Shell maintained that extensive environmental research showed that the contents of Brent Spar would have no environmental impact. Despite emotional arguments put forth by Greenpeace, the scientific community generally remained committed to deep sea disposal.

Greenpeace was determined to generate a great deal of publicity around the issue of deep sea disposal. Its most spectacular actions occurred on April 30, 1995, when four experienced alpine climbers, who were taken to the platform by inflatable raft, scaled the platform and then chained themselves to it.

Directed by its international headquarters in Amsterdam, Greenpeace's offices in Britain, Germany, and Holland maintained continuous coordinated attacks in the media on the British government. Buoyed by the resulting publicity, Greenpeace sparked a boycott of Shell service stations in Germany and in other areas of Western Europe. The boycott led to decreased revenues for Shell's German subsidiary. Once political passions flared, Shell stations were firebombed and shots were fired at a station in Frankfurt. As a result of the boycott, Shell's German sales fell by 20 percent and Greenpeace released the results of a poll that showed that 85 percent of German car owners would boycott Shell over the Brent Spar issue. Not surprisingly, political, religious, and environmental groups, along with the public, were pressuring German officials to stop the disposal and preserve the North Sea environment. In the German parliament, Shell was accused of ". . . endangering the world."

Box 7.3   *(Continued)*

In addition to having an impact on oil revenues in Germany, the environmental organization was able to convince many politicians in Europe that the disposal was a bad idea. At the North Sea Conference on June 8, 1995, ministers from Germany and Denmark, backed by ministers from Sweden, Belgium, and the Netherlands, verbally attacked the British representative, arguing that the plan to dispose of Brent Spar was an ". . . act of environmental vandalism." Pressure was placed on the British Prime Minister to reverse the government's decision.

By the time of the G-7 Summit on June 15th in Halifax, Nova Scotia, the United Kingdom's Prime Minister, John Major, was under substantial public and political pressure to withdraw his government's support for the Brent Spar disposal. During the summit, Chancellor Kohl of Germany personally noted his government's disapproval of the proposed disposal to Prime Minister Major.

For its part, Shell appeared to be a house divided. By Friday, June 6, 1995, a day after a Shell station in Moerfelden-Walldorf in western Germany was hit by six bullets, Peter Duncan, CEO of Shell Germany announced that Shell had postponed the deep sea disposal in an attempt to engage in discussions with concerned parties. Almost immediately this announcement was denied by a Shell United Kingdom spokesperson, who claimed, ". . . there is absolutely no truth at all." On June 20 at the weekly meeting of senior Shell executives, the main topic of conversation was Brent Spar. Dr. Chris Fay, CEO of Shell, U.K., found himself confronted by angry subsidiary executives, especially Mr. Duncan. Fay was persuaded to end the disposal plan.

That evening, just a few hours before it was to sink the platform, Shell announced it would abandon its original plan. Instead, it would seek to dismantle the platform on land (at a greatly increased cost and, by all accounts, with an increased potential of environmental damage). The additional costs could be passed on to U.K. taxpayers. In addition to the potential negative environmental impact of the decision reversal, British governmental ministers were incensed by Shell's actions. The government defended the disposal in the House of Commons just a few hours before Shell's announcement; Shell officials had not informed the government prior to the public announcement. Many media organizations also felt that they had been used and manipulated by Greenpeace, especially after Greenpeace admitted that some of the information it distributed about potential contamination from Brent Spar was significantly in error.

---

simultaneously. Although this increases the level of complexity, the strategic options for dealing with each issue are the same.

Managing multiple issues necessitates analysis of core questions (see Table 7.3) that go to the heart of political strategy and execution. As an example of this complexity, consider some of the major issues Ford Motor Company has to manage simultaneously. Ford has to have a coherent policy on fuel efficiency, automobile air pollution, international manufacture and sales of automobiles, the North American Free Trade Agreement, union negotiations and job security issues, the closed nature of the Japanese market, international competition, and automobile safety. Many of the issues overlap and have overlapping stakeholder interests. The unions are concerned about jobs, salaries, and benefits, but Ford has to consider the costs of the car from a customer's view. It might be cheaper to produce cars in Mexico but what will be the reaction of unions in Detroit? Cars are a major source of air pollution, but to improve their performance requires expensive technology that lowers gasoline efficiency and raises the cost of the car to the buyer. The company must address all of these issues, and many of them will only be resolved in the political arena.

The following sections provide examples of organizations engaging in corporate political strategy. The fundamental organizing theme is the issue, although, as should be clear, managing an issue entails developing strategies for stakeholder management and choice of arena. For ease of analysis, we focus on showing how an organization manages a specific issue rather than how it deals with multiple issues simultaneously.

Managing Early Issue Evolution

It is to an organization's benefit to preempt and contain issues. Although it is difficult to manage emerging issues, organizations always need to consider trying to seize the political initiative by steering the early stages of issue evolution in a direction that favors their own interests. They can do this in a number of ways including, but not limited to, redefining the issue, appealing to stakeholders, or moving the issue to arenas of the organization's choosing.

A well-known example of managing early issue evolution is the action of Johnson & Johnson (J&J) in a case of criminal tampering with bottles of Tylenol, its over-the-counter analgesic product. The stakes for J&J were very high:

- Loss of consumer faith and trust.
- Significant financial losses due to the withdrawal of a market-leading and highly profitable product.
- Potential negative regulatory reaction.

As soon as it became evident that some bottles of its product had been opened and poison hidden in them and that people may have died as a result, J&J immediately pulled all Tylenol from store shelves. This action sent a powerful and unmistakable signal to key stakeholders, American consumers and regulators, that the firm was committed to preserving and protecting not just its consumer franchise but consumer safety and health. This decision was not reached easily. The Federal Bureau of Investigation (FBI), another key actor in this issue, wanted J&J to keep the product on the market. However, when J&J

raised the issue of liability for further loss of life, the FBI backed away from its position. As a result, J&J could choose the arena in which this issue would be resolved—the marketplace.

J&J maintained constant contact with the media, another critical stakeholder. The company's message to the media was that it was committed to solving the crime and ensuring that a similar problem never occurred again. To attain the latter goal, J&J quickly moved the issue to another arena: It began to push a remedy for its problem in the form of a public policy initiative. It suggested that the FDA should immediately require that all products such as Tylenol be placed in tamperproof containers. (One consequence of this initiative was that the costs associated with finding a solution to the tampering problem would be borne by all its competitors.) In addition, J&J strengthened its position with customers as a firm that worries about their safety. As a consequence of its management of the issue, the stakeholders involved, and arena selection, J&J was able to quickly reintroduce Tylenol and recapture its leading market share.

In contrast, Coca-Cola executives responded less speedily than they could have in the Belgium contamination case. According to one analysis, the firm's executives took several days to make the matter a high priority.[3] By that time, the regulatory authorities had begun to shape the issue in the public mind.

Greenpeace, the environmental activist organization, engaged in a carefully orchestrated set of actions designed to attract widespread attention to the potentially negative consequences of disposing of any oil platform in the North Sea. When Greenpeace members climbed aboard an oil platform at sea to protest the proposed scuttling they provided the media with a dramatic photo opportunity. More to the point, the organization was selecting the "court of public opinion" as the arena to resolve the issue.

Delaying Issue Evolution

Another way to manage issues early in their evolution is to deny them access to the agenda in the first place. Agenda setting is the politics of selecting issues for active consideration from the enormous and constantly changing mix of issues that could receive attention. If some branch of the legislature, a regulatory agency, one level of the judicial system, or specific elements of the media refuse to consider an issue (that is, place it on their agenda), then the issue will receive less public debate than it otherwise would. In some instances, it may not receive any attention at all, and thus never become an "issue."

Organizations can choose among several agenda denial strategies. One approach is to refuse to recognize the existence of the problem or to deny that a problem exists. Many companies have adopted this tactic with regard to the issue of bioengineered foods. A second approach involves discrediting the issue by denigrating its supporters. Some scientists have belittled claims that global warming is rapidly reaching dangerous levels by dubbing the evidence supporting such claims as the work of "fringe" groups and organizations. Third, an organization can attempt to coopt the issue by showing symbolic concern with the problem and conveying the impression that action is already taking place or will be forthcoming on the issue. Finally, organizations can pursue high cost and extensive resource commitment strategies to keep an issue off the agenda. They also may adopt actions such as electoral, economic, and legal threats.

We are not endorsing any of these four strategies or tactics. We are merely noting that they have been used successfully to keep an issue off an agenda. Once an issue gets placed on any formal and/or informal agenda it may gain unexpected allies, and the outcome can become uncertain.

Issue Redefinition: Redefining Issues Already on the Agenda

Despite an organization's best efforts, issues will still emerge, evolve, and get to arenas that were not of its choosing. The Mattel-Hasbro merger case showed how difficult it is to win when an issue gets placed in an unfriendly arena. The further the issue evolves, the more likely that many stakeholders are aware of the issue, have developed an understanding or interpretation of it, have assessed their stake in it, and have developed some set of preferences for certain outcomes.

One of the most powerful strategies available to organizations is to redefine the issue, or recast it, for existing and potential stakeholders. By deftly redefining the issue, the organization can change stakeholders' perceptions of their stake in the issue.

The power of redefining or reshaping issues is evident in most of the examples that have been noted. J&J reshaped the issue in the Tylenol incident from product tampering to the protection of consumers' health and safety. Opponents of nuclear power redefined the issue from lower cost and energy independence to safety and security. Greenpeace redefined the issue from safe and economical disposal of oil platforms at sea to one of serious pollution of the sea, a catastrophe they were willing to risk their lives to oppose.

It is also important to define or redefine issues quickly before antagonists can assume and retain the initiative by successfully redefining issues in a way that attracts and energizes a broader base of stakeholders. A classic example is the 1964 grape strike in California led by the late Cesar Chavez. It was not the first strike to be organized against the landowners (an example of an advocacy issue) and the history of such strikes was one of failure. Chavez succeeded where numerous others had failed because he managed the perception of the issue and made it one of universal appeal. Chavez and his followers portrayed the strike as a battle for the rights of the oppressed minority, migrant workers, not just another union-management conflict. In 1964, civil rights was still a sensitive issue, and rights of the oppressed offered a valuable symbol to gain media attention and other support:

"I am here," announced an early arrival in clerical garb, "because this is a movement by the poor people to improve their position, and where the poor are, Christ should be and is." Other supporters . . . said much the same thing in their own way: This was part of their battle against society's power structure.[4]

Moving an Issue Off an Agenda

In many instances, the ideal outcome for organizations is not just preemption or redefinition of an issue, but its total elimination. Once an issue is placed on an agenda, its elimination is normally beyond the actions of a single organization. The cooperation of stakeholders who represent diverse interests is most often required to achieve successful removal. Organizations are provoked to try to "kill" an issue when the consequences of how the issue might be resolved are large (or stated differently, their stakes in the issue are very high).

Many organizations have successfully gotten issues off either formal or informal agendas by reshaping existing stakeholders' stakes and/or broadening the base of stakeholders. A classic illustration of these tactics occurred in Massachusetts in 1982, when a controversial piece of legislation was introduced calling for dramatic reallocation in healthcare costs. The introduction of this legislation arose from federal pressures for changes in Medicare management and payments. The state saw this legislation as a potential opportunity to obtain a waiver from the federal government. Several major stakeholders were involved: the state Business Roundtable, the Massachusetts Hospital Association (MHA), Blue Cross, the High-Technology Council, physicians, the state Commissioner of Insurance, and the Life Insurance Association of Massachusetts (LIAM). A major focus of the legislation was to reduce healthcare costs and erode the dominant position that Blue Cross held in the state. This would improve the competitive position of the insurance companies in Massachusetts in the healthcare field. It was clear to all that the issue was "healthcare cost containment." This had great appeal to business (it would reduce the cost of employee benefits) and to individuals (it would reduce their costs for healthcare). The MHA, the physicians, and Blue Cross were less than thrilled by this proposal, but it had great public, business, and political backing and appeal.

In assessing the situation, Blue Cross noted that if the legislation passed, it would force them to reduce benefits provided to their 300,000 plus elderly subscribers. The group would either pay more for benefits, receive less benefits, or both. Blue Cross called all of these subscribers to let them know of this impact. The subscribers, in turn, caused a massive grassroots movement—an organized campaign of phone calls to public representatives, letters to newspapers, and representation to the electronic media. The resulting publicity stopped the issue dead. The public debate shifted to "erosion of benefits for the elderly" and no group or organization wanted to support that position publicly.

LINKING POLITICAL AND CORPORATE STRATEGIES

As noted at the beginning of this chapter, an organization's political strategy is not disconnected from its business strategy. Indeed, quite the contrary. Political strategy can affect business strategy in myriad ways.

First, political strategy is sometimes essential for survival as a stand-alone economic entity. Had Hasbro not engaged in a decisive political strategy to fend off Mattel's proposed hostile takeover, it would not have survived to develop and execute its own preferred business strategy.

Second, political strategy is sometimes necessary for business strategy success. Many firms have used political strategy to develop the alliances necessary to put in place the technological standards that were central to the marketplace success of their products. IBM has recently announced that it would become part of an industry alliance involving firms such as Compaq, Hewlett-Packard, Microsoft, and Intel, to create better security for electronic-commerce transactions.

Third, political strategy can greatly contribute to or impede execution of specific elements of a firm's operations. Shell discovered to its great surprise how a stakeholder to whom it had paid relatively little attention—Greenpeace—could dramatically intervene in its best-laid plans to dispose of an oil platform in the deepest reaches of the North Sea.

Fourth, political strategy is sometimes critical to gaining access to marketplaces. The European Union effectively prohibited Coca-Cola from extending its reach into the European market through the acquisition of other firms' well-established product lines. For many years, Japanese automobile manufacturers essentially negotiated the extent to which they could enter the U.S. marketplace through the "voluntary restraints" (i.e., the number of cars they could export to the United States) they established with the U.S. government.

Fifth, the corollary of gaining marketplace access is that political strategy can contribute to preservation of marketplace position and protection against new entrants. U.S. automobile and electronics firms benefited from the Voluntary Restraining Agreements with Japan. The well-known difficulties of penetrating the Japanese domestic market provided many Japanese firms with a protected domestic base from which to expand internationally.

SUMMARY

In developing its political strategy, an organization needs to identify the most salient issues, the stakeholders who are likely to be its allies and antagonists, how they can impact the issue and the arenas in which it has a position of advantage over other current and potential stakeholders. The questions noted in Tables 7.2 and 7.3 provide the necessary framework of analysis. Once the most critical issues have been determined, then the organization has to assess and execute the strategy alternatives discussed earlier. Given the current pace of change in the political and social arenas, it seems safe to suggest that managers are going to confront a greater diversity of issues than ever before. Becoming adept at political strategy is no longer a luxury: It is a survival skill.

NOTES

1. Portions of this chapter draw on the following work of the authors: B. Bigelow, L. Fahey, and J.F. Mahon, "Political Strategy and Issue Evolution: A Framework for Analysis," *Contemporary Issues in Business and Society,* ed. K. Paul (Lewiston, NY: Edwin Mellon Press, 1991): 1–26; J.F. Mahon, "Corporate Political Strategy," *Business in the Contemporary World* (November 1989): 50–62; and J.F. Mahon, B. Bigelow, and L. Fahey, *Toward a Theory of Corporate Political Strategy,* paper presented at the Academy of Management national meetings, Washington, DC, August 1989.

2. P.F. Bartha, "Managing Corporate External Issues: An Analytical Framework," *Business Quarterly* (1982), 47: 78–90.

3. Constance L. Hays, "A Sputter in the Coke Machine," *New York Times* (June 30, 1999), pp. C1 and C6.

4. R.W. Cobb and C.D. Elder, *Participation in American Politics: The Dynamics of Agenda Building* (Baltimore: John Hopkins University Press, 1972), p. 72.

PART TWO

STRATEGY INPUTS: ANALYZING THE EXTERNAL AND INTERNAL ENVIRONMENTS

8 MAPPING THE BUSINESS LANDSCAPE

David J. Collis
Yale School of Organization and Management

Pankaj Ghemawat
Harvard Business School

> When an industry with a reputation for difficult economics
> meets a manager with a reputation for excellence, it is usu-
> ally the industry that keeps its reputation intact.
>
> *Warren Buffett, CEO of Berkshire Hathaway*

Managers developing and executing strategy must perform a critical exercise—
the analysis of the business landscape in which their firm currently competes
or may enter. Systematic analysis of this sort can help managers understand
current profitability levels, identify the forces that must be countered or capi-
talized on to improve profitability, test decisions to enter or exit an industry,
assess the effects of major changes (e.g., deregulation), and even identify ways
to alter industry structure.

This chapter describes two helpful complementary frameworks:

1. The five forces framework.
2. The value net framework.

The chapter concludes with a discussion of the *process* of using these frameworks to map the business landscape or industry as an input to strategy development and execution.[1]

171

FRAMEWORKS FOR ANALYSIS

Industry analysis assumes importance because of the considerable evidence that the industry environment in which a business operates has a strong influence on its economic performance (see Figure 8.1).[2] The pharmaceutical industry, for example, has earned far more on average than the steel industry in the United States over the past 20 years. The size and longevity of these differences suggest the value of assessing whether the industry you want to study will resemble pharmaceuticals or steel in terms of its long-term profit potential.

A substantial body of research indicates that the profit potential of an industry is not a matter of luck but depends on its basic conditions (e.g., the price elasticity of demand) and structural attributes (e.g., the number and size distribution of competitors) as well as on the strategies actually adopted by various players. By far the best known application of these structuralist ideas is Michael Porter's "five forces" framework.

The Five Forces Framework

Developed in the 1970s, Porter's five-forces framework broke new ground by looking at "extended competition" for value rather than just competition among direct rivals (see Figure 8.2).[3] More specifically, it shifted attention from two-stage vertical supply chains, each made up of a supplier and buyer, to three-stage chains, made up of suppliers, rivals, and buyers (the vertical axis in Figure 8.2), and it also took account of potential entrants and substitutes as well as direct rivals. We can illustrate the effects of these structural forces on

FIGURE 8.1   Value line industry groups.

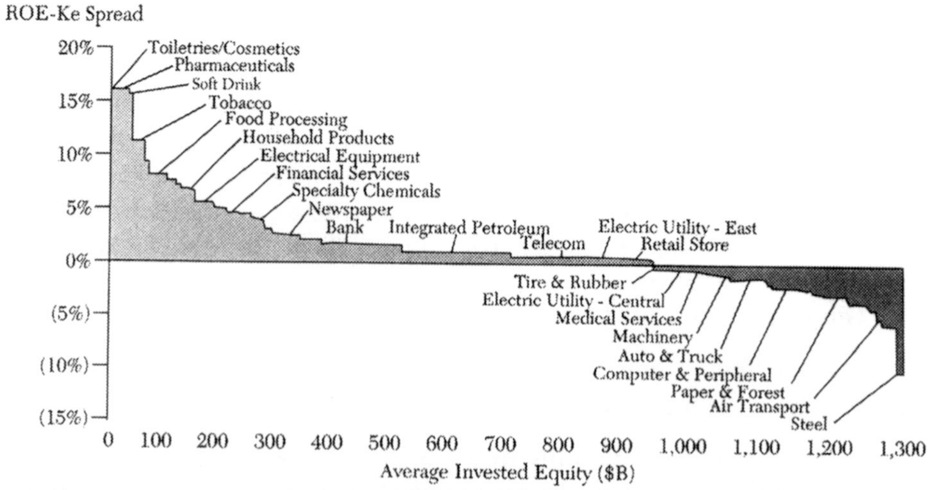

Source: Compustat, Value Line, Marakon Associates analysis.

FIGURE 8.2   The five forces framework.

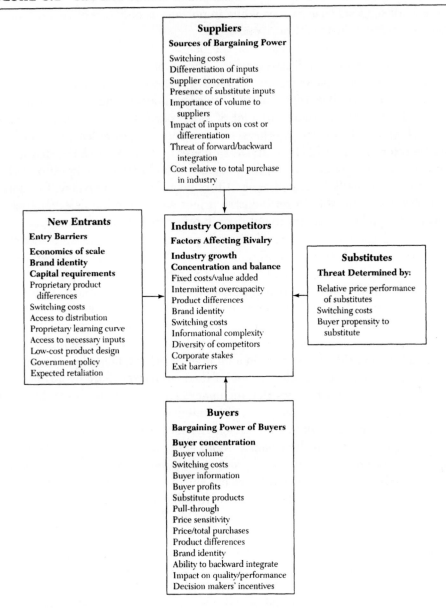

industry profitability by applying the framework to the steel and pharmaceuticals industries.

Force 1. The Degree of Rivalry

The intensity of rivalry is the most obvious of the five forces in an industry and the one that strategists usually address first. Intensity of rivalry determines the extent to which the value created by an industry will be dissipated through head-to-head competition. Remember, however, that the five forces framework suggests that rivalry, while important, is only one of several forces that determine industry attractiveness.

The structural determinants of the degree of rivalry in an industry are numerous. One set of conditions concerns the number and relative size of competitors. The more concentrated the industry, the more likely it is that competitors will recognize their mutual interdependence and so restrain their rivalry. If, in contrast, there are a lot of small players in the industry, each is apt to think that its effect on others will go unnoticed, or at least unpunished, and therefore is more likely to strive to increase its market share, disrupting the market. For similar reasons, the presence of a dominant competitor rather than a set of equally balanced competitors may also lessen rivalry: the dominant player may be able to set industry prices and discipline defectors, while players of equal size may try to outdo each other to gain an advantage.

A good example of these influences is provided by the U.S. steel industry, which reached its height of profitability before World War II. Competition in the prewar period was confined to a small number of domestic players led by U.S. Steel. As the dominant firm, it provided an important source of stability—sometimes through illegal methods. In the 1920s, for example, its chairman, Judge Gary, became notorious for inviting competitors to dinner so that U.S. Steel could make its pricing policy clear to them. Using such techniques, the dominant firm in this industry, as in a number of others, helped prop up prices for several decades despite the erosion of its own market share over time.

A second set of attributes that influences rivalry is more closely linked to the industry's basic conditions. In capital-intensive industries, the level of capacity utilization has a direct impact on the incentive for firms to engage in price competition to fill their plants. More generally, high fixed costs, excess capacity, slow growth, and lack of product differentiation all increase the degree of rivalry. The U.S. steel industry has suffered from all these factors in recent years. The ratio of fixed capital costs to value added is particularly high in steel, labor is largely a fixed cost as well, demand has been essentially flat, and product differentiation has been minimal, so that excess capacity has been chronic and catastrophic in its effects.

The pharmaceutical industry presents a very different picture. Fixed manufacturing costs are limited as a percentage of sales or value added. In fact, gross margins range as high as 90 percent for some breakthrough medicines. Demand has grown at double-digit levels, and differences among products, brand identity, and switching costs—discussed at greater length in the subsection on buyer power—have created insulation among competitors that is reinforced, in some cases, by patent protection.

Finally, the degree of rivalry also has behavioral determinants. If competitors are diverse, attach high strategic stakes to their positions in an industry, or suffer from high exit barriers, they are more likely to be aggressive rivals. In steel, foreign competitors have, by increasing diversity, helped shatter the domestic oligopolistic consensus. In addition, strategic stakes have been high since each domestic integrated steel maker historically focused on steel as its core business, and exit barriers have been compounded by the costs of cleaning up decommissioned sites.

Force 2. The Threat of Entry

Potential as well as actual competitors can influence average industry profitability. To analyze the threat of entry by potential competitors, managers must understand the concept of entry barriers. Entry barriers exist whenever it is difficult or infeasible for an outsider to replicate the position of the incumbents, and act to prevent an influx of firms into an industry whenever profits, adjusted for the cost of capital, rise above zero. Entry barriers most often arise from irreversible resource commitments.[4]

Figure 8.2 illustrates the diverse forms that entry barriers can take. Some barriers reflect intrinsic physical or legal obstacles to entry. The most common forms of entry barriers, however, are usually the scale and the investment required to enter an industry as an efficient competitor. For example, when incumbent firms have well-established brand names and clearly differentiated products, it may be uneconomical for a potential entrant to undertake the marketing campaign necessary to introduce its own products effectively. The magnitude of the required expenditures may be only part of the entrant's problem in such a situation: Years may be required for it to build a reputation for product quality, no matter how large its initial advertising campaign is. Entry barriers can also be contrived by incumbents, as illustrated by credible threats of retaliation.

The effect of entry barriers is apparent in two very different strategic groups or business models within the pharmaceutical industry: research-based pharmaceutical companies and manufacturers of generic pharmaceuticals. Research-based companies have been far more profitable on average, largely because they are sheltered by higher entry barriers. These include patent protection, a development process for new pharmaceutical entities that can cost hundreds of millions of dollars and stretch out for more than a decade, carefully cultivated brand identities, and large sales forces that call on individual doctors. In the generic segment of the industry, in contrast, there is no patent protection, the capital and time required for product development are much smaller, brand identities are weak to nonexistent, and distribution efforts focus on serving large accounts that purchase in bulk at low prices. However, some generic manufacturers have tried to introduce so-called "branded generics," a marketing strategy designed to give these low-cost drugs a distinct identity that conveys quality and reliability.

The history of the steel industry illustrates that barriers to entry can, like other elements of industry structure, change over time. Integrated U.S. steel producers that made steel from iron ore were long protected from domestic entrants by the billion-plus dollars of capital required to build an efficiently scaled integrated steel mill—a barrier that helped ensure that no new integrated mills were built in the United States for nearly 50 years. Since the 1960s, however, integrated steelmakers have come under intense pressure from minimills, which make steel from scrap rather than from iron ore. Minimill technology has essentially reduced the scale required for efficient operation by a factor of 10 or more, and cut the investment required per ton of capacity by another factor of 10. The result has been a hundredfold reduction in barriers to entry! As a result, profitability has collapsed in the segments of the steel industry that minimills have been able to penetrate.

Force 3. The Threat of Substitutes

The threat that substitutes pose to an industry's profitability depends on the relative price-to-performance ratios of the products or services that customers can choose among to satisfy the same basic need. The threat of substitution is also affected by switching costs. These are the costs in areas such as retraining, retooling, or redesign that a customer incurs when switching to different types of products or services. In many cases, the substitution process follows an S-shaped curve. It starts slowly as a few trendsetters assume the risk of experimenting with the substitute, picks up steam if other customers follow suit, and finally levels off when nearly all the economical substitution possibilities have been exhausted.

Substitute materials that put pressure on the steel industry include plastics, aluminum, and ceramics. Consider the substitution of aluminum for steel in the metal can industry. Aluminum's lighter weight and superior lithographic characteristics make it attractive to can producers despite its higher prices. Though the costs to can makers of switching from steel to aluminum probably slowed substitution initially, today steel retains only a small share of the market, succeeding only in niches such as food cans.

Any analysis of the threat of (demand-side) substitution must look broadly at all products that perform similar functions for customers, not just at physically similar products. Thus, substitutes for pharmaceuticals, broadly construed, might include preventive care and hospitalization. Indeed, there is evidence for the pharmaceutical industry's assertions that one of the major reasons for its profitability and growth is that pharmaceuticals represent a more cost-effective form of healthcare, in many cases, than hospitalization.

Conceptually, analysis of the substitution possibilities open to buyers should be supplemented with consideration of the possibilities available to suppliers. Supply-side substitutability affects suppliers' willingness to provide required inputs, just as demand-side substitutability affects buyers' willingness to pay for products. Thus, integrated steelmakers who mix steel scrap with iron ore as inputs into their production process have been unable to hold down scrap prices because of growing demand for scrap from minimills, who use it as their primary input.

Force 4. Buyer Power

Buyer power is one of the two vertical forces that influences who gets what share of the value created by an industry. Buyer power allows customers to squeeze industry margins by compelling competitors to reduce prices, to increase the level of service offered without raising the price, or to add features to the product or service.

Probably the most important determinants of buyer power are the size and the concentration of customers. Such considerations help explain why automakers, in particular, have historically enjoyed considerable leverage in dealing with steelmakers. Other reasons for automakers' bargaining power as buyers include the extent to which they were well informed about steelmakers' costs and the credibility of their threats to integrate backward into steelmaking (a strategy once adopted by Ford). In contrast, none of these sources of buyer power—concentration, good information, or the ability to backward integrate—were evident, historically, in the pharmaceutical industry.

Buyer bargaining power can obviously be offset in situations in which competitors are themselves concentrated or differentiated. Both conditions have helped manufacturers of stainless and other specialty steels achieve higher rates of profitability than large integrated steelmakers. In the pharmaceutical industry, no substitutes are available for many of the drugs that are still on patent, so to get the desired treatment, patients must purchase the products from a single manufacturer. And even when therapeutic substitutes are available, differences in dosage frequency, ease of administration, and side effects can create significant product differentiation.

It is often useful to distinguish potential buyer power from the willingness or incentive to use that power. For example, the U.S. government is potentially a powerful buyer of pharmaceuticals through its Medicaid and Medicare programs. Historically, however, it refrained from exercising its potential power, which was fortunate for the pharmaceutical industry but unfortunate for taxpayers. Only recently is there evidence that the federal government is more willing to flex its muscles on pricing.

To explain why buyers do or do not have the incentive to use their inherent power, it is necessary to look at another, more behavioral set of conditions. One of the most important of these factors is the share of the purchasing industry's cost accounted for by the products in question. Purchasing decisions naturally focus on larger-cost items first. This has been one of the curses of the steel industry: Steel represents a major portion of the costs of many products in which it is used, ranging from cans to cars.

Another important factor is the "risk of failure" associated with a product. In pharmaceuticals, patients lack the information to evaluate competing drugs and so are swayed instead by the potential high personal cost of any substitute's failure. For many years, research-based pharmaceutical companies encouraged physicians and the general public to view generic drugs as a risky substitute. Scandals involving some generic firms' substandard manufacturing practices did not help. As a result, high-price brands have been able to retain significant shares in many product categories even after satisfactory generic substitutes have become available.

The pharmaceutical example also highlights the importance of studying the decision-making process when analyzing buyer power. The interests and incentives of all players involved in the purchase decision must be understood if one is to predict how much price sensitivity affects a decision. Many doctors and patients historically lacked incentives to hold down the prices paid for drugs because a third party (e.g., an insurance company) actually paid the bill. These incentives are changing, however, as the spread of managed care increases price sensitivity.

Force 5. Supplier Power

Supplier power is the mirror image of buyer power. The analysis of supplier power therefore typically focuses, first, on the relative size and concentration of suppliers relative to industry participants and, second, on the degree of differentiation in the inputs supplied. The ability to charge customers different prices in line with differences in the value created for each of them usually indicates higher supplier power (and low buyer power).

None of these considerations has been much of a problem for the pharmaceutical industry in the past. For conventional pharmaceuticals (as opposed to biotechnology-based ones), inputs are usually available from several commodity chemical companies. The U.S. integrated steel industry, in contrast, has been ravaged by supplier power. The suppliers who have mattered the most have been the workers unionized by the United Steel Workers. Through collective action, they were historically able to bargain their wages to levels well in excess of other manufacturing industries while protecting jobs. In the late 1980s, excess compensation and employment swallowed up as much as one-quarter of steelmakers' total revenues! In contrast, there is no union of Ph.D. or physician researchers in the pharmaceutical industry even though the many years required for their education gives them substantial bargaining power.

Relationships with buyers and suppliers have important cooperative as well as competitive elements. General Motors and other U.S. automobile companies lost sight of this fact when they pushed their parts suppliers to the wall by playing them off against each other. Japanese car companies, in contrast, committed themselves to long-run supplier relationships that paid off in terms of quality and the speed of new product development. The importance of cooperation as well as competition is highlighted by the framework for landscape analysis, the value net, discussed in the next section.

The Value Net

The years since Porter first developed his five-forces framework have seen the rearrangement and incorporation of additional variables (such as import competition and multimarket contact) into the determinants of the intensity of each of the five competitive forces. Even more importantly, new types of players have been incorporated into the analysis. The most successful attempt to do so is the value net framework devised by Adam Brandenburger and Barry Nalebuff (see Figure 8.3).[5]

The value net highlights the critical role that complementors—from whom buyers obtain complementary products or services, or to whom suppliers sell complementary inputs—play in influencing business success or failure. The role of complementors mirrors that of competitors (including new entrants and substitutes as well as existing rivals). On the demand side, they increase buyers' willingness to pay for certain products; on the supply side, they decrease the price that suppliers require for their inputs.

To see why it is important to bring complementors into the picture, reconsider the pharmaceutical industry. Physicians have an important influence on the success of the pharmaceutical manufacturers through the drugs that they prescribe, but they cannot, in most cases, be considered buyers because money typically does not flow directly from them to the pharmaceutical manufacturers. Instead, they play the role of complementors who increase buyers' willingness to pay for particular products.

An even more powerful example is the complementarity between computer hardware and software. Windows 97 from Microsoft works more efficiently on a computer with a Pentium microprocessor from Intel than on one with a 486 chip. Even so, Microsoft and Intel might not show up on each other's "five-forces" screens! Common sense nevertheless suggests that Intel and Microsoft should regard each other as an important player in the business landscape. This insight gained importance when recent reports of divergences in the interests of these two players seemed to be creating problems for both of them. Intel has, in fact, started to incorporate complementors into its environmental scans according to its chairman, Andy Grove.[6]

FIGURE 8.3   A value net framework.

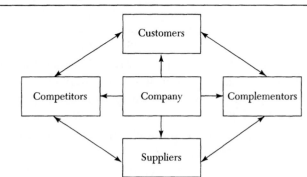

Source: Adam Brandenburger and Barry Nalebuff, *Co-opetition* (New York: Currency Doubleday, 1996): 17.

Complementors are ubiquitous features on many business landscapes. They seem to be particularly important in situations where businesses are developing entirely new ways of doing things or where standards are critical in combining different kinds of expertise into systems that work well. In the early days of the automobile industry, General Motors and other manufacturers, many now defunct, financed and built short stretches of roads to help catalyze the development of the first coast-to-coast highway in the United States. And in the high-tech sector today, the competition between alternate information infrastructures—such as that between Java applets or Unix programs over the Internet versus the Wintel desktop system—makes the role of complements crucial.

The biggest benefit of taking complementors seriously is that they help add a cooperative dimension to the competitive forces approach. As Brandenburger and Nalebuff put it,

> Thinking complements is a different way of thinking about business. It's about finding ways to make the pie bigger rather than fighting with competitors over a fixed pie. To benefit from this insight, think about how to expand the pie by developing new complements or making existing complements more affordable.[7]

When considering cooperation with complementors to expand the size of the pie, be aware that sooner or later your firm will likely be forced into competition with them to claim slices of that pie. Common sense suggests determining the extent to which complementors, as a class of players, are likely to be able to claim their share at the expense of the competitors within an industry. In making this assessment, you need to consider the following:

- *Relative concentration.* Complementors are more likely to have the power to pursue their own agenda when they are concentrated relative to competitors, and are less likely to be able to do so when they are relatively fragmented. Thus, competitors in video games such as Nintendo have deliberately fragmented their base of complementors—independent game developers—to reduce their power.

- *Relative buyer or supplier switching costs.* When the costs to buyers or suppliers of switching across complementors are greater than their costs of switching across rivals, that increases the general ability of complementors to pursue their own agenda. The cost of switching the software on your desktop is likely to be significantly higher than the cost of switching your Internet service provider, with clear implications for how much of the economic pie those two classes of players can hope to capture.

- *Ease of unbundling.* Complements will tend to have less power if consumers can purchase and use products independently of them. This is the reason that applications software programs, while complements to the manufacturers of microprocessors, tend to be less important than the operating system (e.g., Windows). Many categories of application programs can be, and are, purchased independently.

- *Differences in pull-through.* As complementors play a greater role in pulling through demand (e.g., through differentiation) or supply (e.g., through volumes commanded), their power is likely to expand. Thus, in the media and entertainment sector, content providers complement but also cause grave concern for other types of players.
- *Asymmetric integration threats.* Complementors are likely to have more power when their threats to invade competitors' turf are more credible than competitors' threats to invade their turf.
- *Rate of growth of the pie.* From a behavioral perspective, competition with complementors to claim value is likely to be less intense when the size of the pie available to be divided among competitors and complementors is growing rapidly.

This list of the determinants of complementors' power could probably be lengthened. The end result is sometimes depicted as adding a "sixth force" to Porter's five-forces framework. Nevertheless, landscape analysis of the sort advocated in this chapter should not be thought of as simply an extended version of the five-forces framework for industry analysis. Cooperative as well as competitive relationships must be taken into account for *all* players, whichever "force" they might be listed under.

MAPPING BUSINESS LANDSCAPES

Having discussed frameworks for mapping the business landscape, it is time to turn to the process of making such mappings. The first step in the process is to draw boundaries around the part of the landscape to be described in detail, by identifying the types of players that will be taken into account. The next step involves identifying and sometimes calibrating key relationships among the players considered. The final step is adapting to or shaping those relationships to maximize profitability. Although it may be necessary to cycle through these steps more than once, they are most simply considered in turn.

Step 1. Drawing the Boundaries

For most business strategy issues, it is more useful to zoom in on sets of players with a direct impact on the profitability of one's own business model than to look across the entire economy. Operationally, the challenge for the strategist is to decide how broadly or narrowly to look in mapping the business landscape.

The units of analysis commonly used in the business press and by other popular information providers are often inappropriate and therefore need to be redrawn if they are to be helpful. For example, the "auto and truck" industry often used in the business press should be split into "autos" and "trucks" for most purposes since buyers, competitors, and even suppliers differ across those two segments.

Similarly, beware of official statistical definitions such as the Standard Industrial Classification (SIC) code, which has been employed in the United States since the 1930s. Thus, at the 4-digit level, the U.S. SIC code does distinguish between motor vehicles and passenger cars on the one hand and trucks and buses on the other. However, it lumps light trucks with heavy trucks even though the former are frequently used for personal transportation.[8]

These caveats can be supplemented with several positive principles for drawing boundaries:

1. Look beyond direct competitors who use the same suppliers and the same technology to make the same products: also include indirect competitors that offer products or services that are close substitutes for those of your firm. It is easy to overlook current and potential technological substitutability as well as "disruptive" technologies that may fulfill customers' needs in the future if not at present. Such errors of omission can be extremely dangerous. As a result, companies that (potentially) share customers or technologies should be included within the boundaries of the map. Thus, whether it makes sense to analyze cars and light trucks as part of the same map depends on both the degree of demand-side substitutability between the two product lines and the extent to which know-how and production equipment can be cross-utilized (supply-side substitutability).

2. Identify the important complementarities as well as substitution possibilities (as suggested by the value net). This does, however, complicate the picture in one respect that must be acknowledged at this point. The same player may simultaneously enact the roles of competitor and complementor, or may switch from one role to the other—what Brandenburger and Nalebuff refer to as the "Jekyll and Hyde" effect.

3. Players other than the types suggested by the five-forces framework or the value net may need to be included in the analysis as well. In particular, it is often important to account for nonmarket relationships with players such as the government, the media, activist/interest groups, and the public as well as players with whom market relationships exist.

   There are three common pitfalls in identifying the relevant players. First, there is often a tendency to focus on existing players; new or potential ones must also be taken into account. Second, players need to be thought of in terms of detailed subcategories rather than just the broad categories identified in the analytical templates discussed so far. It would be hard to analyze the degree of threat posed by supplier relationships to integrated steelmakers without recognizing that labor represents an important subcategory of suppliers. Third, players need to be clearly and consistently labeled from the perspective of the business that motivates the analysis in the first place. To return to the example of integrated steelmaking, case discussions sometimes confuse rivals with suppliers on the grounds that rivals supply their own buyers!

Most of the remaining ambiguities in drawing boundaries around your firm's business landscape revolve around dimensions of scope:

- *Horizontal scope.* Across product markets.
- *Vertical scope.* Along the value chain.
- *Geographic scope.* Across local, regional, and national boundaries.

Horizontal Scope

Horizontal scope has already been highlighted in the passenger car/light truck example. When it is unclear whether a narrow horizontal definition corresponds to a segment of an industry or a separate industry, it may make sense to analyze the industry based on both narrow and broad definitions. The narrow definition focuses the analysis, and the broad one prevents being blindsided by unexpected new competitors. If it proves very difficult to analyze the broader definition of an industry because of differences among segments, then the industry is properly defined narrowly, not broadly.

Vertical Scope

The key issue of vertical scope is, how many vertically linked stages should be included in the span of an industry? For example, can one analyze bauxite mining, alumina refining, aluminum smelting, and fabrication of aluminum products independently of each other? In general, if a competitive market for third-party sales exists between vertical stages, then the stages should be uncoupled in defining industries; if not, they should remain coupled. In this sense, the tightest coupling in the vertical aluminum chain is between bauxite mining and alumina refining, because most refineries are tied to one source of bauxite. The loosest coupling is between aluminum smelting and fabrication because fabricators can buy aluminum ingot from the London Exchange as well as from different smelters. If competitors specialized to a particular vertical stage thrive, it may make sense to treat that stage as a separate industry.

Geographic Scope

The issue here is, should physically separate markets be treated as being served by the same industry or by distinct industries? For example, does it make more sense to perform industry analysis on just the U.S. pharmaceutical industry or to consider also the global pharmaceutical industry? Such issues can arise around local and regional boundaries as well as national ones. A key criterion in settling them is whether competitive positions in different geographic markets are interdependent. Because of the importance of amortizing their huge research and development (R&D) expenditures, interdependence across markets is higher for pharmaceutical companies than for steelmakers, suggesting that the pharmaceutical industry should generally be defined to have broader geographic scope.

Additional complexities can arise along each of these dimensions if competitors differ significantly in terms of their chosen scope. In such situations, industry definitions may have to acknowledge the differences among competitors. More generally, it may sometimes be helpful to identify strategic groups within an industry—sets of competitors that compete in similar ways for similar customers and interact more directly within each group than with competitors drawn from other strategic groups. In the automobile industry, luxury car manufacturers constitute a distinct strategic group whose performance is partly independent of competition in the mass market for automobiles.

To summarize Step 1, identifying the players who will be kept in as opposed to left out of deep analysis of the business landscape is a considerable challenge for managers. The principles and guidelines offered here should help.

Step 2. Mapping Key Relationships

Identification of the relevant players paves the way for actually mapping the relationships among them. Such maps can be constructed for two very different purposes. Both are encountered in practice though usually not within the same company. One approach is to calibrate relationships in quantitative or at least categorical terms (e.g., low vs. medium vs. high power for one's own side) to yield something akin to a traditional decision support system. The other approach focuses on mental models; it stresses the importance of ensuring that key relationships are understood in some depth by key decision makers. Both approaches have succeeded in numerous practical applications. Both have many of the same implications for mapping the business landscape. Here, we emphasize three common implications.

Information Requirements

Both approaches require the acquisition and integration of a large amount of information about the competitive environment. This challenge is compounded by the need to assess changes in relationships over time or across issues—a need that usually mandates ongoing rather than one-off attempts to map business landscapes. The fixed costs of setting up and operating a system for more-or-less continuous environmental scans are considerable. However, scanning also provides useful inputs into other forms of strategy-relevant analysis such as customer analysis, technology analysis, and evaluation of strategy alternatives.

Cooperative and Competitive Relationships

The cooperative *and* competitive elements of relationships of players in the competitive milieu should also be reflected in the maps that are drawn. While this adds to the difficulty of the analysis, it also enhances the chances of finding win-win strategies, in which the size of the economic pie expands, as opposed to focusing solely on win-lose strategies, which involve redistribution of the shares of a largely fixed pie. The general inattention to cooperative relationships in the five-forces framework is one of the key reasons many strategists have recently argued that it is impossible to define industries satisfactorily, particularly in the high-tech sector, using only the five-forces framework. Attention to the cooperative possibilities highlighted by the value net can help.

Dynamic Thinking

The final reason attempts to map relationships among players can offer both dividends and difficulties is that those relationships tend to change over time and do so partly as a result of the strategies adopted by various players. One obvious implication of such change is that we should map the business landscape the way it will be in the future rather than the way it was in the past. Success at anticipating how the business landscape will change can be extremely valuable, just as a failure to anticipate changes can be disastrous. Several additional guidelines can be helpful.

First, distinguish carefully between short-run and long-run dynamics. Short-run dynamics reflect transient effects but also pick up on phenomena such as business cycles that can be important, particularly in capacity-driven industries. In the U.S. steel industry, integrated steelmakers' attempts to modernize were regularly and debilitatingly interrupted by cyclical downturns, which increased the profit potential for minimills.

Second, pay particularly careful attention to longer-run dynamics such as market growth, the evolution of buyer needs, the rate of product and process innovation, changes in the scale required to compete, in input costs, exchange rates, and so on. A number of possible long-run dynamics are noted in Figure 8.4. Some of the changes involved may cut across more than one set of relationships.

Finally, changes may also be drastic rather than incremental. Many contemporary forces—including advances in information technology, deregulation, and globalization—can subject landscapes in emerging markets as well as developed ones to shocks or discontinuous changes that are qualitatively distinct in their competitive effects from cycles and trends.

Step 3. Adapting to/Shaping the Business Landscape

Having identified the key players and mapped (current and future) relationships among them, the manager's attention must turn to using that knowledge for strategic action. The way in which landscape analysis connects to strategic action is most obvious when the analysis is motivated by a specific choice (e.g., whether to enter or to exit a particular market). Other connections to

FIGURE 8.4 Long-run dynamics.

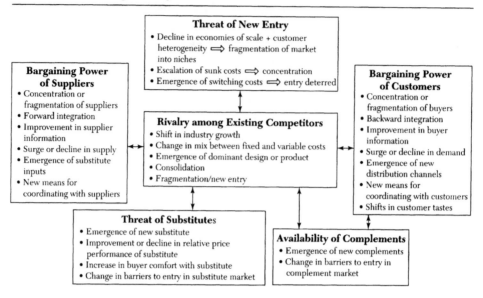

Threat of New Entry
- Decline in economies of scale + customer heterogeneity ⟹ fragmentation of market into niches
- Escalation of sunk costs ⟹ concentration
- Emergence of switching costs ⟹ entry deterred

Bargaining Power of Suppliers
- Concentration or fragmentation of suppliers
- Forward integration
- Improvement in supplier information
- Surge or decline in supply
- Emergence of substitute inputs
- New means for coordinating with suppliers

Rivalry among Existing Competitors
- Shift in industry growth
- Change in mix between fixed and variable costs
- Emergence of dominant design or product
- Consolidation
- Fragmentation/new entry

Bargaining Power of Customers
- Concentration or fragmentation of buyers
- Backward integration
- Improvement in buyer information
- Surge or decline in demand
- Emergence of new distribution channels
- New means for coordinating with customers
- Shifts in customer tastes

Threat of Substitutes
- Emergence of new substitute
- Improvement or decline in relative price performance of substitute
- Increase in buyer comfort with substitute
- Change in barriers to entry in substitute market

Availability of Complements
- Emergence of new complements
- Change in barriers to entry in complement market

action are possible as well. Thus, a map of the business landscape may highlight certain competitive relationships that must be countered or certain cooperative relationships that must be exploited to achieve superior economic performance.

For a current example of adaptation, consider the strategic actions taken by large accounting firms to mitigate the worst aspects of their business landscape. The profitability of their audit business, in particular, was being eroded by rivalry among the traditional Big Eight firms, which were similar in their size and in their intent of becoming number one in the business. Adding to this were pressures from the typical purchaser, the Chief Financial Officer (CFO) of a client, for whom the external audit fee represented the largest item on his or her budget after salaries. Large accounting firms have responded to these pressures in several ways. The Big Eight are now down to the Big Five, with further consolidation likely. They have broadened the scope of their professional services (e.g., by moving into consulting) so as to shift to more attractive parts of the landscape and to increase clients' switching costs. Finally, they have been attempting to shift the purchase of audit services away from CFOs to audit committees of clients' boards of directors, whom they perceive to be less price-sensitive.

Adaptation, while important, is not the only strategic thrust that might be adopted vis-à-vis the business landscape. A business may also take a more active role in shaping its environment to its own advantage—a possibility that has been headlined by a large body of recent literature emphasizing the importance of strategic insight or foresight. Opportunities to shape or reshape business landscapes are most obvious in fluid environments, such as multimedia, but are also evident in older, apparently more mature contexts.

Although strategies that aim to reshape business landscapes often carry high risks, the returns can be remarkable. Consider how Nintendo rebuilt the video game business in the second half of the 1980s, after sales had dropped by more than 95 percent between 1982 and 1985 due to a flood of low-quality software reaching the market. Nintendo paid attention from the very outset to setting up relationships with other players that would allow it both to grow the pie *and* to capture a major share of the value created. Thus, on the supply side, it developed some of its own content, limited the number of titles sourced each year from outside game developers to keep them symmetrical, and required exclusivity of them. And on the demand side, it restricted the supply of game cartridges to retailers and insisted on resale price maintenance to prevent any one of them from achieving dominance over the others.

SUMMARY

Landscape analysis involves taking an extended look not just at direct rivals but also at other classes of players who influence the profit potential for individual businesses. Given the ambiguity regarding who is "in" and who is "out," achieving clarity about the participants' identities is often more important than striving for *the* right way to draw the boundaries of the portion of the business landscape that is to be mapped in detail. Identification of the relevant types of players paves the way for actually mapping the relationships among them. Both cooperative and competitive relationships must be taken into account. Also, the mapping must be dynamic because relationships can and do change over time.

The ultimate objective of mapping the business landscape is to suggest ways in which businesses can adapt to or shape the landscapes in which they operate. That is why landscape analysis is often treated as the starting point for many strategy development exercises.

NOTES

1. For a more detailed discussion, see Pankaj Ghemawat and David Collis, "Mapping the Business Landscape," in *Strategy and the Business Landscape*, ed. Pankaj Ghemawat (Reading, MA: Addison Wesley Longman, 1999), Chap. 2.

2. Figure 8.1 subtracts the estimated costs of (equity) capital from reported profitability (return on equity) and simultaneously displays the size of each industry group in terms of the capital invested in it. This approach therefore links accounting measures of profitability to economic measures of total value created or destroyed. Scott Gillis of Marakon Associates deserves our thanks for helping make these data available.

3. Michael E. Porter, *Competitive Strategy: Techniques for Analyzing Industries and Competitors* (New York: Free Press, 1980).

4. For additional discussion, see Pankaj Ghemawat, *Commitment: The Dynamic of Strategy* (New York: Free Press, 1991), Chaps. 2 and 5.

5. Adam Brandenburger and Barry Nalebuff, *Co-opetition* (New York: Currency Doubleday, 1996): 17. Even Porter is reported to have modified his five-forces framework in ways suggested by the value net.

6. Andrew S. Grove, *Only the Paranoid Survive* (New York: Bantam Doubleday Dell, 1996): 27–29.

7. Adam Brandenburger and Barry Nalebuff, *Co-opetition* (New York: Currency Doubleday, 1996): 12.

8. The Standard Industrial Classification is being replaced with the North American Industrial Classification System, which seems to provide a somewhat improved basis for bounding the business landscape.

MACROENVIRONMENTAL ANALYSIS: UNDERSTANDING THE ENVIRONMENT OUTSIDE THE INDUSTRY

9

V.K. Narayanan
Drexel University

Liam Fahey
Babson College and
Cranfield School of Management

Businesses large and small often have to scramble to respond when the headlines of daily newspapers trumpet portentous events in the political, social, economic, technological, ecological, and institutional milieu—the macroenvironment *outside* the bounds of an organization's industry. Demographic shifts, movement toward an integrated global economy, changes in governments, ecological disruptions, and technological innovations all affect the evolution of industries and influence organizations' strategies. Advance preparation for such macroenvironmental discontinuity should be a management priority. Strategy analysis as practiced in many organizations often gives only cursory attention to anticipating, assessing macroenvironmental change. And only a few leading edge organizations routinely rehearse their strategic responses to environmental discontinuity. In this chapter, we argue that an ongoing analysis of the macroenvironment is essential for crafting and executing sound strategy.[1]

The macroenvironment tends to be shortchanged in both strategy textbooks and practice, even though there are key reasons for managers to monitor, project, and assess it:

- Many transformations and discontinuities experienced by industries are caused by changes in the macroenvironment. As the twentieth century ended, scientific advances, technological developments, deregulation,

189

innovative litigation, and new consumerist laws have unleashed a torrent of opportunities and threats in industries as diverse as airlines, telecommunications, chemicals, food, software. Some predictable demographic changes, such as the aging of the baby-boomer generation, have caused many industries to focus on older age groups as major customer segments. Other complex social transformations—such as the percentage of American households made up of married couples with children, which dropped from 45 percent in the early 1970s to just 26 percent in 1998— have reset the marketing plans of a host of industries.

- Companies that learn to be among the first to perceive and exploit macroenvironmental changes can gain many advantages over their rivals, as the examples in this chapter demonstrate.

- Organizations that rehearse the appropriate strategic reactions to macroenvironmental discontinuities that suddenly present new market opportunities and foreclose others can develop the valuable organizational competency of change management.

Only by seeking new markets created by shifts in the macroenvironment can managers satisfy the *imperative of growth* that now dominates strategy making in most business organizations. Companies recognize that no matter how well they execute restructuring (adding and dropping businesses) and reengineering (improving operating efficiency), the results can't by themselves lead to continued growth in sales, margins, and profits. Managers need to recognize that all too often the best growth opportunities occur as a result of events that subtly remake the macroenvironment and that unanticipated macroenvironmental change can threaten the best-laid plans.

We need to preface this discussion by clarifying what the objective of macroenvironmental analysis is and what it is not. Like any business assessment of the future, the purpose of macroenvironmental analysis is not to predict what will take place. That is an impossible task. Macroenvironmental analysis can, however, do the following:

- Provide an understanding of both *current and potential* changes taking place in any industry's external environment. The role of current changes is often emphasized in practice at the expense of potential changes; however, as many examples in this chapter attest, both are important.

- Provide critical inputs to strategic management. Understanding change is not enough. Although we urge firms to cultivate the ability to recognize and assess change, the truly valuable product of macroenvironmental analysis is its contribution to strategy.

- Facilitate and foster strategic thinking in organizations. An understanding of current and potential social, economic, political, ecological, technological, and institutional change can bring fresh viewpoints into the organization. To cite merely one example, an analysis of technology change can challenge an organization's historic assumptions about its ability to create and launch products that will be superior to those of rivals.

These benefits of macroenvironmental analysis, however, are only realized when those doing the analysis are willing to assume the difficult but necessary task of making judgments about the effects of change. The many examples cited in this chapter show that it is the role of the analyst[2] to interpret and make sense of subtle alterations of in the macroenvironment. In particular, the implications of macroenvironmental change for an organization's current and future strategies is never self evident; it is always the product or outcome of the judgments of those doing the analysis.

In the following sections, we define the macroenvironment and look in detail at its major segments—social, political, technological, economic, ecological, and institutional. Next, we address how to capture macroenvironment change—how to scan, monitor, and project it. We highlight two widely used macroenvironmental analysis methodologies—scenarios and issue impact matrices. We then focus on integrating macroenvironmental analysis into strategy development and execution. We use the case of Monsanto Corporation's move from industrial chemicals (e.g., weed killers) into life sciences (such as genetically enhanced seeds) to illustrate the process and outcomes of macroenvironmental analysis (see Box 9.1).

Box 9.1

Monsanto Corporation: Moving into Life Sciences

Monsanto Corporation, headquartered in St. Louis, Missouri, has committed itself to becoming a leading player in the emerging "life sciences" industry. This new industry, which began to emerge as a distinctive competitive domain during the last half of the 1990s, represents a convergence of more established industries—chemistry, biotechnology, pharmaceuticals, agribusiness, and nutrition. Although many companies have announced their intention to commit significant resources to life sciences, Monsanto is one of only a few firms to dedicate itself substantially to this rapidly evolving domain. In the mid-1990s, the firm began to sell off some of its chemical businesses and then divested them completely in 1997. It also sold off its lawn and garden business and has announced its intention to dispose of its artificial sweetener business that makes well-known Equal and NutraSweet products. It has invested in excess of $8 billion in the past few years in life-sciences firms including DeKalb Genetics Corporation and Plant Breeding International Cambridge Ltd.

Genetically modified crops and seeds represent a dominant focus of Monsanto's involvement in life sciences. Gene-splicing (inserting a foreign gene into a plant's DNA) can lead to crops with new characteristics. Monsanto has succeeded in producing some of the first blockbuster products based on genetic engineering—Posilac bovine growth hormone and Roundup Ready soybeans. The growth hormone, given to cows to boost milk production, is used in roughly 30 percent of U.S. herds. The soybeans, which account for approximately half of the 1999 U.S. crop, survive spraying of Monsanto's Roundup weed killer.

UNDERSTANDING WHAT THE MACROENVIRONMENT IS

To understand the interactions between an organization and its macroenvironment, it is helpful to visualize a firm's environment as shown in Figure 9.1. According to this view, a business operates within several layers or levels of environment.

The *task environment* encompasses the set of customers, suppliers, and competitors that constitute the firm's immediate environment. Much of the day-to-day operations of a firm involves activities or decisions related to its task environment. Thus, a firm may negotiate a new source of capital with potential investors, enter into a component codevelopment agreement with a supplier, or upgrade its service to a particular group of customers. The task environment is more or less specific to a firm, and is not necessarily shared by its competitors.

The *industry or competitive environment* surrounds the task environment. The industry environment is the focus of Chapter 8. Environmental factors at the industry level directly affect most competitors, but not everyone feels them with the same intensity. For example, the threat of new entrants may be a major concern of competitors in one segment on an industry but other segments may be much less threatened.

The *general environment,* or macroenvironment, the broadest and most complex area affecting an organization, is the focus of this chapter. Fortunately, an organization doesn't need to analyze every facet of the social,

FIGURE 9.1   Levels of environment.

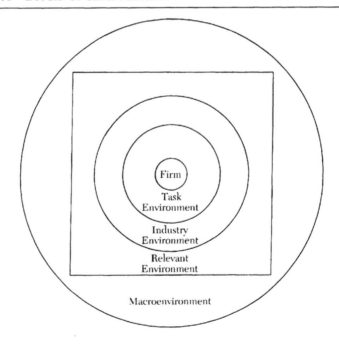

political, technological, economic, ecological, and institutional environments. Indeed, it would be well nigh impossible to do so. Instead, experienced practitioners narrow the areas of interest to their organization to the "relevant environment" described in Figure 9.1.

The relevant environment defines the boundaries of the general environment for analytical purposes based on the key aspects that significantly affect a particular organization. For example, a consumer goods firm and an industrial products firm may define their relevant environments quite differently. Demographics and lifestyles may be of crucial importance to the consumer goods firm but of lesser relevance to the industrial goods firm. All definitions of the relevant environment require judgments, and as noted at the beginning of this chapter, such judgments are necessary for engaging in worthwhile analysis.

Segments of the Macroenvironment

To facilitate analysis, we identify six major segments of the macroenvironment: (1) social, (2) economic, (3) political, (4) technological, (5) ecological, and (6) institutional. The principal elements of each segment are briefly noted in Box 9.2.

The *social* segment includes demographics, lifestyles, and social values. An analysis of this segment considers shifts in the structure and mobility of the population, lifestyle variations, and social values transformations. Changes in the social environment directly affect total market potential for many products, especially consumer products.

The *economic* environment is the general set of economic conditions facing all industries—the aggregation of all the markets where goods and services are exchanged for payment. Economic activity is reflected in levels and patterns of industrial output, consumption, income and savings, investment, and productivity. Changes in the overall level of economic activity directly affect supply and demand in almost all industries.

The *political* segment includes all electoral processes as well as the administrative, regulatory, and judicial institutions that make and execute society's laws, regulations, and rules. This is perhaps the most turbulent segment of the macroenvironment. Few industries are unaffected by change in the electoral, legislative, regulatory, and judicial milieu.

The *technological* segment refers to the level and direction of technological progress or advancements taking place in a society including new products, processes, or materials; general level of scientific activity; and advances in fundamental science (e.g., physics).

The *ecological* segment encompasses the physical and natural resources within a region—the land, sea, air, water, flora, and fauna. Many firms have had to invest millions of dollars to avoid polluting or degrading the physical environment (such as the installation of technology to reduce or eliminate air pollution) or to rectify the consequences of not paying attention to their local

---

Box 9.2

Key Elements of the Macroenvironmental Segments

Social Environment

The social environment consists of demographics, lifestyles, and social values.

Demographics may be segmented into several elements:

Population Size. The total number of people in a given geographic area.

Age Structure. The number of people within different age bands such as 0–10 years and 11–20 years.

Geographic Distribution. Growth rates within and shifts of population across geographic regions.

Ethnic Mix. The mix, size, and growth rates of ethnic groups.

Income Levels. The amount and growth rates of income across demographic/lifestyle groups such as family types, age levels, and geographic regions.

Lifestyles may also be segmented:

Household Formation. The composition, type, rate of change, and size of households.

Work. Whether people work, what type of work, where they work, expectations about work, how long they work.

Education. Type and level of education.

Consumption. What people purchase or consume (or do not purchase and consume).

Leisure. How people spend their spare or nonworking time.

Social Values may be broken into the following values:

Political Values. Reflected in how people vote; how they feel about major political and social issues such as support for the military, abortion, and preservation of the environment.

Social Values. Reflected in attitudes toward work, leisure, participation in organizations, acceptance of other groups, acceptance of social habits (e.g., smoking).

Technological Values. Reflected in acceptance of new technologies, choices between costs of technologies and their benefits.

Economic Values. Reflected in pursuit of economic growth, trade-offs between economic progress and its social costs.

Economic Environment

The economic environment refers to the nature and direction of the economy in which business operates. The following two types of change are especially worthy of emphasis:

Structural Change. Refers to change within and across sectors of the economy such as movements in economic activity from some types of industries to

---

Box 9.2 *(Continued)*

others (such as a decline in steel industry and growth in the electronics industries) and movements in the relationships among key economic variables such as the relative levels of imports and exports as a percentage of gross national product (GNP).

Cyclical Change. Refers to upswings and downswings in the general level of economic activity such as movement in GNP, interest rates, inflation, consumer prices, housing starts, and industrial investment.

Political Environment

The political environment may be segmented into formal and informal systems.

Formal System. The formal system consists of the electoral process as well as the institutions of government: the executive branch, the legislatures, the judiciary, and the regulatory agencies.

The Informal System. Refers to the arenas outside government in which political activity occurs. It includes local community settings and the media.

Technological Environment

The technological environment involves the development of knowledge and its application in "how to do things." It can be broadly segmented into the following domains:

Research. Fundamental or basic research that seeks the principles and relationships underlying knowledge, often termed invention.

Development. Transforms knowledge into some prototype form, often termed innovation.

Operations. Puts the knowledge to use in a form that can be adopted by others, often termed diffusion.

Ecological Environment

The ecological environment involves the stock of the physical and natural resources within a region. It can be broadly segmented into the following domains:

Physical. Land, air, water, and sea.

Nature. Flora and fauna.

Institutional Environment

The institutional environment involves the physical and intellectual infrastructure and all the institutions associated with them. It has the following domains:

Physical Infrastructure. Transportation such as roads, rail, and water systems.

Communications. Mail, phone, and other electronic systems.

FIGURE 9.2   A model of the macroenvironment.

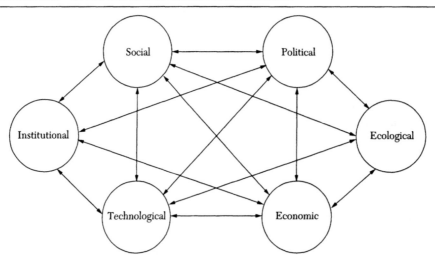

ecology (such as chemical firms creating toxic waste dumps or manufacturing firms fouling rivers and polluting the local water supply).

The *institutional* segment focuses on both the physical and intellectual infrastructure and all the institutions associated with it. The physical infrastructure includes both transportation (e.g., road, rail, and water systems) and communication (such as the mail, phone, and other electronic systems). The intellectual infrastructure comprises scientific enterprises, universities, and other intelligence-generating organizations.

In the model presented in Figure 9.2, multiple linkages exist among the segments; every segment is related to and affects every other segment. The macroenvironment ultimately can only be understood as an interrelated system of segments. However, the model does not specify the types of linkages; these are deemed to be the output of a process of analysis and the judgments of analysts. Analysts discern the key linkages during their efforts to scan, monitor, and project and assess macroenvironmental change. Monsanto's move into life sciences illustrates the breadth and depth of the analysis that can be conducted within each segment as well as the potential interactions across them (see Box 9.3).

ANALYZING THE MACROENVIRONMENT

This section offers a framework of analysis to identify, track, project, and assess change in the macroenvironment. It consists of four analysis stages:

1. *Scanning* the environment to detect ongoing and emerging change.
2. *Monitoring* specific environmental trends and patterns to determine their evolution.

Box 9.3

Macroenvironmental Change Confronting Monsanto as It Moves into Life Sciences

Social. The demographics of most agricultural communities in the United States and Europe are undergoing dramatic change: fewer farmers, larger farms, and so forth. Farm families desire the same standard of living as they observe in urban communities. Social value clashes have come to the fore around the desirability of bioengineered crops and food.

Economic. The economics of farming has changed significantly over the past 20 years in both Europe and the United States. Farmers are actively seeking every possible means to augment their profitability. Both the input and output markets in agriculture are affected. For example, according to the USDA (United States Department of Agriculture) 36 percent of corn and 44 percent of soy crops were produced from genetically modified seeds.

Political. Bioengineered food, crops and plants are emerging as hot political issues. Social activist, community, and some scientific groups have organized protests, demonstrations, and political activity to protest the sale of bioengineered foods, the patenting of seeds that could produce plant crops that are themselves infertile. Some critics have used the label "Terminator" technology for such seeds. Opponents of bioengineered food and crops in Europe have reached such a fever pitch that many biotechnology companies and food firms have given assurances that will not market (and are not now marketing) bioengineered products.

Technological. Many firms are now committing extensive resources to a new wave of research and development in bioengineering. These R&D initiatives reflect a convergence of many heretofore relatively independent industries: biotechnology, agribusiness, nutrition, chemistry, and pharmaceuticals. The resultant "crop sciences" involving genetic manipulation of plant and seed promise new product breakthroughs.

Ecological. Some scientists, social commentators, regulatory bodies, and consumer groups have raised extensive concerns about the environmental impact of bioengineered crops, plants, and food. They have noted many risks associated with altering the genetic makeup of plants could accidentally give rise to genetically altered weeds and pests that prove difficult, if not impossible, to control.

Institutional. Changes in the telecommunications infrastructure, even in less advanced countries, now allow farmers to rapidly upgrade how they perform key tasks such as seed planting through the use of global positioning technologies. Educational institutions in many countries are expending considerable efforts to improving the knowledge and skill levels of those involved in agribusiness.

3. *Projecting* the future direction of environmental changes.

4. *Assessing* current and future environmental changes for their strategy and organizational implications.

For a case in point, at each stage we look at how Monsanto, a major chemical company that elected to transform itself into life sciences company, would have to deal with its macroenvironmental issues.

Scanning

Organizations scan the environment to identify indicators or precursors of current and potential change and emerging issues in the social, economic, political, technological, ecological and institutional environments. Monsanto should scan each macroenvironmental segment (see Box 9.3) for indicators of current and emerging change. Scanning the social and political milieu may alert Monsanto to the change in attitudes and behaviors toward bioengineered products in both the United States and Europe. Scanning the technological environment should draw the firm's attention to current and emerging developments in research and development domains such as subspecialties within chemistry. Scanning the economic environment should alert Monsanto to changes in the way farmers purchase inputs (e.g., genetically enhanced seeds) and sell their finished products (e.g., corn or wheat with special characteristics in demand by the market). Many of the critical questions that guide scanning and monitoring are noted in Table 9.1.

TABLE 9.1   Guiding Questions in Scanning and Monitoring

1. What are the relevant segments of the macroenvironment?
   - Which segments are most important?
   - Which areas within each segment are most important?

2. What are the current and emerging trends?
   - What is each trend?
   - What are the emerging trends?

3. What are the current and emerging patterns?
   - What are the specific patterns?
   - What trends contribute to each pattern?
   - What patterns seem to be on the horizon?

4. What are the indicators of these trends and patterns?
   - What indicator is associated with each trend?
   - Are two or more indicators related to a specific trend?

5. What is the historic evolution of these trends and patterns?
   - How has each indicator changed over time?
   - What is the time period?

6. What is the degree of change within these patterns?
   - Is the degree of change minor or major?
   - How different is the expected change from the present state or a past state?

Scanning alerts an organization to future conflicts or opportunities so that it will have as much leadtime as possible to consider and adopt alternative courses of action. Indeed, the most successful scanning draws an organization's attention to the definitive points in the future—both fortuitous and calamitous—well before other organizations understand their significance.

Scanning feeds *early indicators* of potential technology change into the monitoring and forecasting process. Once an organization has become aware of a potential change, it can begin to monitor its development, project its evolution, and examine its implications.

Often scanning unearths indicators of change that require *immediate action*. For example, a scan may detect that a rival is on the verge of marketing a product based on breakthrough technologies. After pharmaceutical giant Bayer Corporation invested $700 million in a state-of-the-art factory to distill a protein needed to treat hemophilia, its tiny rival Avigen Inc. performed a preliminary test of an injectable gene therapy that could make Bayer's plant obsolete. Should Bayer go ahead with its planned $300 million expansion of its high-tech factory?

Monitoring

Monitoring involves tracking specific macroenvironmental change over time. Analysts observe the evolution of trends (e.g., demographic, economic, and ecological indicators), sequences of events (e.g., technology developments, political election results), or streams of activities (e.g., the actions of regulatory agencies).

The intent of monitoring is very different from that of scanning. Analysts monitor to assemble enough data to discern the emergence of patterns. These patterns are likely to be composed of several new trends. For example, an emergent lifestyle pattern may include alterations in entertainment, education, consumption, work habits, and domestic location preferences.

As part of the monitoring process, analysts should update the organization on the hunches and intuitive judgments about weak signals observed during scanning. These hunches and judgments need to be tracked for confirmation, elaboration, modification, and validation or invalidation.

In the monitoring phase, the data search is more focused and more systematic than during scanning. As monitoring continues, trends accumulate into patterns. A picture of change in progress that may have been hazy and uncertain when first uncovered during scanning will be better understood as monitoring progresses.

Because of its many lines of business, Monsanto will need to monitor indicators in each of the six macroenvironmental segments. For example, it might watch the emergence of new social, community, and consumer groups opposed to bioengineered products as well as the types of activities they engage in as one input to determining the breadth and depth of the social and political antagonism toward bioengineered foods and farm inputs. Monitoring specific technology developments in and around farming such as the speed of adoption of agricultural software and connections to weather satellite information systems would provide key insights into change in farm productivity. Monsanto might also monitor a set of economic variables related to farming such as the changing size of farms, stocks of supplies (e.g., fertilizer, chemicals, seed) going through distribution channels and prices of farm products on futures exchanges. Monitoring change in the institutional milieu—such as plans within different countries to upgrade road, rail and telephone systems, and agronomy education—might help Monsanto anticipate which countries are more likely to witness an upsurge in economic growth.

Projecting

As is evident in every chapter of this book, to make successful strategic decisions, an organization must develop the capability to look at possible futures and think creatively about responding to them. As a start, organizations need a picture of what is likely to take place in their external environment. The intent of projecting is to develop plausible projections of the *scope, direction, speed, and intensity* of macroenvironmental change. Many typical foci are shown in Table 9.2.

A few useful terms describe the characteristics of the change pattern:

- *Scope* refers to the substance of what is being projected: whether it is a narrowly defined trend such as the evolution of a particular performance characteristic of a specific technology or a broadly conceived pattern such as the emergence of a major core technology.
- *Direction* describes the vector of the specific trend and pattern. For example, interest rates may be going up or down; more or fewer individuals may be following a particular lifestyle.
- *Speed* describes how quickly or slowly a trend or pattern is projected to move.
- *Intensity* describes the strength of the forces propelling a trend or pattern.

There are two distinct types of projecting. The first involves *simple projections.* These projections are based on evident trends (they reflect data over some time period) and can be expected (with some margin of error) to continue unabated for some period of time. For example, many demographic trends, such as the number of children entering high school, or the number of people reaching retirement age can be projected with reasonable accuracy. To cite another example, it is often possible to project technological trends in terms of the rates of diffusion of new products, or evolution of a performance characteristic.

The second type of projecting creates *alternative futures.* These are based on fresh interpretations of current trends or new insights regarding events that may take place or that may be made to happen by the firm itself or by other entities such as competitors, customers, suppliers, social and community groups, or

TABLE 9.2   Sample Macroenvironmental Foci of Forecasting

Social

1. How will the demographic structure (the number of people in different age groups) shift over the next 20 to 40 years?
2. What lifestyle shifts might occur as those presently in the age group 25–40 move into the age group 40–55?
   - How will the composition of their household change?
   - How will their consumption patterns change?
   - How will their work patterns change?
   - What changes will occur in how they use their leisure time?
3. How will social values change?
   - Will there be an increase in political conservatism?
   - Will more people manifest agreement with reduced military spending?
   - Will people be more or less willing to bear the costs of curtailing and eliminating pollution?

Economic

1. What will be the level of inflation over the next 3 years?
2. Will GNP increase or decrease over the next 5 years?
3. Which service industries will grow and decline in the next decade?

Political

1. Which political parties will gain/lose strength in the next two or three elections?
2. What significant shifts will occur in governmental policies, laws, and regulations pertaining to specific industries?
3. What decisions at different levels in the judicial system might affect different industries?
4. Will existing social/political movements such as consumerism and environmentalism gain/lose public support?

Technological

1. When and how might recent breakthroughs in basic research lead to commercial products?
2. What linkages among which technologies would have to occur before a specific technological event or breakthrough occurs (e.g., high-definition TV)?
3. What might be some new applications of currently available technologies?

Ecological

1. In which countries will environmental pollution continue to worsen?
2. What events might give rise to an "ecological disaster" and how and why might they occur?

Institutional

1. What bottlenecks might occur in different elements (road, rail, sea) of the transportation system?
2. What changes might occur in telephony over the next 5 years?
3. How might new roles emerge for universities and other centers of learning over the next decade?

governmental agencies. Some leading corporations use sets of scenarios to consider a spectrum of possible alternative futures—a topic to which we return in the next section.

To project changes in the life sciences field, Monsanto might develop simple projections around trends in demographic data (e.g., change in the average age of farm owners), economic data (e.g., changes in farm size or output per farm), social values (number of individual groups opposing bioengineered food), and technology (e.g., advancement in specific technology developments). Monsanto might also develop scenarios of specific alternative futures.

Assessing

To perform assessment, analysts identify and evaluate how and why the ongoing and anticipated changes in the macroenvironment affect strategic management of the organization. During assessment, the frame of reference moves from understanding and interpreting the environment—the focus of scanning, monitoring, and projecting—to specifying what that understanding means for the organization. In linking macroenvironmental analysis and strategic management, the critical question is, What are likely to be the positive or negative impacts of macroenvironmental change on the organization's current and future strategies?

Assessing macroenvironmental change, may force Monsanto to address serious threats to its planned moves into the life sciences.

To explain the concepts of scanning, monitoring, projecting, and assessment, we have introduced them as if they were distinct analysis activities. In practice however, they are intertwined. For example, scanning often generates surprises and indicators of change that lead firms to assess their impact on the industry and the firm's future strategies. Projecting requires initial assessment to ensure that the organization expends its efforts on the most critical issues.

SCENARIOS AND ISSUE IMPACT MATRICES FOR STRATEGY DEVELOPMENT

Many organizations use *scenario development to* conceive and refine sets of *alternative futures*. Such scenarios allow mangers to simulate operating in distinctly different plausible and relevant futures.[3] They typically include trends, patterns, and events, pertinent assumptions, and the dynamics that lead from the present state of the environment to the future state.

Various types serve three purposes:

1. They provide an opportunity for a firm to examine the future by searching for and postulating linkages among different aspects of the macroenvironment. Managers can test how current strategies would work under varied conditions and consider alternative strategies.

2. They serve as an explicit context for identifying assumptions, clarifying perceptions about the environment, and assessing risks and implications of macroenvironmental change.
3. Scenarios also provide a context that allows managers to test other environmental analysis techniques such as Delphi and simulations.

Developing Scenarios

Although there are several techniques for developing macroenvironmental scenarios, the following steps typify how most organizations construct them:

Identify the Strategic Decision Context

Because scenarios serve as a context for analyzing the strategic decisions facing the organization, they should examine how those decisions would play out under a complete range of relevant conditions. Monsanto's decision context might be stated as follows: Given its desire to move into life sciences, what strategies ought the firm pursue?

Identify Individual Macroenvironmental Forces

This step requires managers and others to identify each individual "driving force," or source of change within each macroenvironmental segment, that might affect the firm's competitive future. One way to sharpen this analysis is to ask the following question: What change is occurring or might occur in each macroenvironmental segment that currently affects or could affect the industry or competitive landscape in which the firm competes or wants to compete? Thus, Monsanto would lay out systematically the individual driving forces within each macroenvironmental segment. For example, it should identify all the relevant technology trends unearthed by its scanning and monitoring efforts.

Identify and Analyze Key Macroenvironmental Forces

Individual macroenvironmental forces are always interrelated in multiple ways. Thus, managers and others must sift through the individual forces to identify relevant patterns and to determine which patterns might have the most critical impact on the firm's competitive landscape. Typical questions to consider are:

- To what extent are individual forces reinforcing, opposing, or disjointed?
- In what ways are patterns reinforcing, opposing, or disjointed?

Monsanto might detect a pattern involving the emergence of new social, community, and scientific groups deeply and profoundly opposed to the development and use of bioengineered products.

Ask Fundamental What-If Questions

The ultimate content of scenarios always stems from asking what-if questions. Monsanto managers might ask:

- What if social, political, and ecological forces coalesce to severely retard society's acceptance of bioengineered products? (Let's call this the Bio-Repressed scenario.)
- What if an abundance of scientific evidence emerges that convinces the public and regulatory authorities that bioengineered products are not only safe but that they contribute significantly to human well-being? (Let's call this the Bio-Excited scenario.)
- What if economic conditions in and around farming continue to deteriorate in all major geographic regions of the world leading to worldwide malaise in agribusiness? (Let's call this the Economic Malaise scenario.)

Reflection on these questions leads to the choice of specific scenarios that merit development.

Develop Scenario Plot and Logic

The next step involves developing a story or plot that describes how a scenario would unfold; how we could get from the world of today to the world as delineated at the end of the scenario (a point in time that scenario developers refer to as the end-state). For example, Monsanto might detail what would have to happen for a Bio-Excited world to unfold: what types of research breakthroughs would occur; how the research might be conducted; who would develop them; how they might be communicated to the public; which groups and organizations might support the research findings; and so on. The plot allows the scenario development team—composed of business unit managers, functional specialists, and various experts—to consider what sequence of events would have to happen for a scenario to occur.

Elaborate the End-States

Every scenario results in a description of the relevant world at the end of the time period covered by the scenario—the end-state. Many firms develop detailed economic scenarios describing what the North American economy might look like given distinctly different plots over a 5- or 10-year time period. End-states for the three Monsanto scenarios previously noted—Bio-Repressed, Bio-Excited, and Economic Malaise—are described briefly in Box 9.4.

Implications for Strategic Decisions

Scenarios only generate value for an organization when decision makers use them for the following purposes:

- To identify potential opportunities that could serve as the focus of new strategy alternatives.
- To identify threats to current or planned strategies.
- To test one or more strategies across a set of scenarios.

Box 9.4
Monsanto Scenarios

Bio-Repressed Scenario

In this end-state, regulations in most North American and European countries prohibit the sale of most bioengineered food products. Despite some scientific evidence to the contrary, consumer and many social activist groups vociferously portray the potential dangers of foods "that are unnatural." Some lead distribution channels (including supermarket chains and agricultural supply providers) refuse to handle bioengineered products or the materials required to produce them. A number of companies that had initially invested heavily to move into "life sciences" have severely curtailed, and in a few cases, eliminated entirely their investment programs. A small set of companies continue to conduct research but are careful not to be drawn into public discussion about it. Yet the debate over the benefits of bioengineered products continues to rage.

Bio-Excited Scenario

In this end-state, many firms have launched new bioengineered products and other firms are committing extensive R&D resources in search of new scientific breakthroughs. New claims appearing in the popular and trade press almost on a daily basis announce potential relationships between bioengineered products and health improvement in humans and extensive new efficiencies in crop production. Although regulatory authorities in both Europe and North America are executing rigorous review processes for each bioengineered "breakthrough," they are allowing firms to conduct extensive product trials in carefully controlled experiments. Informed by new labeling laws requiring full disclosure of which products are bioengineered, consumers are increasingly accepting such products.

Economic Malaise

In this end-state, declining economic conditions dominate agribusiness. Farm incomes continue to decline; productivity remains stagnant at best in all sectors of the farming industry; profits decline in all the supply (e.g., fertilizer and pesticides) and distribution industries associated with farming. Farming organizations, however, voice strong support in favor of bioengineering breakthroughs that would result in new crops or greater productivity associated with existing crops. Most consumerist and some environmental groups remain strongly opposed to application of the life sciences to food production, but governmental agencies are taking a "wait-and-see" attitude: They are willing to support R&D and to test products in use in limited trials.

- To develop a common language to facilitate management of a chaotic and rapidly evolving environment.

Companies in industries as diverse as telecommunications, software, oil and gas, and pharmaceuticals use scenarios depicting alternative competitive and macroenvironmental futures to identify, develop, and test a range of strategies.

Monsanto might ask what strategies (what scope, posture, and goals, as outlined in Chapter 1) might be appropriate if each scenario were to result in the end-states briefly outlined in Box 9.4. If the world depicted in the Bio-Depressed end-state were to materialize, Monsanto might have to seriously consider pulling back from many of its investment commitments to develop new products as well as possibly divesting some of its existing product lines or significantly reducing its support for them. Consideration of the strategy implications of this scenario would sensitize Monsanto managers to the need to critically monitor the indicators of the emergence of the Bio-Depressed world.

Issue Impact Matrices

Those macroenvironmental changes or patterns that have already had an impact on the organization's strategies or those that are judged to possess the potential to do so are deemed to be *issues* for the organization.

Identifying crucial issues and ranking them necessarily entails making judgments. Questions such as those posed in Table 9.3 can help managers to eliminate all but the most important issues and set priorities.

Issues can be conveniently arrayed on a probability-impact matrix (see Figure 9.3) with a separate matrix being prepared for each of the three planning periods: short-, medium-, and long-term. Although the scoring system for this assessment of probability and impact can be simple or complex, a general categorizing of high, medium, or low is usually sufficient. The merits of the matrix display are that it provides a *comprehensive, at-a-glance array of issues*, orders them in a manner that facilitates discussion and planning, and places them in time frames appropriate to the allocation of resources and management attention.

LINKING MACROENVIRONMENTAL ANALYSIS TO STRATEGY DEVELOPMENT AND EXECUTION

Before describing the methodology of the assessment phase of macroenvironmental analysis, it is valuable to reiterate three major points about the role of macroenvironmental analysis in strategic management:

1. Macroenvironmental analysis is useful only to the extent that it results in strategy-related actions and decisions.
2. The integration of expectation of change and preparation for it does not just happen; it must be made to happen. Change must be managed;

TABLE 9.3   Assessing Macroenvironmental Analysis Implications

1. How might each change (or issue) affect the organization's industry?
   - General expectations about the industry?
   - Emergence of new products?
   - Sales of existing products?
   - Entry and exit of competitors?
   - Emergence of new suppliers?
   - Entry and penetration of substitute products?

2. How might each change (or issue) affect the organization's more immediate task environment?
   - Demand by existing customers?
   - Changes in existing competitors' strategies?
   - Changes in suppliers' strategies?

3. What might be the implications of each change (or issue) for the organization's current strategies?
   - Change in existing products?
   - Change in existing target market segments?
   - Change in how the firm competes?
   - Change in the firm's current goals?

4. How might each change affect the organization's future strategy choices and their execution?
   - Potential new products?
   - Potential new customers?
   - Potential new ways of competing?
   - Change in strategy choice criteria?
   - Need for new organization structure?
   - Need for new operating processes?

choices and alternatives need to be weighed, the consequences and operating issues involved in actions need to be examined, and resources need to be allocated.

3. Integration needs to take place for short-, medium-, and long-term horizons.

FIGURE 9.3   Cross-impact matrix: An illustrative structure.

Probability and Timing of Events	Event 1	Event 2	Event 3	Event 4
Event 1 (Prob., Timing)				
Event 2 (Prob., Timing)				
Event 3 (Prob., Timing)				
Event 4 (Prob., Timing)				

Corporate Strategy

Macroenvironmental analysis can influence corporate level strategy in at least three ways: (1) patterns of diversification, (2) resource allocation, and (3) risk-return trade-offs.

Patterns of Diversification

Diversification represents the intent of an organization to move into product-market segments unrelated to its existing businesses. As illustrated in Chapter 2, an organization can pursue a number of distinct approaches to diversification, each of which is influenced by both the opportunities confronting the firm as well as its own resource profile.

There are at least three ways in which macroenvironmental change can influence an organization's pattern of diversification. First, corporations differ with regard to the synergies they try to exploit across their business units. These synergies could be upset or enhanced by macroenvironmental change. A number of leading consumer product and food firms such as Proctor & Gamble and Heinz are now experiencing difficulties in maintaining and leveraging the marketing synergies that historically have been central to their corporate strategies. Changing demographics, lifestyles, social values, and increasingly intense rivalry left many consumers increasingly price conscious. As a result, these firms are finding it harder to build and sustain an image of superior "value for money" around their brand names.

Second, the different patterns of diversification developed in Chapter 2 are susceptible to different vulnerabilities. Change in the macroenvironment may amplify these vulnerabilities. For example, a diversification venture based on linkages across certain types of technologies will be at risk if competing technologies gain favor with customers. As a case in point, defense industry firms that diversified around their core technological capabilities now find many of the businesses they developed in the past decade suffering from the same difficulties as their historic core business: a lack of demand due to the end of the Cold War.

Third, macroenvironmental change may open up or close out existing patterns of diversification. For example, political change in form of a new administration often affects enforcement of regulations governing mergers and acquisitions. Thus, mergers that were barred by one administration may be allowed by the next government.

Resource Allocation

Macroenvironmental change has important implications for corporate resource allocation across business units. This is so for at least two reasons. First, as noted, macroenvironmental change gives rise to differential product opportunities across business units. Some business units may need an infusion of resources to exploit these opportunities. The emergence of public antipathy toward bioengineered foods may cause Monsanto to switch resources from its initial commitment to the biosciences to other product sectors. Second, global macroenvironmental change opens opportunities in new geographic areas. In the 1990s, a number of corporations dramatically increased the resources they committed to a strategy of "dipping their toe" in Chinese markets.

Risk-Return Trade-Offs

Political, economic, technological, and social shifts can determine the returns and risks of existing and potential portfolios of business units. Anticipated changes in key economic indicators such as interest rates, money supply, inflation, unemployment levels, and gross national product often critically affect projected returns in both existing businesses and potential new businesses. To cite merely one example, an industry leader in building materials and supplies whose sales always closely correlate with the overall state of the economy, has seen its profits oscillate largely in line with gross national output over the past 20 years. Many technology-related corporations have had to come to grips with the increasing rate of obsolescence of some of their major product lines. Not surprisingly, these firms search for ways to leverage their existing technology into product enhancements or even new products. Many firms now do extensive political risk assessments of foreign countries as an input to initial or continued investment. Some firms have recently announced they plan to scale back investments in Russia due to its political and social turmoil and concerns about their employees' personal safety.

Business Unit Strategy

Macroenvironmental analysis provides critical intelligence in the formulation and execution of business unit strategy in two distinct but related ways: its effects on industry structure and evolution need to be assessed; its implications for various inputs to strategy development can then be assessed.

Implications for Industry Analysis

At the level of industry or competitive analysis, changes in the macroenvironment may affect:

- The boundaries of the industry.
- The forces shaping industry structure, such as suppliers, customers, rivalry, and product substitution, and entry barriers.
- Strategic groups.
- The key success factors.
- The general expectations within the industry.

These elements provide the competitive context within which business unit strategy is developed.

Macroenvironmental change can threaten the *survival of an industry* or specific industry segments. This is perhaps most evident in the way that technological change can obsolete substantial segments of an industry. As an example, advances in the frozen foods technologies have reshaped major sectors of the food industry. For another example, technology developments facilitating linkages among voice, data, and images reconfigured what used to be three distinct industry sectors (called telecommunications, televisions receivers and optics) into today's multimedia business.

Macroenvironmental change directly influences each of the *forces shaping the industry structure:* suppliers, customers, new entrants, and substitute products (see Chapter 8). It can affect the number, type, and location of *suppliers,* the products they offer customers, supply costs, and the competitive dynamics of supplier industries. Global macroenvironmental change has dramatically restructured the supply sector in many industries. To cite one example, the political, economic, and social change that has occurred in Korea and other Asian countries has spawned new competitors for American and European firms that previously dominated many raw material and component businesses.

Changes in demographics, lifestyles, and social values can affect the size, characteristics, and behavior of the *customer base* in an industry or industry segment. Changes in lifestyles and related social values such as greater emphasis on personal health and physical attractiveness generated the necessary consumer base for the array of products now associated with jogging, hiking, and home exercise.

Product substitution and *new entrants* are most often driven by technological change. In the computer and software industries, voice recognition software is likely to replace many types of current software.

Macroenvironmental change differentially impacts *various strategic groups within an industry.* Changes, to the extent that they affect customers' preferences, suppliers' capabilities, substitute products, and so forth, could potentially enlarge or decimate the product-market arenas in which different strategic groups operate. Perhaps more importantly, macroenvironmental changes may afford opportunities for firms in a specific strategic group to overcome mobility barriers, that is, the barriers inhibiting a firm from moving from one strategic group to another. Deregulation of the airline industry in the late 1970s had an adverse impact on longer-haul airlines relative to those with shorter hauls, thus facilitating restructuring of the routes of larger airlines and the capturing of these by smaller airlines.

Macroenvironmental change can potentially affect the *key success factors* in almost any industry or industry segment. At a minimum, such change needs to be assessed in terms of its impact on factors such as desired product quality, product functionality or performance criteria (e.g., reliability and durability), relative cost positions, image and reputation, and resource commitments for major product-market segments. For example, many industry sectors that depended on door-to-door sales have suffered severely due to the rapid increase in the number of women in the full-time workforce.

Issue-impact matrices are a useful means of analysis. These matrices detail the effect of each one of the selected set of macroenvironmental issues on industry-level factors. Matrix displays of the type shown in Figure 9.3 facilitate assessments of these impacts. These assessments should include not only the general direction of change but its timing and intensity. Such assessments help form a common understanding of industry change and prepare managers to formulate responsive business strategies.

Linkage to Business Unit Strategy

At the level of business unit strategy, macroenvironmental analysis together with industry and competitor analysis needs to be assessed for the impact on business unit strategy in these terms:

- Business definition.
- Assumptions.
- General strategic thrust.

Few concepts are more central to business unit strategy than *business definition*. There are three critical elements in any firm's business definition: (1) What customers does the business serve? (2) What customer needs are satisfied? (3) What technologies are employed to satisfy these customer needs? Each of these elements can be affected directly or indirectly by macroenvironmental change. Many businesses have found that demographic and lifestyle changes have altered not just their served or target customer base but also customer needs. The growth in the elderly market has caused all kinds of businesses from insurance and financial services to food and entertainment businesses to either introduce new product offerings or significantly reshape existing products. As a major segment of the population ages, new opportunities to fill its needs and wants develop and other promising opportunities wane.

Because strategy is about winning in the future marketplace, *assumptions* about the current and future environment always underlie any strategy. Key macroenvironmental assumptions (as distinct from industry assumptions) might include expectations about shifts in governmental policies, changes in technology developments, and demographic and lifestyle shifts. These assumptions need to be anchored in a thorough analysis of the macroenvironment surrounding the industry if they are to be realistic and thus useful for strategy formulation.

Because of the importance of macroenvironmental assumptions, the merits of identifying and challenging them need to be emphasized:

1. By defining assumptions, an analyst is compelled to make a critical assessment of macroenvironmental change. It is not merely enough to identify

prevailing change. Assumptions emphasize the importance of projecting and assessing the future direction of change.

2. Consideration of assumptions facilitates and fosters sensitivity analysis. Every strategy alternative is always vulnerable to environmental change. Consideration of assumptions necessarily entails asking what macroenvironmental changes, as noted earlier, might most negatively affect each strategy alternative.

3. Assumption analysis frequently serves to heighten awareness of macroenvironmental change and its importance to strategic management.

Finally, macroenvironmental analysis must be linked to the business unit strategic thrusts identified in Chapter 3. This linkage is related to business definition and assumptions discussed earlier. For example, a market share building thrust presumes some relevant business definition as well as assumptions pertaining to customers, suppliers, new entrants, substitute products. Thus, macroenvironmental change through its impact on industry elements may signal the need for a change in strategy thrust.

Global Strategy

Macroenvironmental analysis is an important input into several global strategy questions: (1) Choice of markets to enter, (2) mode of entry, (3) location of operations.

Choice of Markets to Enter

Market entry into different regions of the world always needs to be preceded by macroenvironmental analysis. Prevailing and anticipated conditions in any single macroenvironmental milieu—social, economic, political, technological, ecological, and institutional—may critically affect the attractiveness of the market in any single country or region. The current legal and institutional context in many countries provides little protection for many firms' intellectual property. The emergence of democratic political processes in many central European countries after the fall of the Berlin wall has made them increasingly attractive markets for many U.S. and European firms which previously had done little if any business in this region. Some firms only decided to enter or actively pursue sales in many South American markets when specific economic conditions dramatically changed during the course of the 1990s. When inflation declined from astronomical levels (in some instances greater than 100 per cent per year) to much more tolerable levels of 10 to 20 per cent per year, many South American countries became far more attractive as places in which to do business.

Political relations between countries and regions can also affect the choice of markets to enter. Free trade agreements such as NAFTA (North American Free Trade Agreement) or trade disagreements (e.g., the recurring disputes between the European Community and the United States) may directly impact the conditions under which products are allowed into specific national markets.

Mode of Entry

Macroenvironmental analysis often provides key inputs to determining the appropriate way to enter foreign markets. Key demographic and lifestyle conditions may dictate which products to provide in each market (and which products are inappropriate for each foreign market). Consider, for example, the large U.S. firm that neglected to study key demographic and lifestyle issues when it decided to export thousands of its largest kitchen refrigerators to Thailand. Only after the first shiploads of the product arrived in Thailand did the firm discover that the average home was considerably smaller than American homes. The large refrigerators failed to sell and had to be shipped back to the United States. Institutional conditions often affect key mode of entry decisions. For example, many firms have been shocked to discover that they cannot develop adequate distribution systems in China unless they are willing to have the "Red Army" be intimately involved in product distribution.

Location of Operations

Changes in local or national economies influence factor costs such as labor, raw materials, and components. A continued rise in the general standard of living in Europe has made many European countries considerably less attractive than they were in the 1970s and 1980s as a location for cheap(er) labor and lower factor costs. A dramatic shift in the monetary and fiscal policies executed by the Malaysian government in 1997–1998 (e.g., controlling the flow of capital into and out of the country) resulted in many European, U.S., and Asian firms switching manufacturing operations to other countries and refusing to do additional business in the country.

As factor costs change across different countries and regions, firms move operations from one country to another and devote considerable attention to developing linkages between operations in different countries. Relationships between countries or regions may also affect organizational choices.

Political Strategy

Chapter 7 details the linkages between key elements of macroenvironmental change and political strategy. Our only intent here is to emphasize that macroenvironmental change gives rise to issues, affects stakeholders and their demands, and influences the arenas in which political strategy is played out.

SUMMARY

Macroenvironmental analysis provides critical inputs into all phases of strategic decision making. Change is the dominant characteristic of the macroenvironment.

Without a thorough understanding of how possible futures in the social, economic, political, technological, ecological, and institutional environments may affect evolution of individual industries, an organization is highly likely to adopt strategies that do not anticipate and leverage environmental change.

NOTES

1. This chapter is largely adapted from Liam Fahey and V.K. Narayanan, *Macroenvironmental Analysis for Strategic Management* (St. Paul, MN: West, 1986).

2. Analyst is the term we use throughout this chapter to refer to any individual engaged in any facet of macroenvironmental analysis. He or she might be a line manager at any level in the organization or a staff person charged with doing macroenvironmental analysis.

3. For a more detailed discussion of scenarios, see Liam Fahey and Robert M. Randall, *Learning from the Future: Competitive Foresight Scenarios* (New York: Wiley, 1998).

A STRATEGIC ASSESSMENT OF AN ORGANIZATION'S ASSETS

10

Liam Fahey
Babson College and
Cranfield University

Understanding the competitive and macroenvironmental landscapes, as discussed in the previous two chapters, can never be sufficient by itself to develop winning strategies. Every organization requires some tangible *assets*, such as money, people, plant and equipment, and technology. Yet tangible assets can never suffice; organizations also require intangible assets such as relationships with suppliers and alliance partners, knowledge of the emerging marketplace, and image and reputation with governmental agencies and customers. Identifying, developing, and nurturing the right assets (and transforming them into capabilities and competencies, as discussed in the next chapter), constitutes one of the fundamental strategy-related challenges confronting every organization.

A good example of a company facing these challenges is Amazon.com, a web-based company that first became famous selling just books. It now wants to become an online retailer with an ever-widening range of consumer products, and it wants to do so quickly. Pursuing this goal places a heavy premium on being able to acquire, develop, and nurture many types of assets: finished products such as books, CDs, videos, toys, consumer electronics, and apparel; personnel to obtain, market, distribute, sell, and service the rapidly growing product range; warehouses to house, sort, and pack products to satisfy an escalating volume of orders; brand name and reputation so that customers will know about the firm and want to do business with it; strong relationships with alliance partners such as product suppliers; and, ever-increasing financial resources.

This chapter outlines a framework that links strategy and assets. It begins by briefly describing the role and importance of assets as an input to strategy making. It then presents a framework for identifying what is in a firm's current stock or inventory of intangible and tangible assets and for determining its asset needs. The chapter then notes critical issues that must be addressed in any analysis designed to relate strategy and assets. It concludes with a discussion of what managers must do to manage asset development programs.

THE ROLE AND IMPORTANCE OF ASSETS

What an Asset Is

For the purposes of making strategy, an asset can be defined as something that an organization *possesses* and *can leverage* for its economic purposes. To create, manage, and leverage assets effectively, an organization must first understand what they are, why it doesn't always need to own an asset, and how assets are valued.

Functioning organizations accumulate both tangible and intangible assets that can be leveraged in the service of strategy. Tangible assets include cash, plant and equipment, buildings, and people. Intangible assets include the knowledge and repertoire of skills of individuals and groups within the organization; relationships with external entities such as vendors, channels, and end-customers; and perceptions by others of the organization and its products (for example, customers that believe the organization provides better value for money than its rivals).

An organization does not need to own an asset in order to "possess it" and to leverage it. For example, Amazon.com does not own any of the portals such as Yahoo through which it reaches many of its customers. Yet the relationship with Yahoo constitutes a critical asset that Amazon.com can leverage to serve existing customers and reach new customers. Moreover, if the relationship with Yahoo was exclusive, Amazon.com would preempt this portal from becoming a distribution channel for any of its online rivals.

Assets have value if they can be leveraged for some strategy purpose.[1] For example, without doubt, Amazon.com's brand name represents one of its most critical assets. Yet that asset becomes more severely tested as Amazon.com begins to sell such diverse products as apparel, toys, flowers, and software. Customers may not see Amazon.com as the best source from which to purchase these products online.

Operating Processes: The Link between Assets and Capabilities

Many firms fail to distinguish clearly between assets and capabilities. Consequently, they have not recognized the assets they actually possess nor have they fully developed and exploited their potential capabilities. Managers bring tangible and intangible assets to life. They do so by understanding that assets always serve as inputs to work practices, procedures, or activities—what have come to be called operating processes.[2] Managers commingle capital, people, plant and equipment, knowledge, perceptions held by external entities, and relationships with them, to establish and enhance operating processes such as new product development, supply chain management; customer relationship management; personnel recruitment, retention and motivation; technology acquisition; deployment; and leveraging. One difficulty in any attempt to link assets and operating processes is that any process can always be integrated into higher level or more macro processes or broken down into further subprocesses. Thus, for example, customer relationship management might be broken down into subprocesses such as identifying potential new customers, learning about product usage and application, developing and executing service programs, enhancing trust and customer loyalty, and managing customer site visit teams.

Over time, operating processes in turn affect the stock of individual assets. For example, the new product development process typically generates increments of new knowledge about customer needs, market change, and technology developments. To cite one more example, the supply chain management process may result in extended relationships with suppliers and vendors, increased volumes of finished products, new manufacturing plant and technologies, and new pockets of knowledge about internal logistics and distribution channels. The organizational work inherent in operating processes continually reconfigures, and sometimes, transforms the stock of both tangible and intangible assets.

Capabilities constitute measures of how well the organization performs specific operating processes, or stated differently, the ability to do[3] something or other. Thus, for new product development, one might judge that a firm is able to generate a new product every year or is able to dramatically upgrade each product line every 18 months. Amazon.com might endeavor to enhance its order-processing capability by improving its order fulfillment from five to three days (the period between when the customer places an order and it is in his or her hands).

Classifying Assets

Managing and leveraging assets requires managers to somehow categorize and classify assets. Different authors, consulting firms, and organizations categorize and classify assets in quite distinct ways. One approach for any organization seeking to identify its assets begins by distinguishing between asset categories, classes, and types, as shown in Table 10.1.

An organization starts by asking itself what its principal asset categories are. This list will always include financial, human, and physical assets. Other broad asset categories such as relationships (with suppliers, distributors, customers, and governmental agencies) and knowledge (of customers, markets, and technologies) are also likely to be relevant to every organization. In the case of Amazon.com, perceptual assets such as customers' expectations of the firm and its products (e.g., Amazon.com can be depended on to provide fast, reliable, and consistent service) and suppliers' perceptions of the firm (e.g., whether Amazon.com shows loyalty to its suppliers) are an important asset category.

Considering relevant classes of assets within each category requires mangers and others to be both specific and imaginative. For example, in delineating classes within knowledge as an asset category, managers might usefully consider knowledge about various external entities or stakeholders[4] such

TABLE 10.1   Asset Categories, Classes, and Types

Categories	Classes	Types

Financial	Debt
	Equity
	Liquidity
		Debt types:
		    With different sources; short-,
		    medium-, long-term

Human	Personnel
	Skills
		Number of personnel by type:
		    Functional level
		    Different skill types

Physical	Plant
	Equipment
	Supplies
	Inventory
	Finished products
		Plant types:
		    Technology processes
		    Product focus

Knowledge	About external entities
	About process/systems
	About things/objects
		Customer knowledge:
		    Location of customers
		    Buying behaviors
		    Purchasing criteria

Political
(Relationships)
	Formal relationships with external entities
	Informal relationships with external entities
		Relationships with distribution channels:
		    In-depth partnering
		    Transactions

Perceptual	Perceptions held by external entities	Competitor perceptions:
		    The firm's products
		    The firm's willingness to
		    retaliate against rivals' moves

Organizational	Systems
	Structures
	Culture
	Decision-making processes
		Systems types:
		    Information
		    Purchasing
		    Control

as customers, channels, suppliers, competitors, governmental agencies, and community groups. They might also consider knowledge about trends and patterns in particular external domains such as demographics, leisure, social values, technology, the legislature, and the economy.

However, as illustrated throughout this chapter, analysis at the level of asset types provides essential inputs to decision making. With regard to competitors as a class of knowledge, managers might need to develop specific knowledge types: knowledge about competitors' marketplace strategies, assumptions, use of technology, and potential strategy options. Each knowledge type may make a distinct contribution to different decisions. Amazon.com, for example, has committed extensive resources to developing detailed knowledge about customers' historic purchases, buying preferences, and potential needs.[5]

Why Pay Attention to Assets?

The short answer to this question is that without developing the assets needed to create operating processes—and as a consequence, failing to foster organizational capabilities—an organization cannot (and will not) function effectively. The following concepts highlight the importance of assets as inputs to formulating and executing strategy:

- The relative importance of asset categories has changed dramatically over the past decade. No longer are "bricks and mortar"(or more generally, tangible assets) the fundamental building blocks of organization's efforts to attract, win, and retain customers.[6] Rather, perceptual assets such as reputation with customers, channels, and even competitors, and knowledge assets such as understanding how and why customers are responding to various rivals' offerings are increasingly critical to how firms compete in the marketplace.
- As is evident in Chapter 11 (and in other chapters throughout this book), assets and how well they are integrated and managed to constitute operating processes are critical ingredients of an organization's capabilities or competencies.
- The best-laid plans of many organizations have floundered because they didn't realize they lacked the key assets to implement their strategy.
- The inability to acquire, develop, or retain the requisite assets is often one of the most debilitating vulnerabilities an organization can suffer.[7]

The Increasing Importance of Intangible Assets

What accounts for the spectacular market capitalization of firms like Microsoft, Intel, Dell Computer, and of course, Amazon.com? Certainly not just the value of their physical assets such as plant, machinery, equipment, buildings, or work-in-progress (that is, products in the process of being manufactured at any one time), or even finished products in storage and inventory. Investors value their stock so highly because of such intangible assets as:

- The knowledge about products, technology, and markets presumed to be locked up inside these firms.
- The reputation and image they have created as product and technology leaders.
- The relationships they have developed with channels and end-customers reflected in their market share, brand equity, and customer satisfaction measures.
- The organizational culture and routines embedded in their organizations that enable them to stay at the leading edge of developing and executing strategies.

These intangible assets offer investors a rationale for expecting a stream of successful product solutions from these firms.

Another reason for the increasing importance of intangible assets often goes unnoticed: intangible assets add to, and in many instances, facilitate the value-generating capability of tangible assets. For example, manufacturing firms' knowledge of customers' changing tastes, buying patterns, and product preferences enable them to adapt their manufacturing technology, raw materials, and components (physical assets) to develop and provide products with the functionality, features, and style demanded by customers. Amazon.com's relationships with suppliers such as book publishers and technology portals such as Yahoo, allow it to create and supply the demand without which its investment in extensive and elaborate warehouses (a physical asset) could not produce financial returns.

Tangible assets (finance, people, and plant and equipment) will always be necessary, but intangible assets have emerged as the critical base of strategic leverage for almost all types of businesses.

Linking Strategy and Assets

A fundamental strategy question increasingly asked by senior managers is: How can this firm leverage the assets (and capabilities) it now possesses or can develop over the next few years? The process of addressing this question greatly shapes and determines the marketplace strategy managers eventually develop and execute. To answer it, an organization must be able to:

- Identify its asset stocks.
- Determine the asset stocks it needs for successful strategy development and execution.
- Identify and assess the critical attributes of current and desired asset stocks.

Box 10.1

Three Strategy Situations (Illustrative Examples)

A software firm (Evergreen Software) has decided to *reinvent* its strategy. This will involve developing a new software product that will offer corporate customers a new solution to a long-standing operational problem. The proposed product differs fundamentally from anything now available in the marketplace. It will allow customers to perform specific tasks more efficiently and more quickly. Senior managers want to get the product to the market within six to nine months.

A distribution and retail organization (Widespread) wants to *renovate* its strategy. It plans to dramatically extend the variety of product lines it carries, to move its posture from an emphasis on low prices to an emphasis on service and customer relationships, and to significantly increase the volume of purchases by each customer (share of customer).

A small industrial components supplier (IndCompSupp) has committed to incrementally extending and improving its strategy. This firm is adding new items to each of its product lines. It has committed to reaching new customer segments, especially customers in industries that it had not previously served. It is continually improving the functionality (performance and reliability) of its products and adding to the product use and application services it offers customers. It aims to double its sales in two to three years.

- Manage the asset development programs necessary to generate the required assets.
- Determine how best to leverage the assets once developed and possessed.

The remainder of this chapter addresses these issues. As well as continuing with the Amazon.com example, we use three strategy contexts (the cases of "Evergreen Software," the "Widespread" distribution and retail firm, and the "IndCompSupp" industrial components supplier) briefly noted in Box 10.1 to illustrate the discussion.

IDENTIFYING AN ORGANIZATION'S CURRENT ASSET STOCKS AND FLOWS

Knowing the current (and anticipated) inventory of and needs for its key asset classes and types helps an organization identify its critical asset gaps, develop appropriate asset development programs, or determine how best to leverage its assets. However, most organizations invest disproportionate time in delineating the stock and flow of tangible assets (financial, human, and physical assets) but neglect to inventory their knowledge or perceptual, political, and organizational assets.

Most organizations find it extraordinarily difficult to determine even approximately the stock, and especially the flow of many asset types. An organization's intangible assets are perishable, yet replenishable. This is especially true for most intangible asset types such as brand image, reputation for delivering quality services to customers, and knowledge of competitors' strategic intentions. Lest you think these are outlandish statements, ask your colleagues to answer the following questions about your firm's intangible assets:

- With which external entities do we have strong or weak relationships? And, are these relationships growing stronger or weaker?
- What do we know about which segments of customers? And, is this knowledge being enhanced or is it atrophying?
- What perceptions do different segments of customers, distribution channels, and suppliers have of our firm? Are these perceptions becoming more positive or negative?

Determining the current stock (or inventory) and the prospects for gain and loss (the flow) of these and other types of assets involves three steps.

Identify Key Assets

This first step requires managers and others to identify the assets that are most critical to the organization's current (and most likely future) strategies. Two complementary approaches are useful.

First, identify your organization's current strategy and ask the types of questions posed in Table 10.2. These questions cause managers to reflect on which asset classes and types are truly important to the firm's current strategy. Even at the level of asset categories, these questions often generate critical insights. Some firms have been shocked to discover that relationships (with key end-customers, channels, and suppliers) were more important to developing new products and to getting them rapidly into the market than financial assets.

TABLE 10.2   Identifying Relevant Assets: From Strategy to Assets

Given our current (and anticipated) strategy direction:

1. In general terms, how does each asset category (e.g., financial, human, physical, knowledge, perceptual, political, and organizational assets) contribute to the firm's current marketplace strategy?
2. How does each asset category affect direction of marketplace strategy?
3. What classes of each asset are required to execute the current strategy?
4. What are the principal types within each asset class and how do they affect execution of the current strategy? And execution of desired strategy direction?
5. What would be the implications for the strategy if the organization suffered constraints in specific asset classes and types?

Real insights emerge at the level of asset classes and types. This is so because only at these levels do managers and others truly understand what assets they possess or don't possess, what assets they require, and how they can leverage them. As the Evergreen software firm ponders how to reinvent its strategy (see Box 10.1), it can develop a list of the distinct types of software development knowledge required to design and develop a potential radical new product. It can also list the relationships it will require with different external entities such as industry associations, channels of distribution, customers, and key providers of knowledge and technology expertise.

Amazon.com, for example, needs to develop many types of relationships: with end-customers, product suppliers, providers of financial capital, sources of specific market expertise, and other online retailers such as Drugstore.com and Pets.com in which it has an ownership stake.

At the level of asset classes and types, discussion of the questions noted in Table 10.2 often generates surprising insights. For example, the credit card business of a leading bank realized that knowledge of its customers' buying habits was a much more pivotal asset than financial assets in its competition with both long-standing and newly emerging rivals.

The second approach involves asking what assets your organization possesses and then assessing whether and how they relate to its current (and potential) strategy (see Table 10.3). This approach encourages managers and others to think broadly about the firm's assets. For example, in one firm, senior human resource managers led an analysis team that was charged with the following task: identify the key types of knowledge possessed by the organization. The team quickly began to recognize how little they knew about the different types of knowledge possessed by different groups, departments, and subunits within the firm, or about ways in which this knowledge might be leveraged by the firm.

TABLE 10.3   Identifying Relevant Assets: From Assets to Strategy

Given specific stocks of assets:

1. What asset categories are germane to our organization?
2. What asset classes seem to be relevant within each asset category?
3. What asset types do we possess within each asset category?
4. What data and information do we possess for each asset class?
5. What gaps exist in our understanding of each asset type?
6. How does each asset class and type enable the firm's current marketplace strategy in terms of scope: the products it offers and the customers it pursues?
7. How does each asset class and type enable the firm's current marketplace strategy in terms of posture: how it competes to attract, win, and retain customers?
8. How does each asset class and type enable the firm's current marketplace strategy in terms of goals: what the firm is trying to achieve in the marketplace?
9. How might each asset class and type contribute to developing and executing new marketplace strategy alternatives?

Identifying relevant asset classes and types typically causes intense and prolonged discussion. For example, managers frequently find it difficult to identify the classes of knowledge and perceptions relevant to the firm. What knowledge do we currently possess about specific product, manufacturing, and logistics technologies? Which of these technologies should be of concern and interest to us? These questions spawn discussion and analysis that otherwise would not occur.

Executing both approaches to identifying key assets should help avoid two common errors. First, managers at all levels in all departments and functional areas typically overemphasize some assets and downplay or even ignore some others. In a recent strategic planning session in a medium-sized firm, the CFO listed all the assets, that in his view, the firm needed to "grow." He did not mention a single intangible asset. Second, some organizations have spent too much time categorizing and classifying assets instead of asking how each asset class or type might be relevant to current or potential strategy.

Estimate Asset Stocks

Once key asset classes and types are identified, the next challenge is to estimate the stock of each asset your organization possesses. Meeting this challenge requires managers to make judgments that vary in difficulty across asset types. This is so in large measure because well-established methodologies are available to determine some asset stock types such as financial and human, but not in others such as perceptual, political, organizational, and knowledge assets.

Box 10.2 provides a brief outline of analysis methods that can be applied to determine the stock of many asset classes. Thus, Amazon.com might use multiple forms of financial analysis to determine its stock of cash, debt, and equity. It might conduct audits to determine the inventory of books, videos, CDs, and so on, that it held at any one time.

It is appropriate to reiterate that a particular asset may have value in one context but not in another. Amazon.com's brand equity as an online seller of books may not carry over to create positive perceptions of the firm as an online seller of medical products or toys. The "IndCompSupp" components supplier firm (see Box 10.1) trying to incrementally extend its product offerings to new industry segments may discover that its knowledge of customers' operations in one industry is of little assistance in designing marketing and sales programs in other industries.

It is simply not possible to reduce asset stock estimation to a few easy-to-use rules. However, irrespective of the asset types, managers need to continually ask three questions:

1. How do we delineate and define the asset type?
2. What are the indicators that might be used to measure both how much we have and how much is enough?
3. What are the relevant data sources?

Box 10.2

Determining Asset Stocks: Some Illustrations

Financial

- Use conventional financial analysis tools and techniques to determine equity, debt, cash-in-hand, etc.
- Use funds flow statements.

Human

- Identify numbers of individuals across departments, subunits, etc.
- Identify skills associated with groups, teams, departments, subunits, etc.

Knowledge

- Ask groups, departments, and functional units to articulate what they know about change in and around external entities or stakeholders such as customers, competitors, suppliers, distribution channels, governmental agencies, and social and community groups.
- Ask the relevant groups and units to delineate what they know about trend and patterns in various external domains such as specific segments of the industry, demographics, technology, and the economy.

Physical

- Delineate what the firm possesses with regard to plant, equipment, machinery, etc.
- Delineate work-in-progress, inventory, etc.

Perceptual

- Conduct customer surveys, interviews, etc., to determine perceptions customers, suppliers, and channels hold about the firm, its products, and services.
- Use third-party studies to discern brand perceptions, brand loyalty, etc.

Political

- Examine actions of external entities to deduce nature of relationship with the firm.
- Ask individuals within the firm to specify the nature of the firm's relationship with external entities and to provide evidence for their judgments.

Organizational

- Analyze the firm's written documents describing its systems, culture, and decision-making processes.
- Ask individuals to provide their judgments about the content of each class (systems, culture, etc.) and how they work.

Consider the example of customers' perceptions, a critical asset class for many firms. Customers' perceptions might be broken down into many types: perceptions of the firm; perceptions of individual brands; perceptions of the firm's service; and perceptions of the firm's responses to complaints, product breakdowns, or failures.

To break the data down for even finer measure, perceptions of the firm's brand(s) might have several relevant indicators: purchases by different segments of customers; postponement of purchases until an announced product line extension becomes available; customers' responses to survey questions about the firm's brand(s), specific comparison to rivals' brands, or brands in general. Relevant data sources might include third-party studies (such as those conducted by J.D. Powers in the automobile industry); in-company customer research; academic research; interviews with past, current, and potential customers.

Estimate Asset Flows

Whether the stock of any asset type is growing or declining gravely affects strategy development and execution. Sometimes, it is relatively obvious that a firm is losing its supply (or stock) of a certain asset, and as a consequence, jeopardizing strategy development and execution. Firms often overlook how a decline in the stock of particular perceptual and political asset types can quickly negatively affect marketplace strategy results. Consider Coca-Cola's experience with product contamination in Europe during the summer of 1999. As soon as the public health authorities in Belgium and France declared that there was an apparent link between some outbreaks of non-life-threatening illnesses and drinking Coke from cans, the positive perceptions of Coke's brand name plummeted. Sales of Coke in some countries declined precipitously.[8]

Because asset flow constitutes the difference between the stocks of a particular asset at two points in time, estimating asset flows relies on the same methodologies as identifying asset stocks (see Box 10.2). Thus, funds flow statements are used to determine cash-in-hand at any one point in time and also track whether cash availability is increasing or deteriorating. Customer satisfaction surveys and interviews with customers provide benchmarks to determine what is happening to such intangible assets as customers' perceptions of the firm and its products.

DETERMINING ASSET NEEDS

The central premise underlying this chapter is that developing and executing strategy requires that an organization must determine the assets it needs, as a prelude to developing and leveraging them. Thus, managers must ensure that the organization engages in specific types of analysis to determine what stocks of which assets need to be developed (and how they might be leveraged).[9] Determining asset needs revolves around three interrelated steps.

Understand and Project the Strategy

Understanding your firm's current strategy, and especially its potential future direction, is the starting point for determining current and potential asset needs. Managers must understand the content, direction, and intensity of any proposed strategy change before they can specify what the financial, personnel, physical, knowledge, perceptual, and organizational asset requirements might be.

The implications of understanding the firm's strategy for determining asset needs can be quickly illustrated by considering the three strategy forms—inventive, renovative, and incremental briefly described in Box 10.1. Reinventing Evergreen software firm's strategy (see Box 10.1) will require:

- New knowledge about software design, without which the new products simply cannot become a reality.
- New knowledge about application of the software in the context of customers' needs and operations.
- New manufacturing technology, plant, and equipment to manufacture the software.
- New personnel who will bring with them and/or can help develop the required new knowledge.
- Relationships with new alliance partners as sources of new knowledge, skills, and access to potential customers.
- New increments of financial capital to fund development of the software.
- New customer perceptions (that will see the value in the new product and in the firm's ability to design, develop, market, and service the new software).

The Widespread distribution and retail organization requires a significant infusion of new financial capital to allow it to add many new product lines and engage in the necessary marketing and promotion. It also requires the development of a whole new stock of knowledge and related skills pertaining to new modes of marketing.

The IndCompSupp firm needs to add to many of its current asset classes:

- Additional cash flow to fund the investments in personnel and marketing required to penetrate new customer segments.
- Additional sales personnel to spearhead pursuit of new customers.
- New relationships with emerging distribution channels.
- New sets of perceptions of the firm and its products (e.g., enhance brand image) with existing and new customers.

As Amazon.com renovates its strategy by moving into multiple new product lines, it will require substantial capital to purchase these products from suppliers, to build modern warehouses, and to fund major marketing and advertising programs.

Determine Specific Asset Requirements

Understanding the direction, intensity, and intent of strategy change guides managers in asking and answering questions pertaining to specific asset needs (see Tables 10.2 and 10.3).

Because the Evergreen software firm is attempting to craft and execute an inventive strategy, its senior managers would have to raise and answer the following questions:

- How much capital do we require to fund each phase of product development?
- What knowledge do we need about rivals' likely product offerings?
- What new knowledge do we need about software codes, architecture, and design?
- What new knowledge about customers and channels do we need before we can take the product to market?
- What skill sets new to the company will we require?
- How many individuals will be required to bring each new type of knowledge and each new skill set into the company at the required level?
- What information technology will be required to facilitate new modes of interaction with channels, customers, vendors, and others?
- What types of relationships might we need with sources of relevant technology knowledge, channels, and customers?
- What perceptions of the new product would customers need to possess to influence them to purchase it?

Incremental strategy sometimes results in asset requirements that may surprise even seasoned managers. As IndCompSupp (see Box 10.1) begins to offer its products to customers in industries it hasn't previously served, it will need to develop knowledge of the manufacturing operations of these firms. It most likely will find that some of these new customers possess manufacturing norms and procedures that are radically different from many of its existing customers.

Determine Asset Gaps

Asset gaps—the difference between the stock of an asset required by a firm to execute a strategy or a major strategy change and the stock of the asset it currently possesses—reveal the supply of each asset type that must be developed. Asset gaps also critically influence whether a strategy or specific strategy change is feasible. If the asset gap is so large that the firm cannot resolve it, then the proposed strategy cannot be executed. If Amazon.com cannot obtain necessary supplies of finished products (such as books, video, CDs), it cannot attain its "stretch" sales goals for the forthcoming Christmas season.

Pivotal asset gaps emerged for the Evergreen software firm. First, senior managers were acutely aware that key pockets of knowledge about the design of the software had yet to be developed. Second, it had little relationship with key pockets of expertise required to develop the new product. Third, it lacked any base of positive perceptions on the part of key corporate customers pertaining to the new product. They simply did not associate the firm with the new form of software product.

The Widespread distribution and retail organization also has several apparent asset gaps. It currently lacks the financial capital to procure the new product lines and to remodel and refurbish the retail outlets senior managers desired. It also lacks the customer perceptions that are critical to upgrading its image among both current and potential customers from a "low-priced also-ran" in the industry to a more "upscale, service-friendly" retailer. Senior managers also flagged another asset gap as critical to the success of their new strategy: there are not enough managers and sales associates who possess the skill sets to create and deliver customer-friendly service.

Analysis Aids in Determining Asset Needs

Determining asset gaps and needs must not be viewed as a stand-alone exercise or as an analysis that managers conduct once-a-year as part of a strategic planning retreat or when the annual budgeting cycle requires some estimates of the capital required to develop specific assets. Also, keep in mind that many types of strategy analysis methodologies can be used to identify asset needs and gaps. Some organizations have found the following two methods particularly useful.

First, scenarios allow managers to pinpoint and assess specific strategies that would be appropriate were the competitive and macroenvironment to unfold in fundamentally different ways. Managers can then determine the asset stocks that would be required for each strategy, as well as the gaps that would be associated with each asset class or type. Amazon.com might develop a set of three or four scenarios that would project radically different competitive conditions over the next two or three years in online retailing. One scenario might envision a spectacular explosion in the volume of business conducted online with a multiplicity of rivals, while another scenario might project a steady increase in business but with only a small of number of rivals dominating the marketplace. Each scenario would allow Amazon.com to develop and test distinctly different strategies and, in particular, to identify the stock of assets required to facilitate and execute each strategy.

Second, simulations allow managers to identify and assess strategy outcomes given different assumptions about competitors' actions, customers' behaviors, overall growth in the market, different types of governmental regulations, and so on. Amazon.com might develop a set of simulations to identify and test the cost and profit outcomes of a specific strategy given different levels of overall market growth, actions of a small set of competitors, and different internal decisions such as whether to build its own warehouses and relevant levels of inventory. As managers change the inputs into the simulations, such as overall online sales, they become sensitive to the asset implications: what stock of particular assets would be required and how large the consequent asset gaps might be.

LINKING STRATEGY AND ASSETS: SOME CRITICAL ISSUES

Identifying and assessing asset stocks, flows, and gaps always generates a set of critical "asset issues" that can affect design and execution of marketplace strategy in multiple ways. Each issue creates another avenue of insight into linking strategy and assets.

Strategy Leverage Points

An unavoidable issue in any consideration of an organization's current and potential assets can be succinctly stated: Which assets provide the critical strategy leverage points? The question can be restated in two separate but interrelated ways: Which assets contribute to competitor-based advantage, that is, to outwitting, outmaneuvering, and outperforming rivals? What assets contribute to customer-based advantage, that is, to creating and sustaining value for customers?

Competitor-Based Advantage

As noted, assets contribute directly to an organization's operating processes, and thus to its capabilities. For example, the knowledge and skills embedded in an organization's sales force and other personnel contribute directly to greater speed and efficiency in an operating process critical to many organizations—order fulfillment. If the organization can perform order fulfillment *faster* than any rival, it possesses a distinct competitor-based advantage: it can do something better than its rivals. Thus, it is imperative for every organization to examine in detail how each asset class and key asset type contributes to enhancing specific operating processes, and thus competitor-based advantage.[10]

Customer-Based Advantage

Many firms have committed to developing and sustaining competitor-based advantages that did not translate into customer-based advantage: they did not create reasons for customers to purchase from them rather than from rivals. Customers may or may not appreciate a faster order fulfillment process: it may not make any discernible difference to them whether they receive the firm's product in two or four days. Thus, some retailers selling products through catalogs have discovered that faster order fulfillment provides them little power to raise prices in the case of many customers—they simply don't care whether they receive certain clothing items in three or five days.

The Widespread distribution and retail organization (see Box 10.1) must ask itself how its refurbished and remodeled stores will help attract and retain customers (who have the alternative of shopping at an information-rich Web site). Compared with the breadth of its product offerings and the service it provides to customers, the physical layout and aura of its stores may prove to be of limited value as a strategy leverage point.

Sustainability of Leverage Points

As they gauge the contribution of individual and bundles of assets to competitor-based and customer-based advantage, managers must also consider whether and how each leverage point is sustainable. For each critical asset, they should ask the following three questions:

1. Is the asset unique to the firm or is it readily available to current or emerging rivals? If Amazon.com can develop warehousing, distribution, and service assets that far surpass any of its rivals, then it may be possible for it to develop operating processes (and thus capabilities) that rivals will not possess.

2. Can the asset be copied? If the Everygreen software firm's emerging knowledge about specific software codes can be duplicated by one or more rivals, its capacity to serve as a key strategy leverage point will be severely circumscribed.

3. Does the asset have (perfect) substitutes? Some firms have discovered, much to their chagrin, that newly emerging rivals could develop substitutes for their long-established sales and distribution assets (the knowledge and skills of their sales force, relationships with retail organizations): these new rivals developed the capacity to sell directly to the end-customer.

Asset Constraints

Much of the discussion throughout this chapter makes it clear that assets can constrain strategy development and execution. Asset constraints can emerge in many ways. First, an organization may not have sufficient stock of specific asset types to imagine and develop winning strategies. The absence of personnel with the appropriate skills and knowledge about e-business has inhibited many firms from developing inventive or renovative e-business-based strategies. The absence of specific knowledge types has inhibited the Evergreen software firm from developing its potential inventive strategy.

Second, the absence of specific asset stocks hinders strategy execution. Many firms have discovered that they did not have the manufacturing capacity to produce the volume of product required to meet their own sales projections. The absence of sufficient knowledgeable and trained sales personnel has inhibited the IndCompSupp firm (see Box 10.1) from entering new industry segments as quickly as it had initially planned.

Third, asset stock deficiencies, if they are not alleviated, can constrain potential strategy options. Even though Toyota had been exceptionally successful in developing and leveraging its brand name in the small and mid-sized segments of the U.S. automobile market, the firm believed that the Toyota brand name would be a constraint on its ability to enter and penetrate the luxury end of the market. Hence, it developed the Lexus brand name as the platform for a range of cars to compete against the long-established rivals in the luxury market segment including Cadillac, BMW, and Mercedes-Benz.

Asset Vulnerability

Many firms have learned a cruel lesson regarding assets: Even though they do not have a current or anticipated constraint with regard to specific assets, asset availability may still be a major problem. Potential constraints may arise due to the unavoidable vulnerability of assets to events within or external to the organization.

In a broad sense, all assets ultimately are vulnerable to internal and external events. Abundant cash-in-hand may get quickly depleted if a major downturn occurs in the firm's product markets. Plant and equipment may be vulnerable to fire or a flood. Some firms learned only in retrospect that a large portion of their plant and equipment was vulnerable to an "act of God" such as lightning or an earthquake.

Managers thus must be especially vigilant in asking the questions in Tables 10.2 and 10.3 about those assets deemed "strategy leverage points," which are critical to facilitating and fostering competitor or customer-based advantage.

MANAGING ASSET DEVELOPMENT PROGRAMS

Asset gaps must be filled. Asset constraints must be ameliorated. Asset vulnerabilities must be anticipated and, if possible, preempted. Each of these imperatives requires every organization to initiate and manage multiple asset development programs. In keeping with the thrust of this chapter, managers must ensure that each asset development program contributes to the firm's marketplace strategy.

Developing (and leveraging) assets is inherent in the life and work of any organization. Almost every action managers take pertains to some aspect or other of asset development—creating and developing new financial, personnel, physical, knowledge, perceptual, political, and organizational wherewithal. Senior managers invest extensive efforts to create new equity capital or debt, and to hire, train, motivate, and lead the right personnel. Managers frequently commit much of their time to creating and extending specific types of knowledge and to sharing it across subunits, functions, and departments. Increasingly, groups of managers work together across organizational boundaries to acquire, develop, and deploy new technologies related to manufacturing, logistics, information, sales, and service. Action programs in marketing, sales, distribution logistics, and service can be viewed as efforts to develop and leverage perceptual and political assets: how customers and other perceive and relate to the organization.

In simple terms, managing asset development programs involves three stages: identification, design and execution, and monitoring of results.

Identify Key Asset Development Programs

Determining current and required asset development programs emerges from many of the analysis steps already addressed, especially, identifying key assets, determining asset stocks and flows, and specifying asset requirements and gaps.

First, as managers identify their organization's current asset stocks and flows,[11] they can ask the following four questions:

1. What is our organization doing to augment the stock of each key asset class or type?
2. To what extent do these actions represent an organized and integrated "program"?
3. Who is responsible for managing each program?
4. What commitments are involved in each program—managerial time and attention, timing, personnel, and other assets such as capital and technology?

Managers can then list the major asset development programs in each of the asset categories noted in Table 10.1. For example, given the asset needs identified earlier for the Evergreen software firm reinventing its strategy, the following asset development programs would seem unavoidable:

- Develop knowledge about software design.
- Develop knowledge about customers' needs and operations.
- Search for, assess, purchase, install, and test innovative and new manufacturing technologies.
- Seek, interview, assess, hire, train, and monitor many categories of personnel with specific types of skills and knowledge.
- Identify, analyze, approve, negotiate, and work with a range of alliance partners.

- Identify and work with new sources of capital.
- Design and execute marketing, sales, and service programs with a view to enhancing brand equity and superior customer relationships.

As noted in the discussion of leverage points in the previous section, current asset development programs may not necessarily lead to either competitor-based or customer-based advantage. Thus, managers must assess whether existing asset development programs will be sufficient to meet the firm's asset needs and gaps. Typically, this assessment leads to two related outcomes:

1. The need to extend and refine existing asset development programs.
2. Identification of new asset development programs.

Once a firm has identified specific asset requirements, as outlined in the previous section, it can ask whether it needs to create an asset development program for each asset class or type.

Design and Execute Programs

Once current and desired asset development programs are identified, managers confront two tasks:

1. Specifying changes to existing asset development programs.
2. Developing new asset development programs.

The Evergreen software firm would need to adapt and extend some existing programs as well as initiating new ones. For example, a program to acquire new knowledge about many facets of software design might be essentially a new program, whereas finding, hiring, and training sets of individuals with specific skills and knowledge might merely require refocusing existing personnel recruitment and development programs.

When Amazon.com decided in early 1999 to dramatically extend the range and volume of products it would make available to customers later in 1999, it was confronted with major distribution problems: Where would it warehouse these products? Should it own its own warehouses or outsource this activity to distribution specialists, as many online retailers choose to do? Should it take on the responsibility of hiring thousands of low-wage workers to staff warehouses and distribution centers? Eventually, the firm decided to build, staff, and manage its own warehouses, thus giving rise to a major new asset development program. Amazon.com's commitment to building warehouses during 1999 amounted to $300 million.

Monitor Program Results

Finally, managers need to monitor the execution and results of asset development programs. The Evergreen software firm can track how well it is progressing in achieving its goals for each of the asset development programs. With regard to personnel recruitment and development, it can track how many potential employees have been identified, how many interviewed, how many hired, how many accepted offers, when they started to work, and so on. Amazon.com can track progress in the design, development, and execution of its advertising program as it tries to extend recognition of its brand name in the critical months heading into the make-or-break Christmas season.

SUMMARY

Developing and executing strategy change presumes that the right assets are available, and in sufficient supply. Frequently, however, firms only pay attention to asset development when shortages arise or when their asset stocks prove inferior to rivals. This chapter has presented a framework of analysis to enable managers to connect strategy formulation and execution to asset identification and development.

NOTES

1.   We emphasize strategy-relevant value here. Sometimes assets, especially tangible assets such as plant and equipment, and partially or finished products, can be sold in the market. Intangible assets, such as brands and many types of information, can also be sold in the market.

2.   Operating processes are fully explored in Chapter 15.

3.   We emphasize "do" here to reinforce the distinction between assets as stocks of something or other, and capabilities as measures of how well an organization performs one or more operating processes.

4.   See Chapter 7 for a discussion of the role and importance of stakeholders as a source of influence on firms' product-market and political strategies.

5.   This is an example of an asset development program, as discussed in the final section of this chapter.

6.   This argument has been forcefully made by many others. See, for example, James Brian Quinn, *The Intelligent Enterprise* (New York: Free Press, 1992).

7.   Assets constraints, and vulnerabilities are discussed in greater detail later in this chapter.

8.   This Coca-Cola episode in Europe is discussed in some detail in Chapter 7.

9.   All the reasons noted earlier under the subsection/heading, "Why Pay Attention to Assets?" reinforce the importance of the need to determine required asset stocks.

10.   This imperative is examined in some detail in Chapter 11.

11.   How to do so was addressed earlier in this chapter.

CREATING AND LEVERAGING CORE COMPETENCIES

11

C.K. Prahalad
University of Michigan

Liam Fahey
Babson College and
Cranfield University

Robert M. Randall
Randall Publishing

A fundamental question lies at the heart of any assessment of rivalry within an industry or competitive space: Why do some firms succeed and others fail? If this question seems naive, why is it that in so many instances the firms that failed seemed to have more advantages than the firms that succeeded. Ask yourself:

- Why have so many firms achieved dominant leadership in their product or market domains only then to lose out to later entrants, smaller rivals, or firms in adjacent product or market domains?
- On the global stage, over the past three decades, why have so many large North American and European corporations failed to develop new businesses?
- Why have so few asset-rich firms pioneered the newly emerging industries or industry segments?

These questions compel us to reconsider the meaning of strategy, and especially growth strategy, and the role of top management in revitalizing firms. This chapter addresses the role and importance of core competence as the source of new business opportunities, and thus of growth strategy. It begins by identifying three distinctly different challenges—including achieving break-through growth strategies—that must be managed if a firm is to enhance its revenues. The chapter then goes on to discuss (1) exactly what core competencies are, (2) the connection between core competency and the governance process, (3) the connection between core competencies and core products, (4) the tasks of managing core competencies, and (5) the importance of core competence in creating new competitive space.

RETHINKING THE SCORECARD

The fundamental business issue as we move into the new millennium is *growth* in revenues. Creating the potential for revenue growth must become the all-consuming focus or agenda for top management. Without revenue growth, organizations cannot invest in their future; they cannot create their future.

Downsizing, restructuring, and streamlining organizations cannot substitute for vigorous, internally generated growth. Downsizing in the form of "reducing headcount" rarely enhances sales revenues. Restructuring by acquiring and/or divesting business units or recombining existing business units without rethinking the focus and agenda of management inevitably leads to further restructuring. Many large U.S. firms have restructured themselves more than once (and some, many times) in the past 10 years. Despite this management effort, the business difficulties that prevent those firms from growing never seem to get resolved.

If growth and new business development are the real issues, *value creation* will be the appropriate scorecard for managers in the years ahead. The scorecard will consist of three parts (see Figure 11.1):

1. *Managing the performance gap.* Organizations must be assessed on how well they improve performance across a wide variety of dimensions, such as quality, cost, cycle time, productivity, and profitability.

FIGURE 11.1 Scorecard for top management: Value creation.

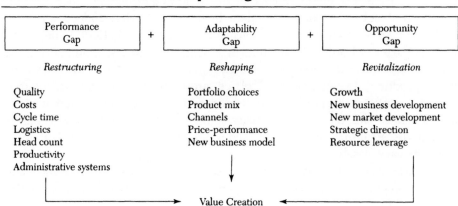

2. *Managing the adaptability gap.* Organizations must be assessed on how well they anticipate industry change and initiate and manage industry transformations. This is dramatically different from managing to enhance performance in an existing industry or being the "best of breed" in a given industry segment.

3. *Managing the opportunity gap.* Organizations must be assessed on how well they create new businesses, pioneer new markets, and discern and communicate strategic direction. The defining challenge for organizations aspiring to global leadership is their capacity to identify, create, and exploit fundamentally new business opportunities that do not exist in today's industry.

The Need to Address Opportunities

This three-part scorecard is necessary because so many industries are undergoing major structural change. Industry change adds urgency to the need to manage the adaptability and opportunity gaps. Merely outperforming existing competitors in terms of product quality, cost, and features is unlikely to provide the basis for breakthrough business opportunities.

Consider how structural change has affected the computer industry. For decades, IBM was the increasingly powerful leader of the computer industry, the epitome of a highly vertically integrated firm: from components, to mainframes, to operating systems, applications engineering, and software. IBM also owned its own distribution channels. Today, the computer industry is "deverticalized." IBM was slow to change as this new industry structure evolved, allowing companies such as Intel, Compaq, and Microsoft to pioneer new segments of the industry. In fact, the entire industry landscape has changed. Now the component part of the industry (for example, microprocessors) is dominated by Intel. The operating system that drives most computers is provided by Microsoft. The applications software is dominated by specialists such as Lotus. There is considerably more variation in distribution channels: from value-added resellers to owned distribution to mail-order houses, to large retail operators such as Computerland and Sears, to new electronic channels.

Such structural change is evident in most industries. Indeed, in many cases, the degree of change is so extensive that it is often difficult to delineate the boundaries or borders of an "industry." Consider the so-called multimedia business. It seems safe to suggest that the dividing lines that distinguish consumer products, professional and office products, computing, telecommunications, software (especially publishing and entertainment), and content providers have blurred. Moreover, because this change is continuous, scenarios of what the structure of the multimedia industry will look like a few years from now vary widely.

Industries are undergoing various degrees of structural change for many reasons: competition from Internet companies, deregulation, excess capacity, mergers and acquisitions, changing customer expectations, and technological discontinuities, to name a few.[1]

The persistent change in and around industries poses one overriding issue for every manager: What is the capacity of my organization to anticipate and manage the transformation of the industry? Unless managers seriously challenge their capacity to understand the project industry change, they are destined to be followers rather than leaders.

Managers can measure the ability to generate industry foresight and change proactively with the *adaptability gap*. Given the evidence that an adaptability gap exists in most large corporations, managers must rethink their business model. The model has two parts:

1. Understanding the environment.
2. Competing to win in the marketplace.

Using this model requires corporations to rethink the logic underlying their business portfolios as well as price-performance assumptions in each business.

While firms are coping with the performance and adaptability gaps, they have to address simultaneously the *opportunity gap*. How are they going to initiate new business opportunities that lie outside the purview of their current product portfolio? They must profitably deploy resources to create new markets and new businesses and establish a broad strategic vision.

During the past decade, management attention has been focused primarily on the performance gap, sometimes on the adaptability gap, and rarely on the opportunity gap. Managing the performance gap—fixing the problems of profitability, cost, quality, cycle time, logistics, and productivity—is the legitimate task of management. Measuring the performance gap, if done well, ought to create a *large investment pool*. The question for managers, then, is how to use the investment pool in the pursuit of new opportunities for growth. To create value, management must address operational improvement (performance gap) and strategic direction (opportunity gap) simultaneously. Value creation is not just a matter of catching up with the competition and eliminating the performance gap. It also must include the active management of the opportunity gap—the development of opportunities not available in the current industry configurations. The remainder of this chapter addresses the role and importance of core competence in developing and exploiting new business opportunities.

UNDERSTANDING CORE COMPETENCIES

It is important to recognize that competition today takes place on multiple planes (see Figure 11.2). To build and sustain market and intellectual leadership on a global scale in the long run, an organization will probably have to win on all planes. First, there is competition for end-product markets and services,

FIGURE 11.2   Competition at three levels.

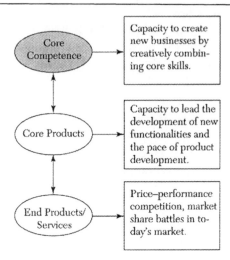

that is, price-performance competition represented by market share battles for today's market. Managers have to fight in that arena. There is also a less visible battle for dominance in core products. These are the building blocks that create the capacity to lead in the development of products with new functionalities. Finally, there is competition for competence—the capacity to create new businesses or new competitive space.

What Is a Core Competency?

The idea is now widely accepted that the diversified firm is both a portfolio of distinct businesses and a portfolio of core competencies.[2] Although they may vary dramatically across firms and even differ among firms in the same competitive space or industry, core competencies always consist of some combination of:

- Multiple technologies (hard and soft).
- Collective learning (multilevel, multifunctional).
- Capacity to share (across business and geographical boundaries).

Examples of core competencies that reflect these three elements include miniaturization at Sony, network management at AT&T, billing at the Regional Bell Operating Companies, user-friendliness at Apple, and high-volume manufacturing at Matsushita.

Some Central Challenges in Managing Core Competencies

Organizations have little option but to enhance existing core competencies, and in many instances, to develop new competencies. In either case, managers will be confronted by new, complex challenges. We merely identify here one key challenge associated with each of the constituent elements of a core competency. In the last part of this chapter, we address the key tasks involved in managing these and related challenges.

Technology

This involves incorporating bundles of technologies that are new to the traditional businesses of the firm. A bundle of related technologies, or a *knowledge stream,* such as software, needs to be blended with more traditional technologies (e.g., electronics and software in a chemical firm). This means that managers must recognize that they have to work with a new logic (e.g., electronics in a traditional chemical firm).

Learning

Learning about new technologies and new customer needs, as well as how to integrate new and old technologies and new and old businesses, must take place in teams that cross functional or departmental lines. The composition of teams will also change over time. Globalization requires that team members *from multiple cultures* must learn as a group.

Sharing

Developing and redeploying core competence across business opportunities, and trying to do so ever more quickly, will force firms to collaborate and transfer knowledge and skills across multiple business units and geographic locations.

The Composition of Competencies

The creation of new competencies by integrating a firm's existing knowledge base with new knowledge streams creates the need to reevaluate the elements that collectively create the system of competencies. Two broad elements can be recognized:

1. People-embodied knowledge—both tacit and explicit.[3]
2. Capital-embodied knowledge—both proprietary and vendor-based.

It is the combination of people-embodied and capital-embodied knowledge that represents the totality of the competence base within an organization. In many industries, such as semiconductor manufacturing, access to vendor-based knowledge (and learning to work with them creatively) tends to be as important as the internally generated proprietary knowledge (see Figure 11.3).

FIGURE 11.3   It is the combination of both people-embodied and capital-embodied knowledge that represents the totality of an organization's competence base.

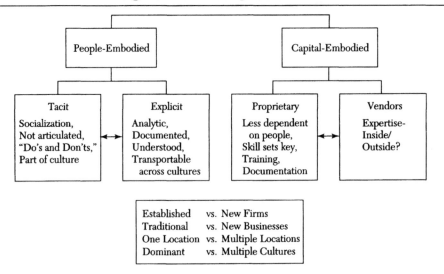

The relative importance of the various elements in the overall composition of a firm's competence profile is important to understand, in order to manage it effectively. The balance is likely to be different between:

- Established and new firms in the same industry (e.g., General Motors and Samsung).
- Traditional and new industries (e.g., cement manufacture vs. digital imaging).
- Firms with one location and those with multiple locations around the world (e.g., the tacit-to-explicit balance is critical in managing multiple locations, which demand more explicit knowledge).
- Dominant and multiple cultures (e.g., if most of the development work is done in one dominant culture, say in Japan, then the group can work with more tacit knowledge).

Achieving balance between the elements requires continuous assessment. As the discontinuities in the competitive landscape evolve, they will have an impact on the nature and composition of the elements of the competence base of the firm. Senior managers will have to constantly evaluate and calibrate these shifts and adjust their focus accordingly.

Identifying Core Competencies: Some Key Questions

How does the organization identify its core competencies? Three simple tests or sets of questions can reveal the key characteristics of core competencies:

1. Is the competence a significant source of differentiation? Does the competence generate distinct value and benefits for the customers? Core competencies manifest themselves to customers in the form of the firm's products and their attributes.
2. Does the competence transcend a single business? Does it cover a range of businesses, both current and new? A core competence should provide access to a variety of product marketplaces.
3. Is the core competence hard for competitors to imitate? Is it difficult for others to learn how the firm does what it does?

All the examples of core competencies noted previously meet these tests: miniaturization at Sony, network management at AT&T, billing at the Regional Bell Operating Companies, user-friendliness at Apple, and high-volume manufacturing at Matsushita. Sony's miniaturization and Apple's user friendliness are the unique signatures of these companies. These competencies underlie the competitive differentiation they have attained across a variety of end products. However, it is difficult for someone to visit Matsushita or Sony and define precisely why one is so good at manufacturing and the other excels at miniaturization.

Few companies are likely to build and sustain world leadership in more than five or six core competencies. The knowledge required to achieve world-class status and the speed of technological change render it difficult for any organization to possess more than a few core competencies. It is little wonder, then, that organizations invest so heavily in alliances and other forms of relationships to acquire the resources necessary to build desired competencies.

Avoiding Misunderstanding about Core Competencies

Because core competence is a term that is often misunderstood, it is important to define precisely what it means. Many managers regard the concept of core competencies as synonymous with core technologies and/or capabilities. Core technologies are a component of core competencies. But core competence only results when firms learn to *harmonize multiple technologies.* For example, miniaturization, which has been the "trademark" of Sony, requires expertise in several core technologies, such as microprocessors, miniature power sources, power management, packaging, and manufacturing. It also requires an understanding of user-friendly design, a knowledge of ergonomics, and an awareness of emerging lifestyles. Sony product designers need to know how and why customers will want miniaturized products such as a radio that is no bigger than a business card.

The example of miniaturization highlights a key characteristic of core competencies: They are more than a collection of technical capabilities. Core competencies involve the *creative bundling* of multiple technologies along with customer knowledge, marketing intuition, and the skill to manage them all synergistically.

A second source of misunderstanding occurs when core competencies are confused with capabilities. Capabilities are, in some cases, prerequisites for participants in a business. For example, just-in-time (JIT) delivery is now a prerequisite to be a "tier 1" supplier to the auto industry. It is the price one has to pay to get into the game. In the terminology of gamblers, capabilities are the equivalent of "table stakes." A capability is crucial for survival but, unlike a core competence, it *often* does not confer any specific differential advantage over the other competitors in that industry. Also, capabilities are often unique to a particular function or group within a business unit and therefore do not carry advantages over other businesses.

Because competencies require (1) the management of complex, iterative processes, (2) the bundling of technologies, and (3) the integration of learning in many parts of the organization, they are difficult to imitate. Managers need to understand that any competence permeates the whole organization. In comparison, technology can be stand-alone (e.g., the design of VLSI—very large system-integrated circuits): Competence, on the other hand, means getting consistently high yields in VLSI production. Competence transcends a specific technology or design capability. The process of converting good designs into high yields requires that multiple organizational levels (e.g., workers on the shop floor and product development engineers) and multiple functions (e.g., applications engineers and manufacturing groups) work together.

Much of the understanding and learning by individuals at different organizational levels and in the different functions that make up a competency is tacit. Leveraging tacit learning requires constant communication across hierarchical and functional boundaries.

CORE COMPETENCE AND THE GOVERNANCE PROCESS

The key to understanding competence is that, although it incorporates a technological component, it also involves the *governance process* inside the organization (the quality of relationships across functions within a business unit or across business units within a multibusiness firm), and *collective learning* across levels, functions, and business units. A core competence can be conceptualized as equal to the multiple of these three elements. According to this definition, the formula for a competence is:

Competence = (Technology × Governance Process × Collective Learning)

Let us examine the implications of this view of competence, using, as a hypothetical example, a typical U.S. firm. The usual assumption is that if a firm's managers pour a lot of money into technology, it will become competitive. Using the preceding equation, consider this hypothetical firm to be rich in technology—commanding, say, 1,000 units of technology. However, assume that the various businesses within this corporation do not work together. They earn just 20 units in the governance process—the capability to work across business and functional unit boundaries. Also assume that, in this firm, the capacity for collective learning is low: 5 units for this dimension. Using the formula, the firm's overall competence score is 100,000 ($1,000 \times 20 \times 5$) units.

For comparison, look at a company that is not blessed with as much technology. It rates only 200 units of technology, using the same scale that was used for the previous firm. However, this firm has fostered the capacity to work across organizational boundaries and is fully focused on organizational learning. It earns 100 units for governance and 500 for collective learning, which leads to a competence of 10,000,000 ($200 \times 100 \times 500$) units. The assertion is simple: Unless accompanied by investments in *governance* and the creation of a *learning environment* at all levels in the organization, investments in technology will remain underleveraged.

This relationship among technology, governance, and learning environment suggests that the logical approach to improving the management of the core competencies for firms is to focus on improving the *quality of their organization.*

The Honda Case

For evidence of the logic underlying this assertion, consider Honda (see Figure 11.4). Honda's multiple businesses depend on a competence in engines. However, if each of its business units behaved as if it were discrete and only focused on (and was willing to pay for) the functionalities (i.e., specific engine design attributes) it needed, Honda's engine competence could be compromised. For example, in power tillers, managers may demand and be willing to pay for a light and powerful machine. However, noise reduction is not a major priority for power tiller managers because they target their products for use in villages in the developing world. On the other hand, the business unit manager

FIGURE 11.4   Honda: Leveraging core competencies example.

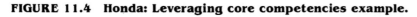

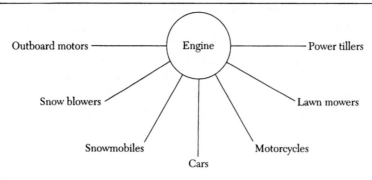

developing lawn mowers for sale in the United States may need a light and powerful engine that is as quiet as possible. Suppose that business unit managers could uniquely define the functionalities that they need. If each Honda business unit merely optimized its own needs without maintaining a perspective on the implications of its parochial approach for the protection and development of an overall competence, the skill base would be eroded.

Competency development is also inhibited by prevailing organizational models. Historically, the dominant corporate model has been that of a portfolio of businesses. If the portfolio model is the only one used, then cost reduction within those businesses will appear to be the primary task, sometimes accompanied by the goal of product-line extensions. However, if we model the corporation as a portfolio of core competencies, as demonstrated in the final section of this chapter, the result will be greater attention to new application opportunities. This will help make new business development top management's priority.

At Sharp, Sony, and Canon, the businesses in the portfolio share core competencies. For example, Canon sells a wide variety of end products—copiers, laser printers, fax machines, cameras, and camcorders. All these businesses share access to core products (or components), such as Canon lens systems and Canon laser engines. To be world-class, these core products depend on Canon's core competencies—miniaturization, mechatronics, and so on. Each end-product business has an independent identity and a specific set of customers and markets. But underlying that market focus is a structure of core products and core competencies that are shared. As a result, within Canon, there is an opportunity for gaining economies of scale in core products and an ability to anticipate new functionalities and leverage technical resources.

FROM CORE COMPETENCE TO CORE PRODUCTS

Core products are often the physical embodiment of one or more core competencies. Compressors at Matsushita and laser printer engines at Canon are examples of core products. Canon not only uses its laser printer engine in several businesses, it also markets it to external customers. Firms such as Canon distinguish among their market share of end products (such as copiers), their manufacturing share (such as share of the market gained by providing manufactured products under private label to others), and their share of core products (such as laser printer engines sold to others). Canon has gained a predominant market share of over 85 percent worldwide in laser printer engines. However, the firm remains a small worldwide player in laser printers—the end product.

Consideration of core competency adds to the need to recognize that competition for core products is distinctly different from competition for end products and services. Consider, for example, the color television business. To succeed, firms must have access to core products such as picture tubes, single-processing integrated circuits (ICs), tuners, and line output transformers. If we disaggregate business to the core product level—say, VCRs, camcorders, or laptop computers—we find that very few Western firms have sought leadership.

Understanding the importance of core products compels us to evaluate competitive rivalry differently. For example, in the VCR business, we can explain why Matsushita and JVC won the battle for their VHS format over Sony's Beta Max. Their combined market share for the end product—VHS VCRs—was only 24 percent. However, their manufacturing share (that is, the share of market gained by providing manufactured products under private label to others) was 41 percent, their VHS format share through licensing was 80 percent, and their core product share for decks was 85 percent. Eighty-five percent of the world's demand for VCR decks was met by one company!

Managers tend to underestimate the power of core product dominance. Such dominance gives rise to a critical issue: Who controls critical technologies? Given the dependence on a foreign supply base for critical core products, what are the chances that U.S. firms can create an indigenous high-definition television (HDTV) business, even if resources are not constrained? The supplier base (and access to and control over core products) is a fundamental part of competitiveness. The key point here for both firms and countries in this: technological superiority (including a world-class supplier system) without a corporate competence will likely be a short-term victory.

The emerging global competitive picture should force senior managers to ask themselves these questions:

- How long can this erosion of core product capability in the West be sustained?

- Who are the custodians of the technological virtuosity of individual companies? Managers of business units, as discussed, have no natural inclination to concern themselves with core product share or competencies.

- How can group and senior executives transcend the concerns of business units and play a role in protecting the basis for long-term competitiveness of their firms?

- Who should protect the disciplines that require multiple business units to work together?

MANAGING CORE COMPETENCIES: SOME KEY TASKS[4]

The task of managing competencies in the new global market place is complex. There are at least five distinct tasks:

Gaining Access to and Absorbing New Knowledge

The most obvious way to gain access to the necessary new knowledge streams is to recruit people with the required (new) knowledge (e.g., mathematicians in a bank, geneticists in a traditional pharmaceuticals firm, or software engineers in a hard-core manufacturing firm). Anyone who has been through this process of new skills acquisition knows how hard it is for these new skills to be accepted and made welcome in an organization. While bankers have to learn the new tools that mathematicians bring to the game, mathematicians also have to learn banking.

This two-way knowledge transfer is critical before a useful blending can occur. However, the tendency in most organizations is to reject these new skills—similar to the response of the immune system to an invading virus. Left to its own devices, the organization is unlikely to absorb these skills. Therefore, one of the critical roles of senior management is to create legitimacy for the new knowledge. Top managers must not only constantly present the strategic direction of the firm to all employees, but also identify the new knowledge that will help to create that future. Further, several levels of the organization must learn and apply the "culture" of that new knowledge. For example, software has a different culture from manufacturing.

The intellectual heritage limits and restricts what a management team can do. For example, why do we not have software upgrades in automobiles? It is equally difficult for those who have operated in a regulated environment to understand the culture and discipline of the capital market. One senior manager from the Eastern bloc, perplexed by the changes in the stock prices on a daily basis, asked: "Which organization fixes the price?" In his country, government agencies set all prices until recently.

It is not enough that the need for new knowledge is recognized and steps are taken to acquire it (including alliances), but fundamental legitimacy and urgency must be assigned to that task. To be successful, the progress of instituting and melding the new knowledge into different traditional intellectual cultures must be continually monitored.

Integrating Multiple Streams of Knowledge

Acquiring new knowledge is difficult and actively integrating it into traditional knowledge to create new business opportunities is even harder. For example, at Kodak, knowledge of chemical imaging must be integrated with electronics and software knowledge to create new hybrid products. Photo compact disks and digital cameras demand a seamless and careful integration of multiple streams of knowledge. Over time, the mingling of these streams creates a new competence.

Organizations learn by doing. Therefore, top managers must set up specific, bite-size projects. Projects are the carriers of new learning. They focus the organization's attention on solving the problems of integrating the new knowledge with the old. Project teams with cross-disciplinary membership are critical for successful learning and application.

Sharing across Cultures and Distance

While the focus thus far has been on intellectual diversity—the culture of various knowledge streams—in a global firm, there is yet another dimension to cultural diversity. This is a result of *multiple country cultures.*

Different cultures have different implicit priorities. For example, the product development philosophy—the priorities placed on quality, cost, time, safety, and performance—among U.S.-trained, European, Japanese, and Chinese designers is likely to be different. No manager lives in a vacuum. Every manager lives in a culture that values some characteristics more than others. This is a result of deep socialization. In some cultures for example, learning is a linear process. It is primarily analytical and based on individual effort. In other societies, learning is much more sequential, experiential, and a team-oriented effort in which intuition plays an important role.

When collaboration is initiated in the context of evolving knowledge, across multiple cultures (i.e., collaboration with teams from three different continents), conflicts and misunderstandings emanate. A deeper and explicit understanding of the socialization patterns of groups involved becomes a necessity. Moreover, managers must avoid stereotyping the other groups. Cross-cultural collaborative activity is emerging as a critical skill in the new economy.

Learning to Forget

It is easy to exhort an individual or an organization to learn. But forgetting may be equally important. The dominant logic of the firm, or the recipes people use to learn, can become a major impediment to learning. Firms (and their managers) must learn to forget, and forgetting is more difficult than learning. In most organizations, the forgetting curve is flat; in an age of discontinuities,[5] a flat forgetting curve is a serious problem.

For example, it takes an enormous amount of effort to move from a "cost plus" view of the business to a "price minus" view of the business. The two formulas are (1) Cost + Profit = Price; and (2) Price − Profit = Cost. The traditional Department of Defense (DoD)-type businesses are characterized by mind-sets, processes, and skill sets appropriate to (1). Commercial businesses are characterized by (2). The transition for a DoD-driven firm to the commercial arena has been one of deep frustration, with few successes. Participants in this different business culture need to forget their old patterns and replace them with new ones.

A similar situation exists in deregulated industries. Previously, the market was the "regulators"; some would argue that competition was also the "regulators." Senior managers paid a lot of attention to regulators, and the process of regulation made most of the firms in the industry look and act exactly the same. The genetic variety, if any, was minimal. In market-based competition, the game is about consumers, differentiation, price-performance, innovation, and competition. This is a very different competitive milieu. To compete in the New Economy, it is essential to forget old patterns.

Deploying Competence across Business Unit Boundaries

The more that the large organizations move toward business unit (BU)-based strategies, measurement systems such as Economic Value Added (EVA), and rewards, the harder it is to focus on sharing across BU boundaries. The motivation for sharing is removed from all the business units and the competence base becomes fragmented.

To have a system of deployment of competencies, all business units must have a common understanding of market and technology evolution. Without such understanding, the conceptual framework for sharing does not exist.[6] But a conceptual framework, without organizational support systems, is unlikely to work. Many firms invest time and energy developing perspectives on the future while clinging to administrative systems that reinforce the business unit orientation to the exclusion of all others. It is as if we were approaching the fourth-generation strategy with a third-generation knowledge base, second-generation managers, and first-generation administrative systems. There is a clear mismatch between "desire," rhetoric, and reality in most firms across this dimension.

CORE COMPETENCE: A STEPPING STONE TO CREATING NEW COMPETITIVE SPACE

Competencies are developed and honed to create and exploit new competitive space—new opportunities in the marketplace. Thus, as an executive team endeavors to manage the performance, adaptability, and opportunity gaps outlined earlier, it must ask itself: How can firms create totally new products or services? Consider new businesses such as personal fax machines, a Global Positioning System (GPS) for hikers, and photo CDs. The *opportunity list* for the next decade, in high-volume electronics alone, could fill several pages. The key question for consideration by senior managers is: What do we have to do to capture our share of new business development?

New business development requires a new mind-set on the part of most enterprises. Such a mind-set has the following three characteristics:[7]

1. *A persistent challenging of existing price-performance assumptions.* Why can't we create a color fax machine that sells for $200? Why should it cost $5,000? Canon, in copiers, and Lexus or Honda, in the luxury car segment,

are good examples of firms that dramatically challenge the prevailing price-performance assumptions in the industry.

2. *An understanding of the meaning of "customer-led."* Most firms have only recently learned to listen to customers and to give them what they ask for. That is important and beneficial but not sufficient. It is also necessary to lead customers. As customers, many of us may not have anticipated, 10 years ago, our emerging dependence on fax machines in our homes. Being a customer-led company is important, but leading customers is what competing for the future is about. Managers must create products with a price-performance ratio that makes them attractive for people to buy.

3. *Ability to avoid the tyranny of the "served market."* Most managers are so focused on their current market that they cannot see opportunities emerging elsewhere. A served-market orientation puts too much emphasis on current businesses and reduces the capacity to foresee opportunities that arise outside the current market scope, especially those that fall in between two or more current business units. If we wish to reignite corporate imagination, we have little choice but to deemphasize the served-market orientation and emphasize exploiting the opportunity horizon. Managers must not just defend markets, but create markets. Managers must not be comfortable with incrementalism in price-performance enhancement but commit stretching price-performance goals. It is not enough just to benchmark the competition; managers must plan to outinnovate it. Firms must move:

- From satisfying needs to anticipating needs.
- From being close to customers to leading customers.
- From thinking in terms of products to focusing on functionality and rapid market incursions.
- From focusing on core business to diversifying around core competencies.

These shifts would constitute radically new aspirations for most firms. Managers have traditionally sought to satisfy current customers, analyze current product-markets, and grow existing business units. But to achieve exponential growth based on core competencies, managers need both a new mind-set and new managerial capabilities. The competency-based view of the corporation allows it to share knowledge and components across business unit and functional boundaries.

SUMMARY

Restructuring and other ways of delayering organizations cannot be the corporate focus. Dramatic growth will not take place if the focus is on technology alone; it will take place only if the focus is on competencies, with technology as a component.

NOTES

1.   Two related frameworks for industry analysis that are intended to identify and analyze the forces shaping industry change and evolution are examined in Chapter 8.

2.   See, for example, C.K. Prahalad and Gary Hamel, "The Core Competence of the Corporation," *Harvard Business Review* (May/June 1990): 79–91.

3.   People-embodied knowledge has received a fair amount of attention with the increasing focus on knowledge management. See, for example, I. Nonaka and H. Takeucki, *The Knowledge Creating Company* (New York: Oxford University Press, 1995).

4.   This section draws heavily from C.K. Prahalad, "Managing Discontinuities: The Emerging Challenges" *Research Technology Management,* Industrial Research Institute, Inc. (1998): 14–22.

5.   Many of these changes and discontinuities were noted in Chapter 1.

6.   The need for such a framework, a strategic architecture, is discussed in Gary Hamel and C.K. Prahalad, *Competing for the Future* (Boston: Harvard Business School Press, 1994), Chap. 5.

7.   For a fuller discussion of the mind-set required in exploiting opportunities, see Gary Hamel and C.K. Prahalad, "Corporate Imagination and Expeditionary Marketing," *Harvard Business Review* (July/August 1991): 81–92.

PART THREE

STRATEGY MAKING: IDENTIFYING AND EVALUATING STRATEGIC ALTERNATIVES

12 IDENTIFYING AND DEVELOPING STRATEGY ALTERNATIVES

Marjorie A. Lyles
Indiana University

Liam Fahey
Babson College and
Cranfield University

Alternative generation, that is, the process of defining the various means by which a goal can be attained, a problem solved, or an opportunity realized, must be carefully and systematically managed. It simply does not just happen. Unless a firm continually generates a steady stream of incremental, renovative, and inventive alternatives, its strategy choices unwittingly become narrower and narrower. When this occurs, there can only be one result—the organization will weaken. Thus, senior managers must be highly attentive to monitoring and assessing not just the quality of the alternatives that are generated but the quality of the analytical and organizational processes that give rise to them.

> An agricultural supply firm was reviewing current and emerging trends that could change its industry. The purpose of the firm's industry and macroenvironmental analysis was to determine what its future strategy options might be. As part of the review process, the analysts asked teams of managers to brainstorm new strategy alternatives—options that had not previously received any serious attention. Quickly the teams identified and developed a series of alternatives including taking the firm's current product line into new geographic regions, selling more of its product range to existing customers, developing new channels of distribution (such as e-business) to reach both existing and new

customers, and acquiring some smaller firms with related product lines. These and other alternatives were then critically assessed by the firm's top management team as part of its ongoing strategic planning process.

Without doubt, identifying and developing individual strategic alternatives—the task assigned by senior management to the teams in the agricultural supply firm—constitute one of the most neglected, and as a consequence, least well-managed facets of strategy making. Most managers readily admit that generating alternatives as part of problem solving or leveraging opportunities is not something they do well. Indeed, when pressed, most managers admit they don't invest a lot of intellectual or emotional energy searching for alternatives.

Yet because organizational and environmental change is so prevalent and so risky to ignore, as is shown in so many places in this book, generating strategic alternatives is both a necessary and critical component in change management. When crafting an organization's future strategic direction, managers typically begin by identifying and considering the organization's principal alternatives. By generating alternatives that can be developed into viable and challenging strategic options, managers increase their organization's chances of winning in the marketplace.

This chapter describes how organizations develop strategy alternatives and how organizational processes can enhance the quality of their choices. First we describe what a strategic alternative is, and then we lay out the analytical and organizational processes involved in generating alternatives. A concluding section reviews how senior management can influence the process of alternative generation.

UNDERSTANDING STRATEGY ALTERNATIVES

What Is a Strategic Alternative?

At the most abstract and general level, alternatives are the means by which a goal can be attained, a problem solved, or an opportunity realized. For example, most businesses have various alternative ways to enter a new geographic market or to introduce a new product to the marketplace or to preempt a competitor's anticipated moves to lure away your customers.

It is critical for managers to understand that alternatives are always "nestled," that is, they occur at multiple levels. To quickly illustrate the concept of nestled alternatives, let us consider a business unit example. Table 12.1 shows distinct business strategy alternatives that might be generated by a business unit. As discussed later in this chapter, a set of managers in any business unit or single business firm can begin with a set of alternatives similar to those outlined in Table 12.1 and ask themselves whether and how it might be possible to create and execute each alternative. For example, many business units, when going over their annual strategic planning processes, attempt to identify which

TABLE 12.1 Business Unit Strategy: Some Generic Strategy Alternatives

1. Gain market share with existing products in current markets.
2. Introduce a new product line.
3. Add new items to individual product lines.
4. Drop one or more product lines.
5. Acquire a related product line from a competitor.
6. Acquire an emerging product line from a newly founded firm.
7. Enter new geographic markets.
8. Enter new distribution channels in existing markets.

new geographic markets they can successfully enter with their existing product lines and which product line extensions would be appropriate and desirable.

However, each strategy alternative noted in Table 12.1 contains sub-alternatives. Table 12.2 outlines some of the options that a business unit might consider to gain a major increment of share in a particular geographic market.

Alternatives typically involve opportunities for shaping an organization's future strategic direction—hence the emphasis in this chapter on strategic alternatives. More specifically, by *strategic* we mean that the alternative has the following characteristics:

- It refers to choices about marketplace strategy.[1]
- The issue is of importance to the organization.
- The outcomes of the choices are uncertain.
- It takes time to develop the alternative.

TABLE 12.2 Strategy Subalternatives: Gaining Share in a Particular Market

"Gain market share with existing products in current markets." [Strategic alternative 1 in Table 12.1]

1. Improve functionality (performance) of the product line.
2. Add new features that would increase the product's appeal for some customers.
3. Seek greater shelf space within each type of retail store.
4. Extend number of retailers.
5. Change incentive structure for distributors to entice them to "push" these products.
6. Add some new distributors.
7. Develop new advertising themes to improve image of both the firm and its products.
8. Provide off-site service that would allow the firm to influence many customers simultaneously.
9. Restructure the sales force by realigning sales territories and modestly changing its incentive systems.

The Importance of Identifying and Developing Strategic Alternatives

It is not an overstatement to assert that the future of any organization resides in its ability to identify and develop strategic alternatives. This is so for at least three reasons:

1. Alternatives define the choices available to a top management team as they contemplate any strategic decision. As illustrated in Tables 12.1 and 12.2, once the alternatives have been defined and detailed, managers can then assess the risks, vulnerabilities, and trade-offs associated with any specific choice.

2. Unless new alternatives are continually identified and developed, managers are likely to fall back on enhancing execution of the current strategy. In the face of pervasive and discontinuous competitive change, as noted in Chapter 1, strategies that do not constantly adapt to a changing environment eventually lead to organizational failure.

3. Many large corporations such as Alcoa, Citigroup, IBM, and Motorola are currently in the news because of their attempts to acquire other firms or specific business units of other firms. Unless what it takes to execute these acquisitions and integrate them into the parent organization is fully detailed and assessed, managers in these firms are not likely to understand what alternatives exist. As a result, the likelihood of bad acquisition choices rises considerably.

Types of Alternatives

Alternatives can differ greatly along key dimensions: the extent to which they are logical extensions of existing strategies; the extent to which they are creative or inventive; and, the extent to which they are unthinkable. By "unthinkable," we mean the alternatives break the current rules of what is appropriate and acceptable within the organization. The strategy forms discussed in Chapter 1—incremental, renovative, and inventive—provide a useful way to categorize and think about strategic alternatives.

Incremental alternatives stem from an organization's current strategies. They are typically extensions or corrections to the thrust of what the strategies are now. Many of the alternatives noted in Table 12.2 fall into the category of incremental alternatives.

Renovative alternatives also take the firm's current strategy as a point of departure, but they are intended to significantly alter its direction and thrust. In the language of Chapter 1, they cause major change to the strategy's scope, posture, and goals. They include new product lines, extensions of existing products, and changing emphasis in differentiation (e.g., moving from an emphasis on product functionality alone to include intimacy in relationships with customers).

Renovative alternatives often require managers and others to challenge the conventional wisdom about the market and existing ways of doing business. For example, committing to undertake an acquisition or an alliance in a firm that historically has shunned acquisitions and alliances as a means to develop new products or enter new customer segments, requires managers to openly confront and discuss long-held beliefs and assumptions. A key question: In such a situation, can the top management of the alliance partners learn to trust and work well with their allies and to share profits and learning?

Inventive alternatives, on the other hand, always lead to radical change in the firm's strategy. They embody a new approach to winning in the marketplace and frequently entail new products or solutions. They sometimes represent distinctly new ways of competing against rivals. Thus, they represent a conspicuous departure from the organization's historic mind-set and ways of doing things. They always require new modes of thinking and analysis: The "business case" required to support inventive alternatives often fundamentally conflicts with the rationales underlying current strategy.

Inventive and some renovative alternatives, have been labeled "unthinkable" alternatives in some organizations. However, inventive alternatives are "unthinkable" not because no one in the organization thought of them (or could think of them) but because they contradict a corporation's implicit or explicit rules for making choices. Middle managers begin to assume that inventive alternatives will always be outside the bounds of possibility for any organization or see them as incompatible with the organization's culture and way of doing things. It is precisely for these reasons, however, that it is appropriate to include some inventive alternatives in the early stages of any decision- or strategy-making process. Inventive alternatives frequently can jump-start new lines of thinking throughout the organization. They do so in part by illuminating the status quo in a radically different light. The underlying hope is that they will provoke managers to develop and propose creative solutions resulting in new product breakthroughs and new ways of doing business.

Identifying and Developing Alternatives

Identifying an alternative—incremental, renovative, or inventive—is one thing. Developing it into information that is useful for managerial decision making is quite another. One reason renovative and inventive alternatives are sometimes so quickly dismissed and discarded by managers is that they don't fully understand what the alternative is. Alternatives constitute possibilities: a strategy direction that a firm might pursue. Thus, the alternatives noted in Table 12.1 might be considered only theoretically possible. Until, for example, an inventive alternative such as a new way of delivering services to customers has been described in detail, it is not ready to be assessed and evaluated. [2] Managers would need to know what types of services would be offered to which customers, how the services would be developed, what organizations would be involved in doing so, how the services would be delivered to customers, what roles customers and others would play in the design and development of the services. Table 12.3 illustrates how strategic alternative 7 in Table 12.1 might be probed for its actual potential to the company. Only after alternatives receive the due process of "pretrial discovery" and a creative hearing can they be reasonably evaluated. For brevity, we shall refer to alternative identification and development as alternative generation.

When Are Alternatives Generated?

The pervasive and discontinuous change noted in Chapter 1 and in so many other chapters throughout this book, dictates that alternative generation should be a never-ending activity in every organization. Paradoxically, this may be especially so when managers consider there is not a need for alternatives: They may be becoming complacent and thus are likely to miss the opportunities inherent in current and emerging change. Two major reasons underlie the need for continued alternative generation:

1. Organizations should always be looking for ways to enhance the returns from its existing strategies. The persistent search for both incremental and renovative alternatives provides a sharp focus to any organization's effort to continually monitor and project change in its industry or competitive context, and in its broader macroenvironment. However, unless the organization makes a commitment to seek the opportunities embedded in such environmental change, it is highly likely that they will not be captured.

2. The fundamental strategic challenge noted in Chapter 1—the need to build for tomorrow while exploiting today—necessitates the development of both renovative and inventive alternatives that will allow the organization

TABLE 12.3   Exploring a Potential Strategic Alternative

"Enter new geographic markets" [Strategic alternative 7, Table 12.1]

Identify markets to be entered.
Identify depth and breadth of customers in each market.
Determine purchasing power of each customer segment.
Identify which products should be launched in which markets.
Determine distribution channel options.
Determine appropriate advertising programs.
Determine appropriate sales promotions programs.
Determine use of the firm's own sales force.
Estimate revenue flows.
Estimate costs associated with program of expenditures.
Specify sequence in which markets should be entered.

to position itself for the future marketplace. Unless renovative and inventive alternatives are developed with some frequency, the organization cannot expect to edge ahead of, much less leapfrog, its rivals in the race for leadership in the marketplace.

Alternatives are more necessary at some times than others. When there is a clear need for a strategic change (e.g., there is a continued deterioration in performance), a list of alternative courses of action must be generated.

How Are Valuable Alternatives Generated?

Most companies do not have sophisticated analytical and organizational processes for alternative generation. Even organizations with a systematic approach may not get high paybacks from mere diligence.

At the risk of oversimplification, here's how many firms go about identifying and developing valuable alternatives: several individuals are assigned the task, they dutifully identify a set of alternatives, prune the initial set down to a few that are more fully developed, identify those that are "doable," and perhaps arrive at a small set that are described in terms of actions, consequences, and resources. Yet, in the same organizations, alternative generation is a significant and spontaneous part of decision making. Alternatives are crafted rather quickly, without attempting to identify whether they are "good" or "bad," and without seeking the input of others outside or inside the organization, about which alternatives might be worth considering.

Because there are no simple algorithms for alternative generation, the next two sections detail some key analytical and organizational approaches to identifying and developing alternatives. Before we do so, however, it is important to consider what is meant by a quality alternative.

What Are the Qualities of a Superior Alternative?

We noted that organizations seldom attempt to determine whether alternatives are good or bad. The purpose of evaluating alternatives, as discussed in Chapter 13, is to determine which alternatives are best for the organization. It is also important for anyone involved in alternative generation to understand what constitutes a truly valuable alternative. This understanding leads to more efficient alternative development processes and to alternatives that are more likely to enhance organizational performance.

Although there are no definitive criteria for judging the quality of any individual alternative or set of alternatives, organizations have found the following guidelines helpful:

- *The variety of the alternatives.* Having wide-ranging alternatives is important because the merits or flaws of one alternative or a set of related alternatives often only become apparent whey they are judged against other alternatives.

- *Differences among the alternatives compared to the present situation.* Among other things, such differences compel decision makers to reappraise the quality of the present strategy.
- *The costs and difficulties of implementation.* If the alternatives are too easy to implement, it is most unlikely that any significant renovative or inventive alternative has been identified.
- *Do they challenge existing goals?* Superior alternatives cause managers to challenge existing expectations, aspirations, and objectives. As a consequence, long-held assumptions and beliefs may be challenged.

A set of superior alternatives presents different viewpoints and assumptions. A good list therefore creates real choice: Decision makers can select from among distinctly different alternatives. To the extent that alternatives are mutually exclusive, they should help decision makers avoid locking into a particular alternative too quickly.

Some Common Errors in Alternative Generation

Although they are implicit in this and other chapters, some common mistakes in the way organizations go about alternative generation are worth noting. Eliminating each mistake saves time and contributes greatly to developing quality alternatives:

- Sometimes, neither renovative alternatives involving significant strategic change nor inventive alternatives are developed. Thus, managers' understanding of the present and the future is not challenged.
- Too often, the incremental or renovative alternatives considered are merely variations on a theme. For example, a group of product managers spent considerable time developing alternatives to enhance the firm's competitive posture. Each alternative emphasized price reduction. It was only when they considered an alternative built around enhancing the product's functionality and associated service that real insight accrued. They stumbled on an alternative that could lead to a viable action plan for a price increase rather than a price decrease.
- Managers and others sometimes lock into specific alternatives far too quickly. Generating and evaluating alternatives is not a process that easily occurs as managers take a series of steps. In practice, generating alternatives often gives rise to new information which in turn sheds further light on the strategic issue at hand. Indeed, new information may lead to the generation of new alternatives. One firm that was seeking alternative ways to enter a foreign market discovered that some of its competitors might be interested in selling their business "if the price was right." This information led to the generation of a new alternative: the acquisition of one or more competitors who already had a presence in the relevant foreign markets. The issue definition switched from one of "going it alone"

to procuring a business that was already in the market. The intensity of the search for new information depends on the importance of the issue to the future of the firm.

- Many organizations, regrettably, confine alternative generation to one phase of the strategic planning process, or restrict the activity to one subgroup or task force, or confine initiating the search for alternatives to one or a small team of executives. As a consequence, the contributions and insights of many organizational members and groups are simply lost to the process of alternative generation.

The analytical and organizational processes outlined in the following two sections are intended to help managers avoid these or related errors.

ANALYTICAL APPROACHES TO IDENTIFYING ALTERNATIVES

Because so few organizations have honed the art of identifying and developing alternatives, managers need some form of systematic analysis approach to ensure that they do not fall into the errors previously noted. Although analytical approaches to alternative generation can be categorized in multiple ways, we shall group the approaches based on the organization's strategy context: its current market strategy, business unit strategy, and corporate-level strategy. Each strategy context allows us to connect to the types of strategy alternatives noted earlier: incremental, renovative, and inventive.

Before we detail the various analytical approaches, three critical considerations need to be emphasized:

1. The alternatives that emerge are shaped by organization's understanding of its business issues. If senior managers believe that only incremental alternatives need to be considered, then renovative, and certainly inventive, alternatives are not likely.

2. Organizational context and goals influence the process. If managers are trying to dramatically increase financial performance, they are very likely to search for and approve development of alternatives that satisfy the enhancement of financial returns.

3. Current and future strategy choices involve complex issues: changes in technology, competitive environments, global competition, and host governments. Thus, managers need to be willing to spend considerable time teasing through these complex issues to detect latent opportunities—strategy alternatives.

The analytical aspects of the alternative detection and development can be challenging. Beware of simple alternatives arrived at quickly using only one narrow approach to alternative generation.

Extensions of Current Strategy

The current strategy provides a logical basis for generating both incremental and renovative alternatives. Table 12.4 illustrates many possibilities for extending the scope and posture elements of a firm's current strategy. These alternatives are aimed at extending the firm's market share within both end-customer and distribution channel segments by extending its current product lines and/or penetrating existing and new customer segments.

Although the alternatives noted in Table 12.4 are obvious in the sense that they represent the ones that most firms should (and usually do) consider on an ongoing basis, they may also lead to developing and executing alternatives that mark significant departures from the firm's historic strategy. Such renovative alternatives may involve dramatic shifts in the firm's scope, posture, and goals. Consider the recent change in America Online's strategy in Great Britain. Largely in response to the free offerings of its rivals, America Online introduced its own free Internet service, known as Netscape Online, thus breaking with its long tradition of only offering its service for a fee or monthly subscription. By offering the new service under the Netscape Online name (itself a joint venture between America Online and Bertelsmann AG, a large German media conglomerate), America Online aims to differentiate it and not cannibalize its content-rich subscription services like AOL UK and Compuserve. Presumably, America Online identified and analyzed a variety of alternatives such as those noted in Table 12.4 before it chose to offer a subscription free service under a new brand name.

TABLE 12.4 Alternatives Stemming from Current Strategy: Scope and Posture

Scope

1. Add new product lines.
2. Extend the variety of models, styles, or types of each product within each of the firm's product lines.
3. Penetrate more customers in existing markets.
4. Obtain greater share of existing customers' purchases of these product categories.
5. Seek customers in new geographic markets with existing products.
6. Seek customers in new geographic markets with new products.
7. Penetrate new distribution channels with existing products.

Posture (Differentiation)

1. Enhance functionality of products.
2. Add new services around the core product.
3. Improve relationships with all customer groups.
4. Upgrade image and reputation of the company and its products.
5. Improve the price/value relationship for customers.

As illustrated in the America Online example, alternatives that extend the firm's current strategy inevitably must address competitive posture, that is, how the firm distinguishes itself from its competitors in the eyes of customers.[3] The emphasis is on identifying potential ways in which the firm can differentiate itself in each of its product-customer segments. While the sources of differentiation may vary considerably, from unique skills and capabilities to market position (market share and reputation), the intent in identifying differentiation alternatives is to develop specific means to get and keep customers.

Generating differentiation alternatives requires the organization to ask the types of questions noted in Table 12.5. These questions are likely to spawn alternatives that result in a combination of the dimensions shown in Table 12.4.[4] Such alternatives may range from customization (customizing the firm's offering for each customer) to mass marketing the firm's product line at the lowest possible price.

Obvious extensions of a firm's current strategy sometimes serve as stepping-stones to more inventive ones. For example, an organization can develop innovative ways of reaching its customers with its existing products or new products. Often such alternatives represent a major departure from the normal modes of operating or the conventional wisdom within an industry. Many firms are now spending considerable time figuring out how they can use

---

TABLE 12.5 Generating Differentiation Alternatives: Sample Questions

1. What are our current customers' needs and wants?
   How do they appear to be changing?
   What might they be in two, three, or five years?

2. What are the needs and wants of our competitors' customers?
   How are they changing?
   How different are they from those of our current customers?

3. What are the needs and wants of our substitute competitors' customers?
   How different are they from those of our customers?

4. To what extent are customers falling into clearly identifiable segments based on buying behaviors, volume of purchases, demographic considerations, or other criteria?

5. What are some of the key trends in customers' buying behaviors?

6. What opportunities might be suggested by these needs and wants?

7. Given answers (however tentative) to the preceding questions, how might the firm differentiate itself in terms of:
   Product line width.
   Product features.
   Functionality.
   Service.
   Availability.
   Image and reputation.
   Selling and relationships.
   Price.

e-business to connect directly to customers or end-users and avoid the interventions and bottlenecks represented by many of the channel members (distributors and retailers) that currently separate them from those who "pay the final bill."

Revenue Enhancement and Cost Reduction

Another distinct analysis approach to alternative generation addresses ways the organization can enhance revenues and/or reduce costs. These alternatives are not mutually exclusive: Alternatives that enhance revenues often also lead directly to unit cost reduction.[5] Also, many of these alternatives are closely related to those that are extensions of the current strategy.

Revenue enhancement alternatives, a constant goal of managers, aim to increase revenues within the current business. The alternatives noted in Table 12.4 can be viewed as means of revenue enhancement.

Many consumer goods, food, and beverage firms are now actively seeking to attain greater shelf space from retailers and/or greater returns per square foot of shelf space. This goal has contributed to the identification and development of previously unrecognized or little considered alternatives. Consider, for example, Pepsico's recent efforts to develop a "power aisle" on a trial basis in selected large supermarkets. The company wants to reserve both sides of a regular aisle in a supermarket and stock it with Pepsico products including Pepsi soft drinks and Frito-Lay snack foods. The intent is to lure consumers to choose a variety of related products simply by having them walk down the reserved aisle.[6]

Cost minimization builds on the philosophy of being the low-cost producer and generating alternatives that keep the cost structure low. More intense rivalry in many industries has compelled many organizations to seriously

---

TABLE 12.6   Identifying Cost Minimization Alternatives

1. How can the organization reduce manufacturing or operations costs? Is it possible to extend capacity utilization? Is it possible to reduce or eliminate waste?
2. How might the organization reduce or control raw material and input costs?
3. What might be some lower cost sources of components, raw materials, and other supplies?
4. What possibilities might exist now or at some point in the future to use substitute components, materials, or supplies?
5. What might the firm outsource to reduce costs?
6. What purchasing policies might be changed?
7. What distribution efficiencies might the firm be able to affect?
8. Where might further economies of scale exist?
9. How might the firm partner or align with others (e.g., vendors and distributors) to lower costs?

search for cost reduction alternatives. Many of the questions that typify the search for cost minimization are noted in Table 12.6 on page 266.

Many industries could be cited as examples in which cost minimization strategies have emerged as critical to the survival of individual firms. Consider the U.S. airline industry. Many airlines have had to consider reducing capacity, decreasing the number of personnel, and canceling orders on new aircraft. Several airlines have lowered costs by reducing the number of hubs that they supported.[7]

Lots of companies seek out alternatives that achieve not just cost savings but simultaneously give rise to added capability to deliver value to customers, often through augmenting their capacity to differentiate from rivals. Oracle Corporation, for example, is only one of many corporations that recently announced major cost-saving initiatives such as shuttering close to 40 data-processing centers worldwide and placing its financial and human resource systems in just two locations. These actions would enable its new online software sales processes to reach more new customers and serve them more quickly and more efficiently.[8]

Generic Corporate Strategies[9]

The corporation gains as much from the identification of strategy alternatives as the business units do. As discussed in Chapter 2, many corporations are now dramatically shifting their strategies. Thus, at some earlier stage, corporate managers must have identified and assessed their options, and chosen a change of course. The following are some of the major alternatives.

Diversification provides an analytical framework for corporate expansion in both related and unrelated business areas. Some firms find their major business area maturing and unable to provide the sustained growth that shareholders want. Consideration of diversification inevitably follows. Conglomerate or unrelated diversification creates a wide spectrum of alternatives that can be generated. Firms can identify and explore almost every imaginable option pertaining to entry into businesses that are new to the corporation. One large U.S. conglomerate has claimed that at one time or another it has investigated the possibility of diversifying into almost every industry that exists.[10]

The importance of continually generating and considering corporate strategy alternatives is well illustrated by the many firms that adopted conglomerate diversification in the 1960s and 1970s but found themselves desperately trying in the 1980s to identify the alternative that would best refocus them on their core businesses. On the other hand, some firms such as Dow Chemical, have been successful at conglomerate diversification. Dow needed to identify alternatives that would overcome the cyclicality of its commodity chemical business, and it did so with the acquisition of drug and specialty chemical operations.

Acquisition or merger is a generic corporate strategy that opens the door to many alternatives.[11] It is obviously an alternative that has found favor in many corporations: during the 1980s, $1.3 trillion was spent in the United States on mergers, acquisitions, and takeovers.

The failure rate in mergers and acquisitions suggests the importance of analysis in identifying potential merger and acquisition candidates. It has frequently been noted that many of these failures occurred because the merger or acquisition decisions relied too heavily on the input of financial analysts for both generating and evaluating the alternatives.[12] The better deals were based on strategic analysis and addressed alternatives that had a fit alongside the current corporate strategy. Examples of successful acquirers (and their acquisitions) include General Electric (RCA), May Department Stores (Associated Dry Goods), and Quaker Oats (Stokely-Van Camp). Before making an acquisition, a firm usually does a detailed analysis of potential targets. American Telephone & Telegraph studied Digital Equipment Corporation, Hewlett-Packard, and Apple Computer as potential alternatives, before launching a hostile takeover bid for NCR Corporation.

Divestment is often initially an unthinkable alternative because it is hard for management to even contemplate divesting a business after spending many years cultivating it. The reality, as evidenced in the large number of corporations shedding one or more substantial business units, is that divestment is a viable and highly appropriate corporate-level decision.

Frequently, divestment is identified as an option when it has not been fully studied. This seems to be especially true when the business unit is profitable or in a growing market. When the alternative to divestment is thoroughly scrutinized, management may realize that the particular business unit does not fit with the corporate intent or vision.[13] Proceeds from the sale of the business unit may be urgently needed to fund and develop other, more viable business areas.

Global Strategies

As discussed in Chapter 4, organizations must develop alternatives that address the increasingly important global business arena. Typically, consideration of global strategy involves the generation of myriad alternatives: selection of different countries and regions; the products suitable for the selected areas; how best to enter these areas; what strategies to pursue in penetrating these markets.

Sara Lee is a firm that has globalized its strategy in almost all its product domains in the past decade including apparel, personal-care items, and baked goods. What alternatives might it have considered? That is, what alternatives might have been responsible for quick penetration of major national markets overseas? Acquisitions was one alternative that it identified and fully developed: Recent acquisitions have added to its businesses in many countries in recent years.

Another alternative might have been the extension of its products across national borders. This potential alternative flies in the face of considerable conventional wisdom. The food industry traditionally has been dominated by adherence to unique national tastes, customs, and eating habits and practices. Thus, products had to be designed specifically for individual markets. But Sara Lee and other food companies are beginning to find that certain products can be offered successfully "as is" in many national markets.

Inventive Alternatives

Inventive alternatives, as noted, require decision makers to break out of their mental models, assumption sets, and predictable way of thinking about businesses. Unless they do so, there is little chance they can reinvent their business, that is, create ways of doing business that are new to the marketplace. As argued in Chapter 1, strategic reinvention requires developing strategic alternatives that are premised on an understanding of possible futures and not on how and why the organization's strategies were successful in the past.

Managers must systematically identify and develop inventive alternatives for at least two reasons:

1. If they don't do so on their own initiative, they may be forced into doing so. The actions of competitors have compelled many organizations to seriously consider what previously might have been seen as unthinkable. Some firms simply would not consider divestment or merger until their circumstances were so dire (through the loss of market share to rivals) that the only choices were one of these alternatives or going out of business.

2. Once formerly unthinkable alternatives are identified, they may prove on reflection to be quality alternatives. For example, both Apple and IBM found it very difficult to seriously consider any form of cooperation or alignment due to the intensity of the rivalry between the organizations. Yet once an alternative in the area of technology development was explored, it became apparent to both organizations that the alternative had strong potential to be a "win-win" relationship.

Cooperative Strategies

Cooperating with current or potential competitors is an increasingly employed alternative. Many different types of alliances, relationships, and networks are reported in the business press every day of the week. Many of these cooperative relationships represent options that many firms would never have considered a few years ago.

One of the challenges in identifying and developing cooperative alternatives is that so many distinct possibilities potentially exist: joint ventures, cooperative R&D, integrated marketing and distribution, cross-licensing of technology, outsourcing of manufacturing, to name but a few. One of the dangers of these cooperative alternatives is that in gaining an ally, an organization may also be creating a future competitor. Thus, it is important to consider in advance the consequences of cooperating with current or potential competitors. Many American firms have discovered much to their surprise that cooperative agreements with their Japanese counterparts have greatly enabled the Japanese firms to learn about the business, the technology, and the customers—precisely, the knowledge they needed to displace the American partners from the market.

ORGANIZATIONAL PROCESSES TO AID IN ALTERNATIVE GENERATION

The design and development of appropriate organizational processes and procedures can aid and abet alternative generation. Among the many such processes that could be discussed, several have proven their usefulness in aiding alternative development. These may be employed at any of the various levels (corporate, division, or business unit) within the firm. They are useful to any manager who wants to stretch the thinking of the individuals involved in the alternative generation process.

A Designated Team

Many firms create a team or a task force and charge it with identifying and developing a set of strategy alternatives that can be evaluated later, often as part of the strategic planning process. The team is asked to apply many of the analysis processes described in the preceding section. Teams often begin by identifying incremental opportunities that would modestly extend the current strategy in new directions. They then proceed to identify renovative opportunities aimed at reconfiguring the firm's industry or some segment of it. Finally, the team assumes the task of thinking about creative opportunities that would result in products or services new to the market.

Alternative Teams: Using Assumption Analysis to Manage Conflict

Rather than employing only one team, a few firms have used two teams or task forces to generate alternatives. The importance of this organizational process is that different and sometimes conflicting assumptions underlie different alternatives. Distinct sets of assumptions—for example, about the future growth of specific product-markets, competitors' strategies, the evolution of technology, governmental policies, and the organization's own cash flows—may underpin distinctly different alternatives such as internally developing a radical new product or merely extending existing product lines. If these assumptions are not identified, explicated, and critiqued, they unwittingly influence the identification and development of alternatives.

There are two philosophies about the management of assumption conflicts:

1. They need to be acknowledged, channeled, and managed.
2. They need to be stimulated to enhance the probability of generating quality alternatives.

It is widely accepted that conflict stimulation can enhance the alternative generation process. Mason and Mitroff[14] suggested that managers are frequently unaware of the assumptions they hold and that examining them through debate or conflict generation can lead to a rich understanding of the prevailing problem frame within organizations. Research suggests that structured conflict helps to confront basic assumptions and to improve the decision-making process in generating and evaluating alternatives.

Two specific processes are useful:

1. "Devil's Advocacy," a process in which an alternative is examined with the perspective of heaven and hell reversed. In addition to searching the proposal for inconsistencies, inaccuracies, and irrelevancies, the Devil's advocate must critique the proposal from the contrarian perspective, at least in part.[15]
2. "Dialectic Inquiry," a utilization of groups to present the most divergent alternative views of the issue. Individuals are often grouped based on building the most heterogeneous viewpoints across groups. The groups develop alternatives and then debate them. An important aspect of this process is the identification of underlying assumptions.

Scenario Generation

In recent years, cutting-edge firms have experimented with developing sets of scenarios in a formal process that allows managers to envisage and detail alternative pictures of the future of an industry, of a number of related technologies, or of the economy. Using this scenario process, managers address what the future might be, what could be, and why it might arise. Scenarios allow any group of decision makers to envision the future without being constrained by widely held and possibly incorrect assumptions. This scenario process usually generates four alternative pictures of the future simultaneously, as shown in Box 12.1. This helps managers see, experience, and practice managing in a set of unique, relevant, and possible futures before they take place.

Each of the scenarios may give rise to distinct strategic alternatives. For example, a firm may develop a set of scenarios that consider massive upheaval in its industry (such as the entry of substitute products that replace a large percentage of current competitors' product lines), or the introduction of a range of new products stemming from one or more technology breakthroughs, and a baseline scenario that is a continuation of the industry's key current

---

Box 12.1

Different Industry Scenarios as Inputs to Generating Strategic Alternatives

Scenario 1. The industry will experience a rate of growth over the next five years double that of the past five years. A host of new products will be introduced by new rivals and by some existing rivals. Major new customer functionalities will be established.

Scenario 2. The industry will experience a rate of growth well in excess of the past five years but it will be driven solely by the emergence of a single new product. All rivals will quickly develop largely similar varieties of the new core product.

Scenario 3. The industry, as currently configured, will slowly but surely succumb to the emergence of one or more substitute products. Some of the dominant current rivals will exit the business. Technology will continue to drive and refine the substitute products.

Scenario 4. The industry will continue to be dominated by existing products and modest extensions of them. As a consequence, overall industry sales growth will plateau and begin to decline due to penetration of the major customer segments. Over time, price competition begins to replace product differentiation as the primary focus of winning customers.

---

trends. The organization then develops specific alternatives that would allow it to prosper in the competitive environment sketched out in each scenario. In the second scenario just noted, the firm might craft an alternative around the development of a new product that no one in the firm had previously envisioned. Thus, it is no surprise that many of the alternatives generated through scenarios not only give rise to renovative strategy possibilities but also to inventive strategy options. Consider the following examples:

- A healthcare company developed four scenarios detailing distinctly competitive contexts over a five-year time frame. One scenario emphasized the potential for a number of entities in the industry supply and delivery chain to combine into a new type of organizational network. The firm then developed a highly inventive alternative: what that network would look like, how it might be created, and how it might function.

- A software provider developed a set of scenarios outlining potential strategies that might be pursued by some of its current rivals. One implication of these scenarios was the need for new products. As things now stood, the current rivals could decimate each other's financial results through many different types of aggressive marketing. After studying this scenario, the firm generated alternatives involving different types of new software offerings, using both its own skills and competencies and those of potential alliance partners.

Scenarios allow firms to think backward from a future. That is, to develop pictures of some future with a totally different operating environment and then think of what has to happen for that future to come to pass or to be made to happen. Scenario development fosters an organizational environment in which creative and unthinkable alternatives are likely to be identified and developed.

Simulations

Simulations are computer-based models that allow decision makers to test multiple interactions among a set of variables. It is not uncommon to include 20 or 30 variables representing differing levels of activity in sales, manufacturing, operations, marketing, and service, in a simulation. The appeal of simulations resides in their ability to test the consequences of different assumptions about (for example) sales results, cost dynamics, and competitors' marketing programs. The results often give rise to issues and possible alternatives that could never be gleaned simply by eyeballing a set of numbers. Simulations testing the revenue enhancement or cost reduction consequences of changes in the rate of product introduction by competitors, and in their marketing program expenditures, as well as the firm's own marketing, sales, and service programs, may lead to marketing alternatives that managers may not have previously considered.

Brainstorming

Sometimes managers need organizational processes that are less formal than scenario development and simulations, and are designed specifically to help generate creative and perhaps unthinkable alternatives. An environment conducive to such creative processes must offer openness, trust, freedom from criticism for failure or nonconformity, and playfulness.

Brainstorming is one such creative process. According to its rules, participants can come up with any alternative without fear of criticism. Four rules are usually suggested: (1) no criticism, (2) no bounds on the nature of the ideas, (3) no limit on the number of ideas that can be generated, and (4) no restraints on using ideas to create new ideas.

Brainstorming is especially useful when individuals have found it difficult over some period of time to get beyond obvious alternatives. For example, a group of managers should try to brainstorm if the alternatives generated appear to be merely incremental alternatives.

Complex Adaptive Systems and Chaos Theory

Scenarios and simulations demonstrate the difficulties inherent in trying to anticipate and project emerging and future change in the external context of any organization. A number of authors have advocated a theory of understanding organizations and their interactions with their competitive context under conditions that stem from the principles and premises of complex adaptive systems.[16] Its critical principles relevant to organizations include (1) it is impossible to predict a planned or envisioned future because the linkages between cause and effect are tremendously difficult to trace, (2) stability in relationships between a firm and its customers, competitors, vendors, is likely to be a precursor to failure (because others will see and react to change faster), and (3) complexity arises because entities can interact in multiple, and often surprising ways, thus creating unexpected events and patterns. Recognition that every organization is itself a complex adaptive system that must live "close to the edge of chaos" encourages managers not only to accept the inevitability of change, but also to work assiduously to achieve and sustain multiple internal cultures, and to deal wisely with conflict around issues, lack of cohesion, and lack of consensus.

Using this approach, alternatives are created in a spontaneous manner. They address the unwritten issues, aspirations, and challenges to which key groups of managers are attending. By addressing these strategic issues, managers create instability in the existing system. Through an informal process of discussion and debate, they choose an alternative that shatters the existing order. Thus, alternative generation becomes a spontaneous process for challenging and changing relationships in the firm, and success depends on destabilizing the current organization.

Group Work Support Systems

Several different types of organizations are utilizing computer tools to facilitate interaction among groups of individuals in alternative generation. Indicative of this thrust is work developed by the University of Arizona, which uses a room with 24 workstations and a variety of media equipment. It allows a group of managers to generate ideas and surface assumptions utilizing computers and other media. A facilitator, providing expertise in decision making and group dynamics, helps to lead the group through the stages of alternative generation.

In the Electronic Brainstorming (EBS) technique, ideas are generated anonymously and entered into the computer. By having the ideas submitted anonymously, the status of the individual submitting the idea has no bearing on the attention the idea gets. The files are shared from workstation to workstation to allow others to build on the ideas. Ideas can change, grow, or inspire other ideas. The resulting ideas are then categorized and grouped according to issues. Out of this mode of interaction come potential alternatives that probably would not be crafted by any individual working alone.

The Strategic Planning Process

The annual strategic planning process, now utilized by most firms in one form or another, serves as a logical focal point of alternative generation. Many of the processes previously discussed—scenarios, simulations, brainstorming—are frequently used in the early stages of strategic planning to identify potential alternatives.

However, the strategic planning process lends itself to many organizational processes for the purposes of alternative generation. One large computer firm asks each executive team to identify its list of "alternative business models" when it submits its long-range plans to corporate headquarters. Each alternative business model describes in detail how the business unit might "do business differently." Thus, it shows how the firm might develop new products differently, or manage integrated logistics in an entirely different manner, or how it might create a network of relationships with new suppliers, technology houses, and distribution channels. Each business model thus becomes the source of new strategy alternatives.

A large energy firm asks a team of managers to identify the strategy that they believe would be most successful as a rival against their own firm's strategy. Managers then examine the strategy for clues to alternatives that may have been omitted or downplayed in the firm's own strategy analysis work.

ROLE OF TOP MANAGEMENT IN ALTERNATIVE GENERATION PROCESS

Alternative generation is poorly executed in many firms because it is not considered important by top management for several reasons:

- It is not seen within the organization as the job of top management; instead, it is viewed as falling within the domain of middle management. Top management's role is to choose among alternatives, not to develop them.
- It is too time consuming. Top management simply does not have the time to become involved with alternative development.
- Top management does not have the knowledge to develop alternatives in sufficient detail.

Yet, top management can influence alternative generation in multiple ways:

- Top management must remove organizational obstacles to generating renovative and inventive alternatives. In some organizations, senior managers ask that a listing of such alternatives be included in the early phases of the annual strategy review process or in the early stages of discussions about specific strategic decisions.
- Senior managers can designate resources specifically for the alternative generation process. They can fund many of the organizational processes noted earlier such as scenario or simulation teams. They can authorize ad hoc teams to identify and develop distinctly different alternatives, especially inventive alternatives.

- Perhaps most importantly, senior managers through their words and deeds, should emphasize the need for alternatives that stretch and create learning rather than those that extrapolate the present into the future. They can challenge middle-level managers and functional groups to develop renovative and inventive alternatives that would enable the firm's vision and mission to become a reality. A vision should provide a challenge for the future and give members of the firm the opportunity to generate new possibilities that stretch the current organizational analytics and mind-set.

SUMMARY

Unless managers carefully nurture the identification and development of strategic alternatives, those that are subjected to the available strategy evaluation methodologies, as discussed in Chapter 13, are not likely to move the organization in the direction of inventive and renovative strategies. Managers must help create both the analytical and organizational processes that are instrumental in evoking creative strategy alternatives.

NOTES

1. These are the principal foci of Chapter 1: Winning in the marketplace and building the strategic organization.

2. Since the evaluation of alternatives is the focus of Chapter 13, this chapter only addresses the identification and development of alternatives.

3. For a detailed discussion of competitive posture or differentiation, see Chapters 1 and 3.

4. This is in keeping with the observation in Chapter 1 that posture that attains some degree of sustainable differentiation almost certainly results from the integration of the dimensions shown in Table 12.5.

5. For a detailed discussion of business unit strategies, see Chapter 2.

6. Constance L. Hays, "An Aisle Unto Itself: Pepsi's Vision: All of Its Eggs in One Shopping Basket," *New York Times* (July 31, 1999), pp. B1 and B14.

7. See "Ready to Soar Again? The Big Flyboys May Be Bouncing Back at Last," *Business Week* (April 26, 1993), pp. 26–28.

8. See "Oracle: Practicing What It Preaches," *Business Week* (August 16, 1999), pp. 74–76.

9. See Chapter 2 for a discussion of corporate strategies.

10. This is largely a true statement if one accepts that the provision of suppliers or raw materials constitutes involvement or participation in an industry.

11. Acquisitions and mergers are the means by which firms often execute their diversification strategy.

12. The difficulties in integrating financial and other considerations in evaluating strategy alternatives is explicitly considered in Chapter 13.

13. The notions of corporate intent and vision were discussed in Chapter 1.

14. R.O. Mason and Ian I. Mitroff, *Challenging Strategic Planning Assumptions* (New York: Wiley, 1981).

15. See C. Schwenk, *Essence of Strategic Decision-Making* (Lexington, MA: Lexington Books, 1988).

16. See, for example, R.D. Stacey, *Managing the Unknowable: Strategic Boundaries between Order and Chaos in Organizations* (San Francisco: Jossey-Bass, 1992); and Howard Sherman and Ron Schultz, *Open Boundaries: Creating Business Innovation through Complexity* (Reading, MA: Perseus Books, 1998).

13 EVALUATING STRATEGY ALTERNATIVES

George S. Day
University of Pennsylvania

Unless we change our direction we are likely to wind up where we are headed

—*Ancient Chinese proverb*

Poor choices of strategic direction are costly. They dissipate scarce financial resources, consume time, and cause management to neglect other opportunities as they struggle to contain the damage. Consider the high costs of these initiatives:

- Disney built a theme park in France based on the assumption that visitors would behave—at least in some ways—like the tourists in its U.S. and Japanese parks. They didn't, and Euro-Disney came close to bankruptcy.

- British Satellite Broadcasting based its television broadcasting strategy on the development of a transmission technology that was superior to what was available. Their delay gave an opening to Sky Broadcasting, which used an older but adequate technology. Sky won because they were first to market and locked in customers with their receiving equipment. Most customers wanted a choice between programs, not technologies.

- Next Software Inc., the company Steve Jobs launched after losing Apple, targeted the university segment and developed powerful, elegantly designed workstations with advanced features researchers would like. The college and university market, however, had little money for high-priced computers. Next was ultimately bought out by Apple.

Each of these flawed strategies was based on bad assumptions that were not rigorously challenged. The purpose of this chapter is to offer a series of test questions that can reduce the likelihood of bad choices. They are also

278

useful for improving strategies, by identifying weaknesses to be overcome and ensuring that the implementers have a common understanding of the key success factors.

How can managers reduce the likelihood of bad decisions and encourage good decisions? The strategy development process that is the backbone of this book suggests three answers: understand the situation fully, surface a rich set of alternatives, and subject these alternatives to a rigorous strategy review. This chapter contributes to the process by proposing a series of challenging questions that must be asked during these reviews.

Had the management of Convergent Technologies squarely confronted these test questions before they rushed their Workslate notebook computer to the market (see Box 13.1), they might have avoided a costly debacle that forced their withdrawal from the burgeoning personal computer market. We refer to the Workslate experience as we develop the logic of a strategy evaluation framework.

Despite the excellence of the Workslate product, prospects for successful implementation of the entry strategy were never good. What questions should have been asked to help reveal these problems? Each of the test questions formulated in this chapter addresses the credibility of a proposed strategy; the answers determine whether senior management has confidence in realizing the promised returns on the investment.

These questions work best when there is a rich array of strategic alternatives from which to choose. There is mounting evidence that superior strategic choices are made when the decision makers explicitly search for and debate several alternatives at a time. The variety gives managers a basis for comparison and enhances creativity by suggesting combinations of different strategies. However, the debate over which alternatives should be chosen will be productive only when the alternatives are compared in terms of three fundamental issues that underlie creation of shareholder values. These issues are dealt with in the four tests included in this chapter.

The first fundamental issue addresses the prospects for superior profitability. These prospects depend on the attractiveness of the market opportunity (Test 1), and the ability of the business to gain and sustain a competitive advantage (Test 2). These two sources of profits can be seen schematically in Figure 13.1, which displays the distribution of profits of all the firms in a market at a given time. The bell curve indicates that a few are doing well, some are doing poorly, and the majority of firms are being bunched around the average.

The second fundamental issue is whether the *intended* strategy, which promises superior—or at least acceptable—profitability, has a reasonable chance of being *realized* (Test 3). Is this a strategy that can be implemented with the skills and resources at hand? If not, can the deficiencies be overcome without too much extra cost or time delay?

The third issue asks whether the risk-reward ratio is acceptable (Test 4). Specifically, what things might go wrong and can the potential damage be

Box 13.1

Convergent Technologies Learns an Expensive Lesson

In 1983, the company was a well-regarded designer and manufacturer of powerful workstations, which were sold through other brand names. Management was anxious to diversify into other computer markets to reduce their exposure to a single volatile market. They also wanted to establish their own brand name, and capitalize on the promise of rapid growth and high volumes in the emerging personal computer market. The Workslate computer was their first foray into a mass market under their own name.

The initial reception left no doubt the Workslate was an outstanding product, with a substantial lead over the Japanese competition. The designers had managed to package a powerful small computer into a shape the size of letter paper and one inch thick. They accomplished this feat in less than a year by skipping field testing and going straight from design to manufacturing.

Soon after its introduction, the Workslate appeared on the covers of three major computer magazines, was featured in the American Express Christmas catalog, and touted in various mailings. One computer retailing chain forecast they could sell everything that could be made. When the company saw this reception, it made ambitious plans to sell 100,000 units in the first year, at a retail value of $90 million. So confident was management in these signals of acceptance that it was decided that research into the market was not necessary, and would only delay proceedings. For the same reason the president rejected the marketing manager's request for a $7 million launch budget, and only reluctantly agreed to spend $700,000.

The first cracks in the plan emerged when the project ran into production difficulties. The company was a manufacturer of workstations for large computer suppliers, and was unused to large-volume production of standard units. As a result, the factory soon fell a month behind schedule and missed most of the Christmas season. Lack of production wasn't the real problem; customers weren't buying what was available. In fact, it wasn't clear this was a consumer product that could be sold as an ordinary personal computer. The company used a totally new sales force to reach a mass market consumer and ignored the existing sales network of business sales teams and distribution that might have delivered steady sales. Confusion was also created in the market by frequent price changes; starting at $900, the retail price soared to $1,300, but soon dropped to $1,100 in face of buyer resistance. It appeared the accountants were responsible for the price hikes after they discovered that even at the most optimistic production levels it was not profitable at a unit price of $900. Costs were high, because of very high expenses, including 50 engineers in the R&D budget.

Only 1,000 units were sold in the first quarter of 1984. The losses were mounting so rapidly that the company was forced to cease production by July and take a $30 million write-off. As serious as the cash loss was to the

---

Box 13.1   *(Continued)*

company, this sum did not begin to reveal the true extent of the damage. Because senior management and the R&D group were so distracted by this problem, they neglected their core workstation business and lost ground in a fast-moving sector that they have never recovered. Worse, the company lost a chance to become a significant player in the booming PC market, because "once bitten (they were) twice shy" as the old saying reminds us. Although these "opportunity costs" did not appear in any financial statement, the management was appropriately held accountable for the bad judgment that was the cause.

---

contained? Will credible forecasts of revenues, costs, and investments yield profit returns that warrant taking these risks?

VALUE-ADDING STRATEGY REVIEWS

Management did not subject the Workslate entry to a rigorous review before making major financial commitments. The go-ahead decision was made by advocates who were simply validating their conviction they had picked a winner. The result was collective delusion, a condition that permitted management to ignore some awkward realities. An effective, tough-minded review by

FIGURE 13.1   Distribution of profits across rivals.

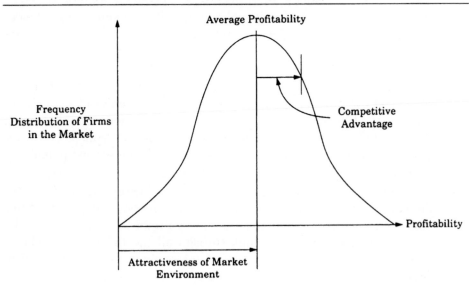

an informed and objective top management group would have led to a search for an entry strategy that better suited the capabilities and assets of the firm.

The root of the Workslate debacle was the unwarranted belief by the development team that the excellence of the product would sell itself to all comers. This belief is seldom justifiable, no matter how good the product, but it is especially dangerous when it obscures the need to take the product to the right market through the right channels. Because neither the Workslate team nor the parent management had any experience with retail chains, they did not consider the lack of match between what their product could do and the needs of the market they were trying to reach. Had they realized this earlier, they might have seriously considered other strategies using available channels to reach business markets, or partnerships to gain market access.

A strategy review should be much more than a detailed scrutiny of financial projections as the basis for a go or no-go decision. To add value to the strategy development process, the review should serve four functions:

1. Provide top management with a sound basis for resource allocation decisions and for the negotiation of performance objectives. There will be modifications of the proposed strategy alternatives as insights into strengths and vulnerabilities are revealed. By the end of the review process, the relative merits and drawbacks of each alternative should be evident, so a fully informed choice can be made.

2. Focus the business team on the drivers of profitability and shareholder value. If the focus is on the financial forecasts, it is very hard to know whether the numbers have been arrived at by the simple expedient of working backward from the profitability requirements to be satisfied before funding is approved. If the company requires a two-year payback and a 15 percent internal rate of return, then the forecasts of prices, costs, growth, and share will be subtly massaged to exceed these targets.

3. Serve as a forum for surfacing and testing critical assumptions. Choices among alternative strategies are arguably the least structured decisions that managers make. To cope with the inherent ambiguity, all participants in the decision make assumptions about how customers, competitors, channels and costs will respond, and how well the organization will implement the programs. Good decisions are based on valid assumptions and grounded in defensible evidence, not on faulty, uninformed guesses. Only through relentless questioning can the valid assumptions be distinguished from those that are unexamined, possibly wrong, and potentially misleading.

4. Help to isolate risks, contingencies, and control factors. We can be virtually certain that the actual results from the chosen strategy will differ from the forecasts. To minimize the damage from these "surprises," the management team needs to think through all the things that could go wrong, and prepare contingency plans for minimizing the likelihood of these surprises or containing the damage when they occur. This line of

thinking will help to identify control factors that can be monitored as early indicators of trouble, which will trigger remedial action.

A key presumption of a value-adding strategy review is that the top management reviewers and decision makers, as well as the business team developing and proposing the strategy alternatives fully understand the fundamentals of the strategy. These fundamentals are addressed with the following test questions, which can be used in any competitive market:

Test 1   How attractive is the market opportunity?
Test 2   Can the strategy achieve a sustainable competitive advantage?
Test 3   What are the prospects for successful implementation?
Test 4   Will the forecast financial results be achieved with acceptable risks?

TEST 1: HOW ATTRACTIVE IS THE MARKET OPPORTUNITY?

Market attractiveness depends on the balance of threats and opportunities uncovered during the situation assessment. Included here is the anticipated impact of events and trends in the aptly named PEST environment (the political, economic, social, and technological domains covered in previous chapters).[1] Supplementing these factors are the specific attributes of the competitive market to be served:

- Market size and growth—where is the product in the life cycle?
- Cyclicality of market demand—will forecast demand be steady with small fluctuations or be vulnerable to economic swings or the fortunes of related industries?
- Present and prospective intensity of competition, as revealed in the industry analysis? Here we employ the methods of Chapter 8 to assess the forces of competition: direct rivalry, bargaining power of suppliers and customers, substitutes, and threats of entry.
- Degree of market fragmentation, which determines the presence of protected market segments?
- Ease of channel access—is this going to be a high- or low-cost market to serve?
- Social and regulatory constraints and opportunities?

The better the market opportunity measures up on these criteria, the higher the long-run average profitability of all the players in the market. The potential of high average profitability provides a degree of encouragement, for if the strategy falls short of its market penetration objectives, there might still be some profit possibilities. However, each competitor will have a different perspective on the optimum levels of each attribute. Small companies will value smaller markets (with numerous protected niches they can safely occupy) quite

TABLE 13.1 Comparison of Customer Segments by a Manufacturing Firm

Criteria	Segment B (Large, Global Customers)	Segment D (Midsize Nationally Focused Customers)
Size ($, units)	Large	Medium
Growth (average for next 3 years)	+5%	±1%
Cyclicality	Moderate	Moderate
Intensity of competition	Moderate	High
Access of channels	Easy	Easy
Break-even share	Moderate	High
Costs to serve	Low	High
Overall attractiveness	+ + +	−

differently than will large companies. Incumbents will celebrate high barriers to entry, which are very costly for new entrants to surmount. These same costs may make it completely unattractive for outsiders. Even a high forecast growth rate is not always a good thing if it draws in an overabundance of competitors and erodes the overall profitability.

The management of Convergent Technologies spent relatively little time on this test; after all, industry pundits were unanimous that prospects were favorable. The current high rate of growth seemed to support the belief that there would be plenty of room for new entrants. Management might have reflected on the relentless pace of technological change and the implications of unforeseen entrants and continuous downward pressure on prices. Further inquiry into the volatile nature of customer behavior might have sent up a warning flag about the pivotal role of access to distribution channels to reach and assure prospective customers about product performance, reliability, and service support.

Full-fledged assessments of market attractiveness must attend to events and trends in the macroeconomic and industry environment as well as conditions within the segments of the market the strategy proposes to target. After all, it is within the market segments that the competitive war will be waged. In Table 13.1, we see how one manufacturer viewed prospects in two segments and justified a growing emphasis on segment B, which was large, global customers. This decision was a major departure from their previous strategy of emphasis on midsize, nationally focused customers.

TEST 2: HOW SUSTAINABLE IS THE COMPETITIVE ADVANTAGE?

Economists who take a long view of markets have a bleak answer to all questions about the sustainability of advantages. Called the Law of Nemesis, this tenet holds that nothing good lasts indefinitely; that is, other competitors will invariably find ways to share the wealth of the market leader. Attractive opportunities always induce competitors to try to match, leapfrog, or offset the advantages the leader has achieved. Thus the anticipated extra profitability that a competitive advantage promises may not materialize or may quickly dry up.

This law is vividly illustrated by the Japanese consumer electronics market where new products—usually variants in a theme—are matched in months or less. Sony has had to introduce hundreds of models of their Walkman to withstand the onslaught of followers. Their innovations are copied within 6 to 12 months. The frenetic pace of "innovative imitation" ensures that closely matched competitors who understand each other well, and closely match each other's moves, can anticipate and respond rapidly. The only basis of sustainable advantage appears to be continuous innovation. This raises daunting questions when customers, no longer valuing the blizzard of features and minor variations, start to buy for other reasons.

At the other extreme are those firms with highly durable advantages based on a resource or capability that is unique and tightly secured within the organization. A classic example is the patent-protected pharmaceutical industry which usually has the best return on capital of all U.S. industry groups. Another revealing example is the Microsoft MS-DOS operating system, with an unassailable position based on the "first-mover" advantage of being able to set standards and create high customer switching costs. Some of the most durable advantages are derived from close personal relationships such as those investment bankers often achieve with their clients. The actual investment products—investment advice, merger screening, balance sheet management—are sophisticated but readily available elsewhere. However, in a pressured, high-stakes deal environment, the clients are only willing to work with those advisers they know and trust. Such confidence is earned over a very long period of time.

Evidence of Sustainability

The pessimism of the economists' Law of Nemesis notwithstanding, sustainability is a matter of degree. Most advantages are contestable, especially price advantages, for competitors can rapidly counter them. Most product innovation is also quickly matched. It is estimated that competitors are able to secure detailed information on 70 percent of all new products within a year of introduction. Even improvements in internal processes are hard to protect—60 percent to 90 percent of all learning eventually diffuses to competitors. Five conditions tend to make an asset or capability a sustainable source of advantage:

- It is *valuable*, in that it makes a significant contribution to superior customer value.

- It is *durable* and not vulnerable to rapid depreciation or obsolescence because of the pace of technological change, shifts in customer requirements, or the depletion of nonrenewable assets.
- There is *causal ambiguity;* it is unclear to the competition how the source of advantage works. This is usually because the source of advantage embodies a lot of tacit knowledge that is accumulated through experience, and requires a complex pattern of coordination among many interdependent activities.
- Even if the competitors understand the advantage, they still can't *duplicate* it, either because they cannot amass the same assets or capabilities or they cannot find different resources to serve the same purpose.
- The early movers are able to deter efforts at duplication with a credible threat of *retaliation.*

The last three conditions—causal ambiguity, duplicability, and credible retaliation—create the barriers to imitation that permit advantages to persist. They help explain why Chubb Corporation has continued to realize returns on shareholder equity of 20 percent in the property and casualty market, while the rest of the competition has seen average returns slide below 5 percent. Chubb focused on insurance coverage for expensive houses and competed by offering attentive and highly knowledgeable personalized service. For example, Chubb clients can have all their worldly goods valued by an agent at the same time they are buying the insurance, thus eliminating the usual inconvenience of finding an appraiser, getting an evaluation, and then calling the insurance company. Chubb also has a reputation for settling claims fairly and quickly.

Chubb's competitors continually pursue this affluent market, but have not been able to incorporate the detailed knowledge of this market into their organizations, emulate the complex systems, or hire and train the right kinds of people. Chubb's competitors may not be fully aware of all the processes that underlie Chubb's advantage, and this causal ambiguity makes it harder for them to create similar capabilities. Chubb's rivals also cannot duplicate those parts they understand. And, even if a competitor could pass these first hurdles, it would face a threat of retaliation if it directly confronted Chubb in this affluent market. Thus, Chubb continues to sustain this advantage in full view of its competitors.

TEST 3: WHAT ARE THE PROSPECTS FOR SUCCESSFUL IMPLEMENTATION?

The first two tests ask about the attractiveness of the market opportunity and the likely payoff from the *intended* strategy. This test asks whether the intentions can be realized. Three conditions must be fulfilled before we can be satisfied that a strategy can deliver the promised results: (1) feasibility, (2) supportability, and (3) consistency.

Feasibility: Does the Business Possess the Necessary Skills and Resources?

If the business doesn't have the skills and resources, is there time to acquire or develop them before the window of opportunity closes? Financial resources (capital funds or cash flow requirements) and physical resources are the first constraints against which a strategy alternative is tested. If these limitations are so restrictive that undertaking a strategy would actually jeopardize the competitive position, then the strategy has to be modified to overcome or live within the constraint or perhaps be rejected. Imaginative solutions may be needed—innovative financing methods using sale and leaseback arrangements or the tying of plant mortgages to long-term contracts.

The next constraints to be tested are access to markets, technology, and servicing capabilities. Do we have adequate sales force coverage? Is the sales force capable of the selling job demanded by the strategic alternative? Is the advertising effort likely to be sufficient? What about the cost efficiency, and coverage of the present distribution system including order handling, warehousing, and delivery? Are relationships with jobbers, distributors, and/or retailers strong enough to support the proposed new strategy? Negative or uncertain answers should trigger a search for modifications to overcome problems, and may lead to eventual rejection of the strategy. The Workslate project described earlier clearly failed these tests.

The most rigid constraints stem from the less quantifiable limitations of individuals and organizations. The basic question is: Has the organization ever shown it could muster the degree of coordinative and integrative skills necessary to carry out the change in strategy? Any strategy that depends on accomplishing tasks outside the realm of reasonably attainable skills is arguably unacceptable.

Supportability: Do the Key Implementers Understand the Strategy and Are They Committed to It?

A broad-based commitment to successful implementation requires two conditions:

1. The premises and elements of the strategy must be readily communicable. If they are not understood, then not only will the strategy likely be flawed, but its capacity to motivate support will be seriously compromised. A good strategy can be easily understood by all functions, so they are not working at cross-purposes. For this reason, the elements and logic of a good strategy can be adequately explained in two or three pages.

2. The strategy should challenge and motivate key personnel. Not only must the strategy have a champion who gives it enthusiastic and credible support, but it must also gain acceptance by all key operating personnel.

If managers have serious reservations about a strategy, are not excited by its objectives and methods, or strongly support another alternative, the strategy must be judged infeasible. This test must be applied with care however. The Convergent Technologies case warns us that excessive enthusiasm by a highly placed champion can be counterproductive. Apparently, the president in particular overrode criticism and suppressed any doubts about the soundness of the strategy.

Consistency: Does the Strategy "Hold Together?"

To achieve consistency, there should be minimal conflict within each level of strategy, and between the levels. The first question is the fit of the elements of strategic thrust with the supporting functional strategies. Table 13.2 is an example of how the functional elements might mesh with the alternative investment strategies. This chart was developed by a manufacturer of process equipment to aid in testing the suitability of individual functional programs.

The second level of fit addresses the couplings among the functional strategies. Without an acceptable degree of fit, effective coordination cannot be achieved. The obvious price is management energy needlessly devoted to resolving organizational conflict, and functional "finger pointing" to shift

TABLE 13.2 Alternative Functional Strategies

	Strategic Thrust				
Functional Elements	Invest/ Build	Selectivity/ Growth	Maintain/ Protect	Selectivity/ Manage for Earnings	Harvest/ Divest
Product design	Lead, Differentiated ←			→	Cost Reduction
Product line	Proliferate ←				→ Prune
Pricing	Value Oriented, Build Experience ←			→	Generate Margin
Distribution	Exclusive, Selective ←			→	Margin Oriented
Promotion/Sale	Create Demand, Capture Share ←			→	Least Cost
Service	Quick Fix, Applications ←			→	Only for Profit
Technology	Innovate ←			→	Minimum Necessary
Costs	Pursue Scale Benefits ←			→	Ruthless Cutting
Capacity	Lead Demand ←			→	Divest for Utilization
Inventory	Anticipatory ←			→	Minimum Response
Risk	Accept, Contain ←				→ Avoid

blame. A less obvious price is the diffused and uncertain impression of the business in the market. The customer has the best view of the inherent contradictions in the strategy—a quality claim contradicted by shoddy packaging, or a service-intensive selling program without the essential back-office support to expedite deliveries and troubleshoot problems.

The consistency test is seldom pivotal; few strategies are conclusively rejected for inconsistency. However, this test can be useful in improving and refining the strategy to ensure that all elements are pointing in the same direction. This test may also indicate that the degree of change necessary to bring the elements into line is simply not feasible with the available resources. Functional managers can only cope with a few changes simultaneously while trying to maintain continuing operations. Thus it may not be possible to upgrade old product lines, enter new markets, modernize the costing system, and build a new manufacturing plant all at once.

TEST 4: WILL THE FORECAST FINANCIAL RESULTS BE ACHIEVED WITH ACCEPTABLE RISKS?

All strategy alternatives must eventually be tested for their financial attractiveness. The raw materials for this test are valid assumptions about future revenues, costs, and investment requirements of each alternative. These in turn are based on persuasive evidence of sustainable competitive advantage. Which yardstick should be used for judging the financial merits of these strategies? There is growing evidence that conventional yardsticks such as return on sales, revenue growth, and earnings offer inferior guidance by ignoring risk and timing considerations.

A more defensible yardstick judges a strategy alternative by its ability to enhance shareholder value. The basic premise of this approach is that the market value of stock depends on investors' expectations of the cash-generating abilities of each business in the firm. This means that investors willingly invest in a firm only when they expect management can get a better return on their funds than they could get on their own—without exposing themselves to any greater risks. Their minimum expected return is the firm's cost of capital.

These ideas apply neatly to strategy evaluation, because any strategy needing new investment will be justified only if the promised returns are greater than the cost of capital. To account for differences in the timing and riskiness of financial benefits and up-front costs, the overall value of the strategy is estimated by discounting all relevant cash flows. The discount rate is the cost of capital adjusted to take into account the riskiness of the strategy alternative compared with other investments the firm could make. The best strategy for a business—if there are several choices—will create the most value. Interested readers will find more details of this evaluation method in Box 13.2.

Cash flows have the advantage that they are not distorted by the accounting conventions that afflict forecasts of net earnings. Suppose a business maintains

---

Box 13.2

The Valuation of Strategies

There is a close affinity between shareholder value based methods of strategy evaluation and the familiar discounted cash flow (DCF) methods widely used to evaluate capital investment projects such as the addition of plant capacity. The extension of the DCF method to the comparison of business strategies had to wait until business units had their own profit and loss statements and balance sheets. These are the necessary conditions for the estimation of annual operating cash flows that are the raw material of this method. These cash flows reflect the sales, profit, working capital, and fixed capital investment consequences of a strategy alternative within a particular environmental scenario.

The total shareholder value a business expects to realize from a strategy has three components:

1. The present value (PV) of cash flows during the planning period. This period may be three to five years depending on the industry. The discount rate used to bring future cash flows to the present depends on the parent's cost of capital, and the riskness of the strategy being proposed. A radical departure from the present direction will have a sizable risk premium, whereas a continuation of the current strategy in a low volatility environment will have a low risk premium.

2. To this present value is added a "residual" value, which is the present value of the cash flows to be received after the end of the planning period. In effect, this is what the business is worth at the end of the planning period. For many strategies, especially those that require heavy up-front investments, this may be the largest source of total value.

3. From these two present values is subtracted the market value of debt assigned to the business.

This calculation results in an estimate of total shareholder value. This is also equivalent to the initial shareholder value, plus the value created by the proposed strategy. This initial value is essentially what the business is worth today without taking any account of the value created by prospective investments.

---

market position by allowing customers increasingly long periods to pay. Even though accounting profits are realized, the business may not have enough cash inflow to pay for the increase in working capital as well as other investments. Rapid sales growth may turn a business into a heavy cash consumer. A distributor of medical lasers had to file for bankruptcy after a year in which sales trebled. Although reported earnings were high, the accounts receivable grew even faster. The company found itself so short of cash, because of this surge in working capital needs, that it had to write down its receivables, which eliminated most of the next year's earnings. This was a dramatic evaporation of shareholder value, but any business that persistently needs more cash than it generates is eating into shareholder value.

Because the estimates of value are so dependent on the quality of assumptions about market share revenues, costs, and timing, a business would be unwise to use the results as the ultimate arbiter of strategic decisions. These methods are better used as a defensible framework for a sensitivity analysis of key assumptions. How much would prices, market share, timing of entry, costs, and so forth have to change for a strategy to become unattractive? Whether this scenario can be reasonably anticipated depends on an understanding of the competitive situation, the prospects for sustainable advantage, and the ability of the business to implement the strategy. This approach shifts the emphasis back to where it belongs—to an understanding of the fundamentals that create shareholder value.

Are the Risks Acceptable?

The overall level of risk reflects the vulnerability of key results if pivotal assumptions are wrong or critical tasks are not accomplished. For example, an aggressive build strategy that increases investment intensity also elevates the break-even point. This makes the strategy alternative more sensitive to revenue shortfalls than a "manage for current earnings" strategy.

Overall risk reflects the combined threats from *environmental* uncertainties (can competitors match, offset, or leapfrog the prospective advantage? Will the target customers respond as anticipated? Will the government regulations be more restrictive than expected?) and the *internal* uncertainties about the ability of the business to implement the strategy. Both sources of risk proved too much for the Workslate computer. Either would have crippled the undertaking; in combination they were lethal.

Assessing Risk

The usual procedure begins by identifying the major environmental and internal uncertainties. These could result from events "e.g., we can't launch the new product in time for the annual trade show" or trends (e.g., growth of the target market segment doesn't materialize). Essentially the risk is a joint function of the probability of the adverse event or trend happening and the consequent effect on long-run performance. The outcome of this analysis is an identification of the key leverage points, as shown in Figure 13.2.

A risk assessment should not stop with an enumeration of all the things that might go wrong. The value of this evaluation comes from helping the management team take precautionary steps to reduce the probability of bad things happening. If there is a significant risk of a major customer back integrating (leaving the supplier with unused capacity, and adding to the available capacity serving the market), what can the supplier do to lessen the probability of this happening? Sometimes it is not possible to take effective precautionary

FIGURE 13.2 Key leverage points.

Competitive Response		Expected	More Attractive	Less Attractive
	Greater			Acid Test
	Less			
	Expected	Plan		

Market Opportunity

activity, especially with events and trends that are beyond management's control. In such circumstances, the best that can be done is to put contingency plans in place. These are plans that are only triggered when some kind of threshold is reached. A contingency plan might be stated, "If demand falls 20 percent below forecast levels we will do the following—cut prices selectively, reduce the workforce, and accelerate the new product activity."

Robust versus Fragile Strategies

Some of the riskiest strategies will achieve desired results in only one environmental scenario. Success is then highly dependent on certain conditions—high growth being realized, currency levels remaining stable, or competitors behaving as they have in the past. If the expected scenario doesn't materialize, then performance results are likely to be disappointing. This is the hallmark of a fragile strategy—it withers under adversity. The acid test that reveals just how fragile a strategy is, asks, "What if the fundamental assumptions about the attractiveness of the market opportunity are excessively optimistic, while the major competitors' reaction is far more significant than expected?" Conversely, a robust strategy is one that may underperform the fragile alternative if the expected scenario unfolds. However, a robust strategy will succeed in a variety of scenarios because it won't be nearly so damaged by undesirable events.

ASSUMPTIONS: THE ACHILLES HEEL OF STRATEGY FORMULATION

Anyone who undertakes to test a strategy must be constantly on the alert for the deep-seated optimistic bias that managers bring to their forecasts. Such a bias is usually the outcome of the following habits managers have developed for coping with ambiguity:

- *Anchoring.* Decision makers tend to "anchor" on a particular outcome they believe will occur. This expected outcome dominates their thinking and suppresses consideration of uncertainties. As a result, downside risks are understated.

- *Selective perception.* Several biasing elements work together to foster selective perception. For example, people tend to structure problems in light of their past experience (e.g., marketing people will interpret a general management problem as a marketing problem). Another cause of this bias is that people's anticipation of what they expect to see will influence what they actually see. As a consequence, conflicting evidence will be disregarded.

- *Illusion of control.* Planning activities may give decision makers the illusion that they can master and control their environment. At the same time, decision makers have a tendency to attribute success to their own efforts and failures to external events and "bad luck."

- *Availability.* Emphasis is usually given to facts and opinions that are easy to retrieve. Often these are hard data about past successes, which are given greater weight than soft assessments of future adversity. As a result, the ability of new competitors to gain market acceptance and penetrate previously secure markets is often underestimated.

A rigorous strategy review (1) recognizes that the quality of strategic thinking depends on the quality of the underlying assumptions, and (2) uses the tough questions to identify the critical assumptions and challenge their validity.

SUMMARY

A major telecommunications firm conducted a postmortem of its failed diversification activities, so that it could avoid repeating the same mistakes. These were expensive lessons, for the cumulative loss on the six ventures exceeded $56 million. The firm concluded:

- The plan review process led to unrealistic profit projections. Year 1 was an operating plan, with the numbers in years 2 to 5 simply adjusted to meet known criteria. Everyone knew they had to break even in 3 years; therefore they backed into their projections . . .

- There was a built-in lack of accountability that encouraged people to put together and approve unrealistic long-term plans . . .

- We didn't know what we didn't know. The reviewers didn't have the expertise or market experience to add value in the review process. As a result the reviews were based more on format than on content.

This is certainly a damning indictment of a misguided effort to diversify into markets where the firm had few competencies. It is also symptomatic of strategy evaluations that don't add value because they suffer from several deficiencies. Senior managers are disconnected from the early development of the strategy, so they don't appreciate the range of possible alternatives or the trade-offs to be made. Instead the business team makes the choice among the alternatives they have chosen to consider. By the time the team proposes its preferred strategy, team members are completely committed to that direction and have foreclosed other possibilities. During the strategy review, the emphasis tends to be on the financial forecasts, which deflects attention from the strategic fundamentals emphasized in this chapter. When approval is given, it is often to accept the performance objectives, but to provide less funds than requested—partly because there are not enough funds available, but also because the reviewers suspect that the resource requirements have been inflated. This leads to an unhealthy amount of games-playing as the business teams anticipate that they will be cut back and adjust their estimates accordingly.

A healthy strategy evaluation process should be an integral part of the planning process, not a single event at the end of the strategy development process. A well-informed senior management team will provide guidance, using the test questions to probe the strategy at several stages during the planning process. During the early stages, the emphasis is almost exclusively on the qualitative factors covered by the first three tests, and the validity of the underlying assumptions. As the feasible alternatives are refined, attention turns to quantifying the performance results, capital investments, and risks. In this approach to strategy evaluation, management is more deeply involved and can exercise a leadership role throughout the process, while still coaching the business team on the important factors to consider and communicating their expectations. For this entire process to be productive, both the reviewers and those being reviewed must be working with the same mental model of the attributes of a sound strategy. All parties must fully understand the four test questions and their underlying premises. This uniformity ensures the complete transparency of the strategy evaluation process. The payoff is realized in informed and committed managers, who will implement sound strategies with above-average prospects for success.

REFERENCES

Day, George S. 1990. *Market-Driven Strategy: Process for Creating Value.* New York: Free Press.

Day, George S., and David B. Reibstein. 1998. *Wharton on Dynamic Competitive Strategy.* New York: Wiley.

Porter, Michael E. 1985. *Competitive Advantage.* New York: Free Press.

Rappaport, Alfred. 1998. *Creating Shareholder Value: A Guide for Managers and Investors.* New York: Free Press.

NOTE

1.   These domains as well as the ecological and institutional domains were addressed in detail in Chapter 9.

PART FOUR

MANAGING STRATEGIC CHANGE: LINKING STRATEGY AND ACTION

STRATEGIC CHANGE: HOW TO REALIGN THE ORGANIZATION TO IMPLEMENT STRATEGY

14

Russell A. Eisenstat
Center for Organizational Fitness

Michael Beer
Harvard Business School

The technology for developing business strategy is formidable. Over the past 20 years an armory of sophisticated strategic planning techniques has been employed—including competitor analysis, market segmentation, and product positioning. Chief executives have also had assistance in the use of these powerful tools. Most large firms have high-level strategy and planning advisers available internally. In addition, U.S. businesses spend billions of dollars annually on strategy consulting.

All too often, companies discover that the strategies devised with the help of these specialists fail to be implemented effectively. Millions of dollars spent in analysis and strategy formulation may yield little more than fancy presentations and reports. The operations and behavior of functional departments, staff groups, or workers who need to adjust to new competitive realities remain largely unchanged. Why?

Successfully implementing business strategy requires a general manager and his or her team to not just identify opportunities for competitive advantage in the marketplace, but to also develop an organization capable of realizing these opportunities. By capability, we mean much more than the competence of the many employees who make up the business unit. The organization as a whole must be capable of coordinating the efforts of individuals and groups in a way that allows it to sense what the market demands and to respond as a unified whole. This is far easier said than done, as the case of Honeywell's Commercial Aviation Division, detailed in Box 14.1, illustrates.

297

Box 14.1
Honeywell CAvD Case

Honeywell's Commercial Aviation Division (CAvD) was floundering in its efforts to commercialize a new technology for aircraft navigation developed for its defense business. Convinced that the new technology had commercial applications that could propel Honeywell into a major new business, top management created a new division. After two years, little progress had been made. New commercial products were long overdue. Customers were so angry they threatened to cancel their orders. Losses threatened Honeywell's return on investment. The future of the business was in doubt. What was the problem?

When John Dewane was appointed to replace the first division manager, he found a top team that did not work well together. The general manager and the director of marketing had developed business strategy without involvement of the full staff. Little consensus about the strategy or commitment to it existed. The result was conflicting directions from functional managers and unclear priorities.

Communication was extremely poor. Dewane found that directions discussed at the top did not get to lower levels, possibly due to an excessive number of levels in the organization.

Consistent with practices that worked in the defense business, engineering designed the product with little influence from manufacturing and then, according to managers in manufacturing, "threw an incomplete product over the wall to manufacturing." Many costly engineering changes were required to make the product manufacturable at the specified cost. All these changes created cost overruns in manufacturing for which they were held accountable. Consequently, manufacturing distrusted engineering and viewed them as arrogant.

The commercial business required rapid product development, but it also required greater responsiveness to customer needs and lower costs than the military business. Locked in a competitive battle brought about by deregulation, airlines put pressure on aircraft manufacturers to reduce the cost of an airplane. They in turn pressured subcontractors like Honeywell's CAvD to lower cost. Simultaneous demand for rapid product development and lower cost could only be met by close interfunctional coordination, particularly between marketing, engineering, and manufacturing.

The demand for a lower cost product required a production workforce committed to lowering costs while maintaining quality. A history of distrust between management and the union still blocked cooperative efforts.

CAvD's hierarchical and functional approach to management fostered little of the teamwork required by the new business environment. Though CAvD had many talented technical individuals, the organization as a whole lacked the capability to respond to increased competition. John Dewane quickly realized he had to develop new capabilities in response to new market demands and that this would require organizational as well as individual change. How he should go about realigning the organization with strategy was less clear. It presented a challenge with which Dewane struggled for several years.

Over the past decade we have studied strategy implementation in a range of business units across different corporations. We found that at the core of the more successful efforts were general managers who were able to effectively blend analysis and action. These managers could perform two difficult tasks:

1. Develop a comprehensive and coherent organizational road map of the capabilities required for effective strategy implementation.
2. Orchestrate change initiatives in a way that built partnership and learning.

The first task identifies *what* changes need to be made, the second identifies *how* these changes need to be made. In this chapter, we use the Honeywell Commercial Aviation Division case to show how a manager can effectively accomplish each of these tasks.

DEVELOPING THE ROAD MAP: ANALYZING ORGANIZATIONAL CAPABILITY TO IMPLEMENT STRATEGY

Just as successful strategy formulation requires a comprehensive scanning and assessment of the external competitive environment, effective strategy implementation demands an equally rigorous assessment of the organization's internal environment. The analysis should answer whether the organization possesses the capabilities it needs to achieve the chosen strategy, and if not, what the barriers are that prevent the development of these capabilities, as well as how these barriers should be surmounted.

Unfortunately, many managers do not apply rigorous analysis to the question of how and why their organization is not implementing strategy effectively. One reason is that they do not possess an analytic framework for asking the right questions. Figure 14.1 is a systemic framework for making an organizational

FIGURE 14.1 Assessing the readiness to implement strategy.

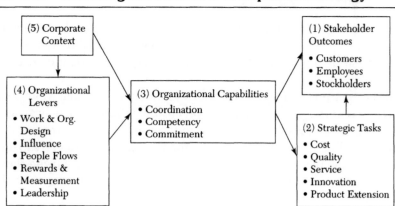

diagnosis. As will be discussed in more detail below, because implementing strategy usually involves asking organization members to act in new ways, success is far more likely if those who will be affected are involved in the diagnosis, analysis, and redesign efforts.

The model, summarized in Figure 14.1, is based on five simple premises:

1. Organizations, to survive and prosper, must meet the needs of their stakeholders—their customers, employees, and investors.
2. Business strategies must be articulated in actionable terms. What are the key tasks the organization must accomplish to satisfy stakeholder needs?
3. Success in accomplishing a given strategic task requires three organizational capabilities:
   a. Coordination among relevant individuals and groups.
   b. Appropriate technical and managerial skills.
   c. Shared commitment to accomplishing the task.
4. The nature and extent of these capabilities is in turn shaped by how the organization is designed and managed—its structure and systems, who has a say over key decisions, the types of individuals who are hired and promoted, its information and reward systems, and the character and behavior of its leaders.
5. How the organization is designed and managed, as well as its capabilities, are shaped by the larger corporation of which the business unit may be a part.

Table 14.1 outlines diagnostic questions for each element of the model. These will enable you as a manager to assess systematically all aspects of your organization's readiness to implement a proposed business strategy.

Stakeholder Outcomes

How adequately is the organization meeting the needs of its stakeholders— customers, employees, and investors?

For a business organization to remain viable, customers must be willing to buy its products, employees must be willing to provide their labor and their intellectual commitment, and investors must be willing to provide the necessary financial capital.

Market share is a proxy measure of customer satisfaction. More sensitive and direct measures include surveys of customer satisfaction, warranty returns, and customer loyalty. In response to the competitive environment, many firms are developing multiple methods for measuring customer satisfaction. They are learning that when these measures show a downward trend they indicate that the firm will have difficulty meeting its financial targets in the future. Consider the shock of a new general manager who studied a company's

TABLE 14.1   Assessing Organizational Readiness for Strategy Implementation

Stakeholder Outcomes

How adequately is the organization meeting the needs of all its stakeholders—customers, employees, and investors?

Strategic Tasks

What are the strategic tasks for the organization?
Is the top team clear on and in agreement with the strategic tasks?
Is the rest of the organization clear on and in agreement with the strategic tasks?

Organizational Capabilities

Does the business have appropriate levels of coordination or teamwork among the individuals and groups critical to accomplishing a given strategic task?
Does the organization have access to the necessary technical and managerial competencies to accomplish the task?
Is there the necessary level of commitment to accomplish the strategic task?

Organizational Levers

- The Organization of Work
  How do each of the following either support or hinder accomplishing the strategic tasks?
    The formal organizational structure.
    The presence and quality of cross-unit mechanisms such as meetings or formal teams.
    Specification of individual roles, responsibility, and relationships.

- Influence
  Are decisions made with appropriate influence from relevant functions and business units ?
  Are decisions made with appropriate influence from all organizational levels?

- People Flows
  Do individuals in key organizational positions have the appropriate skills and abilities?
  Does the management succession process reward the appropriate behaviors?

- Information, Measurement, and Reward Systems
  Do the information and measurement systems provide the data needed to monitor and manage strategy implementation?
  Do the measurement and reward systems motivate the right behaviors?

- Leadership
  Do the actions of the general manager and his or her top team reinforce effective performance on the business's strategic tasks?

Corporate Context

Do the policies, procedures, or culture of the larger corporation help or hinder the business unit in implementing its strategy?

---

financial measures and thought he was inheriting a healthy business, only to find that customer satisfaction was low and declining.

The ability of the firm to attract and keep employees is a proxy measure of employee satisfaction. Labor markets are not perfectly efficient, however. Employees do not always choose to leave when they are unhappy, and their lowered commitment can hurt the firm's capacity to implement its strategy. Other measures of satisfaction such as surveys of employee attitudes, grievances, legal suits regarding fair treatment, desire to unionize, and/or the relationship of the firm with the union, must, therefore, be used as indicators of employee satisfaction. It is important to recognize that a firm's policies can satisfy top management and not lower level managers or workers. For this reason, data about employee satisfaction must be collected from all levels.[1]

The interests of investors are generally defined by financial measures such as return on investment, and stock price appreciation. In the 1970s and 1980s, investor interests may not have been adequately represented in the financial measures utilized or the goals set. In the 1990s, boards of directors, pressured by shareholders, have exerted considerable influence on management to adopt more ambitious financial targets. Because the Internet now permits both large and small shareholders to deliver messages to the CEO in seconds instead of days, this trend is likely to gain momentum.

A firm takes a big risk by satisfying one stakeholder in the short run at the expense of others. Paying a dividend while laying off employees and decreasing investments in new products puts investors ahead of employees and customers in a way that is apt to harm long-term competitiveness. Retaining employees on the payroll when profits are inadequate puts employees ahead of investors with potentially equally damaging consequences. A major challenge facing general managers is balancing these interests in such a way that the business will prosper over time.

Strategic Tasks

What are the strategic tasks for the organization?

The foundation for strategy implementation is a clear, shared understanding of the strategic tasks of a business. Strategic tasks are simple statements of what has to get done in a business to create or sustain a competitive advantage in the marketplace. In Honeywell's Commercial Aviation Division (CAvD) the strategic task had changed from developing an innovative high-quality product without much regard for time or cost to developing products rapidly with careful attention to cost as well as quality.

The accomplishment of a given strategic task depends on the organization's ability to accomplish certain key work processes. For example, developing high-quality and lower cost products rapidly at Honeywell's CAvD was strongly dependent on a process that translated a technical innovation in engineering into a manufacturable and commercially viable product. This process involves many trade-offs between marketing, engineering, and manufacturing.

Strategic tasks can be defined at any organizational level. Within a manufacturing plant, accomplishing the strategic task of improving product quality requires coordinated effort across the various parts of the plant. Within a business unit such as Honeywell's CAvD, the strategic task of product development required work processes spanning many functions. Corporate strategic tasks are accomplished through work processes that span multiple businesses. These tasks define ways the corporation as a whole contributes to the competitive advantage of its various businesses, through such work processes as multidivisional sales to large customers, or through the transfer of technologies from domestic to overseas businesses.

Is the top team clear on and in agreement with the strategic tasks?

In many organizations, despite the enormous amount of time spent developing strategic plans, there is no consensus within the senior team about their business's strategic tasks. Strategic planning documents contain discussions of long-term trends in technology and customer buying behavior and incisive analyses of competitors' strengths and weaknesses. Yet they say little that would help an employee decide on a day-to-day basis what activities on his or her part would be most helpful in making the business successful.

One division we studied developed the following strategy statement: "Fortify our quality, product cost, and market share strengths, while also transforming the industry through expanded customer knowledge and product/service innovation." Undoubtedly the business must do all of the things in the statement, but not all of them are equally important for competitive advantage. The strategy statement provides little organizational guidance as to which of the factors—quality, cost, or product and service innovation—is more or less important, and why.

Just as often what substitutes for clarity on strategic tasks is a list of quantitative business objectives such as profitability, sales growth, return on assets, and market share and/or a list of programs and projects for achieving them. This is very different from providing a sense for the overall tasks the organization needs to complete if it is going to be successful in the marketplace.

A common reason strategic tasks are not better defined is that senior teams are uncomfortable about making tough choices. Functional heads who make up the top management group of a business unit each stand to gain or lose based on strategic choices made. An emphasis on decreasing product cost will tend to tip the balance of power toward manufacturing, while an emphasis on innovation will move power toward R&D; VPs of quality will push for increases in product reliability, while VPs of sales will be especially interested in increasing market share.

Many top teams tend to paper over their differences, rather than directly confront hard trade-offs. The results are vague statements that incorporate too many strategic tasks or rely on numbers, but provide little direction to the larger organization. Not surprisingly, the response of employees is strategic confusion.

Is the rest of the organization clear on and in agreement with the strategic tasks?

Communicating a business's strategic tasks allows those responsible for implementation to work from a common strategic story. This story explains to individuals and groups how their job activities are contributing to critical work processes, and how the quality of these processes in turn relate to long-term success in the marketplace. These tasks help guide action as unforeseen problems arise.

Clearly defined strategic tasks do not and should not eliminate conflict. Discussions can be contentious, with different parties debating how the strategy applies in particular circumstances. Short-term financial pressures are a reality in most organizations. They can cause managers at all organizational levels to act in ways perceived as inconsistent with accomplishing strategic tasks. Clearly articulated strategic tasks can, however, force a debate about these inconsistencies.

As this discussion suggests, the articulation and communication of strategic tasks has the potential to change the fundamental relationship among the parts of an organization. Without a shared understanding of strategy, those at lower levels have little choice but to do as they are told. Conversely, when a shared understanding exists front-line managers have a basis for independent judgments and entrepreneurial actions that will further the objectives of the enterprise.

Organizational Capabilities

Making the strategy clear is a necessary first step. It is not enough, however. Successful strategy implementation requires organizational capabilities. Managers in Honeywell's CAvD knew that product development was the key to their success, but this knowledge did not enable them to develop products at the cost and speed required. Knowing the strategy merely identifies the competitive game. It does not determine whether it is a game that the organization knows how to win. Winning depends on three critical organizational capabilities—coordination, competence, and commitment.

Does the business have appropriate levels of coordination or teamwork among the individuals and groups critical to accomplishing a given strategic task?

Few sources of sustainable competitive advantage can be realized through the efforts of one function. Knowledge and expertise can be bought. However, the capability of the organization to implement strategy through teamwork between different parts of the organization cannot be purchased. Increasingly, teamwork is required not just within the firm, but with customers, suppliers, and industry partners as well. At Honeywell's CAvD, product development was impeded by lack of teamwork between engineering, production, and marketing and this was a reflection of lack of teamwork at the top of the division.

Does the organization have access to the necessary technical and managerial competencies to accomplish the task?

Successful strategy implementation requires two types of competence—technical/functional and managerial. These competencies can either be developed within the firm, or through alliances with external partners. Honeywell's CAvD required and had engineering talent to solve technical problems. Highly competent engineers were not enough, however. Managerial and interpersonal competencies were needed at the top and lower levels for the functions to co-ordinate their efforts effectively. John Dewane's top team in CAvD had to de-velop new competence in resolving conflict constructively. They also had to develop skills and methods for prioritizing programs and allocating resources across programs. To implement programs, lower level employees needed to de-velop skills in project management and group decision making.

Is there the necessary level of commitment to accomplish the strategic task?

Effective teamwork at lower levels cannot be ordered from the top. They need to understand what accomplishments will help a firm achieve its important goals. Employees must be willing to work cooperatively with each other to "do the right thing" for the firm as a whole, rather than attending solely to their local interests. In many industries, such as computers and telecommunications, firms increasingly face the added challenge of developing an alignment of interests and motivations with external partners who may also be competitors. In CAvD, engineers had to become interested in meeting customer needs as opposed to just making technological enhancements to the product. Production workers had to be motivated to identify quality and cost improvement opportunities, and to communicate these to engineering and other relevant departments.

Coordination, commitment, and competence are all three needed to implement strategy. A deficit in any one will lead to failure. The problem is not unlike that facing every basketball team coach. Players with the right skills are needed (competence), but they must also understand how to play as a team (coordination) and they must possess the dedication to win (commitment).

When failures of strategy implementation occur, one or more of the three strategic capabilities is inevitably lacking. For example, companies seeking to decrease time to market for new products often create cross-functional product development teams. After teams are created, however, they are apt to discover that team effectiveness is undermined by low commitment to the new organization from strong functional heads whose authority is threatened. They also may find out that effective teamwork requires competence typically not developed in a strongly functional organization. Skills in project management, conflict resolution, and leadership are missing.

Organizational Levers

What is a manager to do when confronted with a deficit in commitment, coordination, or competence? To determine the most appropriate course of action, deficits in organizational capabilities must be traced back to their root causes.

Figure 14.1 shows five organizational design levers with strong influence on the development of organizational capabilities needed to implement strategy. Their role in causing lower than desired levels of coordination, commitment, and competence must be analyzed:

- The organization of work.
- The amount of influence on decisions of different levels, parts, and functions of the organization.
- The flow of people into, up and out of the organization.
- The measurement and reward systems.
- Leadership of the general manager and her or his top team.

The Organization of Work

How do each of the following either support or hinder accomplishing the strategic tasks?

- The formal organizational structure.
- The presence and quality of cross-unit mechanisms to integrate parts of the organization.
- Specification of individual roles, responsibility, and relationships.

The Formal Organizational Structure.   The structure of reporting relationships and operating unit boundaries has a major impact on levels of coordination, competence, and commitment. For example, consider the differences in the typical capability profiles of businesses with two of the most common organizational designs—a centralized functional structure versus a decentralized business unit structure.

Because functional organizations encourage specialization, people in such organizations are apt to develop high levels of skills in their particular function or technical specialty, but a narrow perspective in their approach to business problems. Narrow job descriptions can lead to problems of commitment and competence. They can rob employees of the sense of meaning and accomplishment that comes from completing a whole task. They emphasize technical over interpersonal skills. This is particularly true at lower levels of the organization and the result is often poor customer service. This syndrome of problems has given rise to methods for reexamining the design of jobs.[2]

The narrow perspective functional organizations encourage makes it difficult to create the cross-functional coordination required to accomplish most strategic tasks. When problems emerge between R&D and manufacturing, or marketing and sales, the general manager becomes the only individual with the formal authority to resolve them. This is the problem John Dewane faced at Honeywell. Recurring conflicts between manufacturing and R&D landed on his desk. He had limited time and expertise, however, to make decisions for all new product development efforts.

One way this problem can be solved is through decentralization. Decentralized organizational structures make it easier to coordinate around key tasks; a corporation divided into a set of focused business units is more apt to be responsive to the needs of distinct market segments than one which is functionally organized. However, decentralized organizations also have their costs.

Instead of one director for each functional area, several are now needed. Further, it is unlikely that each of the functions would be as able to develop or afford the depth of expertise that was available in the previous organization. For example, one large functional organization could more easily afford a marketing manager who specialized in conducting customer focus groups, while the new smaller business units would be less likely to need this specialized work in sufficient quantity to justify the manager's compensation.

Added expense and diminished functional depth are not the only challenges of decentralization. While decentralization facilitates coordination within each of the new business units, coordination among units is more difficult. For example, decentralized businesses organized by product may share common customers. Such companies must find a way to deal with a host of issues that would be more easily managed within a larger integrated organization—from how to coordinate sales calls, to how to price bundles of products and cross-divisional services for key accounts.

As the examples demonstrate, the functional organization is good at developing specialized skills but incurs problems of focus and coordination as the organization develops new products and enters new markets. The decentralized organization solves problems of focus and coordination, but incurs problems of cost while also creating potentially new problems of coordination across business units—particularly when resources must be shared. Neither organizational structure is perfect.

Presence and Quality of Cross-Unit Mechanisms to Integrate Parts of the Organization.   When growth requires the organization to focus on multiple products and markets, but it cannot afford decentralization, another solution must be found. Increasing competition is forcing more companies into this position.

To deal with this complexity, functional and decentralized organizational structures are often supplemented by ad hoc mechanisms such as cross-functional teams. These teams can be created to facilitate more effective coordination along any of a number of organizing dimensions. For example, Honeywell's division manager sought to decrease time to market through the use of new product development teams. Team members retained their functional affiliation and reporting relationship while adding a new affiliation and accountability as business or product team members. In other cases, corporations with decentralized business units have created functional teams that include experts from the various businesses, to encourage best practice sharing and technical excellence. In still other instances, where divisionalized firms are attempting to serve global corporate customers, key account management teams span multiple product lines and geographies.[3]

Specification of Individual Roles, Responsibility, and Relationships.   Even if the appropriate formal organizational structure or cross-functional teams are in place, the intended levels of teamwork and commitment may not necessarily result. Formal organizational charts and cross-functional team rosters are too crude to capture the complex patterns of coordinated behavior required in any successful business. Similarly, the organizational chart for a basketball team tells the players who is playing center, forward, and guard, but this barely begins to specify each player's role, or how they need to work with one another to have a winning team.

A common cause of coordination breakdowns is that individuals are not clear about their roles, responsibilities, and relationships, and or they have not accepted them. For example, in the Communications Products Division of Alpha Corporation, product development teams were introduced to decrease time to market for the business's high-speed modems. A year after the teams began work, however, managers were frustrated that the organization seemed no more productive than it had been in the past. The problem was that while the teams existed on paper, the roles and responsibilities of the key players who had to make the system work—the team leaders, team members, and functional heads had still not been defined and accepted. Members of the organization were still struggling with such questions as:

- Who should have the responsibility for committing functional resources, the team representatives for a functional area or the functional head?
- Who should be responsible for evaluating the performance of a functional representative on a team, the team leader or the functional head?
- What should the role of team leaders be? Facilitators of the team's efforts? Or the individual with primary responsibility and accountability for driving for results?

Unless these difficult questions of roles, relationships, and responsibilities are clarified, even the most elegant organizational design is unlikely to achieve its intended effects. The answer is not a set of centrally defined job descriptions. Organizational members must sit down and discuss their perceptions of roles and negotiate them. A typical tool used to facilitate this process is the responsibility matrix. For each anticipated decision, the matrix shows how functional heads, team leaders, and team members agree on who will have the authority to make the decision, who must be consulted, and who must approve.

Influence

Are decisions made with the appropriate influence from all relevant functions and business units?

One of the most subtle, yet powerful factors affecting the success of strategy implementation efforts is the pattern of organizational influence—what individuals or groups have a say in decisions. To the extent that those who know the most have the most to say in decisions, the organization is able to make the best possible use of the competence it possesses to get the job done.

Changes in strategic tasks usually require changes in the amount of influence exerted by various parts and levels of the organization. These shifts are often difficult to make, given the natural human tendencies for those with high influence and power, typically in the larger established parts of the business, to want to retain their prerogatives. The result is the failure of firms to adequately respond to emerging opportunities and threats. Xerox's failure to adequately capitalize on the computing innovations coming out of Xerox PARC, and IBM's failures in the 1980s to adequately capitalize on its early successes with the personal computer represent two well-known examples.

The new emphasis on rapid development of new products with competitive manufacturing cost required Honeywell's Commercial Aviation Division to boost the influence of production and marketing on decisions relative to engineering. As many companies struggle to become less inwardly focused, and more oriented toward customer needs, they find that there is a need for a shift in relative influence, from the previously dominant manufacturing and R&D functions toward marketing and sales.

Are decisions made with appropriate influence from all organizational levels?

When the implementation of strategic tasks requires delegation of authority to lower organizational levels, upper levels must relinquish power. For example, the successful introduction of cross-functional product development teams typically requires functional heads to remove themselves from day-to-day decision making. This is often a difficult transition.

These problems were well illustrated in the new product development teams established at Alpha's Communications Products Division. While the teams existed on paper, they were not able to accomplish very much. Team meetings were frustrating and inconclusive due to functional heads who prevented their representatives from making commitments for their function. Very quickly, the team leaders discovered that if something had to get accomplished in manufacturing or R&D, the person to speak to was not the functional representative, but the functional head. Since the functional heads refused to allow team leaders a role in the performance appraisal of team members, team leaders had little recourse when functional representatives did not complete team responsibilities on time or even failed to attend meetings.

When external consultants informed the senior team of these problems, team members acknowledged their unwillingness to cede authority. Although they had been frustrated by their work overload before teams were formed, they found it difficult to change their roles. If they delegated decision-making responsibility to the teams what would be left for them to do? What would this mean for their careers? Their perception that corporate management was evaluating them on their knowledge of business details only increased these concerns.

Assessing mismatches between levels of influence and the demands of the strategic task is not easy. Assumptions about the level of influence certain functions and levels of the organization should have tend to be deeply ingrained. It is also natural to assume that the most influential functions and people have the greatest level of competence. This assumption is reinforced by the tendency for the most competent individuals in an organization to gravitate to functions that have traditionally been most influential.

Close examination of the management approaches taken in other companies can be valuable in coping with issues of power. Many companies have improved union-management relationships by sending joint union and management groups to visit Japanese companies. There they have developed insights into a different model of influence. In other cases, assumptions about "who gets to decide what" are so deeply ingrained that more radical steps are needed. Many executives, including GE's Jack Welch, have cut organizational levels and radically increased spans of control to force the delegation of authority. In other instances, the replacement of managers who refuse to loosen their grip on the reins of authority may ultimately be required.

People Flows

Do individuals in key organizational positions have the appropriate skills and abilities?

People flows—the systems for hiring, promoting, and developing employees—have a vital impact on an organization's ability to implement its business strategy. If these systems have been effectively managed, they provide the organization with a core resource—a supply of talented and motivated employees—that will facilitate the implementation of virtually any business strategy. Corporations such as General Electric have prospered in different industries on the strength of their recruitment and management development practices.

Implementing a new strategic direction requires key organizational players to act in very different ways on the job. Defining a new organizational design may specify the behaviors required, but employees often do not have the competence to practice these behaviors or to train others to behave in the desired manner.

This is particularly true when managers in functional and strongly hierarchical organizations attempt to implement strategies that require extensive cross-functional coordination. As pointed out earlier, in functional organizations individuals often progress from job to job within a function. This career progression does little to provide managers with the general management orientation or interpersonal and conflict management skills needed to manage outside the formal chain of command.

When confronted with gaps in skills and motivation, executives must make a difficult assessment—can key managers be developed or do they need to be replaced? Managers have available to them several techniques for assessing managerial skills and competence, ranging from observation of on-the-job behavior to off-site assessment centers, or paper-and-pencil tests.

Does the management succession process reward the appropriate behaviors?

Promotion decisions send strong signals to employees about what is valued. It will be very difficult to gain wide-scale commitment to the behaviors required to implement a new strategy if the old criteria for promotion remain in place. This is an area where it is critical to look not at what an organization says, but what its practices are. The CEO of a consumer products company was frustrated that business unit managers were not moving faster into new products and markets. At the annual retreat for the company's top 100 managers, the CEO declared that the company needed to hire and promote managers who were entrepreneurial and willing to take risks. Over drinks that night, the business unit managers talked about how unlikely it was that they would heed the CEO's words. So long as those promoted continued to be only from mature businesses where it was easy to deliver high margins, there would be no incentive to take risks or to hire others to do so.

More generally, an organizational realignment that reduces career development and promotion opportunities is unlikely to develop commitment to change. Concerns about the consequences for their careers were an important reason the senior management team of the Communications Division of Alpha Corporation was unwilling to share power with the new product development teams.

Organizational changes prompted by a new strategy must therefore be examined from the point of view of the professionals and managers affected and appropriate thought given to how the value proposition for key employee groups should be redefined. Many strategic changes require that the organization restructure and employees be laid off. Such reductions change the psychological contract between employees and the organization, reducing loyalty and increasing employee self-interest. How much help those laid off receive and how they are treated is key to the attitudes of survivors. The company's ability to redefine its psychological contract, from security in return for loyalty to personal and career development in return for high performance, will determine the commitment and the competence the company will be able to obtain in the future.

Information, Measurement, and Reward Systems

Do the information and measurement systems provide the data needed to monitor and manage strategy implementation?

Information and measurement systems provide the data that allow managers and other employees to assess how well they are doing in accomplishing the strategic tasks. Shifting strategic direction without the appropriate information and measurement system is about as easy as driving a car down a dark country road without headlights.

When new strategy requires a major shift in patterns of coordination, it is safe to assume that changes in the organization's information system will be needed. The information and accounting system of functional organizations does not typically consolidate data by product, customers, or market, but only by function. The introduction of new product development teams may be a first step in creating the coordination needed to reduce time to market. However, the teams will be limited in their effectiveness unless the accounting system is modified to allow each one to track the costs of the functional resources it is utilizing.

Thus it is important that the information and measurement system have an appropriate level of flexibility and breadth.[4] Asea Brown Boveri (ABB), a global electrical equipment manufacturer with over 4,000 profit centers worldwide, has been remarkably successful in achieving the benefits of decentralization—razor-sharp product market focus and responsiveness, along with the benefits of worldwide product excellence and scale, in part because of its extremely flexible and responsive information system. This system, known as ABACUS (Asea Brown Boveri Accounting and Communication System), allows rapid access to key financial measures for each profit center, region, and product business.[5]

Do the measurement and reward systems motivate the right behavior?

Information and measurement systems also have a powerful effect on the levels of organizational commitment. Providing individuals with information on the consequences of their actions is a strong internal motivator for improving performance. Measurement systems also establish an organization's scorecard. They help managers figure out the actions on their part that will be valued by the organization.

Do financial rewards have to be tied to performance measures and goals to motivate behavior? It is well established that linking rewards to the achievement of goals will cause people to make an effort to attain them. Salespeople who receive higher commissions for selling certain items will be more apt to pitch these items to their customers. The extraordinary creativity and economic value creation that has issued from California's Silicon Valley undoubtedly has been fueled by the opportunity for dramatic personal financial gains that come with liberally bestowed stock options.

We have also observed all too many instances in which companies design complex incentive systems intended to drive specific employee behaviors. Too often employee energy then becomes diverted into figuring out how to "game" the system. There is also evidence that motivating through commissions and bonuses makes people compliant and reduces internal motivation and creativity.[6] A third difficulty is that it is hard to find the right balance between individual and collective incentives. For example, many companies have found that financial incentive systems that emphasize individual divisional performance are a significant impediment to creating cooperation needed to implement corporate strategies that span business units.

Given these problems, it is often better to use information, involvement, and measurement to motivate while making an effort to pay equitably. When management reviews performance against agreed to measures and goals, people make a good faith effort to achieve them. Accomplishment is rewarded through satisfaction from a job well done, recognition, and the prospect of career advancement. These inducements produce motivation without dysfunctional consequences. Of course, people must be paid fairly, consistent with their market value and performance. But this can be accomplished through long-term adjustments in their pay and through promotions.

Leadership

Do the actions of the general manager and his or her top team reinforce effective performance on the business's strategic tasks?

The organizational levers previously described have a powerful impact on whether the levels of commitment, coordination, and competence needed to implement strategy exist. Organizational structure and systems alone do not assure that desired capabilities will be developed, however. We have observed many instances in which organizations with similar strategic tasks have used similar organizational designs to facilitate implementation of their strategy with very different levels of success.

The difference is leadership—the behavior of the general manager and the top team. It is difficult for managers at middle levels of the organization to work effectively together when the heads of their functions are unable to reach a meaningful consensus, set priorities, or agree on the behavior they want to reinforce. Commitment at lower levels is also directly affected, as illustrated earlier, by the amount of authority the senior group is willing to delegate.

Conversely, the actions taken by an effective general manager and top team can make up for flaws in organization design. Consider how the new plant manager of a glass plant faced up to his problem. He inherited an organization in which the various parts of the plant were at war with each other. To solve the problem, first he developed a cohesive top team and then they as a group broke down some of the barriers to cooperation by serving as facilitators for regular shift meetings. The plant manager also spent a great deal of his time coaching managers on his staff. They in turn coached those at lower organizational levels on how to develop the competence demanded by the new organization. Shared commitment to improving quality was developed, without changing the formal reward system, which rewarded productivity rather than defect reduction.

Corporate Context

Do the policies, procedures, or culture of the larger corporation help or hinder the business unit in implementing its strategy?

A business unit cannot realign its organization with strategy without considering the corporate context in which it operates. Consider a general manager of an electronics business where rapid product development must be led by the marketing function. The larger corporation imposed a control system that measured manufacturing plants on gross margin. Not surprisingly, plant managers were reluctant to introduce trial runs of new products in their plants. To do so would have interrupted their long manufacturing runs and reduced gross margin. Often the businesses that are most creative in redesigning their organization for effective strategy implementation are farthest from corporate headquarters.

The constraints imposed by the corporation on a division should not be used as an excuse for inaction. General managers must devise strategies for convincing corporate management to allow them to do what is right for their business.

We have described a systematic framework for diagnosing organizations. But, how does a manager actually go about redesigning the organization and making changes? The steps Honeywell's manager, John Dewane took to turn around the company's aviation unit, outlined in Box 14.2, provide an instructive model. Dewane involved members of the organization in analysis and change. The result was not only an organization that was formally aligned with strategy but employees who were committed to learning how to work within the new alignment.

Box 14.2

Honeywell's Change Program

Honeywell's Division manager, John Dewane, began his change effort by working with his top team. His staff, which had never been part of the strategy formulation process, spent many meetings reviewing data about the competitive environment—market trends, customer reactions to CAvD's product, and financial goals—and ended with consensus on the strategy. It defined its strategy as first developing the new commercial product, then developing good customer service, and finally reducing cost once the unit established its volume goals. In the first few years, product development was the key.

During the same period Dewane also held several off-site meetings, facilitated by a consultant, to discuss relationships among the staff. At the meeting, the directors discussed their views of themselves, how they viewed their jobs, and their approach to managing. Dissatisfaction with the current organization and its management practices grew as a result of these discussions. Dewane recalled that the group evolved toward agreement with his view, "This is garbage, why the hell are we living is a mess like this? There should be some pleasure in this work."

Once Dewane and his staff had decided to seek some type of change, they formed a team of volunteers to visit other companies and Honeywell plants to identify a model that could be used at CAvD. The team included a cross-section of people from a union steward to a director reporting to Dewane. The team was impressed by a visit to Honeywell's Chandler plant. Employees were working in teams with cooperation between management and union. A production employee remarked, "After seeing and feeling that atmosphere at Chandler, I realized what an improvement it would be in Commercial Aviation . . .

Box 14.2   *(Continued)*

to be able to ask for engineering support and get it, and to find everyone genuinely concerned about solving problems . . . with everyone having a chance to contribute to the whole."

Back home, a discussion developed about the barriers CAvD's functional organization posed to the development of new products and how Chandler's team approach might be used to overcome these problems. In response, Dewane appointed a design team composed of management and production employees. Their task—identify organizational barriers to product development and recommend a new model for organizing and managing to overcome barriers.

The design team quickly concluded that all work in CAvD, but particularly product development, cut across functional lines. They proceeded to recommend a team structure at the divisional and plant level that brought people together around tasks. Product development teams that brought engineering, marketing, manufacturing, and other functions together were the most important part of the proposal.

The design team formed a larger "core group" composed of 90 employees. Their assignment was to review the organizational model developed by the design team, to suggest modifications and to craft a statement of values for the division. At the end of a week, the core group agreed on a new organizational model and the values that would drive it. After reviewing these, Dewane and his staff assembled all employees in a theater where the design team and core group presented their recommendations. What came to be known as the Total Involvement Program (TIP) was born.

In the second year of change, it became apparent that employees at several levels did not fit the new model of management. The Operations manager agreed to transfer out to another part of the company. He was not replaced, reducing the number of reporting levels in the division. Several supervisors who found it difficult to work within the new framework were given different jobs or transferred. The union president objected to the new approach to management, but the local union steward convinced him that the approach was one to which production employees were committed.

By the end of the second year, it was clear that the transformation effort was succeeding. Cross-functional coordination, the central objective of the organizational realignment had improved markedly.

The realignment of the organization with strategy also produced a dramatic improvement in business performance. Three years into the transition, CAvD had become the market leader in inertial reference and inertial navigation products (IRS/INS). The division estimated that 80 percent of IRS/INS systems installed on air transport airplanes and 95 percent of the IRS/INS systems installed on business aviation jets were made by Honeywell. Customers thought Honeywell's systems were three times as reliable as competitors' products. The division's reputation for customer service was excellent. Honeywell's cost of producing products was estimated to be quite a bit lower than that of its competitors. The division also had become profitable for the first time.

ORCHESTRATING CHANGE INITIATIVES IN A WAY THAT BUILDS PARTNERSHIP AND LEARNING

Why Partnership Is Important

The case of the Commercial Aviation Division suggests that the foundation for effective strategy implementation is partnership. A way must be found to rally employees in different levels and parts of the organization around the implementation of strategy.

Competition is forcing most companies to find ways to improve coordination and partnership among various parts of the organization. Few sources of sustainable competitive advantage can be realized through the efforts of any one function. As the CAvD case illustrates, product quality and cost is affected not just by manufacturing but also by R&D where the product is designed for manufacturability, as well as by purchasing and logistics that ensure raw materials consistently meet specifications. In fact, partnership must go beyond the boundaries of the firm to include suppliers and customers.

Partnership is necessary not just in the newly aligned organization, but also in the change process itself. Why? Senior management, because of its knowledge of both the external environment and the overall business, can define a broad strategic direction. However, the top management group cannot do it alone. Those closer to the front line tend to have a better sense for the specific barriers that must be addressed if implementation is to be successful.

For all these reasons creating a partnership for implementation across organizational levels and between different parts of the organization is essential.

Why Building Partnership Is Difficult

The problem is that many of the most important barriers to implementation can't be discussed easily in management forums. For example, barriers to cross-functional coordination at CAvD were rooted in the arrogance within the engineering function. In the military avionics business, the military customer valued technical solutions so highly that it made sense for engineers to be in complete control of design decisions. This translated into a dictatorial style at every level and to hostility and distrust between the heads of manufacturing and engineering.

Deep-seated issues of this type are difficult to surface and discuss publicly. Without the capacity to surface them, however, the organization is unable to redesign and correct its structure and management practices. If general managers have grown up in the organization, as had John Dewane's predecessor, they may be blind to these problems. Even if they are vaguely aware of problems, they may have a difficult time assessing their significance. These are "iceberg issues"—the issues below the surface of the organization's public conversations that are most likely to sink new strategic initiatives. This is a case where what you don't know can hurt you.

Just as often, the barriers to partnership are in vertical relationships. Employees and/or the union may distrust management, preventing them from engaging in the kind of open dialogue and cooperation that identifies problems and develops commitment to solutions. The use of top-down programs to change the organization also reduces commitment. Consider the response of the union president at CAvD to John Dewane's preliminary ideas about change, well before he decided to involve lower levels, "You do it that way, you can count me out. We have really had enough of all these damned programs that come and go, and they have no support from the people."

When the barriers to strategy implementation are the attitudes and behavior of top management, these issues are even more difficult to discuss. Ways must be found to make a dialogue possible or the organization cannot realign itself with strategy.

How to Build Partnership

The most effective way to develop an organizational partnership for strategy implementation is by building a consensus around the business's strategic tasks. This consensus must be created both within the senior management team, as well as in the larger organization. To develop this consensus, key individuals must be convinced that certain actions are good for both the overall business and for them. Dewane helped his top team understand the business problems facing them and the importance of developing new products more quickly and at lower cost through a series of off-site meetings to review the business. Information about customer dissatisfaction and its potentially disastrous consequences helped develop commitment to change. So did the realization, triggered by the visits to the Chandler plant, that there was a better way to manage.

If the top team is committed to accomplishing a common set of strategic tasks, those lower in the organization are less likely to receive conflicting direction. However, this does not necessarily ensure widespread organizational commitment. Developing this commitment usually requires sharing the information which led the top team to decide on a common strategic direction with those at all levels of the organization. In many companies, it often involves sharing far more information about competitors and customers than had been customary. It also requires some imagination and creativity. For example, some companies have arranged visits to customer facilities for production workers as well as salaried workers. In other cases, customers have been invited to demonstrate how the product is used. In still other instances, competitive products have been displayed on the shop floor for all employees to inspect.

The competitive crisis that Dewane faced made it relatively easy to align individual and organizational interests. The problem is more difficult when the external crisis is less severe—individual interests are less likely to align with those of the overall organization. In these instances, it is all the more important that the top team engage the organization in a joint process of data collection and analysis. It allows them to come to a common understanding of both the risks, as well as the opportunities inherent in the new strategic direction. The general manager must also send the message that members of the team will be evaluated on their willingness to act for the good of the overall organization, not just on their functional or subunit performance.

Over the past few years, a number of companies, including Becton Dickinson, Honeywell, Merck, and Hewlett-Packard have put in place a disciplined process for developing a partnership for strategy implementation, known as Organizational Fitness Profiling. After completing its strategic plan, a business unit enlists the help of an employee task force to assess the organization's capabilities to implement its strategic tasks. The task force conducts interviews with employees and feeds back to the top team the results about organizational strengths that should be leveraged and barriers that need to be addressed in accomplishing these tasks. Problems in interfunctional cooperation, top team effectiveness, changing priorities, and uncoordinated resource allocation, as well as deficiencies in technical and managerial competence are typical issues that surface.

The task force is able to present these potentially embarrassing and threatening problems by means of a carefully crafted process intended to promote a nondefensive discussion. Members of the task force sit in the middle of the room in what is called a "fishbowl," where they discuss their findings with each other while top management sits in an outer circle listening. They engage the task force in a discussion about findings under commonly agreed to ground rules for nondefensive dialogue. A trained facilitator helps both groups follow the ground rules.

The top team then develops a diagnosis of why and how the organization is not aligned, as well as a model of how the business unit should be organized and managed to support the strategy more fully. Employee teams are enlisted to help develop particular parts of the change plan. Organizational Fitness Profiling enables business unit managers to examine deficiencies in the organization's capabilities to implement strategy that were hidden or that could not be discussed.[7]

Sequencing Change

The shared desire to implement strategy can be a powerful source of positive energy for change. Having generated this positive energy, how does a manager actually go about redesigning the organization? Should changes in formal organization design be made first? Must people be replaced before any meaningful change can occur?

Figure 14.2 presents a list of interventions or actions managers can take ranging from changing structure, to replacing people, to training. We have classified these interventions into those that require little or no change in formal organization and those that affect the formal structure, systems, and policies

FIGURE 14.2 Sequencing interventions for learning.

	Level of Focus	
	Unit Level	Individual or group level
Informal Behavior	(1) Redefinition of roles Responsibilities and relationships	(2) Coaching, counseling Training Process consultation Team building
Formal Design	(4) Compensation system Information system Organizational structure Measurement system	(3) Replacement Recruitment Career pathing Succession planning Performance appraisal

Intervention seeks to modify

(top and bottom quadrants respectively). We have also classified the interventions into those that affect the organization as a whole and those that focus on the individual or group (left and right quadrants respectively). The resulting two-by-two matrix provides the manager with clusters of interventions.

The exact sequencing of these interventions is to some extent situation specific (See Chapter 17 for a description of many of the relevant contingencies). However, the sequence of interventions specified by the numbered quadrants in Figure 14.2 is particularly well suited to building a partnership for change.[8]

Specifically, after employees are involved in defining the strategic task and making a diagnosis of barriers to change, the top management team, with the help of design teams composed of key employees or union leaders, commits itself to a new strategically aligned model of the organization. That model does not specify changes in formal structure or systems. Instead, it defines an ad hoc organization—task forces, committees, and changes in management process at the top and lower levels that bring the right people together to work on the right things at the right time, regardless of formal affiliation (quadrant 1 in Figure 14.2). Its aim is to improve coordination around the strategic task. Honeywell's CAvD started with this approach. Dewane and his top management team committed themselves to a team-based organization recommended by a design team and elaborated by the "core group."

If the right people have indeed been assigned to do the right thing then strategic tasks will begin to be implemented more effectively. Team members will begin to feel that they are making a difference where the former organization failed. That raises their commitment and enhances teamwork. As the new pattern of working together takes hold, new required competencies—skills in teamwork and problem solving, and a less parochial attitude—are developed in real time. Coaching and training (quadrant 2 in Figure 14.2) further enhances learning. Training at an earlier point—before the new ad hoc organization is put in place—is hard for people to apply.

Honeywell's Commercial Aviation Division followed the sequence we recommend. Engineers, production managers and workers, and marketing representatives on teams began to learn new attitudes and skills from their experience on teams. This learning was supported by six human resource specialists who sat in on early meetings and coached the teams as well as by a training program in interpersonal communication. Dewane's top team utilized an outside consultant at several off-site meetings to facilitate their development into an effective team.

The organizational learning process that unfolds in this sequence is one to which people become increasingly committed. But, it also exposes the capability of people to fit into the new pattern of management. It is inevitable that some people will be unable to learn rapidly enough or at all. These are the people who will have to be replaced after a certain period of time. But their departure will be seen far differently than if they had they been fired at the very beginning.

High-level replacement decisions do not just affect the competence level for an individual position, but also have symbolic value for the larger organization—a decision to replace a senior manager can either energize an organization or demoralize it. Employees can either view the manager who makes the replacement decision as finally having the courage to confront a personnel problem that has been acting as a roadblock for the whole organization, or as "killing off" a valuable co-worker. If the sequence in Figure 14.2 is followed, the former is more likely to be the perception. By the time managers are moved, employees are committed to the new organization and removal of employees who have not adapted is perceived as necessary and fair.

At Honeywell's CAvD, several staffing changes occurred between the first and second year of change. The Operations manager, a member of the team, was helped by Dewane to see that he would not fit into the new pattern of management and was transferred. Several leaders of teams were ineffective and had to be replaced. Slowly, a new standard for hiring and promotion took hold in the division.

As the pattern of management proves itself effective, as it should if it aligns with strategy, changes in the formal organizational levers can be made as needed. Now these changes simply ratify and reinforce behavior already learned. At Honeywell's CAvD, formal structure was modified organically as people left. The Operations manager was not replaced and the structure flattened. The need for better information and a measurement system for new product development teams was becoming evident after two years and plans were being made for change in them.

The preceding sequence of activities maximizes readiness for change. There is more agreement in most organizations on the necessity for confronting core business problems than on the need for a structural reorganization, or for personnel replacements. When changes in the formal organization are made, it comes only after they have been identified as barriers to the new pattern of management. Similarly, personnel changes are made only after it is obvious to all that certain individuals will not or cannot change.

SUMMARY

The successful implementation of a business strategy requires both an accurate assessment of internal capabilities, as well as the mobilization of a broad partnership to make needed changes in organizational structure and systems. This requires accurate and fact-based information to flow freely both up and down the organization.

This approach to strategy implementation is much easier to describe than to enact. While, it is easy to intellectually acknowledge the importance of getting at the barriers to strategy implementation below the surface of the iceberg, actually surfacing and dealing with these issues may be painful and uncomfortable. Similarly, many managers are not used to engaging in a rigorous causal analysis of the human barriers to strategy implementation. Many of the managers who are most skillful in using the analytic tools of strategy formulation face the highest learning curve in taking a similarly dispassionate and logical approach to the emotionally messy issues that can arise during a discussion of how the organization needs to be realigned to implement strategy.

Even the most skilled managers cannot fully anticipate the consequences of the actions they set in motion. This makes strategy implementation less a linear sequence than an iterative one; certain organizational actions are taken, the consequences are assessed, and appropriate modifications are initiated. The iteration and interaction between diagnosis and action represent the organizational learning process needed for continuous improvement. It is the only way the organization can improve organizational capabilities of coordination, commitment, and competence—the essential ingredients for strategy implementation—while also developing the capacity to make further adaptations when the competitive environment again demands them.

REFERENCES

Beer, Michael, Bert Spector, Paul R. Lawrence, D. Quinn Mills, and Richard E. Walton. 1981. *Managing Human Assets.* New York: Free Press.

Beer, Michael, Russell A. Eisenstat, and Bert Spector. 1990. *The Critical Path to Corporate Renewal.* Cambridge, MA: Harvard Business School Press.

Beckhard, Richard, and Rubin T. Harris. 1987. *Organizational Transitions: Managing Complex Change,* 2nd ed. Reading, MA: Addison-Wesley.

Dennison, Daniel. 1990. *Corporate Culture and Organizational Effectiveness.* New York: Wiley.

Eccles, Robert, and Nitin Nohria. 1992. *Beyond the Hype: Rediscovering the Essence of Management.* Cambridge, MA: Harvard Business School Press.

Galbraith, Jay. 1994. *Competing with Flexible Lateral Organizations,* 2nd ed. Reading, MA: Addison-Wesley; and Hackman, Richard, and Greg Oldham. 1980. *Work Redesign.* Reading, MA: Addison-Wesley.

Mohrman, Susan, Susan Cohen, and Allan Mohrman. 1995. *Designing Team-Based Organizations.* San Francisco: Jossey-Bass.

Nadler, David A., and Michael L. Tushman. 1997. *Competing by Design: The Power of Organizational Architecture.* Oxford, England: Oxford University Press.

Schaffer, Robert H. 1988. *The Breakthrough Strategy: Using Short Term Successes to Build the High Performance Organization.* Cambridge, MA: Ballinger.

NOTES

1. In *Corporate Culture and Organizational Effectiveness* (New York: Wiley, 1990), Dan Dennison demonstrates that employee survey data correlate with financial performance in future years.

2. See Richard Hackman and Greg Oldham, *Work Redesign* (Reading, MA: Addison-Wesley, 1980), for a powerful analytic framework managers can use to systematically analyze jobs for their power to motivate.

3. See Jay Galbraith, *Competing with Flexible Lateral Organizations,* 2nd ed. (Reading, MA: Addison-Wesley, 1994); and Susan Mohrman, Susan Cohen, and Allan Mohrman, *Designing Team-Based Organizations* (San Francisco: Jossey-Bass, 1995), for two useful resources on the effective design and use of cross-boundary teams.

4. See Robert S. Kaplan and David P. Norton, "The Balanced Scorecard" (Boston: Harvard Business School Press, 1996), for a useful set of tools to develop a broad set of metrics to measure a businesses most critical pulse points.

5. See Asea Brown Boveri, *The Abacus System* Case 9–192–140 (Harvard Business School), for more information on ABACUS.

6. Alfie Cohen makes this argument quite strongly in "Why Incentive Plans Cannot Work," *Harvard Business Review* (September/October 1993).

7. See Michael Beer, Russell A. Eisenstat, and Ralph Biggadike, "Strategic Change: A New Dimension of Human Resource Management," in *The Handbook of Human Resources Management,* Gerald R. Ferris, Sherman D. Rosen, and Darold T. Barnum, (Eds.) (Oxford, England: Blackwell, 1995): 115–138, for a fuller description of the fitness profiling methodology.

8. See *The Critical Path to Corporate Renewal,* by Michael Beer, Russell A. Eisenstat, and Bert Spector (Boston: Harvard Business School Press, 1990), for a more in-depth discussion of the issues in this section.

STRATEGIC CHANGE: RECONFIGURING OPERATIONAL PROCESSES TO IMPLEMENT STRATEGY

15

Ellen R. Hart
Gemini Consulting

Business in the United States is entering an era of networked competence, particularly in processes. How well firms implement their strategies will depend in large measure on how well they manage key business processes. To successfully implement strategies in this new era, managers must make everyone in the firm aware of the need to transform the organization:

- From a focus on structure to a focus on process.
- From a vertical to a horizontal orientation.
- From being a service provider to being a network facilitator.
- From a primary emphasis on procedures and efficiency to an understanding of the importance of flexibility and adaptability.

The new drivers of business will be innovation, speed, and flexibility. All employees must be made aware that processes are the means by which their company delivers value, and therefore there is no more crucial task in implementing strategy than process design and the integration or coordination of action.

A case in point: Federal Express (FedEx) focuses its strategy on a particular customer value: To provide speedy and reliable delivery of packages. Every process within the organization has been designed to achieve this objective. For starters, the company created a hub in Memphis and centralized all shipments to it. Further, Federal Express owns and operates a fleet of planes to achieve the desired level of service, though this requires a much larger investment than renting space on passenger airlines.

Instead of just looking for ways to mechanize and improve on traditional methods of sorting and delivering mail, FedEx combined changes in infrastructure, information technology, and traditional processes (distribution and logistics) in innovative ways that created a new customer value. In doing so, the company opened a new market for high-value, high-priority mail. FedEx's package tracking system, a main differentiator from the U.S. Post Office and United Parcel Service (UPS), offers customers a way to know where their packages are at every stage of shipping. Because customers can go on the Internet to have this package tracking information at their fingertips, they become, in effect, their own customer service reps. As Federal Express became world class at developing and operating these processes, it proved attractive to more and more customers. It's not hyperbole to credit FedEx with rewriting the rules of its industry (what customers can have) and then reinventing that industry (the processes that delivers what customers can have).

Another way companies can establish a potent competitive advantage is to combine a superior process with superior manufacturing capability. The result: a competence network, a unique system for providing customer value.

Here's how one major company linked world-class process and manufacturing capabilities: National Semiconductor made a strategic decision to establish assembly plants in Southeast Asia. The logistics and distribution aspects of its facilities would obviously be critical to the success of the entire venture. Rather than build its own capabilities to ensure reliable delivery of semiconductors, National Semiconductor contracted with Federal Express Business Logistics Services to store, inventory, and ship its goods. The direct net savings: National Semiconductor closed nine warehouses. But more importantly, by contracting with Federal Express, the company achieved a level of excellence in logistics and distribution far beyond its own capability. As a result, National Semiconductor could offer customers a unique value combination: its manufacturing process and Federal Express's excellent distribution processes.

This chapter discusses the historic link between strategy and operations, some of the factors that have exposed the deficiency of that approach, and the changes that have brought about the necessity of focusing on process management. The chapter then reviews the elements of a business process focus and provides examples of ways to strategically leverage those processes. Moving from concept to practice, the chapter provides a framework for rethinking how core processes can provide competitive advantage.

Asking a company to focus on process rather than on structure (i.e., organization subunits and departments or functional areas) is a radical step for traditional companies that are organized into specialized functional baronies—R&D, sales, marketing distribution, manufacturing, and customer service. The history of corporate organizations in the twentieth century is largely about the rise in power of such specialized functions that sometimes feuded, and often had trouble working together. That's why integrating process and strategy—and in doing so, inventing the modern corporation—is such a significant development.

TRADITIONAL LINKAGES BETWEEN STRATEGY AND OPERATIONS

The linkages between strategy and operations have their origins in the Industrial Revolution. Typically, "strategy" was broad and defined in terms of financial objectives, for example, to use the corporation's assets to return a target level of performance for shareholders. Each functional area within the company—sales, marketing distribution, manufacturing, customer service—was charged with managing its costs and revenues to achieve its portion of the target level of financial contribution.

The operational strategies pursued by the functional area flowed from the concepts developed by Frederick Taylor, a top manager at General Motors and the "father" of industrial engineering. Taylor essentially sought to simplify and standardize work through the decomposition and measurement of tasks. He believed that there were optimal ways to perform discrete tasks; specialization in the performance of each task would result in efficiency improvements. In recent years, management innovations such as benchmarking, best practices, business process redesign (BPR), total quality management (TQM), and continuous improvement often inadvertently reinforced the "machine age" approach to operational performance improvement pioneered by Taylor decades ago. However astute such new approaches were, they all subscribed to a general theory: fix the parts and somehow the whole will improve. What companies discovered was that "fixing" may simply bring a company to parity in a narrow area; it does not necessarily create competitive advantage. The "post-reengineering" era (i.e., the past few years) brought countless examples of businesses that had made enormous process improvements along a dimension, such as cutting claims processing time, while market share and profits declined. Nor is the need for process reconfiguration and improvement likely to go away. As noted by well-known commentator Peter Keen:

> The gap in operating capabilities between industry leaders and their competitors is currently very high as measured by profits and sales per employee, two indicators of process capability [the gaps between the leader and the median performer average more than 50%]. So the pace of change is likely to accelerate—and the need for business process improvements will be greater than ever.[1]

While in the 1970s and 1980s, dramatic operational improvements were in the 10 percent to 20 percent range, in the decade of the 1990s, 10- to 20-fold increases became possible as whole new configurations of core processes and capabilities emerged. As we enter the first decade of the twenty-first century, such leaps are becoming commonplace. The most successful companies will be those who strategically link those processes to their unique positioning within their industry.

What Changed?

A confluence of factors has led to a revolution in our expectations both of strategy and of business operations, and in our understanding of the power of the linkages between them.

- The nature of competition has changed drastically. There are simply more and smart competitors who can quickly replicate virtually any one-dimensional advantage. Competition is open, tough, global, and relentless.[2]

- The digital world and increasingly powerful technologies are altering the role of time, space, and boundaries. Rather than technology simply being an automator or facilitator of business processes, it fundamentally alters how and where business is conducted. For example, in the 1980s, ATMs quickly made platoons of tellers redundant, and in the late 1990s Internet banks challenged traditional banking. In addition, Internet technology has changed the underlying economic model for doing business (e.g., Amazon.com has made it possible for people to purchase books from a virtual bookstore with an almost limitless selection).[3]

- The window of time available to a company to execute its strategy is shorter. The average Web site start-up time is just three months. The re-action to intelligence or signals from the marketplace must be virtually instantaneous and pervasive. As one observer of the marketplace put it, "You must be able to change tires while the car is still moving."

- There are smarter workers available, with increasingly powerful tools to assist them. Every ounce of talent in an organization must be harnessed productively and synergistically.

- There are better educated, more demanding customers and consumers. Customer behavior is in flux due to greater customer connectivity, control, and knowledge. Old analysis models based on clustered patterns or segments may no longer be accurate in predicting future behavior.

- The focus of information technology moved from the back office efficiency and administrative functions to customer interface role.

As a result of these changes, what has emerged are firms like Li and Fung,[4] Hong Kong's largest export trading company, no longer just brokers providing access and guidance for their customers (primarily American and European retailers) within new territories but now a company that assembles a customized value chain to meet their customers' needs. Or firms like Solectron, a contract manufacturer, who represents "a sort of extended enterprise—a set of partnerships between product developers and specialists in components, distribution, retailing, and manufacturing."[5] This extended enterprise model allows their customers to focus their investment dollars on research and marketing, while Solectron hones their manufacturing expertise.

A PROCESS-BASED APPROACH AND
THE VALUE NETWORK

A business process orders and ranks activities/tasks, decisions, information, and material flows over time. It takes an input (such as raw materials, information, or a customer's order), adds value to it, and provides a specific output (e.g., a finished product or a product delivered to a customer on time and in the right place). A process-based approach systematizes the activities of a business into a horizontal flow of suppliers, processes, and customers. Core business processes or end-to-end processes are the value-adding series of activities for the principal *external customer*. Examples of these processes are "product realization" that can include not only the way a product is developed, but also marketed and serviced; "order to delivery" that helps focus on the customer order, not the multiple departments or entities it must pass through to be fulfilled.

Whether in the services or manufacturing arena, each company usually has only a few truly critical business processes. In retailing, for example, only four major processes link supplier, distributor, store outlet, and consumer, and directly impact consumer needs for product, convenience, and price:

1. Ensuring ease of shopping and optimum variety at the retail level.
2. Replenishing product (ensuring product is there when needed).
3. Communicating the value (creating demand and pull-through for the product).
4. Introducing new products.

While each of these processes could be improved in isolation by each player in the value network (suppliers, product providers, channels, retailers), the productivity and revenue improvement possible through cooperation is much greater. Just as intracompany advances require cross-entity cooperation (whether departments, functions, plants, regions, etc.), so intercompany advances require the optimization of the whole, for the good of the customers. In the *introduction of new products,* detailed point-of-sale information on consumer buying habits and tastes allows the suppliers to create niche products that their market research may not have identified. In the *replenishment* dimension, the more synchronized the retail store, the distributor, and the supplier are in terms of real consumer demand, the more they can reduce inventory and capital costs across all three.

Procter & Gamble, a manufacturer, supplies Wal-Mart, a retailer. The business processes of both firms are driven by a similar mission—to get the right products to the consumer. A critical business process to Wal-Mart is inventory management; a critical business process to P&G is order processing. Their performances depend on the same information: how quickly are Wal-Mart's consumers buying P&G products? Information connects the business processes of both companies to track sales and ensure that the Wal-Mart customer doesn't have to go to Kmart to buy a box of Tide, a P&G detergent. This linkage of core business processes does not mean that the two companies have to operate in the same way, only that they share a resource—information—to support each other's business processes and anchor them to the customer. The salient commonality is that each knows when and what to do if Wal-Mart is running low on Tide. (In contrast, in many ways, Kmart's strategic goals have been set in response to Wal-Mart's dominance in key processes. Kmart is in catch-up mode, as are many companies with traditional business models that are trying to replicate "digital" models.)

Successful companies need a thorough understanding of the shifting business environment and innovations outside their industry, not just within their own industry or business. To enable strategy, leaders need to think less about structure and functions and focus more on the processes that control the value they intend to deliver to their customers. Peter Keen, the author of several books on knowledge management, argues: "There are fewer and fewer sustainable product advantages, protected market advantages, national advantages. That means there are fewer and fewer ways of creating and sustaining market differentiation. I can't see any other way of making a firm stand out other than by process."[6] In the 1980s, Michael Porter proposed the concept of a value chain to connect the upstream and downstream components of a business, but today a value "network" may be a more apt description of the interrelationships

FIGURE 15.1   Networked value web.

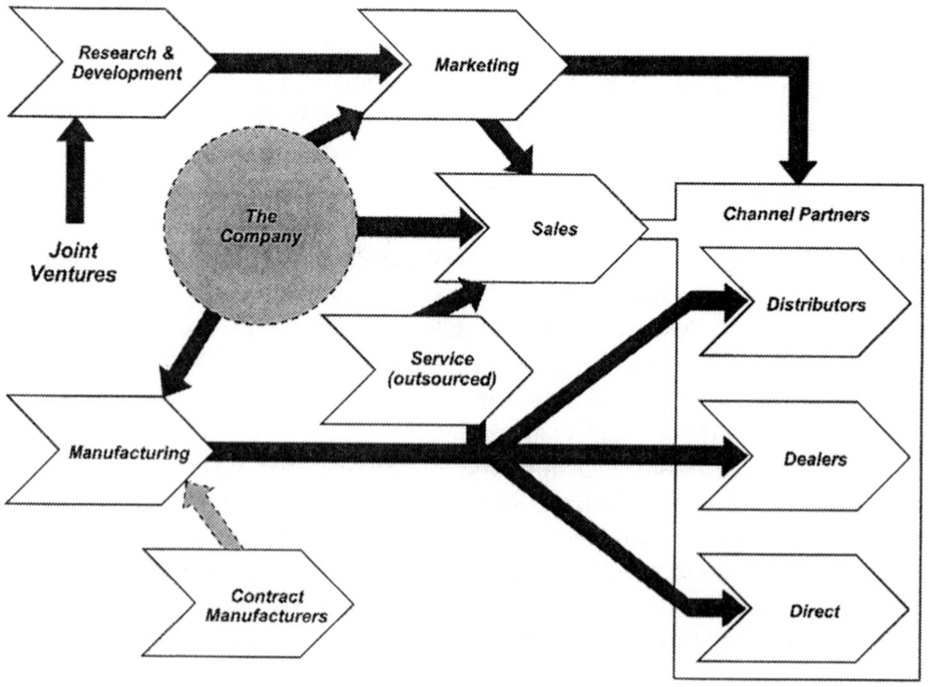

TABLE 15.1   Approaches to Strategically Leveraging Processes

Approaches to Strategically Leveraging Processes*	Examples
Intensification: improving processes to serve current customers better	Many companies' reengineering efforts focused here; Harley-Davidson reduced its delivery time from 360 to 3 days through cell manufacturing.
Extension: using strong processes to enter new markets	Amazon.com moved into selling videos and music.
Augmentation: expanding processes to provide additional services to current customers	Dell provides on-line ordering and tracking of customized PCs; Avis provides personalized car return process.
Conversion: taking a process that you perform well and performing it as a service for other companies	Federal Express does logistics for other companies. Fingerhut does order fulfillment for new "e-tailers."
Innovation: applying processes that you perform well to create and deliver different goods or services	American Express provides purchasing services to business; McDonald's does international site selection for other companies.
Diversification: creating new processes to deliver new goods or services	Schwab provides web-based trading, money management, and research to its customers.

* Categories were identified by Michael Hammer in *Beyond Reengineering.* New York: Harper Business, 1996.

of companies and customers. A company can choose to operate anywhere within the value network (see Figure 15.1 on page 328), but astute strategists select the part in which their company can excel.

There are multiple approaches to strategically leveraging processes (see Table 15.1), as demonstrated in the many corporate examples discussed in this chapter. However they accomplish it, to remain dynamic, companies continuously need to ensure their processes fulfill their strategic purpose. The next section describes six steps for renewing or reconfiguring processes.

RECONFIGURING CORE BUSINESS PROCESSES

The six steps central to renewing and reconfiguring core business processes are:

1. Envision the future.
2. Identify and select core business processes.
3. Design new processes.
4. Assess current processes and analyze the gap.
5. Plan the transition to the future.
6. Implement the change programs.

While each of these steps is described as if the steps are discrete phases, there is a need throughout the effort to operate with the end (the future) in mind, to learn from each phase, and to mobilize the people who are critical to successful implementation. The following subsections describe the steps and the questions they help to answer, as well as provide guidelines for accomplishing each phase.

Envisioning the Future: Scenario Planning for Strategic Processes

As a first step in aligning strategy and processes, you must identify and understand which environmental trends will strongly influence your business. Next, you must create a set of scenarios for the future that are unconstrained by current ways of thinking. Speculate about revolutions in technology, customer preferences, and how your product or service could be created, accessed, delivered, or used.

In the late 1980s, Michael Dell envisioned that savvy computer users would be willing to buy their computers directly by phone through a catalog (in other words he foresaw the next generation of computer buyers). He believed that his company could offer these customers a mass customized product; that is, Dell could build computers to each phone customer's exact specifications. The "traditional" computer sellers, IBM and others, and even the newcomers, Compaq and Apple, rejected Dell's approach. Michael Dell created Dell and the requisite processes such as customized manufacturing and direct distribution to customers, which allowed them to dominate catalog selling and customized configuration of orders. Because Dell only built computers that had been paid for, it also shifted the economic model of the business; Dell's order to cash process is 24 hours, whereas a competitor like Compaq is 35 days (see note 3). When others tried to catch up, Dell leveraged its order taking and fulfillment processes into a new channel (the Internet), to offer not only an alternative to placing an order but to allow online customization and tracking of one's own computer as it is being built. Dell grew from start-up to over $18 billion in sales in its first decade based on insights about the evolution of buyer behavior and preferences, *linked to the execution capability their core processes provided.*

When competitors imitate successful companies—Compaq doing direct selling like Dell, United or Delta trying to be a no-frills carrier like Southwest Airlines, or Barnes & Noble building an online store like Amazon.com—they don't automatically gain the same advantage. This is because these pioneering firms always interlinked their processes to their strategy. For example, Dell started as a master of the direct selling approach (whether it was by phone, catalog, or Internet). Likewise, because Amazon.com's processes were conceived and developed to support their strategic positioning on the Web, companies that merely imitate one of their processes don't gain instant parity.

Using the scenarios of the future as a testing ground, your management team should try to conceive processes that will give the company a competitive advantage in the long term. After mergers or acquisitions, many companies try to either merge or pick the best processes from each entity. However, due to heightened politics and compromise, what often occurs is a dilution of process capability that serves neither original company well, nor does it position either for advantage. In designing processes for the future marketplace, it is crucial not to be hampered by existing ways of thinking or by the inability to differentiate between industry adaptations (e.g., Local Area Networks—a valuable adaptation) and industry shifts (e.g., the Internet—a technology capable of transforming many industries). It is also necessary to take an outside-in (consider the "as yet to be realized" customers and the product/service value they will seek), as well as an inside-out view (what are the core capabilities you must build to serve those future customers?) Breakthrough results in processes are possible if organizations keep in mind the dictum: "Don't play for safety. It is the most dangerous game in the world."[7]

Identifying and Selecting Core Business Processes

The identification and selection of core business processes must be proceeded by an articulation of strategy, the factors which are critical to the success of that strategy, and sources of competitive advantage. Together, these describe the larger business network, where boundaries of businesses are not fixed. The company should spell out the criteria that will be used to select which processes are most significant. As a rule, the key processes are the ones most directly linked to the customer, ones which both make a business unique, and provide a meaningful competitive advantage, such as a potential for breakthrough performance. As business guru Peter Keen said, "Salient processes are the processes that most relate to the firm's identity—those that visibly differentiate it from its competitors—and the priority activities that keep the engine of everyday competitive performance running."[8] To identify your business's key and nonkey processes, look over the following questions, discuss them with managers in as many functions as possible, and draft a brief status report:

- What business are we in and what is our place in the value network?
- What is the value we need to deliver to the customers we've selected?
- What are the business processes we need to perform exceptionally well to deliver that value proposition?
- Which processes although valuable to our customers, can be offered more effectively by other partners?

Designing the New Processes

As a result of these discussions, the organization should begin to have a vision of the competitive performance levels it must achieve, an understanding of customers' expectations around performance and the value they can expect, and a vision of the processes that would enable the company to gain a competitive advantage. Defining the next evolution of business processes involves benchmarking relevant best practices, identifying breakthrough performance levels, developing alternative models of delivering those performance levels, and then prototyping a new process. The broad objectives for new processes are that they be:

- *Effective.* They deliver the intended result.
- *Efficient.* They consume the least amount of resources for the intended value.
- *Flexible.* They can change as customers, market forces, and technology shift.

Breakthrough performance levels should be identified through a thorough knowledge of benefits sought by customers. The current performance level and the breakthrough performance target are like two fingers with a rubber band stretched between them. If the fingers are too far apart, the rubber band will snap; if they are too close, the rubber band will go slack and create no tension. Reach must exceed grasp when setting performance levels, but overreaching can be counterproductive.

Critical to reconfiguring core business practices is the need to identify the unique value proposition. A value proposition is a statement of the benefits a company chooses to provide to its customers and the price it charges for them. It implicitly makes a choice between customer segments the company will and will not pursue. In contrast to traditional demographic segmentation—for example, serve the middle-age upscale male market—the value proposition describes customers in terms of the benefits the customer values. Charles Schwab and Co. has been successful by learning to "serve customers who value ease of access." How the benefits will be delivered is often the focus of the design effort.[9]

Because many firms have adopted ERP (Enterprise Resource Planning) systems and because of the critical role of information technology in most core processes, "best practices" (or at least common practices) are often embedded in the functionality of the systems or modules. This can greatly reduce time and complexity of design and implementation. But it may also lead to a "commoditization" of core processes within industries, where uniqueness becomes harder to leverage.[10]

Design imperatives for the new or improved process should be explicit. When Ford was recreating itself in the 1980s, its vision included a major emphasis on quality. Its slogan: "Quality is job 1." As a design imperative, this might reveal itself through the agreement that customers and their perception of quality will be the final determinant in a conflict situation about the design of a process.

The new process should be designed without regard to current organizational lines, political or emotional constraints, players, or personalities. Taking an even more radical stance, some managers believe that breakthrough processes need to be developed separately, and in protection from, the current dominant processes. Futurists Stan Davis and Bill Davidson suggest:

> . . . that not-yet-existing business is the best source of information for what the future organization should look like . . . *The best place to look for the basis of organization change is in the future business, and the worst place to look is in the current organization.* The present organization, however, may be a good predictor of what will *prevent* you from developing the kind of organization you will need. Like all creatures, it has a vested interest in continuing to exist.[11]

However much autonomy the process team has, it is important that someone (or some team) with significant status within the organization knows they will "own" and be accountable for the entire process being created. The people who will be accountable for the oversight and control of the process should have an important role in designing it.[12] Use the design selection process to achieve buy-in. Some organizations design only one model, others design several alternatives. Creating a prototype allows you to walk through the new process, determine how it actually would alter the business, and test it to ensure that it meets your criteria. The following criteria might be applied in selecting among alternative design options:

- Provides competitive advantage.
- Maximizes use of assets.
- Is customer anchored and customer friendly.
- Maximizes the company's distinctive value-add (e.g., access, speed, reliability, low cost, quality).
- Is measurable in ways that promote continuous improvement.
- Is adaptive, flexible.

Benchmarks can be established by looking within your own organization, at competitors, and at other industries. In understanding how people operate and how processes have been reconfigured in other organizations, it is important not only to see what people do, but also to seek out the transition history— how they got there. It helps to adopt an anthropologist's perspective: honor the native culture, understand that the process of observation alters the observed, see the behavior within their world, not yours, and consider what in their environment made their behavior possible and supportable. Without such a view, companies often adopt ideas or approaches as if they were silver bullets with magical properties. Not surprisingly, the magic fix seldom works. When United and Delta tried to replicate the no-frills/low prices approach of Southwest Airlines, they underestimated how hard it would be to deliver this new value proposition. Their attempt taught them to respect the mastery with which Southwest has woven together a strategy, outstanding operational execution, and a culture.

An aligned measurement system keeps strategy and operations in sync over time through clear and widely understood measures of both in-process and end-of-process performance objectives, customer satisfaction, and financial contribution metrics.[13] Inherent to the success of any measurement system is that everyone knows the measures, receives frequent, consistent information, knows how the pieces they touch contribute to the whole, and feels able to affect the results.

Assessing Current Processes and Analyzing the Gap

"Things are the way they are because they got that way," is the tautology offered to explain how and why many business processes evolved to their current state. Detailing the "as is" situation (i.e., the current way that work is *actually* accomplished, not the procedural or ideal descriptions of how work is supposed to be done), creates an accurate baseline for measuring operations in relation to time, cost, resources consumed, volume, and so on. Comparison of the "as is" to the "could be" demonstrates the magnitude of the gap that needs to be closed and forms the foundation for the transition plan.

The following are some of the dimensions to examine to assess the magnitude of the gap:

Skills/capability—current and future	Roles and responsibilities/organization
Information technology	Decision processes
Reward systems	Culture
Measurement system	Speed at which the change must occur
Infrastructure	

The purpose of analyzing the gap is to identify the capabilities, technologies, information, measurement systems, and organizational dynamics that separate breakthrough performance levels from today's reality. Is incremental change required—or is a quantum leap necessary? Which elements of the gap provide the greatest challenge? Where is the organization closest to the desired performance levels? Which changes are within your grasp from an operational perspective, but daunting from a cultural or political perspective? Analysis allows an organization to establish targets and objectives, determine the specific changes necessary, and begin thinking about timing and sequencing.

Some changes require only a feasibility study of the capabilities and resources required and a transition plan to set up the new process (e.g., when Barnes & Noble, the bookstore giant, created its Web store to compete with Amazon.com).

If it becomes apparent that the makeover or new venture will cause disruption and pain, commitment to the magnitude and speed of the change can become seriously challenged. In 1996, when Schwab, the discount broker, launched its online unit, e-Schwab, the company set up separate staff facilities. But more importantly, they allowed the new unit to cannibalize their core business. Such choices are not without risk, and the counteraction from the core business can be daunting to start-ups. In this case, the gamble worked and Schwab eventually aligned the process of the units rather than keep them separate. During this transition stage, an organization's ambition and fortitude are tested. The enormity of the required change can cause an organization to lose its willpower and make compromises that shortchange its future potential. When this happens, visions become platitudes. To be successful, leaders of major change efforts should anticipate and manage the need for periodic recommitment.

Planning the Transition to the Future

Transition planning does not occur as an isolated "fifth step." Throughout the prior phases, wholehearted commitment to change can be fostered through a push/pull tension: (1) by creating a vision of the future worth achieving (the pull), and (2) by demonstrating that current ways of doing business produce competitive disadvantages (the push).

Transition plans anticipate and address what hurdles and enablers will be crucial to managing change. A good transition plan takes into account that a change in one part of the "system" will likely alter other parts of the system. The design or redesign of any process requires appreciating the impact of the redesign on other processes. For example, the transportation group often wants to wait till the truck is full before shipping any product to its destination because they are measured on cost per mile transported. Conversely, customer service is judged by the ability to make the order-to-delivery cycle time as short as possible, and would like the truck to leave as soon as the product is available, whether the truck is full or not.

Those who craft the transition plan should have a realistic understanding of how successful change has been implemented in the organization in the past and whether that approach will be sufficient this time. Speed to market—not just of product or service, but of supporting processes as well—will become increasingly important. It is also helpful to do postmortems on some failed change efforts to understand the factors that contributed to them. Postmortems often indicate that human, cultural, and managerial factors were to blame.

Implementation

In some change efforts, this is the first phase where those closest to the work are required to alter their behaviors, not just their attitudes or ideas. It is realistic to anticipate new waves of resistance, although if the prior phases have been well handled, it should not be a "show stopper." The most effective change management approaches are inclusive rather than exclusive, multiperspective, iterative, and validated by both the "doers" of the work and the "customers" of the output. The degree of resistance to change is often in direct proportion to:

- The degree of involvement of people impacted by the change (i.e., the degree of mobilization and buy-in you have generated throughout the prior phases).
- The magnitude of the change required.

TABLE 15.2   Transition Management Principles

- Incremental adaptations can occur without senior level focus; major change cannot. Do not delegate accountability for major changes.
- Let your customer, especially your future customer(s), be the drivers of change.
- Help people understand the emerging model of business, i.e., network of business processes and capabilities organized to provide superior value to customer(s).
- Simulate multiple frame-breaking events; cultivate the outsider's objectivity.
- Create a shift in strategic focus and an ambition that requires stretch to achieve. Strive for breakthrough performance levels, but build in interim successes.
- Articulate and be consistent with a change model that people can understand and that helps them anticipate the process. Be systematic in understanding whether barriers are rational, political, or emotional.
- Make progress visible and publicly reward changed behavior and improved results. Create multiple feedback processes; orchestrate an early alert system.
- Plan investments in education, training, and alterations in people support processes (e.g., career pathing, compensation).

If possible, the implementation should begin with a pilot project, although this may require more time than some organizations dare take. Ideally, the selection of the optimum pilot area should be based on the probability of a visible and transferable success. The deck can be stacked in favor of a successful pilot by peopling it with a critical mass of committed leaders and influencers, by providing the necessary training and coaching for people to feel emerging competence as early as possible, by creating communication and feedback loops that identify issues and reinforce progress, and by rewarding new behaviors as quickly as possible. Successful transition management should adopt the principles outlined in Table 15.2.

LEADERSHIP AND THE LINK TO STRATEGY

> Beginnings are always messy.
>
> —*John Galsworthy*

Some senior managers believe that setting direction sufficiently fulfills their role as leaders. But if processes are at the heart of strategy and processes are *what you do* as a company, then leaders must be doers too. Business success can't be just based on good choices (targeting the right markets, products, services, etc.); it also depends on management's exceptional skill at defining processes.

Senior management must be the catalyst for broad-based change efforts for these reasons:

- They have the big picture view and are accountable for the strategic direction of the firm.

- They have access to the resources to make it happen.
- Their stewardship can be focused on the optimization of the whole over the part.
- Without their commitment and participation, the change may be stonewalled or eviscerated.

Leadership is also critical because organizations seldom succeed at getting out ahead of their leadership for extended periods of time. More typically, organizations wait to see if something is "real" by observing the behavior, not just the rhetoric, of their leadership. Leadership's role relative to change involves serving as *catalyst* to set things in motion, as *champion* by continuously communicating the message and acting in concert with the chosen direction, as *coach* in shaping new behaviors. Management in every layer of the organization must take on the role of catalyst, champion, and coach, for broad-based change to succeed.

Building advantage through linking core business processes to strategy is a big job—one that affects virtually every aspect of an organization. The actual dimensions of the initiative are bounded only by the needs of future customers and their concepts of value. But the success of the effort will be driven by the organization's ability to lead change.

SUMMARY

When reconfiguring its business processes, a firm should focus its strategy implementation efforts on improving the execution of tasks central to its success—developing new products, managing the supply chain, and managing customer relationships. But keep in mind that process improvement alone is not enough to provide competitive advantage. To meet the challenge inherent in identifying, selecting, and designing new processes that will foster significant advantages, a firm must first envision its future competitive context. By using scenarios and other future-oriented methodologies to discern future marketplace conditions, managers can then identify which processes would be critical to establishing and sustaining value propositions that will attract, win, and retain customers. After they assess what processes the firm will need in the future compared to the processes used today, managers can develop an action plan for making the transition. Underlying all strategy implementation in the future will be this ongoing management initiative to define, build, activate, and adapt the processes that will enable a firm to serve its future customers better than its competition.

NOTES

1.   Peter Keen, *The Process Edge; Creating the Value Where It Counts* (Boston: Harvard Business School Press, 1997).

2. Microsoft had to wait a decade to "prove" its concept and become profitable (it earned $24 million in the year before its IPO) before it could move to an IPO. The current generation of Internet and biotech start-ups are being funded by the capital generated by the IPO, *Fortune* (February 15, 1999).

3. The largest "real space" bookstores, such as Barnes & Noble, carry 175,000 items, whereas Amazon.com, an "e-space" bookstore handles 3.1 million books, 24 hours a day, 7 days a week. Sales per employee are $375K versus $100K for Barnes & Noble. While the traditional store receives and pays for inventory, then gets cash as the customer buys, Amazon gets the cash up front then "finds" the books, shifting the inventory burden to the publisher or distributor. This frees capital to invest in technology and to build brand and market share. Barnes & Noble launched its Web site in 1998, but for them the Web is another channel, whereas Amazon.com is using a different model. While Amazon.com has early mover advantage, the race is still on. The challenge for Barnes & Noble, who has "real space" bookstores, is to build a link between online and local services, not necessarily to win at the low-price game.

4. Joan Magretta, "Fast, Global, and Entrepreneurial: Supply Chain Management, Hong Kong Style," *Harvard Business Review* (September/October 1998): 102–114.

5. *Business Week* (August 31, 1998).

6. See Keen, *The Process Edge*, p. 163.

7. Attributed to Sir Hugh Walpole in *Fortune* (May 3, 1993).

8. See Keen, *The Process Edge*.

9. Charles Schwab and Co. has successfully made the shift from pioneer discount brokerage firm to market leader in online brokerage, while not dropping its price to match the newcomers who are trying to build market share (e.g., E-Trade, Ameritrade). Besides delivering the normal features of a web based personal trading process, they have combined more than 1,000 mutual funds into "One Source" where ease of use and access make them the broker of choice. Currently 1 in 20 stock trades in America pass through the Schwab system.

10. Tom Lloyd in "SAPping the Strength of the Species" points out that the general convergence of ways of doing business caused by the spread of such large systems, "and by the 'best practices' embedded in them, (may not turn out) to be a 'good thing' for the corporate species as a whole. The ERP systems allow and in many ways, oblige companies to assume a 'concentric' shape, in which a nested set of operating and coordinating elements, encircle a central core that directs the whole company." This apparent strength may turn out to be a weakness because such organizations may become vulnerable to threats from "eccentric enterprises that have no central core and are therefore more adaptable." *Transformation* magazine (June 17, 1999), p. 46.

11. Stan Davis and William Davidson, *2020 Vision* (New York: Simon and Schuster, 1991): 113.

12. The process focus represented in this article will enhance company performance when it is embedded as a primary approach to business. See, for example, Frank Ostroff, *The Horizontal Organization: What the Organization of the Future Looks Like and How It Delivers Value* (New York: Oxford University Press, 1999).

13. See Keen, *The Process Edge*, for a description of an EVA approach to valuing processes: "Evaluating process improvements in terms of their potential to create value is the only way to judge if investing in them makes economic sense" (p. 161).

STRATEGIC CHANGE: MANAGING STRATEGY MAKING THROUGH PLANNING AND ADMINISTRATIVE SYSTEMS

16

John H. Grant
DocPlanet.com, Inc.

Nandini Rajagopalan
Marshall School of Business
University of Southern California

Systematic procedures for managing strategy making can reduce the chances of serious omissions or misguided actions involving the many important activities that provide the critical information and understanding that should underlie strategic action. Planning and administrative systems (PAS) offer mechanisms for coordinating strategy development and execution on either a regular or ad hoc basis to achieve intended organizational objectives.

The role and importance of a PAS often only become evident in an organization when there is a serious communications breakdown between members of the management team. This happened in a business unit of a large financial services firm, which found itself considering an inappropriate strategy alternative that had consumed many person hours of staff time for research and development.

The root cause of this PAS problem was that unit's strategic planning system did not afford senior managers an opportunity to review a list of potential strategy initiatives before they were pruned down to the final set of alternatives. As a result, all the alternatives were fully developed by the planning department, with the help of many middle-level executives, in preparation for a final decision by the senior management team. Because there was no review process, the planning department and the middle managers spent a great deal of time and effort on one alternative that had already been rejected by the business unit's president earlier in the year. At that time, the president had judged it too risky and not consistent with the business unit's vision and mission. But the business unit's issues management system and its information system failed to capture the choices made by the president and his senior management team and so they weren't communicated to the strategic planning department and other middle-level managers. After several months, when the senior management team met to make a final decision on their options, they found to their consternation that the rejected strategy was back on the table again! Well-designed planning and administrative systems would have prevented this embarrassing waste of management resources.

The goals for this chapter are:

- Introduce the purposes, characteristics, and scope of PAS, to familiarize readers with such systems and their potential contributions to improved organizational performance.
- Illustrate the applications, design trade-offs, and effects of PAS in selected organizational settings.
- Outline procedures for designing or evaluating such systems in an organizational context.

This chapter can be studied and used as a separate document, but important materials in other chapters relate to the content given here. Planning and control subsystems relate to both the industry analysis in Chapter 8 and the macro-environmental analysis in Chapter 9. The organizational analyses in Chapters 10 and 11 are important components of each PAS cycle described here. The generation of strategic alternatives, detailed in Chapter 12, comprises important input to the PAS processes. The design of PAS is expected to be valuable to the implementation and reconfiguration processes described in Chapter 15, and to be an important component of the transformation and reconfiguration options presented in Chapter 17.

PLANNING AND ADMINISTRATIVE SYSTEMS: SOME BASIC IDEAS

The planning and administrative systems (PAS) described in this chapter are more than just sets of formal documents, rigid meeting schedules, and computer support. Our working concept of a PAS is much broader. It includes the diverse conditions, activities, and facilities that can be managed to produce desired future behavior and organizational performance. Data availability, senior management leadership, the perceived value of risk taking, employee educational levels, and many other elements contribute to and interact to compose the total PAS.

The design goal is not to make planning and administrative systems more comprehensive and detailed, but rather to make them more effective and efficient in economic, organizational, and human terms. In practice, it is possible to paralyze and eventually bankrupt organizations with overly detailed and excessively formalized PAS. Managers must strive to make the systems agile, flexible, and resilient enough to meet changing organizational needs.

Planning and administrative systems contribute substantially to the quality, timeliness, and structure of information that general managers have readily available for important decisions. Without such systems, executives may fail to recognize shifting consumer tastes, changing output quality, rising investor expectations, or other trends in critical success factors (CSF) for the organization. Or, they may learn the proper lessons but not in time to be first to market or to take corrective strategic action. In many Internet markets, where quality and timeliness of information are increasingly important to profitability or other performance measures,[1] the proper design of the PAS can be crucial to both the recognition of opportunities and the capacity to act effectively.

One purpose of this chapter is to provide guidelines for the design and uses of planning and administrative systems as well as their adaptation over time to the changing requirements of particular organizations and their leaders. Design trade-offs are difficult because they involve the balancing of components along at least four crucial dimensions:

1. Technological feasibility.
2. Behavioral effects.
3. Scheduling sequence.
4. Economic costs and benefits.

Technology brings both speed and efficiency to many planning and administrative systems components, but there remain limits to the analytical technologies of forecasting, data gathering, and the monitoring abilities of computer-based scanners. Technologies can aid managerial judgment, but they cannot substitute for it.

The behavioral effects of different PAS configurations are often difficult to predict. Managers at the same organizational level may react very differently to the same incentive system. Decision makers provided with the same data from a strategic issue analysis may draw distinctly different action implications.

Given the interdependence of PAS components, the scheduling sequence demands attention. For example, if new computer systems are installed before operators are trained, old subsystems may be discontinued before new ones have been tested, so valuable data may be lost rather than being made more accessible.

Managers with responsibility for economic evaluations of a PAS must include balancing employees' needs for stability in their work environments against the task needs for frequent changes. Constant minor adjustments can be costly to communicate and confusing to those affected. On the other hand, lack of periodic refinement allows operations to become unresponsive or insensitive to new management perspectives, particularly in dynamic marketplaces.

Linkage to Specific Organizational Contexts

Planning and administrative systems exist in every organization, whether by deliberate design or by a process of evolution—document flows, human interaction over time, and customer and supplier transactions require them. Our discussion focuses on ways to improve PAS. To provide varied organizational contexts for applying these concepts, Box 16.1 presents data on two major organizations with various PAS needs: General Electric Company (GE) and Ciba-Geigy, before it was merged with Sandoz to become the current Novartis. GE is a very large, highly visible, U.S. firm with global operations and a reputation for giving active attention to seeking improvements in its management systems.[2] Ciba-Geigy is a major Swiss firm that sells the vast majority of its numerous chemical-based products outside its relatively conservative and somewhat secretive home county. Ciba-Geigy recently merged with Sandoz, another Swiss-based pharmaceutical firm with international operations.

Individuals and Organizational Performance

Before discussing the ways to coordinate human actions for organizational purposes through planning and administrative systems, we should acknowledge the important insights being offered in related literature about the valuable contributions that come from "empowered individuals," "teams," and "learning organizations."[3] Nothing we have to say about "systems" should be construed to imply that organizational participants must be "harnessed and controlled" to be productive organizational contributors. On the other hand, books have been written about the difficulties that arose when the PAS did not help an automotive manufacturer isolate and highlight production cost of quality problems, nor help mainframe computer manufacturers understand the consequences of smaller, networked computers for many of their customers' uses.

The extent of personal knowledge and commitment that individuals can add to the work of an organization represents a vital component of the overall PAS. To the extent that a firm develops the capacity to combine and share the insights of many creative people through systems for organizational learning, that firm is well on its way toward the much-sought objective of continuous quality improvement (CQI). The balance between internal or intrinsic components and the external or extrinsic ones used by a company or any other type of organization depends on the types of people attracted to it. This in turn determines whether the capabilities of a firm are to be stored and transferred through individual development and training or through more mechanical means like reports, computer programs, and instruction manuals. The following section describes some of the system components that can constitute PAS for managers.

Box 16.1

General Electric (GE) and Ciba-Geigy (C-G)

General Electric (GE) is a diversified manufacturing and service firm with more than $60 billion in sales from such sectors as power systems, financial services, aircraft engines, and industrial systems. In more than a decade of CEO Jack Welch's leadership, the company has acquired, divested, and restructured billions of dollars in assets and tens of thousands of jobs.°

The design of planning and administration systems (PAS) that provide motivation and delegation without significant loss of control in resource allocation and risk taking is a continuing challenge. Extremely effective PAS design is crucial in a publicly traded firm operating within an aggressive capital market like that of the United States. Many firms that once operated in GE's markets became the subjects of hostile takeovers and breakups when the corporate headquarters were viewed as detracting from, rather than adding to overall corporate value.

The scope of products and services offered by GE has been changing in recent years, but the characteristics of the PAS have perhaps been altered even more. Extensive documentation of the plans of strategic business units (SBUs) has been greatly reduced, the responsibilities of general managers have been increased, the decision-making cycles have been shortened, and the rewards or incentives for innovation have increased.

The changes in the characteristics of GE's PAS have been influenced by:

- Customer reactions to the technological changes surrounding many of GE's SBUs.
- Heightened competitive pressure—often from international sources.
- Demand from capital markets.
- Expectations of employees.

The driving objective has been to strengthen selected market positions to attract the capital, customers, and employees necessary to perform effectively over extended periods of time. There is every indication that, as competitive arenas evolve, top management will continue to rearrange the elements of GE's PAS so the company can either perform well or divest itself of those operating units that cannot.

Ciba-Geigy (C-G), a pharmaceutical company based in Basel, Switzerland, is a publicly held firm (which recently merged with Sandoz to form Novartis) that produces and sells hundreds of products of varying complexity in dozens of countries around the world.† Because of the difficulty of predicting changes in the technical and political environments for all its ethical drugs, chemicals, and agricultural products, C-G needs to retain timely centralized awareness about certain aspects of the business. At the same time, the corporation must delegate a substantial degree of local autonomy to managers operating in many different cultures.

(Continued)

Box 16.1   *(Continued)*

Among the challenges in PAS design at the firm are those associated with technical and regulatory risk sharing, measurement across fluctuating currencies, and communication through many different languages and cultures.

The stimulus for a recent major change in the PAS at C-G was an environmental disaster at a competitor's plant in Europe during the autumn of 1986. When large quantities of toxic compounds spilled from a chemical plant into the Rhine River during a fire, there was public resentment toward the entire chemical industry. This inspired the management of C-G to make fundamental reassessment of the assumptions underlying its operations. The detailed control system of the past was replaced by an information system that provided more division-level flexibility. New procedures shortened the decision cycles, and central service units (CSUs) had to become fully competitive against outside suppliers. To provide greater opportunities for younger employees, a policy of mandatory retirement for all employees at age 60 was implemented. To adapt to the changes in the European Community (EC), C-G restructured its operations around specific geographic regions where it expected competitive characteristics to be similar.

---

* Based on materials from "General Electric (1984)" #9-385-315 and "GE—Preparing for the 1990's" 1990, #9-390-091 (Boston: HBS Pub.); M. Dickson, "All for One & One for All," *Financial Times*, September 3, 1992; N. Tichy and R. Charan, "Speed, Simplicity and Self-Confidence," *Harvard Business Review*, September–October 1989, 112–121. "GE Capital: Jack Welch's Secret Weapon," *Fortune*, November 10, 1997, 116–120.
† Based on material from "Ciba-Geigy (A)," #184-185 (HBS Pub. Div.); C. Kennedy, "Changing the Company Culture at Ciba-Geigy, Long Range Planning" (1993) 26:18–27.

SYSTEMS FOR INTEGRATING STRATEGIC PROCESSES

PAS are organizational and functional subsystems that directly or indirectly contribute to the development, implementation, and evaluation of strategic decisions as well as the overall strategy of the firm. Strategic decisions are those that affect the overall performance of the firm and have significant resource implications. The overall strategy of the firm is reflected in its choice of businesses to be in (corporate strategy), its competitive positioning in the product markets it serves (business-level strategy), and the pattern of resource allocation across the key functional areas that support its competitive positioning (functional-level strategy). Accordingly, PAS can be broadly divided into two types:

1. Organization-level PAS that cut across functional areas, strategic business units, and other organizational subunits. Organization-level PAS include

environmental scanning, strategic issues analysis, capital resource assessment, capital budgeting, information, and measurement, evaluation, and reward subsystems.

2. Functional PAS that are more restricted to specific organizational functions and/or subunits. Functional subsystems include operations, technology development, human resource development, and demand management subsystems.

An overview of PAS components can be seen in Figure 16.1. For a description of the components in Figure 16.1, see Box 16.2.

To implement the overall PAS framework within a given organization, it is necessary to assign activities to specific individuals or groups and to allocate their performance over time. The A-I-T-L (activity-involvement-timing-linkages) chart in Figure 16.2 is a useful way of presenting such relationships.[4]

FIGURE 16.1 Planning and administrative system: Overview.

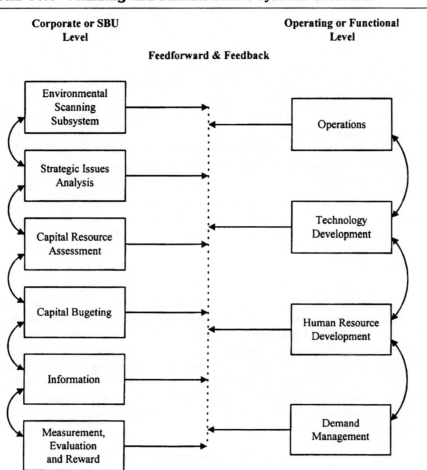

Box 16.2

PAS Component Descriptions (see Figure 16.1)

I. Organization-Level PAS

Environmental Scanning Subsystem The process of identifying key trends and events in the firm's general as well as industry environments that have implications for the firm's short-term and/or long-term performance. The scanning subsystem provides external information for a more focused identification of opportunities and threats to future performance. This information also constitutes relevant inputs into the strategic issues analysis subsystem.

Strategic Issues Analysis Subsystem The processes and activities by which internal and external data and stimuli are translated into focused issues and these issues are further analyzed for their impact on the firm's performance. Strategic issues analysis often forms the basis for a more focused identification of strategic alternatives and can act as a catalyst for incremental or radical strategic change.

Corporate Resource Assessment Subsystem The process of comparing a firm's physical, human, financial, and technological resources with those of competitors and with the best known to exist. The process of locating and measuring against the best available for application is often referred to as benchmarking. The resource assessment subsystem provides information on internal strengths and weaknesses and constitutes the basis for identifying internally oriented strategic issues.

Capital Budgeting Subsystem A subsystem of activities that identify and evaluate financial investment opportunities, whether directed toward plant expansion and equipment, major marketing programs, acquisition opportunities, or other such commitments where the returns are expected to extend a few years into the future.

Information Subsystem The systems, processes, and specific devices for gathering, sorting, storing, and transmitting data between external parties and various parts of the company that are essential for the effective functioning of the PAS. While some of the devices consist of computers and telecommunication devices, others are written reports, and even informal verbal exchanges.

Measurement, Evaluation, and Reward Subsystems° The processes and activities involved in the assessment of managerial performance. Components of this subsystem include the measurement time horizon (frequency of measurement and interval between successive measurements), evaluation criteria (quantitative/qualitative, accounting/market-based, strategic/operational), and incentive mechanisms (cash/stock bonuses, short-term/long-term incentives, proportion contingent pay). Evaluation criteria can also be linked to the measures used by the organization to judge its performance from the perspectives of various stakeholders; often called the critical success factors (CSF) or key performance indicators.

Box 16.2 *(Continued)*

II. Functional PAS[†]

Operations Subsystem The processes and activities involved in ordering supplies, assembling materials, scheduling production, carrying out production, warehousing and inventory management, shipping and delivery of finished products and services, and collection of invoices from the daily operations of the organization.

Demand Management Subsystem All the activities and processes involved in understanding customers' needs and fulfilling these needs as efficiently and effectively as possible. It typically includes market research, promotion, advertising, sales, packaging, and bookings. It is obviously related to, but much larger than the traditional business function of marketing.

Technology Development Subsystem The research and development activities involved in the development of product and process innovations. It includes the quality of working relationships between R&D personnel and other departments, the timeliness of technology development activities in meeting critical deadlines, the quality of laboratories and other facilities, and qualifications and experience of laboratory technicians and scientists.[‡]

Human Resource Development Subsystem Should be given special attention because of the mobility of most personnel and the substantial knowledge and investment many of them represent. It includes systems and processes for enhancing the reputation of the firm as an employer; recruitment, training, and promotion systems; employee incentive programs; and career development and counseling programs, succession planning, and outplacement services.

° For an empirical examination of the performance implications of matching evaluation and reward systems to firm strategy, see N. Rajagopalan "Strategic Orientations, Incentive Plan Adoptions and Firm Performance: Evidence from Electric Utility Firms," *Strategic Management Journal*, November 1997, 761–785.

† See A. Miller and G.G. Dess, "Internal Analysis," in *Strategic Management*, 2nd ed., Chap. 3, for a detailed discussion of these and related processes.

‡ See M.E. Porter, *Competitive Advantage: Creating and Sustaining Superior Performance*, New York: Free Press, 1985, for an elaboration of the role of technology in competitive positioning and strategy implementation.

The interrelated subsystems are constructed of many components; a brief description of the A-I-T-L elements will aid the subsequent discussion.

Key PAS Definitions

Activities The various tasks and procedures performed during the analysis, coordination, and implementation of the PAS. They can be undertaken by various individuals or groups inside the organization or by consultants hired for specific purposes. Illustrative activities might include environmental scanning, budget simulation, reward distribution, decision making, or other managerial tasks.

FIGURE 16.2 A-I-T-L (activity-involvement-timing-linkages) chart.

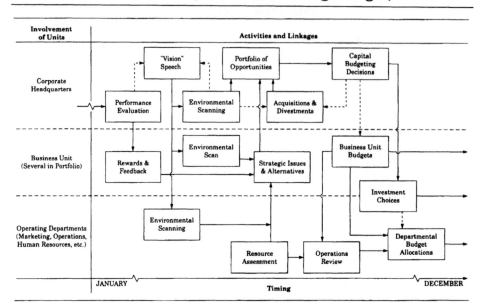

Source: Based on J. Dermer, *Management Planning and Control Systems* (Homewood, IL: Irwin, 1977).

Involvement The participation of various people and organizational units in the development of assumptions and issues, the execution of activities, and the assessment of results. Degrees of involvement will vary from continuous full-time commitment to ad hoc part-time responsibility for gathering data, organizing analyses, participating in decisions, or other activities.

Timing The calendar sequence for the performance of particular activities by those involved. Some activities should occur sequentially; others may be performed simultaneously during the PAS cycle. Although the timing of most PAS activities should be determined by the nature of the businesses involved, some activities are efficiently linked to external reporting requirements and others are dependent on the competitive actions of rival firms or important customers. A cycle is a sequence of various processes involving linked subsystems that address related activities over time. Although some subsystems are activated on a regular daily, monthly, or annual basis, others, like personnel selection, may be cycled only when there is a specific stimulus for action.

Linkage mechanisms Devices that tie together the activities and subsystems. They may be as structured and rapid as computer software that combines databases and analytical models, or as unstructured and time-consuming as a series of negotiation sessions aimed at reconciling investment requests with available financing. Other examples include individuals who convert reports into instructions for personnel, calendars that require the allocation of time to tasks, and speeches that seek to orient employees' energies to a common purpose.

Interdependencies

It is crucial to understand the interdependencies between the planning and administrative systems identified in Box 16.2 (these interdependencies are represented by the bidirectional arrows in Figure 16.1). The first type of interdependency exists between PAS that are classified within the same level (i.e., organizational or functional). To illustrate, the strategic issues subsystem utilizes the information and analyses generated by the environmental scanning subsystems and corporate resource assessment subsystems, an example of the interdependencies between various organization-level PAS. Similarly, the operations subsystem depends on the demand management subsystem for production estimates and order requirements just as the demand management subsystem uses the capacity and inventory data from the operations subsystem in planning sales and promotion campaigns.

The second type of interdependency links organizational PAS to functional PAS and vice versa. To illustrate, a comprehensive assessment of corporate strengths and weaknesses (an output of the resource assessment subsystem) cannot be conducted without relevant information from each of the functional PAS. Similarly, organization-level measurement, evaluation, and reward subsystems need to be reflected in appropriate procedures within the human resource development subsystem.

Illustrating a PAS

Various components of a PAS, as they could be used in a company during a given period of time, can be illustrated in multidivisional firms such as GE or C-G. These firms might begin an annual PAS cycle early in their fiscal year with a statement by the CEO or other officer at the corporate headquarters (CHQ) level. The statement might emphasize or revise the vision or mission of the entire company, based at least in part on the performance evaluation of the preceding year or another recent period. Employees at the corporate level might then gather environmental and competitive trend data for various sectors from capital markets, government agencies, and other sources, and division-level employees might scan and interpret technological developments, customers' preferences among competitors' products and services, and other factors of specific interest to a given division.

At the same time the environmental scanning is occurring, other analysts might summarize the relative quality of the tangible and intangible resources of the firm. By combing the resource analysis with the environmental scan, managers can describe the strategic issues and options as the key future choices facing the company. (The strategic issues analysis subsystem deserves special attention and is covered in a subsequent section.)

In a diversified firm, managers must combine the sets of strategic options from the various business units to provide the portfolio of investment and divestiture opportunities available at the corporate level. It is at this point that managers can make important changes in a company's strategy and then communicate their decisions clearly to competitors, customers, employees, investors, and other stakeholders.

Capital budgeting subsystems are used to evaluate alternative investment patterns as a method of improving profitability and retaining financial flexibility. When managers pursue large projects, changes in the firm's capital structure may have to be synchronized with the overall cash flow requirements of the firm.

Simultaneous with capital budgeting decisions, managers develop and integrate the business unit and departmental operating budgets so that the firm may forecast the expected financial performance a year or more into the future.

Ongoing performance analyses from the departmental levels are periodically aggregated at the business unit level. Changes in marketing programs and production levels then can be accomplished on a timely basis.

Linkage Mechanisms and Performance Criteria

As noted, linkage mechanisms are those structured and unstructured devices that tie together the activities and subsystems. It is particularly important that they be related to measurement criteria and performance levels because of the wide differences in the goals and associated performance measures across functions and between levels within the organization.[5] For example, at the corporate level in a publicly traded company, the CEO and board of directors might aspire to a particular earnings level or stock price. On the other hand, a team in a production department might seek to make a product that meets certain quality and cost standards.

A framework for associating different linkage mechanisms and performance criteria to various stakeholders and organizational levels, from the individual employee through the corporate and nation-state levels, is shown in Figure 16.3. On the horizontal axis are criteria ranging from individual attributes to government regulations. For example, if a manager at GE or Ciba-Geigy is interested in improving the company's stock price, a logical question is: What actions will improve investors' perceptions of the future potential of our company? Two quite different actions might be implied in the framework: (1) seek to improve the return on assets (ROA) or the economic value added (EVA) of divisions within the company or (2) redeploy the portfolio toward industry sectors where the company might find opportunities for successful innovations.

In another example, managers might consider whether investment programs designed to enhance market share might improve the ROA and whether standard costs might be reduced without sacrificing quality. Those analyses would inevitably lead to the most micro level in Figure 16.3: The assessment of individual personnel to see whether they have the skills and technology needed to perform as effective competitors in the external marketplaces.

On the diagonal of performance criteria, upward from the corporate level are the critical success factors (CSFs) that society uses to evaluate individual

FIGURE 16.3   Linkage mechanisms and performance criteria.

| | Internal Technical Emphases ———→ Capital Markets ◄——— External & Societal Criteria | | | | |
| | **Performance Criteria** | | | | |
Levels	Individual Atttributes	Product Markets & Costs	Financial Markets	Industry Structure	Government Regulations
Nation-State					Taxes Emission Control Employee Safety
Industry				Concentration Ratios Innovation	
Corporate			Stock Prices		
SBU or Division			ROA or EVA		
Product Line		Market Share			
Department		Standard Costs			
Individual	Skills Values				

firms. Pharmaceutical firms like Ciba-Geigy, for example, may be asked whether their branded (ethical) drug products are as innovative and cost-effective as alternative treatments for various types of patients' diagnoses.

At the level of a nation's entire economy, the criteria become tax rates, monopolistic practices, consumer fairness, polluting emissions levels, employee safety, and other pervasive concerns of citizens. The organization must ask whether it is meeting the expectations and demands of the myriad stakeholders who constitute the macroenvironment.

The planning and administrative systems within and surrounding a firm will determine how directly these various measures are linked. However, the trade-offs for both managers and government officials are between the rigidities resulting from tight linkages versus the apparent injustices arising from overly loose connections. In general, the PAS should seek tighter linkages over internal relationships because most are more directly controllable. On the other hand, most government policies and regulations are adjusted slowly in democratic societies, so managers will have both opportunities and constraints that may be out of phase in the short term with the technical possibilities in their markets.

PAS designers should be careful to incorporate valid measures of performance, rather than simply convenient ones. Ciba-Giegy made substantial changes in its financial measurement system to avoid using historical book values for assets; it estimated current replacement or market values to calculate performance ratios. Newer EVA and value-based planning procedures seek to incorporate the real economic costs of assets into their calculations rather than permitting valuable but depreciated assets to imply higher-than-actual economic ROAs.[6]

As managers develop ideas for taking action based on the performance criteria that have been analyzed, a next logical step is establishing priorities and assigning responsibilities. If this step is not handled properly, some future options may be precluded or the time of expensive, senior people may be wasted. Hence, a mechanism for deciding which activities are most critical or important to the future well-being of the organization and which must be accomplished first can be a valuable decision aid. If more detailed analyses are warranted at a subsequent stage, the PERT (Program Evaluation and Review Technique) charts or CPM (Critical Path Method) diagrams can be developed and urgency dimensions sorted properly.

As analysts and managers examine external trends and the evolving resource base inside the firm, there is a need to interrelate critical factors in meaningful ways. One way to organize data effectively is to identify key internal developments and a similar list of external trends and arrange them in matrix form, as shown in Figure 16.4. The third axis should be a measure of time: Appropriate technical, legal, and other expert personnel can be asked to

FIGURE 16.4 Strategic issues subsystem.

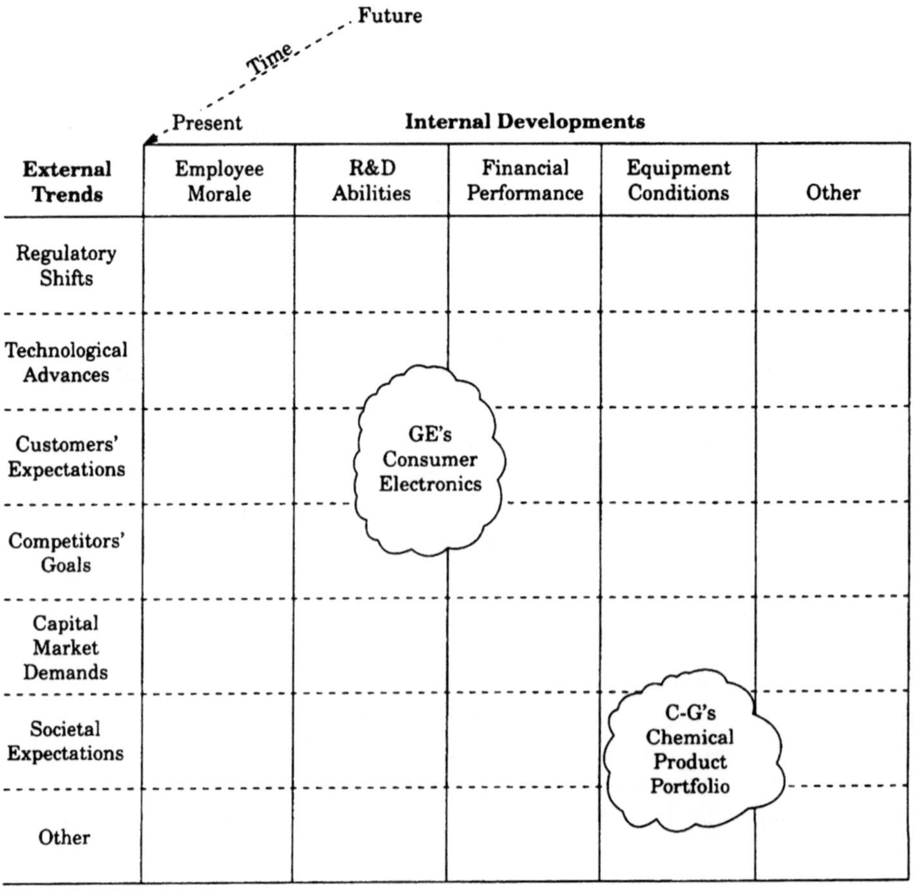

monitor trends and interrelationships over periods of years or months, depending on the rates of change.

For example, when toxic waste spilled into the Rhine River from a competitor's plant fire, it triggered a strategic issues analysis at Ciba-Giegy. Managers recognized that their macroenvironment had changed because of the public's new environmental sensitivity. A macroenvironmental analysis also had a profound impact when GE was assessing the future role of consumer electronics following its acquisition of RCA. Management realized that prospective customers' expectations for design, performance, and price made it seem unlikely that GE's R&D, manufacturing, and distribution systems could compete effectively over the long term. As a result, management decided to divest the consumer electronics operating unit. In the contemporary Internet economy, the announcement of a major new strategic alliance or new high-speed information search engine can create a major strategic issue demanding quick responses from many firms.

Strategic issues subsystems may function on a routine annual cycle as long as the organization's industries and the broader macroenvironment are relatively stable. However, as discussed in Chapters 8 through 11, change is the dominant feature of most organizations' environments.[7] Moreover, analysis should not focus on isolated events or environmental segments: The connections and linkages among the segments of the environment give rise to opportunities and problems. For example, a change in the political environment, such as the election of new national leadership or a change in regulations, may alter customers' expectations. Pharmaceutical operations like those at Ciba-Giegy should closely scan for indicators of potential change and should monitor emerging attitudes in the healthcare industries of major industrialized countries, as government officials and representatives of many healthcare industry stakeholders[8] debate alternative cost, quality of care, and availability considerations. Strategic issues subsystems must have the flexibility to respond to both anticipated and unanticipated events that might have strategic importance.[9]

Crisis management systems exist in many organizations to deal with strategic issues that executives feel are so critical and urgent that most normal operating procedures cannot cope with them.[10] Under such circumstances, the PAS design typically allows for the delegation of much greater authority to individuals with particular skills. For example, a faulty GE jet engine that caused a fatal crash would be expected to trigger the crisis management system in GE's jet engine unit, and a major drug-tampering incident or toxic waste spill at Ciba-Giegy would initiate the same reaction.

The capacity of the organization to identify strategic issues on a timely basis and to act on them efficiently and effectively is highly dependent on the availability and use of reliable information systems.

Information Systems

An organization's information system includes a broad array of data types (financial, technological, marketplace, personnel, etc.) gathered from many

FIGURE 16.5 Data varieties for PAS.

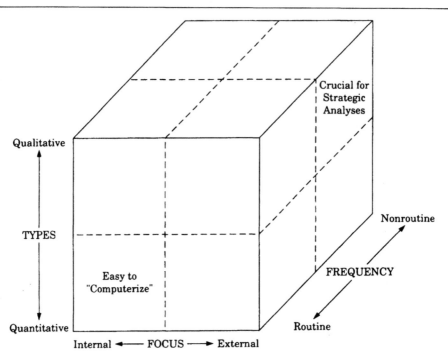

different sources and stored or retained by many different means. In many firms, much of the information needed for strategy development and execution resides in the memories of individual employees. Increasingly, a large quantity of data is stored in computer-based systems.

For purposes of PAS design and evaluation, it is often helpful to visualize a three-dimensional "data cube" (see Figure 16.5). The axes in Figure 16.5—focus (internal versus external), types (qualitative versus quantitative), and frequency (routine versus nonroutine) provide managers and others with a useful means to identify distinct data categories.[11]

An overriding benefit of the data cube shown in Figure 16.5 is that it helps to avoid data use that is driven primarily by availability—a situation found in many organizations today. For many managers and analysts, PAS often become dominated by data that are in the quantitative-internal-routine cell because such data are typically easy and inexpensive to process through computerization. However, the data in the qualitative-external-nonroutine cell are often most critical to strategic issues identification and thus to major shifts in resource allocations. The early indicators of political, regulatory, social, economic, and technological change—a statement by a government official, an announcement of breakthrough findings by scientists, or a major change in consumers' behavior—almost always fall into the qualitative-external-nonroutine cell.[12]

When refining an information system designed to support other PAS components, two other dimensions are often important:

1. Distribution (personal versus shared).
2. Availability (archival versus real-time or online).

Because information tends to convey power or strategic position and direction in many organizational situations, the need for secrecy or personal control over the distribution of certain types of data can be crucial. Hence, information subsystems designers need to determine the breadth of access to data at various points in time. The mode of availability is equally important because it will determine the speed, geographic distribution, and multiplicity of uses of particular data. For example, customer account data on a time-sharing computer system or Internet Web site can be used by marketing researchers, financial planners, and accounts receivable personnel for very different purposes and from dispersed locations simultaneously. On the other hand, an uncopied paper file describing an acquisition candidate is available to only one person in a single location at a particular time.

The importance-urgency activity framework shown in Figure 16.6 can be used to sort and integrate activities on a timely basis and with reference to the person or organizational unit responsible under radically different circumstances.[13] This framework should help PAS designers and managers think effectively about the ways their associates are asked to use their time and energy. For example, the CEO or managing director of a major firm or business unit must expect that a portion of his or her schedule will be disrupted by critical

FIGURE 16.6   Importance-urgency activity framework.

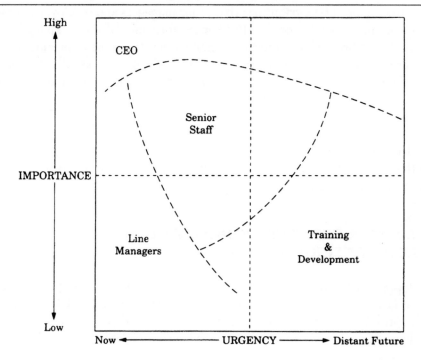

events that arise without forewarning—a hostile takeover threat, a major toxic waste spill, or a promising change in regulations that demands testimony at a congressional hearing. Other line managers should be assigned responsibility for urgent matters that have low importance individually but are collectively crucial to organizational performance.

Such a framework can help in the design of information systems that must be prompt, even though approximate; an example is Ciba-Giegy's hot line to corporate headquarters for technical or political crises. Alternately, product-testing procedures in laboratories at GE must provide precise and reliable data if new components are being considered for mass-produced home appliances or medical equipment.

Measurement, Evaluation, and Reward Systems

Measurement and evaluation processes are crucial because of their impacts on the rewards for information sharing, the motivation for risk taking, the resulting organizational learning, and other factors. Educating diverse employees as to why the performance criteria vary across job descriptions is important for maintaining morale and cooperation, particularly in loosely linked professional organizations like research laboratories, orchestras, hospitals, and similar institutions.

Incentives and penalties must be related to desired behavior, and this relationship must be clearly conveyed to all members of the organization. Thus, it is becoming increasingly common for high-performance executives to use stock options, quality awards, innovation bonuses, and other mechanisms to communicate the important contributions that other managers and employees in many arenas can make to enhance the strategic performance of the company.[14]

In diversified, related-product organizations, the transfer pricing process often creates particular evaluation problems.[15] Firms such as Ciba-Giegy and GE, which hope to benefit from the sharing of knowledge or other assets across subunit boundaries, frequently encounter difficulties distributing the related costs or investments in ways that are viewed as equitable. The specific techniques for balancing market prices and administered costs are too complex to address here, but it is crucial that managers with PAS responsibility recognize that if they do not give special attention to these matters, major dysfunctional consequences can result.

BUILDING A PAS: KEY CHOICES AND DESIGN CONTINGENCIES

Developing a PAS for a particular organization involves making decisions on several key design features in a manner that best aligns the PAS to critical organizational and environmental contingencies. Major variables include: the degree of complexity of individual subsystems, the connections between organizational and functional subsystems, the timing and frequency of activities and processes within each subsystem, the involvement of people and organizational subunits in the day-to-day implementation of the subsystem, the extent to which the subsystems are integrated through formal linkage mechanisms, and the degree to which the PAS allows for quick adaptations to changing contextual conditions (i.e., the extent of flexibility). In making these design choices, the organization needs to be cognizant of the following key contingencies.

Environmental Contingencies

Complexity of the Firm's Operating Environments

How diverse and sophisticated is your firm's product-markets, the geographic distribution of its sales, and the number and types of economic sectors in which its businesses participate? In general, the greater the environmental complexity of the firm's businesses, the more elaborate and complex the overall PAS may need to be.

Rate of Change in the Firm's External Environment

How rapidly do the different parts of your firm's environment (e.g., customer needs, technological discontinuities, and deregulatory trends) change and to what extent does the change in one element of the environment trigger changes in another? Rapidly changing environments necessitate greater frequency in PAS-related activities as well as greater overall flexibility to accommodate diverse and novel information and quick response capabilities. In the world of Internet-based electronic commerce, industry boundaries are drawn and redrawn not on an annual or even monthly basis but may be changed on a weekly or daily basis. The real-time emergence of new customer segments, the rapid entry of new competitors with innovative electronic distribution channels, and the relative cost efficiency of electronic information transfers, have all but rendered obsolete traditional PAS in organizations which have not updated them since an earlier era of lower-speed, higher-cost information technologies.

Degree of Uncertainty

To what extent are current events and trends reliable predictors of your firm's future operating conditions and the changing importance of different elements of the firm's environment as sources of uncertainty? High levels of environmental uncertainty necessitate quick-response PAS with greater levels of frequency in key activities and greater, more complex linkages between organizational and functional subsystems such that information and analyses originating in one subsystem are rapidly reflected in all other systems within the PAS.

Organizational Contingencies

Firm Size and Age

How big and how old is your firm? In general, the larger and the older the organization the more time-consuming and difficult it is to implement widespread changes in the PAS. In such cases, modifying existing PAS through key design changes, and then making the widespread communication of those changes a top priority, may be a better approach than designing a fundamentally new PAS. In contrast, the smaller and younger the firm, the greater its ability to redesign substantial parts of the PAS both at the organizational and the functional levels.

Extent and Type of Diversity in the Firm's Business Portfolio

Are your firm's businesses interrelated? Firms with multiple business units with low levels of interbusiness interdependencies may find it more efficient to operate multiple organization-level PAS with each business unit controlling its own PAS. In contrast, firms with low levels of business diversity and/or highly interdependent businesses may benefit from the design of multiple functional subsystems (corresponding to each individual business) but single, integrated organizational PAS.

Competitive Strategy of the Firm

To what extent does the firm emphasize cost efficiency or product/service differentiation as its main competitive weapons in distinguishing itself from industry rivals.[16] The key challenge for firms emphasizing cost-based competitive strategies is how to produce and distribute goods or services as efficiently as possible. The PAS for such a firm needs to reflect the stability and efficiency criteria central to a cost-based strategy; however, such a PAS may not be well suited to locating and responding to new product or market opportunities. In contrast, the PAS for a firm pursuing differentiation-based competitive strategies should be capable of locating and exploiting new product and market opportunities. Low levels of routinization, decentralized control, and horizontal rather than vertical information systems characterize the ideal PAS for such firms.

Stepping-Stones to Build a PAS

Building a PAS typically involves the following steps.

Develop the Internal Information Requirements

Managers must maintain efficient core operations and provide basic data for quick strategic initiatives. Core operations extend from the acquisition of materials, employees, and financing through the value-adding processes that involve manufacturing or operations, and on to the sales and collection stages. Managers should consider the following typical questions:

- What are the key operating processes in the organization?[17]
- Are the basic economics understood in relationship to competitors?
- For each key operating process, does the organization have thorough and timely data? For example, what is the quality of the organization's data pertaining to production planning, procurement efficiency, and inventory management?
- Can the economic costs associated with each operating process or activity be calculated to perform effective benchmarking?

Identify the Key External Information Requirements

This is often a difficult task, although some critical information needs—customer locations, purchasing patterns and preferences, components and raw materials suppliers' price changes, entry and exit of competitors, and competitors' behaviors—are available through straightforward research methods. Key questions include:

- What are the most relevant changes taking place in the organization's environment (its industry and macroenvironment)?
- Does the organization have procedures for tracking/monitoring and projecting competitors' product/service developments, customers' behaviors, and distribution channel changes?
- Can the organization effectively scan and monitor important technological developments, regulatory changes, and other macroenvironmental trends in ways that permit timely identification of strategic issues?

Identify Critical Success Factors

Critical success factors (CSF) are particularly required for measuring the short-term performance of the business unit. Typical factors include sales patterns, production volumes and quality, order backlogs, margins on sales, and employee turnover. After the essential data requirements are developed, the manager must select those people who will need to be involved either because they will possess key data or because their participation will aid implementation steps. Typical questions include:

- What are the critical success factors? Do they vary from one business unit to another? Do they vary from one geographic market to another?
- Given the objectives of the organization, which key stakeholders must be satisfied with what measures of performance? What profit measures do owners want to see and with what frequency and timeliness? Do contributors to a charity want evidence of services provided?

- How do CSF relate to one another over time? For example, does reduced employee turnover lead to better customer service and does this in turn lead to more profitable sales?
- What persons within the organization possess critical data with regard to each CSF? How can they be motivated to contribute to developing and sustaining each CSF?

Identify the Key Reports or Other Outputs

Planning and administrative systems are designed for the purpose of providing outputs that are useful to decision makers. Thus, it is imperative to determine what types of outputs are required by which decision makers, and what will be needed in terms of information characteristics, schedule of preparation, and sequence of distribution. Key questions include:

- Among the decision makers, who will require written reports? Who will need face-to-face verbal communication? And, who can be contacted via computer systems or video conferencing?
- What schedule of information distribution is needed to help each decision maker perform his or her task both effectively and efficiently?
- Ideally, what information should departments, levels of management, and key individuals receive?

Assess Technology Requirements

When it works, technology can play a definitive role in achieving desired PAS outputs. Thus, technology must be assessed in terms of its cost-effectiveness for the various subsystems, given the expected volume of data and the resources available for handling it. Key questions include:

- How computer-literate are various employees, suppliers, and customers? What is their current state of computer technology?
- Does the business require the speed and precision of integrated computer systems, or should most systems be less structured and seemingly more personal?

Develop Initial Systems

At some point, systems need to be operationalized or put in motion. Thus, the elements of the strategic issues, information, measurement and evaluation, and other systems must be put in place. In the early stages, these systems can be tentative: The intent is to learn from their execution. As learning progresses, each system can be refined and enhanced. Key questions include:

- What minimum systems will be required to satisfy various regulatory agencies, including tax authorities, employment monitors, pollution control agencies, and so on?

- What documentation will be helpful for new employees if the business expands and more complex PAS components or new operating locations need to be added?

SUMMARY

PAS design and characteristics provide crucial infrastructure for the effective strategic management of organizations. When they are well designed, they facilitate and improve decision making. However, when changes in the environment render them obsolete or creaky, they need to be overhauled expeditiously. Many PAS appropriately deserve attention, but neither managers nor analysts must be attracted to system fixes only because of their quick and easy implementation.

PAS are not ends in themselves. Their purpose is to facilitate attainment of the organization's goals; indeed, they can contribute to management's ongoing process of identifying what the goals of the organization should be. Strategic issues, planning and control, and information systems should generate the data necessary for analyses that will challenge whether the organization is pursuing only easy-to-reach goals or stretching its resources to seek higher-yield opportunities.

PAS must not be allowed to become obsolete. Change in the environment always tests the validity and relevance of existing systems. Changes in technologies that cause a shift in the types of products offered in the marketplace often provide a test case as to whether and when they were identified by the strategic issues subsystem. PAS must be continually assessed, refined where appropriate, and redesigned as needed.

NOTES

1. D. Yoffie and M. Cusumano, "Judo Strategy: The Competitive Dynamics of Internet Time," *Harvard Business Review* (January/February 1999): 70–81; and W. Gates, *Business @ the Speed of Thought* (New York: Warner Books, 1999).

2. General Electric was discussed at some length in Chapter 1.

3. For further details, see J.H. Grant and D. Gnyawali, "Strategic Process Improvement through Organizational Learning," *Strategy and Leadership* (May/June 1996), 24(3): 28–33; and J.C. Camillus, "Crafting the Competitive Corporation," in *Implementing Strategic Processes*, P. Lorange et al. (Eds.) (Oxford, England: Blackwell, 1993).

4. See J. Dermer, *Management Planning and Control Systems* (Homewood, IL: Irwin, 1977); and A.P. de Geus, "Planning as Learning," *Harvard Business Review* (March/April, 1988): 70–74.

5. Distinct levels of goals were noted and discussed in Chapter 1. Different types of goals in the case of business units were noted in Chapter 3: 34–38.

6. See a basic discussion of EVA (economic value added) in S. Tully, "The Real Key to Creating Wealth," *Fortune* (September 20, 1993): 38–40, 44–45, 48, 50; and

further analysis is available in K. Lehn and A. Makhija, "EVA and MVA as Performance Measures and Signals of Strategic Change," *Strategy and Leadership* (May/June 1996), 24(3): 34–38.

7. Worth repeating here is the argument in Chapter 1 that change is the central concept in strategic management. See N. Rajagopalan and G. Spreitzer, "Toward a Theory of Strategic Change: A Multi-Lens Perspective and Integrative Framework," *Academy of Management Review* (January 1997), 22(1): 48–79.

8. For a discussion of the role and importance of stakeholders in understanding environmental change, see Chapter 7.

9. For more discussion, see J.E. Dutton and S.E. Jackson, "Categorizing Strategic Links to Organizational Action," *Academy of Management Review* (January 1987): 76–90; and J.E. Dutton, L. Fahey, and V.K. Narayanan, "Toward Understanding Strategic Issue Diagnosis," *Strategic Management Journal* (1983), 4: 307–323; and J. Camillus and D. Datta, "Managing Strategic Issues in a Turbulent Environment," *Long Range Planning* (April 24, 1991): 67–74.

10. P. Shrivastava and I. Mitroff, "Strategic Management of Corporate Crises," *Columbia Journal of World Business* (spring 1987): 5–12; and G. Siomkos and P. Shrivastava, "Responding to Product Liability Crises," *Long Range Planning* (October 1993): 72–79.

11. Adapted from J.C. Camillus, *Strategic Planning and Management Control* (Lexington, MA: D.C. Heath, 1986); J.H. Grant, "Indicators of Strategic Performance," Working Paper, University of Pittsburgh, 1975; R. Saberwahl and J.H. Grant, "Integrating External and Internal Perspectives of Strategic Information Technology Decisions," in *Strategic Management and Information Technology*, J. Henderson and N. Venkatraman, (Eds.), vol. 1 (Greenwich, CT: JAI Press, 1994).

12. Readers are referred to Chapter 9 for a detailed discussion of the scanning and monitoring that are necessary to detect and develop the early indicators of macroenvironmental change. Processes for coping through the use of various types of strategic options are discussed by M. Amram and N. Kulatilaka in "Disciplined Decisions: Aligning Strategy with the Financial Markets," *Harvard Business Review* (January/February 1999): 95–104.

13. See J.H. Grant and W.R. King, *The Logic of Strategic Planning* (Boston: Little, Brown, 1982).

14. For an analysis of recent research findings, see N. Rajagopalan, "Strategic Orientations, Incentive Plan Adoptions and Firm Performance: Evidence from Electric Utility Firms" *Strategic Management Journal* (November 1997), 18: 761–785; and M. Bloom and G. Milkovich, "Relationships among Risk, Incentive Pay and Organizational Performance," *Academy of Management Journal* (June 1998), 41: 283–297.

15. R.G. Eccles, "Control with Fairness in Transfer Pricing," *Harvard Business Review* (November/December 1983): 149–161; and E.J. Kovac and H.P. Troy, "Getting Transfer Prices Right: What Bellcore Did," *Harvard Business Review* (September/October 1989): 148–154.

16. Michael E. Porter's *Competitive Strategy* (New York: Free Press, 1980) offers an extensive discussion of various competitive strategies and their appropriateness in different industry environments.

17. Operating processes are the primary focus of Chapter 15.

17

STRATEGIC CHANGE: DEVISING A CONTEXT-SENSITIVE APPROACH TO IMPLEMENTATION

Julia Balogun
Cranfield University

Veronica Hope-Hailey
Cranfield University

You don't implement a new strategy by flipping a switch. To put strategy into action, someone in the organization, or a team of the company's star performers, has to manage a variety of interrelated programs, such as developing a new product, redesigning distribution logistics, or executing a series of sales promotions. Each program in turn depends on the completion of a several projects. For each program and its set of projects to be a success, the team of managers must design, manage, and execute significant change *within the organization*. Thus, managers must understand how to manage organizational change if they are to successfully implement their preferred strategy. This chapter provides managers with a framework for strategy implementation that emphasizes their role as managers of change within and around their organization.

After extensive research conducted on how best to implement strategy, we have arrived at a fundamental premise that guides the proposed change framework: There is no "one best way to create and execute change." Leading academics and the most effective consultants and practitioners now recognize that for any strategy implementation to be successful, it must be context specific.[1] For example, how IBM or Toyota successfully implements strategy might cause organizational conflict among hierarchical levels or organizational subunits in your organization. The strategy implementation approach adopted by fast-moving small software firms might throw many large consumer goods firms into total organizational chaos. Don't expect to find any simple "change formula" to guide the design and management of your strategy implementation efforts.

The lack of a universal change formula, however, and the complexity of the changes inherent in strategy implementation often tempt managers to apply an "off the shelf" solution to their own organization. It is seductive to experiment with "cutting edge" models for managing strategy implementation developed by distinguished academic researchers or renowned management consultants. These models, as chronicled in the business press, seem to offer a way of improving our understanding of how change takes place in organizations. These "change prescriptions" appear to make highly complex decision making simpler and more manageable. Time and again, however, companies become disappointed when they try to apply to their own organization the approaches that have worked in another organizational context.

Wise managers should be extraordinarily cautious about extracting guidance for their own strategy implementation efforts from descriptions of how other organizations have successfully executed strategy. Instead of identifying "best practice" solutions, they need to start looking for "best questions." They should begin by examining their own organization's internal and external context. Only then are they in a position to determine the appropriate strategy implementation change process.

Informed contextual judgment becomes the competence required of those charged with strategy. Beware of experts steeped in the know-how of a particular change formula, or even several formulas. Just as important, leaders of strategy implementation also need to be aware of their own personal preferences and biases. We all develop beliefs and assumptions about the best way to do things as a result of our previous experiences and our preferred ways of working. Too often, these beliefs and assumptions may prejudice our decisions. They can cause any manager involved in any facet of strategy implementation to make inappropriate change choices, to filter out important questions, and to adopt inappropriate alternatives.

UNDERSTANDING THE STRATEGY IMPLEMENTATION CHANGE CONTEXT: THE CHANGE KALEIDOSCOPE

The change kaleidoscope (see Figure 17.1) enables change agents[2] to make sound judgments about their change context. The outer ring of the kaleidoscope addresses the wider *organizational strategic change context;* the middle ring addresses the more specific *contextual features* of the change situation; and the inner ring exhibits the menu of *design choices* open to change agents when attempting to implement change.

First, the strategy changes to be executed need to be seen in a broader strategic context. In the terminology of Chapter 1, this general context

FIGURE 17.1   The change kaleidoscope.

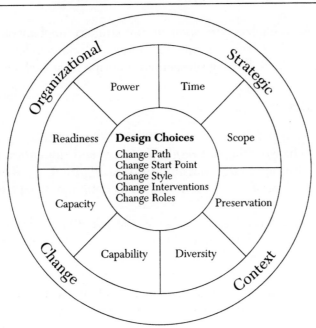

represents change in marketplace scope, competitive posture, and goals: the what, the how, and the why of strategy change.

Next, the contextual features of any change situation, the middle ring of the kaleidoscope, can be extracted partially from the broader strategic context. These features include multiple facets of the organization's culture (e.g., the values and norms guiding behaviors), how power is allocated and shared, the capabilities exhibited by the organization, and the readiness of the organization for change. Managers responsible for strategy implementation should consider each of these features as part of the process that readies them for the third stage, selecting a change approach from the menu of design choices.

Managers need to especially note that the kaleidoscope does not offer particular configurations that can be used to *prescribe* strategy implementation change formulas for particular contexts. Just as a real kaleidoscope continuously reconfigures the same pieces of colored glass to reproduce many different images, the eight contextual features remain the same but are constantly reconfigured to produce different pictures for each organizational change situation. Therefore the change designs will also vary. Furthermore, the organization's context evolves as change progresses, and therefore the choices made at one point in time will need to be reconsidered.

This chapter explains the design choices first, and then the contextual features. Finally three mini cases are used to illustrate how the contextual features of any change situation shape the feasibility of certain design choices.

MAKING DESIGN CHOICES

Five main design choices are open to any strategy implementation change agent (see Table 17.1). These design choices are not independent; each one affects the others. The following subsections describe what each choice entails.

Change Path

Organizations can, and often do, choose distinct types of strategy change. Two dimensions of change—the *end result of change* and the *nature of change*—generate four distinct change possibilities (see Figure 17.2). The *end result* represents the extent of change required on a continuum from transformation to realignment.

Transformation involves a change in the taken-for-granted assumptions and "the way of doing things around here." It is a fundamental change within an organization that cannot be handled within the existing organizational culture. Shell, the world's second biggest company, embarked on an intended transformational change in the late 1990s. The intent was to establish a fundamentally new culture throughout the organization. Key management leaders wanted to replace the traditional bureaucratic, slow, and consensual decision-making processes—the hallmarks of which were predictability and stability—with improved creativity, flexibility, and innovative thinking. A critical desired consequence was that commercial competence would be recognized as being more important than technical competence.

A *realignment* does not involve a fundamental reappraisal of the organization's central assumptions and beliefs. Yet, the strategy change could still be substantial; for example, it might involve the introduction of new products. The organizational change might also be substantial; an example would be a major restructuring.

TABLE 17.1   Definitions of Design Choices

Design	Definition
Change path	The type(s) of change to be undertaken in terms of the nature of the change and the desired end result.
Change start point	Where the change is initiated and developed, for example, top-down or bottom-up, but other choices include pilot sites and pockets of good practice.
Change style	The management style of the implementation, which may vary from highly collaborative to more directive.
Change interventions	The range of levers and mechanisms to be deployed, including technical, political, and cultural.
Change roles	Who is to take responsibility for leading and implementing the changes.

FIGURE 17.2   The change path.

End Result of Change

	Transformation	Realignment
Incremental	**Evolution** Transformational change implemented gradually through different stages and interrelated initiatives. Likely to be planned, proactive change undertaken in response to anticipation of the need for future change.	**Adaptation** Less fundamental change implemented slowly through staged initiatives.
Big Bang	**Revolution** Transformational change that occurs via simultaneous initiatives on many fronts, and often in a relatively short space of time. More likely be forced and reactive, due to the changing competitive conditions the organization is facing.	**Reconstruction** Change undertaken to realign the way the organization operates, but in a more dramatic manner than realignment. Often forced and reactive due to a changing competitive context.

Nature of Change

The *nature of change* encompasses the subject of how change will be implemented. Think of the nature of change as a continuum, with the big bang of all-at-once change at one end, and step-by-step incremental change at the other extreme.

Strategy change initiatives implemented by organizations are frequently heralded as *"revolutions"*—big-bang transformational change. Yet many of these initiatives are more often what we refer to as *reconstructions*. They may involve strategy renovation,[3] but they do not lead to a significant shift in an organization's culture. The organization may need to reengineer the way it operates to become more efficient, yet it does not need to dramatically alter its core values, beliefs, norms, and practices.

However, managers need to be aware that many strategy change initiatives intended to deliver *revolution* often only generate *reconstruction*. This occurs in large measure because the change agents are unable to achieve the desired cultural and attitudinal shifts. For this reason, the kaleidoscope refers to *paths of change* as opposed to *types of change*. The eventual aim of an organization may be to achieve transformation, but the organization may lack the resources, skills, or financing to deliver such extensive change. Alternatively, an organization may be in a crisis, its stock in a death spiral. In this case it needs a quick fix, even if it's painful, before any longer term change can be undertaken. In these circumstances an organization may start with a realignment, via either adaptation or reconstruction, and then move on to deliver more fundamental transformational change.

Consider the case of British Airways (BA). In the 1980s, BA effected a frequently cited strategy and cultural transformation by a change path of reconstruction followed by evolution. In 1981, BA was losing large amounts of money and could only continue operating because it was heavily subsidized by the British government. After Lord King was appointed chairman of the board, his declared goal was to effect a turnaround so that BA could quickly be privatized. In the first phase of the turnaround, from 1981 to 1982, King directed a significant and dramatic downsizing of the workforce. There was also a pay freeze, route closures, the halt of cargo-only services, and cuts to offices, administration, and staff clubs. Only then, in autumn 1982, did BA turn its attention to changing the airline's image and culture from a transportation business to an organization focused on customer service.[4]

General Electric (GE) provides a distinctly different example. GE's CEO, Jack Welch, began to initiate extensive strategic and organizational change in the early 1980s. Until 1988, the organizational changes largely fell into the category of reconstruction, such as altering the GE infrastructure, its working practices, and its political makeup. But before it could deliver a genuine organizational transformation, GE needed to change the culture as well as the infrastructure. In the late 1980s, the firm initiated a 10-year program called "Work-Out" to extend the early organizational change initiatives and also to establish a radically new culture that prized change above all else. Only by anticipating and leveraging change in the marketplace could GE catapult past its rivals. Only by designing and executing massive change in how it did things within its own organizational walls could the giant corporation achieve the operating efficiencies that top management was demanding.[5]

Insiders who participated in the turnarounds at BA and GE learned that genuine revolutions involving both strategic and organizational components are painful and difficult to implement. They involve changing the way subunits and individuals within an organization think and behave. Thus they take enormous amounts of time and investment. This is why transformation may be achieved more gradually and less painfully through an evolutionary approach. This process requires a longer-term program of reconstructions or realignments that build the infrastructure, resources, and capabilities required later for more fundamental change. Others take a more radical approach. When ICI decided to change from a chemicals company into a sensory perception products company, its CEO, Charles Miller-Smith's program changed whole populations of employees. Old businesses were to be sold off and new ones acquired.[6]

Change Start Point

Change start point refers to the locus of control and influence of the change process. The change kaleidoscope offers managers four approaches: top-down, bottom-up, prototypes/pilot sites, and pockets of good practice. The first three approaches are well known. A top-down approach is advocated by much of the prescriptive change literature. The direction, control, and initiation of the changes come from the top management team. Bottom-up change emerges from the middle and lower levels in the organization. It encourages responsibility for change initiation and implementation from all levels of staff. The intent is to generate a wider ownership of and commitment to the required changes. It is also possible to combine a top-down approach with a bottom-up approach.[7] Advocates of this approach argue that some change activities, such as mobilizing support for implementing a particular strategy, often require top-down direction, whereas others, such as creating a vision for change, require extensive involvement of many organizational levels.

Prototyping involves implementing change in just one department, function, or process. Sometimes it requires using a new start-up site.

The approach called pockets of good practice[8] is less well known. An individual within one unit or department initiates some type of change. A sales manager might alter the way that salespersons make calls on new customers. Other changes might include modifying individual projects, initiating pilot schemes to enhance organizational performance, or reshaping the interpersonal dynamics and culture within teams and departments. Keep in mind that these pockets of improved practice will only lead to further organizational change when they are studied and executed by other individuals or units.

Change Style

Over time, managers leading strategy implementation often adopt or take on one or a combination of distinct change styles. Our kaleidoscope model suggests a continuum of five styles, ranging from highly collaborative to highly directive (see Figure 17.3). More directive change styles result in separating the thinkers from the doers. Those leading strategy implementation make the majority of decisions about what to change and how. They then "sell" these changes to the doers, who are supposed to implement the plans. Lower level employees are not invited to contribute to the goals or means of change, except in a limited way. Such approaches are most likely to be effective when there is a sense of crisis within the organization.

It is important for managers at all organization levels to recognize that multiple combinations of change start point and style are possible. Top-down

FIGURE 17.3   Change style continuum.

Education and Communication	Collaboration	Participation	Direction	Coercion
Use small group briefings to discuss/ explain change. Aims to equip employees with an understanding and an ability to initiate changes.	Widespread involvement of employees in decisions about both what to change and how.	Consultation of employees about how to deliver change.	Change leaders make decisions. Leaders use authority to direct change.	Use of power to impose change.

change is often presented as directive or coercive, yet it can also be highly collaborative. The CEO of Eisai, a Japanese pharmaceutical company, wanted to change the focus of the company from manufacturing drugs, to improving the quality of life for elderly sick people. He put his managers through a training program to encourage them to become more innovative and to develop new products and services in line with his strategic intent for the organization. These managers were then expected to use their learning to propose and implement new products and services.[9] This was a participative process, yet the initiation and control of the change process was retained at the top of the organization.

Change Interventions

Strategy implementation ultimately involves the deployment of a range of levers and mechanisms. Organizations comprise several interconnected and interdependent subsystems:

- The technical subsystem (structures and systems).
- The political subsystem (who influences what and whom).
- The cultural subsystem (interpersonal dynamics and style).[10]

Managers instinctively know how difficult it is to change facets of one subsystem without encountering issues involving the other subsystems. In particular, transformational change initiatives, requiring a change in the shared assumptions and beliefs of an organization, are more likely to fail if change agents apply a change recipe which concentrates on the use of levers and mechanisms from just one organizational subsystem. The type and extent of the change required always influences the choice of levers and mechanisms, as illustrated in Figure 17.4.

Realignments typically require a change in the nature of work individuals do and its intended outcomes such as productivity improvement, sales growth, or customer responses. They do not require a fundamental change in the way employees think. Thus, an organization can change rewards and performance measures to focus employees on the achievement of different outcomes and ways of doing things, or it can put in place interventions to change the way people work within the organization, or it could attempt to do both. Such interventions could include changes to organization structure (particularly roles and responsibilities) and changes to control systems to support and measure desired behavioral changes. However, mutually supportive changes may still be needed in all organizational subsystems to ensure that employees do not receive contradictory messages. In the early 1990s, for example, many organizations undertook change through a mixture of restructuring, downsizing, and business process reengineering initiatives. Employees frequently complained that they received mixed, and indeed, contradictory messages about the intent of the change. Managers loudly proclaimed the value of innovation, quality,

FIGURE 17.4   The range of change interventions.

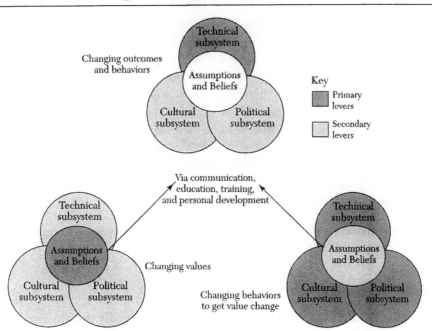

and teamwork, yet they continued to punish mistakes, cut costs, and reward individual performance in ways that suppressed doing things in new ways, taking risks, and doing small experiments intended to augment learning.

In contrast, transformational change, involving a dramatic shift in the way employees behave and in how they think about their work and the organization, typically requires the use of all available levers and mechanisms. Many communication, education, training, and personal development interventions are required to help employees understand what is expected of them in the new culture. These interventions need to be supported by changes to all other subsystems, to create a mutually supportive and consistent organizational system, which will enable and reinforce behaviors appropriate to the new values. However, intense debate persists among researchers, consultants, and practitioners over whether it is best to force behavioral change that will then lead to value change, or whether employee values should be targeted directly. This affects the choice of which levers and mechanisms to emphasize (see Figure 17.4).

Change Roles

Strategy implementation involves multiple individuals, often organized into project teams, task forces, and (informal) committees. Different individuals assume different roles and responsibilities. Indeed, for any one individual or team, these roles may change as the implementation of a strategy takes place over time.

Leadership

Initiating as well as carrying through strategy implementation change programs often hinges on the guidance and persona of a key, pivotal figure. Jack Welch, CEO of GE, is often given credit for spearheading many of the firm's well-known change initiatives such as the Work-Out programs. The leader may be the CEO, the general manager, or another senior manager acting as the internal change agent, or another director such as the human resources director. If the individual championing change is not the CEO or the managing director, then to push change through that person will need to gain the support of more powerful individuals within the organization.

External Facilitation

Firms sometimes use external consultants as advisers. In some instances, they may actively participate as project or team members.

Change Action Team

Some companies designate a team of individuals, typically drawn from multiple functional areas, to lead strategy implementation. However, if the team does not include senior managers, it is likely to require the highly visible support of one or more members of the top management group.

Functional Delegation

Frequently, individual functional areas such as human resources, marketing, or operations management, are asked to take responsibility for executing specific strategy implementation programs or projects. It is more appropriate to do this when specific strategy implementation programs or projects fall within the purview of a particular function or department.

LINKING DESIGN CHOICES TO CONTEXT: THE CONTEXTUAL FEATURES

As noted earlier, contextual features influence change design choices. We briefly discuss each contextual feature (see Table 17.2) and illustrate how they can impact design choices.

Time and Scope

When surveying the change path for an organization, managers must analyze in advance the scope of change—the extent of the alteration in culture, posture, and goals, the three elements of marketplace strategy[11]—as well as extent of

TABLE 17.2 Definitions of Contextual Features

Feature	Definition
Time	The time an organization has to achieve change. Organizations in crisis have less time than those concerned with long term strategic development.
Scope	The degree of change required in terms of re-alignment (within paradigm change) or transformation (paradigmatic change). Scope is also affected by whether change is restricted to a particular division or department or is organization wide.
Preservation	The extent to which it is necessary to maintain certain ways of working, retain particular groups of staff or preserve specific tangible and intangible assets or competencies.
Diversity	The degree of diversity in terms of values, norms and attitudes among the staff groups who need to undertake change. There may be subcultures or national cultures within the groups. Different departments may have their own distinct characteristics. Some staff groups may identify strongly with their team or department, others with their division or the whole organization. Professionals may identify more with their profession than their employing organization.
Capability	The level of ability within an organization to manage change of the type(s) required, and the ability of staff to handle individual change.
Capacity	The resources available, in terms of time, cash and people, to invest in the proposed change.
Readiness	The extent to which staff are both aware of the need for change, and willing to change.
Power	The amount of power, or autonomy, the key change agents have to implement change as they wish.

change. Along with the time over which the strategy implementation will take place, the scope of change is a primary determinant of the type of change required and the change path.[12]

When an organization needs to undergo a realignment, the choice of change path is relatively straightforward. If the organization has time on its side, then it may undertake an adaptive change process. If the strategy change is more urgent, then it will have to undertake a reconstruction. When managers want to execute a strategy and/or organization transformation, then the choice of change path becomes more complex. If the organization is in a crisis situation, with rapidly declining sales and profitability, then immediate action is required. Strategy turnarounds often initially involve *realignment,* in the form of a *reconstruction.* Once the organization is financially viable, it is then possible to put in place other change initiatives to achieve longer term and more fundamental transformation, just as British Airways and General Electric did. Other organizations may try to effect an immediate revolution. The urgent need for action (lack of time) spurs organizations to use more top-down and directive change approaches.

An organization implementing preemptive transformational change, with time on its side, may first undergo some type of adaptation or reconstruction to build the capabilities for fundamental change and an organization-wide awareness of the need for change. Then the organization can move to an evolutionary change approach. The Glaxo case, outlined later in this chapter, describes such a change process. The absence of time pressures also allows a range of design choices. In the absence of any obvious strategic or organizational crisis, managers can employ participative approaches, one benefit of which may be the ability to build the case for "the need to change."

The following example occurred in the early 1990s in the United Kingdom. At KPMG, the international firm of accountants and management consultants, the partner in charge of the southeast region, initiated extensive organizational change through a series of workshops and meetings designed to gain buy-in to the need for change.[13] He perceived a need for the firm to become more client-focused. At the time, the firm's financial results did not suggest any apparent or urgent need for change, but by persuasively building a consensus, this partner enabled the firm to make a significant cultural transformation.

Preservation

Strategy implementation sometimes requires a redirection of the organizational assets and capabilities a firm needs to generate and sustain value for customers. To prevent long-term harm, organizations need to safeguard assets and capabilities that are unique and difficult to imitate. British Telecom, in the early 1980s, and IBM, in the early 1990s, put in place voluntary workforce reduction programs. In both companies, highly valuable skills and knowledge walked out of the door when many talented managers took early retirement. As proof of this point, many former employees soon had to be rehired at consultants' rates.

If a particular group of employees who can easily find work elsewhere need to be retained, more collaborative change approaches are required to maintain their support and cooperation. Alternatively, if strategy implementation centers around transformational change and old ways of thinking and behaving to which employees may be emotionally attached, managers must be shaken up and change leaders may have little choice but to be directive in executing the requisite organizational solutions. Usually this means that some personnel may be let go if they are involved in work the organization no longer needs to undertake. For others, a process of unlearning old ways of doing things through extensive education and training programs may be required.

Diversity

Managers spearheading strategy implementation must recognize that organizations are not homogeneous. Distinct local cultures are the hallmark of departments and subunits in almost every large organization. Diversity among local cultures results in part from differences between national cultures, and also from differences in objectives, background, and tasks between departments or divisions. Also, different professional or occupational groups, such as engineers and salespersons manifest distinct values and behavioral norms.

Choice of change path and the types of interventions required must take into account the breadth and depth of cultural diversity. If managers need to merge culturally diverse companies or even divisions within a single company, the initial change initiatives may need to be directed toward unifying the culture of the groups involved. An organization implementing change across both sales and research and development divisions, for example, is likely to find very different cultures and sources of motivations in the two divisions. Bisto, the supplier of gravy products, found this out when they moved their marketing staff to share offices with the company's production and technical staff. The purpose of the move was to increase product innovation. However, an ongoing source of friction was that marketing believed that production did not understand customers, and production thought marketing spoke in jargon. These attitudes impeded collaboration. Change required interventions aimed at building cross-functional teams that could work purposefully together before progress was possible.[14]

Diversity can also create the need for multiple change approaches in different divisions, and may impact the choice of change roles. If there are diverse professional groups within an organization, such as doctors, nurses, and administrators within hospitals, it is wise to involve representatives from these groups, and particularly the most powerful groups, in an active change role. Furthermore, if the groups are accustomed to high levels of autonomy, behavioral prescriptions are unlikely to be well received. Teachers, doctors, scientists, architects, inventors, and lawyers, to name a few examples, are likely to react negatively to the imposition of directives that limit their discretion.

Capability and Capacity

Strategy implementation frequently founders because an organization lacks the required assets and capabilities. Capability to manage strategy implementation exists at three levels within an organization—individual, managerial, and organizational. Individuals need to be able to manage the personal change that may be required of them. Managers need to be able to aid and assist those under their charge to adopt and manage the change expected of them. The *organizational* level concerns the presence or absence of specialist change resources: individuals who understand how to design and manage a change process.

Transformational change, of course, places the heaviest burden on individual, managerial, and organizational change capabilities. If an organization lacks the appropriate change capabilities, initial change efforts must involve some type of realignment to build the requisite capabilities, as shown in the examples of W H Smith News and Lendco discussed later in this chapter.

Personal development programs can be used to build both the individual capabilities to undertake change effectively and also the managerial capability to help others through change. New systems may also need to be established to aid business planning and performance management during the change process. External consultants can be used in the absence of specialist in-house change resources with the needed expertise to establish appropriate training and development, and design the strategy implementation change process. Particular change styles may also involve particular skills. Collaboration requires experienced facilitators to design and run workshops.

Capacity issues have caused strategy implementation to stagnate in many organizations. Strategy implementation consumes assets: financial, human, knowledge, physical, technological, perceptual, and organizational resources. All strategy implementation programs and projects require managerial time and attention. The more extensive the strategy and organization changes, the more need for senior and middle management involvement. Yet, many managers simply feel overburdened by the change inherent in strategy implementation. In truth, the workload is considerable: they must manage change initiatives; contribute to enhancing current operations; and undertake extensive personal change. More participative change approaches require higher levels of capacity in terms of time, cash, and personnel.

Readiness for Change

A core truth bears repeating: strategy implementation occurs more quickly when the organization is committed to and ready for change. The new British Library opened in London in 1998. Staff members who had previously worked in 20 different buildings in their own areas of expertise were now expected to work as an integrated unit. However, the completion of the new library took three years longer than expected. A restructuring of the senior management and an announcement of changes to staffing levels and work patterns led to job insecurity. A training program did not overcome the staff's fears and concerns; nor did it help them understand how to deal with change or build commitment to the changes. The lack of commitment and motivation to change meant time had to be set aside to enable staff to air grievances and come to terms with the proposed changes.[15]

When there is a low readiness for change, as in the case of the British Library, it may be necessary to adopt a directed or coercive style, especially if there is little time. Alternatively, if key strategy implementation changes do not place a premium on time, initial efforts may be aimed in part at making personnel aware of the need for more extensive change. A low readiness for change may also necessitate a strong change leadership role, and an initial top-down approach, or the use of pilot sites in parts of the organization where there is greater readiness. More bottom-up or collaborative approaches usually require a degree of willingness to undertake change. However, participation can generate a readiness for change, as described at KPMG.

Power

If managers involved in strategy implementation lack the authority to dictate specific facets of desired change, they need to select a change approach, probably involving collaboration and education, to win the support of other powerful stakeholders—specific senior managers, peers, and employees with critical skills or knowledge.

Sometimes, the requisite power to execute change may be limited by a parent group, as in the example of W H Smith News (see Box 17.2 later in this chapter). As was done in this example, the change leader may undertake a realignment change phase first, in which the levers and mechanisms deployed are primarily political, with the intent of winning the needed power.

The reaction of external stakeholders can also restrict the decision-making power of organizations. In 1995, Shell announced that it planned to sink its Brent Spar oil platform in the Atlantic Ocean. Greenpeace, the environment protection group, began a highly visible public relations campaign with the avowed purpose of preventing the dumping. The campaign captured popular support that took the form of a consumer boycott of Shell in many parts of Europe. In addition, because of the reaction of some European governments, Shell was forced to abandon its plans.[16]

DEVISING CONTEXT-SENSITIVE APPROACHES TO STRATEGY IMPLEMENTATION

Strategy implementation always requires change agents to take contextual features into account. The following cases illustrate how our kaleidoscope model works in practice. The first step in each case is to identify the key contextual features, or the key enablers and constraints, presented by the change context. Only then can consideration be given to the appropriate design choices for that change context.

Case 1. Glaxo Pharmaceuticals

Contextual features make the Glaxo strategy implementation case distinct (see Figure 17.5 and Box 17.1). The firm's desire for more efficient and integrated strategy implementation was enabled in at least three ways. First, there was no great urgency for change, although management needed to shake staff out of its complacency. Second, the firm was cash rich; it had extensive capacity to invest cash in a significant change program. Third, the sales division where most of the change was to occur, manifested a high degree of cultural homogeneity (low diversity), as well as a traditionally strong sense of commitment to Glaxo. Employees were highly educated, however, and thus could not be treated as if they had no minds of their own. Finally, it seems fair to suggest that the proposed changes worked because they involved a process of realignment rather than transformation.

FIGURE 17.5 Glaxo Pharmaceuticals key contextual features.

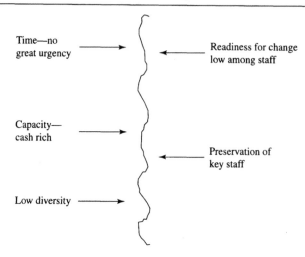

Two key constraints were evident: the low awareness of the need for change among employees, and the need to preserve as many of the talented workforce as possible. The vast pool of knowledge dispersed among the workforce would not be easy to replace.

The change process selected matched this context. An initial *big-bang reconstruction* was picked to destroy employee complacency. It was really a precursor to more fundamental change. A *top-down* approach *led by the senior managers* was taken to overcome the low readiness. Also *consultants* were used where necessary to overcome gaps in managerial capability. The style was *participative* to increase the awareness of the need for change, create some sense of ownership of the proposed change, and recognize employees' need for some degree of autonomy and their need to feel that they were in control. *Management development initiatives* helped managers realize that organizational change meant personal change and were supported by *symbolic office changes.*

Case 2. W H Smith News

W H Smith News faced a situation in which most of the contextual features indicated potential strategy implementation difficulties (see Figure 17.6 and Box 17.2). The only feature aiding change was the homogeneity of the firm's culture and workforce. The ultimate scope of change required was transformation, for which the organization lacked both the capacity and the capability. The change path selected by the HR manager was therefore one of adaptation followed by long-term evolution. In the *adaptation* phase, the HR manager endeavored to gain the power she needed, both in terms of position power and personal power, to effect long-term change, and build a capability and readiness for change.

Box 17.1

Glaxo Pharmaceuticals

In 1988, the senior management team for the sales divisions within Glaxo UK contemplated the combined threat posed by the expiry of its patents and changes within its core customer base, the National Health Service, in the 1990s. An attitude survey had identified high staff complacency, (unsurprising given good business results), and slow decision making exacerbated by strong functional divides. There was little sense of shared responsibility for the changes that would be necessary to ensure future success.

Focusing on the behaviors necessary for the future, a change program called RATIO was introduced. Each letter of RATIO represented a desired behavior (e.g., Role clarity). The directorate went through a team building and development course held outdoors and put together with the assistance of consultants, which enabled them to understand and experiment with the new behaviors that they were going to require from staff. This was so successful that a similar experience was put in place for 700 other members of staff. Staff were invited to revise the behaviors in terms of their own roles so that each characteristic could be customized.

A series of complementary change initiatives were implemented: a values statement was issued stating the values that should underpin the behaviors; cross-functional project groups were introduced; and Glaxo's planned relocation allowed them to make full symbolic use of the interior open plan design of the new building to reinforce the new behaviors. An HR initiative also incorporated RATIO within a new set of managerial competencies.

All these initiatives unfroze the complacency within the organization and enhanced staff's readiness for change. In the mid-1990s, a more radical change program was introduced focusing on business process reengineering and Glaxo merged with Wellcome to form one of the world's most successful pharmaceutical corporations.

Source. Adapted from V. Hope-Hailey and J. Hendry, "Corporate Cultural Change." *Human Resource Management Journal,* (1995), 5(4): 61–73, and L. Gratton et al. *Strategic Human Resource Management: Corporation Rhetoric and Individual Reality.* Oxford University Press: Oxford, 1999.

The adaptation phase effectively reconfigured the contextual features to create a climate more conducive to evolutionary change. However, given the power of the key staff, the *evolutionary* phase still needed to involve *participation* of this staff group. The *start point* still could not be *bottom-up* given the low capability and the low readiness of the wider workforce. Also, some managers were likely to be more ready for change than others. These conditions suggests a *start point* of *pilot sites* or *pockets of good practice.* The lack of cash and a compliant workforce would point to the use of *change levers* aimed at

FIGURE 17.6   News division key contextual features.

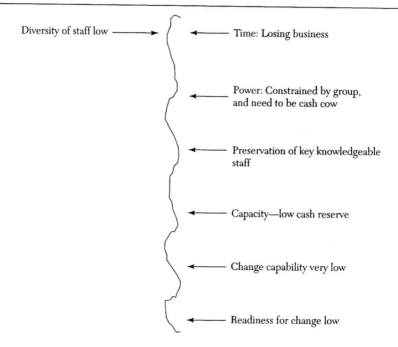

achieving initial *behavioral change* with subsequent interventions to aid attitude change.

Case 3. Lendco Banking Group

Three key enablers facilitated strategy implementation in Lendco (see Figure 17.7 and Box 17.3). First, senior managers recognized the consequences of not successfully executing significant cultural change. Second, the firm possessed an abundance of cash to buttress significant investment. Third, the firm is reasonably culturally homogeneous.

However, key change constraints were also evident. Senior managers' power in relation to the branch managers was limited due to the geographic distances. A low awareness of the need for change was evident among employees, in large part, due to the current success of the organization. Branch staff also exhibited a low change capability: They had little experience in undertaking personal change or in managing organizational change.

Yet, Lendco ultimately must confront an extensive scope of change: It needs to achieve a transformation from a traditional local bank to a retailer of financial services. Although time currently is not an issue, it may become so if change does not take place.

Like many other organizations, Lendco first needs to create an awareness of the need for change and to build a change capability if eventually it is

Box 17.2

W H SMITH NEWS

W H Smith News, part of the W H Smith Group whose business is built around retailing and distribution, was the largest distributor of newspapers and magazines in the United Kingdom by both market share and turnover. This Division had 4,300 employees in 72 wholesale houses and over 22,000 retail customers. Although the Group only set broad financial targets, the division's autonomy was constrained by its role as cash cow within the Group. In 1989, the Group instigated a process of cultural change in response to the loss of £40 million of business to its nonunionized rival, TNT.

The change aimed to introduce a managerial style of "directness, openness to ideas, commitment to the success of others . . . and the strong development of teamwork and trust" to deliver the strategic intent of enhanced customer focus and increased productivity. This contrasted with the prevailing style of management, described as autocracy tempered with paternalism, underpinned by values of loyalty, security, and obedience to orders. The clear message was not to challenge a wholesale house manager's authority. Yet staff were motivated and loyal to this family-based employer.

In part the responsibility for this change was given to the HR function. The newly appointed HR manager found that the house managers were the key to achieving change. They could not be overtly attacked, however, as they were the people who ran the business and made the money, and, as such, possessed tacit knowledge about "the way things are done around here." The absence of any division-wide human resource management systems meant that a textbook transformational change would be difficult to achieve. If the HR function *demanded* a strategic role, then potentially this would have alienated the house managers and an erosion of staff loyalty was a risk to short-term business success.

The HR manager set about formalizing and centralizing human resource management systems while also taking some of the administrative burden of HR away from house managers. She delivered quality training and introduced a management style survey. The data generated gave her the legitimacy to implement changes. By seeking to assist rather than confront, she made few enemies and was invited to join the executive board.

Source. Adapted from W H Smith Group plc annual report, 1998, and L. Gratton et al. *Strategic Human Resource Management: Corporation Rhetoric and Individual Reality.* Oxford: Oxford University Press, 1999.

FIGURE 17.7   Lendco key contextual features.

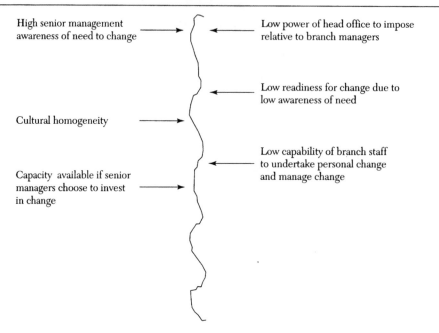

to deliver a transformation. It cannot jettison large numbers of existing staff because their knowledge underlies enhancing current operations. This points to the need for initial reconstruction, involving visible, symbolic interventions to make the inevitability of change apparent, as was the case at British Airways. Change would have to be led initially in a top-down fashion by the senior managers, although over time change action teams could be put together as the readiness and capability for change grew. Similarly, early change would need to be directive, consistent with the dependency culture. Longer-term participation would be needed to support a cultural shift to greater self-responsibility for staff. Early interventions could not just be symbolic, but would have to include creating systems to support change, such as performance management and communication. Behavioral change could be given an impetus by creating a focus on changed performance outputs for managerial staff.

SUMMARY

Given persistent and discontinuous environmental change, strategy implementation necessarily involves managing extensive change within organizations. Managers therefore must become increasingly context sensitive: They must possess the ability to understand the environment they are operating in and to devise approaches to change that will be effective given a particular set of conditions. The change kaleidoscope presents a framework that can help

---

Box 17.3

Lendco Banking Group

This case study focuses on the retail banking division of Lendco which was struggling against intense competition fueled by the success of both its peers and new entrants into the marketplace, and also the impact of new technology. In response, it embarked on a cultural change program with the intention of moving the bank away from what senior management described as an authoritarian culture which had bred a childlike dependence within staff and a general climate of fear and blame. The directors sought to instill a culture that encouraged individual responsibility and excellent people management. They believed this was the means of achieving improved customer service.

The major problem for the bank was that the strength of the old culture was inextricably linked to the type of staff who had chosen banking as a career before the 1990s. These people wanted the stability and predictability that the old culture offered them, and any transition away from the familiar was problematic. The senior management team failed to offer an attractive alternative vision with the result that every change they implemented felt like a fatal blow to the old culture rather than a better alternative for the future.

In the branch network, bankers continued to stick to banking, and contradictory messages about the importance of business targets versus softer people management objectives meant that the former, in practice, gained supremacy in managers' minds. Many branch managers felt that the management of people was what the personnel management department did. Finally, the shift to seeing the branch as a retail outlet rather than an autonomous profit center contributed to lower morale and perceptions of declining status among this managerial group. Therefore, while the branches were critical in delivering the new culture and the new business model, they lacked the capability and motivation to deliver this change.

Source. Copyright Veronica Hope-Hailey, 1998.

---

change agents align organizational change and change in marketplace strategy. The framework aims to encourage questioning and informed judgment, not provide a series of universal answers.

NOTES

1. For a more detailed discussion of the need for change to be context dependent, and the framework used in this chapter—the change kaleidoscope—see, J. Balogun and V. Hope-Hailey, *Exploring Strategic Change* (Englewood Cliffs, NJ: Prentice-Hall, 1999).

2. In this chapter, we use the notion of a change agent as a shorthand for any manager charged with affecting change or implementing strategy.

3.   The notion of strategy renovation, and how it differs from strategy invention and strategy incrementalism, was developed in Chapter 1.

4.   See L.D. Goodstein and W.W. Burke, "Creating Successful Organization Change," *Organizational Dynamics,* (1991), 19(4):5–17; and J. Leahey and J.P. Kotter, "Changing the Culture at British Airways," Case 9–491–009 (Harvard Business School 1990).

5.   The story of the transformation at GE led by Jack Welch is told in N.M. Tichy and S. Sherman, *Control Your Destiny, or Someone Else Will* (New York: Doubleday, 1993).

6.   See H. Connon, "Developing a Taste for the Sweet Smell of Success," *The Observer* (April 5, 1998) Business Section, p. 6 for a report on the repositioning of ICI.

7.   For a description of how to combine a top-down approach to change with a more bottom-up approach, see M. Beer, R.A. Eisenstat, and B. Spector, *The Critical Path to Corporate Renewal* (Boston: Harvard Business School Press, 1990).

8.   For more information on pockets of good practice, see D. Butcher, P. Harvery, and S. Atkinson, *Developing Business through Developing Individuals* (Cranfield School of Management, 1997).

9.   P. Strebel, "Why Do Employees Resist Change," *Harvard Business Review* (May/June 1996): 86–92.

10.   See N.M. Tichy, *Managing Strategic Change: Technical, Political and Cultural Dynamics* (New York: Wiley, 1983). Also N.M. Tichy, "The Essentials of Strategic Change Management," *Journal of Business Strategy,* 3:55–67.

11.   For a discussion of these elements of marketplace strategy, see Chapter 1.

12.   This does not mean that other contextual features should be ignored. Features such as capability and capacity exert a strong influence on the type of change required and the change path.

13.   See the case studies on KPMG in G. Johnson and K. Scholes, *Exploring Corporate Strategy, Text and Cases,* 5th ed. (London: Prentice-Hall, 1998).

14.   See J. Pickard, "Aah, Teamwork," *People Management* (November 6, 1997): 37–39.

15.   See V. Morrow, "Coping with Change at the British Library," *Information World Review* (April 1998): 32–34; and J. Welch, "Turmoil Takes Toll on British Library Staff," *People Management* (January 9, 1997): 12–13.

16.   For a more detailed discussion of this case, see Chapter 7.

18 THERE IS NO UNIVERSAL STRATEGY FORMULA

Ian Wilson
Wolf Enterprises

Good planning employs a multidimensional strategy. It does not call for making false choices, such as that between growth and cost reduction or between meeting customer needs and beating the competition. Good planning derives strength from a "both/and" philosophy instead of an "either/or" dichotomy. In a fundamental sense, the strength of strategy lies in its ability to harness the power of opposites—objectives, strategies, policies, or actions that may seem, on the surface, to be contradictory and mutually exclusive—to work together. The best evidence for this conclusion can be found by surveying the 30 years of strategic management history.

A SHORT HISTORY OF STRATEGIC PLANNING

For the first 30 or so years of its history, strategic planning has constantly evolved as it was alternately embraced and rejected by leading corporations in the United States and Europe. Through periods of diversification or divestiture, growth or recession, regulation or deregulation, the best and the brightest academicians and management consulting firms convinced corporate managements to adopt a succession of strategic theories or processes, each vaunted as a single formula for success. Over the years, scores of these management concepts such as benchmarking, customer segmentation, value chain analysis, scenario planning, reengineering, quality management were enthusiastically adopted by a few cutting-edge corporations as the answer to the strategy problem of the moment. Many of these management tools worked well for a time in certain corporate settings, only to fail sooner or later when they were applied

385

as "universal curealls." Eventually, each approach was supplanted by another methodology with more promise.

Over these past three decades, the one cardinal management sin that spans national and industry boundaries has been the persistent belief that there is a single formula for corporate success, coupled with rapid shifts in conviction as to what exactly that formula might be. One would not expect that supposedly rational executives would so easily succumb to the "strategic perspective of the month" fad, yet they do. "What's in? What's out?" *Business Week* asks every year.

The Four Phases

In Phase 1, from the late 1960s to the late 1970s, strategic planning enjoyed widespread, almost unqualified, acceptance. The emphasis then was on the creation of a new staff planning function, the development of elaborate planning processes and procedures, all supported by an array of new analysis techniques and methodologies such as the experience curve, the growth/share matrix, and PIMS (profit impact of market share). The fatal flaw in this approach was that the staff took over the strategy-making function from line managers; in time, the process, with its elaborate methodologies and documentation, came to dominate the staff; yet little or nothing changed operationally.

Inevitably perhaps, all this planning technology set the stage for a reaction that came in Phase 2, starting in the early 1980s. The turning point came with the recessions of 1980 and 1982, downturns that strategic planning had neither foreseen nor prepared for. Faced with this "implementation problem," many companies simply walked away from the planning process entirely, dismantling planning staffs, abandoning the analysis methodologies, and shifting the balance of decision-making power back to line managers. The trouble with this approach was that, as Professor Michael Porter of Harvard pointed out, "the need for strategic thinking has never been greater,"[1] but without a strategic framework for their planning, line managers fell back on familiar habits, making tactical decisions based on short-term factors.

The power and prevalence of systemic changes in the business environment have confirmed Porter's thesis of the need for strategic thinking, and Phase 3, in the mid- to late-1980s, saw a hesitant return to strategic planning (renamed "strategic management"). Its proponents attempted to correct the original defects by simplifying the process, streamlining the documentation, and placing the main responsibility for strategy development—and most importantly, for execution—in the hands of management teams at the corporate or strategic business unit (SBU) level. However, this was an era of corporate raiders, mergers and acquisitions, and financial deal-making. In such a climate, strategic planning could not help being stunted and skewed toward the needs of this financial approach.

The beginning of Phase 4 was heralded, in the early 1990s, by the advent of a cluster of new, well-hyped approaches to strategic success, including TQM (total quality management), core competencies (or capabilities), and, most notably, reengineering. Reengineering in particular attracted management attention with its implied promise of combining strategic restructuring (based on processes rather than functions) with the tactical benefits of cost reduction. The trouble with this approach was twofold. In the first place reengineering, sweeping though it was in scope and concept, could never, by itself, provide the broad strategic repositioning and the new visions of the future that preparing for rapid technological change and global competition required. And second, its execution turned out to be more demanding and difficult than was initially supposed. Many reengineering projects were abandoned in midstream; and even its leading proponents admitted they had underestimated the importance of the human factor in redesigning processes. Once again, the quest for a one-size-fits-all solution seemed to have led executives into a blind alley.

This setback did not, however, end the search. By 1996, *Business Week* heralded the arrival of Phase 5 with the headline "Strategic Planning—It's Back!"[2] "Reengineering consultants with stopwatches are out," the magazine proclaimed: "strategy gurus with visions of new prospects are in." Thus far, the prospects for this latest attempt to "get it right" seem more encouraging. There appears, for instance, to be a greater willingness to acknowledge two factors essential for strategic success. One is that strategy is a highly complex phenomenon that can't be managed according to any single-track, simplistic formula. Instead strategy requires managers to blend together many diverse (sometimes seemingly conflicting) objectives, factors, and methodologies. The other is that the pace and complexity of change require that strategic planning should not be viewed as a "sometime thing" that can be turned on and off and still be effective. A few years ago, the widely respected consultant Gary Hamel observed: "Strategy is not a once-a-year rain dance, nor is it a once-a-decade consulting project." Since the Internet era began, strategic planning, especially in successful business units, has speeded up and taken a short-term focus. In fact, some companies now see it as a continuously evolving process in which planning, experimentation, modification, and execution are the essential ingredients.

The Continuing Need for Strategic Planning

In the late 1980s, when strategic planning was still under a cloud, Professor Porter pointed out: "There are no substitutes for strategic thinking. Improving quality is meaningless without knowing what kind of quality is relevant in competitive terms. Nurturing corporate culture is useless unless the culture is aligned with a company's approach to competing. Entrepreneurship unguided by strategic perspective is much more likely to fail than succeed."[3] Porter's assertion was right then, it is right now, and it is likely to continue to be right for as far into the future as we can see.

The converging forces of globalization, technology, deregulation, and economic restructuring combine to make strategy and strategic thinking an essential weapon in the corporate armory. Incremental change can generally be dealt with by incremental responses. Radical change of the kind that we are now experiencing requires a radical rethinking of strategic direction and a transformation of capabilities, production, structure, and relationships. This is not exclusively a challenge for high-tech companies. In his book, *Only the Paranoid Survive,*[4] Andy Grove, the chairman of Intel during its years of stellar growth, argues that virtually every industry now confronts a series of "strategic inflection points"—crisis moments when the tectonic plates of the business landscape shift. And strategic thinking and planning are essential when industry maps are being rewritten and business is anything but usual.

And yet, the suspicion persists that executive understanding and support for strategic planning is fragile and will last only until the "next big thing" comes along. Sustained commitment will come only from a radical reperceiving of the true nature and role of strategy. Strategy should be holistic in its scope and its approach. It deals, not with any one particular aspect of the business, but with the business-as-a-whole and its relationship to both the macroenvironment and microenvironment. It derives its power, not from an either/or focus on long-term positioning *or* short-term results, product quality *or* process redesign, but rather from a both/and approach and an ability to harness the power of opposites.

HARNESSING THE POWER OF OPPOSITES

The greatest benefit of strategic planning is that it encourages, indeed forces, managers to consider and take action on multiple fronts, moving from one strategic issue to another. For example, many corporations are confronting the problem of how best to manage, simultaneously, both their traditional business model and their new ventures in e-commerce. Their efforts to do so reinforce the notion advocated at the beginning of this chapter.

The first step in strategy development is, typically, a situation assessment (or SW/OTs analysis). This calls for us to identify *both* the opportunities *and* the threats posed by the current and future environment, *both* the strengths *and* weaknesses that the organization currently brings to the competitive fray. We don't look only at the opportunities and our strengths: we turn the coin over to look at the threats and our weaknesses. Strategy then calls for us to seize the opportunities, avert or minimize the threats, leverage our strengths, and correct our weaknesses—all at the same time (although the emphasis on each of these thrusts will not always be identical). It has to deal, simultaneously, not with a single strategic issue but with many. A corporation typically confronts about half a dozen strategic (make-or-break, life-or-death) issues at any one time. In practice, strategy making and implementation is a highly complex task, taking its cues from the market and competitive environment, and leading to the adoption of multiple courses of action. A business strategy is not a single cord, but a cable made up of the intertwining of multiple cords (a marketing strategy, manufacturing strategy, technology strategy, organization strategy, public affairs strategy, and so on).

Almost from its inception, strategic planning has been undermined by a false dichotomy in both its theory and its practice. Theorists have divided into the intuitive (Mintzberg) and the analytical (Ansoff) schools; yet experience is clear that strategic planning will falter if it is not a blending of the two. Similarly, corporate and consulting practice has all too often tended to emphasize one objective or one methodology—reengineering, total quality management, growth, share owner value, core competencies—to the neglect of others and the detriment of the whole.

In both theory and practice, "both/and" is a far sounder guiding principle than "either/or." Admittedly, both as individuals and as managers, we seem to find it easier to make decisions based on simple either/or choices. However, in the complex world we live in, solutions cannot be this simple. Most frequently, the best, if not the only viable, solution forces us to embrace opposites. Consider, for example, the eight pairs of "opposite" strategies described in the following subsections.

1. Achieving Sales Growth versus Controlling Costs

Perhaps the definitive statement on the fallacy of a growth-cost control choice is one made by Roger Enrico, when he was vice chairman of Pepsico:

> The people who go through restructuring and downsizing without a plan for growth are the people who consume assets rather than invest in them.[5]

Several years ago, business publications began to opine, "Managers are beginning to realize that repeated cost-cutting is no longer the path to sustained profitable growth." Set aside for the moment the implausibility of the belief that cost-cutting ever could have been considered a realistic path to *sustained growth*. If cost reduction or downsizing is an immediate strategic issue, management still has to determine which costs to reduce, what objectives downsizing should serve, and how to distinguish between organizational fat that must be trimmed and organizational muscle that the company must preserve, even strengthen, for future growth.

Stephen Wolf, CEO of US Airways, evidently sees the perils in such false choices. He is confronting the twin imperatives of reducing the airline's costs (which are substantially above industry average) and promoting international expansion and alliances. He may not succeed, but the two-pronged strategy is most surely the correct one.

2. Meeting Market/Customer Needs versus Beating the Competition

It is almost inconceivable that this dichotomy should ever have attained the measure of respectability that it has. Yet, if we read or listen carefully to executive pronouncements (particularly those in corporate annual reports), two schools of thought emerge. There are those who emphasize consultant Tom

Peters' dictum of "getting close to your customer," arguing that understanding what your customers truly need and value is the essential basis for strategic success. And then there are those who take their cue from Michael Porter in emphasizing the critical importance of identifying and responding to current and future sources of competition.

It is surely obvious that a market, by definition, is created by the interaction of *two* groups of people—buyers (who create demand by competing for the opportunity to buy) and sellers (who compete for the opportunity to supply). In the words of the song about love and marriage, you simply "can't have one without the other." It stands to reason, therefore, that any strategy must address both opposites in this equation, at the same time. There are obvious dangers inherent either in focusing on serving the customer without paying attention to what competitors are doing, or in single-mindedly striving to do what the competition does—only better. This simple fact tends, however, to get neglected in corporations' search for a single strategy formula. This is not so much the fault of gurus such as Peters and Porter as it is of their followers who seem to mistake the part (a commendable focus on an admirable course of action) for the whole (the total strategy).

3. Holding to a Strategic Vision versus Flexibility in Tactical Action

The tension between these seemingly polar ideas derives from the larger debate about the relative roles of luck and foresight in market success. Once again the answer is "Both!" In a *Long Range Planning* article, "Realizing the Power of Strategic Vision,"[6] I argued the case for developing a powerful and coherent strategic vision, noting that a vision that is well communicated and well understood throughout an organization *increases, rather than decreases, that organization's ability to act flexibly* in response to changes in the tactical situation. With a clear idea of where, ultimately, that organization wants to be, managers at every level are better able to determine the best course of action in the immediate situation. Without a clear vision, the risk is, "If you don't know where you're going, it doesn't matter how you get there." A sound strategic vision provides "both the readiness and the 'aim'—as in 'Ready, aim, fire'— for both strategic and operational decisions."

This argument is not always well received or understood. When Lou Gerstner took over as chief executive officer of IBM in 1993, he made frequent statements to the effect that "the last thing IBM needs right now is a vision." Certainly, the case for immediate tactical action on cost reduction and improved market focus was obvious and unarguable. But the need for an answer to the question "After restructuring, what?" was equally obvious. Eventually, Gerstner did develop his vision—"network-centric computing[7]—and has used it to unify and motivate a slimmed down, more agile, and rejuvenated company.

One of the essential characteristics of a viable vision is its flexibility: it must always be open and responsive to change. Flexibility does not mean abandoning the vision: It simply recognizes the need to tune the vision continually to the requirements of an ever-changing business environment.

4. Leading versus Following the Market

This pair of opposites reflects the old question in marketing strategy, "Is it better to be the market leader, or a quick follower?" With all the talk these days about the strategic importance of "reinventing industries" and "changing the rules of the game," one might think that the answer had been given, clearly and definitively, in favor of market leadership. And the success of change leaders as varied as Dell Computer, Nike, Home Depot, Enron, and Starbucks Coffee would seem to put this answer beyond argument.

Yet the closer we look at such successes, the clearer it becomes that they are the result of *both* restructuring markets and industries *and* following the latent desires and needs of their customers, frequently developing product and service attributes that customers hadn't even thought of or didn't think were possible. In a fundamental sense, market leaders have, in effect, followed the dictates of the latent or potential market

5. Lower Price versus Higher Quality

In the old typology of competitive strategies one had to make a choice between these options: Quality came at a higher cost, and quality products, therefore, had to be marketed to customers who were prepared to pay a higher price. With the coming of information technology, however, in many cases such a choice is no longer necessary: one can produce and market a higher quality product at a lower price. An obvious example of this phenomenon is offered by the microprocessor industry which has, over several generations of products, followed Moore's Law of doubling capacity and halving price every eighteen months. Less well known is the case of Alaska Airlines which, in face of the entry of low-fare competitors into its markets, successfully executed a strategy that combined maintaining its top-notch service while slashing its fares. The lesson here, at a minimum, is that we should hesitate to assume that these opposites are totally incompatible—desired by customers, but deemed impractical by producers.

6. Acting on Rational Analysis versus Operating on Intuition, Insight, Hunches

This is a continuation of the debate between the Ansoff and Mintzberg schools of thought regarding the fundamental nature of strategic planning.[8] But if one thing is clear from the experience of the past 20 years, it is that innovative strategies do not emerge from sterile analysis and number-crunching: they come from new insights and intuitive hunches. Equally clear, however, is that intuition, if it is to be strategically helpful, must be grounded in facts. Traditionally, the intuitive entrepreneur has always had an instinctive grasp of the facts of his market. Now, in dealing with current complexities, today's strategist must supplement instinct with more explicit analysis.

7. Social Responsibility versus Economic Realities

In the traditional management view, social responsibility was defined as community relations, charitable donations, and aid to education—nice things to do, if one could afford them, but definitely peripheral to the main thrusts of strategy, which were to deal with the hard facts of market and competitive realities.

Now, however, with changing social, economic, and political conditions, social responsibility (or, more accurately, social responsiveness) has been redefined in terms that are central to corporate strategy. In my recent book, *The New Rules of Corporate Conduct*, I identified the six key thrusts of a social strategy for corporations as the issues of corporate governance and legitimacy, environmental strategy, the new employment contract, public-private relationships, equity, and ethics.[9]

Whatever position a corporation might take on these issues, it must deal with them with the same level of importance and executive attention, as the pressing needs to respond to radical shifts in markets, competition, and technology. Doing good and doing well are more closely linked than ever before in an era when public interest groups are multiplying and class action suits routinely seek damages for hundreds of millions of dollars. Both corporate strategy and executive leadership now need to deal, equally and simultaneously, with both social and competitive measures of corporate performance, once conceived as opposites and contradictory, but now as parallel and intertwined requirements for corporate success.

For more corroborative evidence, consider the case of Douglas Ivester, CEO of Coca-Cola Company. Described by the *Wall Street Journal* as a brilliant and driven financial strategist, the Coke board saw him as the logical successor to Roberto Guizeta as chairman and CEO. Yet almost from the outset of his tenure, it became apparent that he lacked the ability to manage social strategy, having what the *Journal* termed "a tin ear" for public and political nuances. His clumsy handling of one public relations and political flap after another cost him the board's confidence and led him to announce his intention to step down and make way for fresh leadership. Significantly, the board then selected Douglas Daft, an executive with a stronger record of dealing with both the competitive and sociopolitical aspects of strategy.

8. Long Term versus Short Term: The Classic Debate

Perhaps the best-known, and most debated, pair of opposites is long-term and short-term perspectives. Too often, U.S. CEOs claim they must have only a short-term focus because they cannot buck either the market or the security analysts whose only interests are in the next quarter.

Such a response first accepts the validity of the charge and then attempts to explain the reasons for this situation. But, as *Fortune* noted many years ago, this argument, "widely accepted as gospel, poses just one problem: It isn't valid."[10] The article quoted research showing that investors do, in fact, place considerable value on profits that won't materialize for 5 to 10 years, and that the market does not necessarily hammer a stock that reports disastrous quarterly results, if investors perceive the dip as a one-time quirk. The article cites the work of Alfred Rappaport, Professor of Accounting and Finance at Northwestern University's Kellogg School and a leading student of stock values, who developed a model of how the market sets stock prices based on such key "value drivers" as expected sales growth, operating profit margins, investments necessary to sustain growth, taxes, and the cost of capital. According to Rappaport, "You can't justify today's stock prices without looking at profits into the 21st century." And this argument could be also applied to the valuation investors have placed on leading Internet company stocks.

But, quite apart from the market's evaluation, the strategic record of the past 20 years demonstrates the need for companies to attend to long-term and short-term issues at the same time. Business history is replete with examples of companies such as General Motors, IBM, and Sears in the United States, Michelin in France, and Philips in the Netherlands that were once brilliantly successful in producing short-term results but failed to consider long-term changes in their markets and competition. The opposite can also be true. In the early 1990s, CEO Richard Ferris's failed vision for Allegis Corporation (as he renamed United Airlines) as a full-service travel company was conceptually sound, but it collapsed in part because of his failure to deal with the immediate problems of poor financial performance. Many "dot.com" ventures have had the right long-term vision but have stumbled in their handling of short-term problems of production costs and consumer marketing.

In all these cases, an either/or strategy failed. To succeed, executives need both a long-term perspective to give vision and relevance to future strategy and short-term attention to the immediate problems that might otherwise derail the strategy.

SO WHAT SHOULD WE DO NOW?

The central message of this chapter is twofold. First, a major reason for the erratic history of strategic planning has been management's futile search for a single strategy formula. And, second, if we are to get the best out of strategic planning, we must recognize that it requires a sustained commitment, an understanding of its complexity, and a harnessing of strategic opposites. This final point has been articulated in various ways by a variety of authors. Richard Pascale has written a book on "how the smartest companies use conflict to stay ahead,"[11] avoiding balance and the middle ground, cultivating creative tension. Thomas Stewart has described the "Nine Dilemmas Leaders

Face,"[12] and Percy Barnevik, former CEO of ABB (Asea Brown Boveri), made a positive virtue out of three "contradictions" in his company's strategy:

> We want to be global and local, big and small, radically decentralized with centralized reporting and control. If we resolve these contradictions, we create organizational advantage.[13]

If strategic planning is to continue to make the contribution to corporate success that it can, we need to move further and faster toward a holistic, both/and approach to these (and other) interlinked elements of strategy. It is not, I think, a matter of *balancing these opposites,* for balancing suggests an equilibrium, a middle-of-the-road strategy, an equal pursuit of the two poles. *Harnessing the power of opposites* better conveys the idea I have in mind. We examine each pole in turn to determine what power it can bring to bear on the strategic issues we face, and then harness that power to help drive the overall business strategy.

The question then arises: What should we do to get the full benefit of strategic planning? This examination of past erratic history conveys at least four cautionary messages to us:

1. *Strategic planning is not a "sometime" thing: it cannot be turned on and off like a faucet and still be effective.* Strategy requires and deserves a long-term commitment. The "on again/off again" approach of the past 20 years has to stop. This is not to say that the process should be frozen for all time, that no improvement in the methodology should be allowed—although an argument can be made that we have all the methodology we need, if we would but use it effectively! However, we need to make a long-term commitment to strategic planning, and stabilize the situation so that no longer will *Business Week* or *Long Range Planning* feel compelled to report yet another death (or rebirth) of strategic planning.

2. *Any strategy that aims to be sustainable over the long haul requires the harnessing of "opposite forces."* Attention to one force while neglecting its opposite will, inevitably, lead to a deficiency and, ultimately, disruption, in the organization's performance.

3. *Focus less on the process, more on the creative thinking, the strategic capability, that it should generate.* To this extent Mintzberg was right: most managers are overly enamored of neat processes: strategy-by-the-numbers. But the creative process at the heart of good strategy development is not that tidy. What we need is a process that is sufficiently tight to give structure to our thinking, but sufficiently loose to give fullest expression to our intuition and imagination.

4. *"Beware the next big thing."* Predictably, new methodologies will be developed, and touted as the next big thing, as TQM, reengineering, core competencies and shareholder value have been in the past, and as market migration analysis and knowledge management are currently. What we need to recognize is that these and other methodologies are

not substitutes for strategic planning; they are part of it and must be viewed as such. It is always a mistake to adopt a new methodology indiscriminately, without tailoring it to the needs and culture of the organization. But the worst mistake of all would be to junk strategic planning—yet again—in the belief that the "new new" methodology is the magic formula we have all along been seeking.

NOTES

1. In "The State of Strategic Thinking," an article in the *London Economist* (May 23, 1987).

2. On the cover of *Business Week* (August 26, 1996).

3. In "The State of Strategic Thinking," an article in the *London Economist* (May 23, 1987).

4. Andrew S. Grove, *Only the Paranoid Survive: How to Exploit the Crisis Points that Challenge Every Company and Career* (New York: Currency Doubleday, 1996).

5. Quoted in *Fortune* (March 7, 1994).

6. *Long Range Planning* (October 1992), 25(5).

7. "The View from IBM: Lou Gerstner Does Have a Vision," *Business Week* (October 30, 1995).

8. See, for example, Henry Mintzberg, "The Design School: Reconsidering the Basic Premises of Strategic Management," *Strategic Management Journal* (1990), 11: 171–195; and, H. Igor Ansoff, Critique of Henry Mintzberg's "The Design School: Reconsidering the Basic Premises of Strategic Management," *Strategic Management Journal* (1991), 12: 449–461.

9. Ian Wilson, *The New Rules of Corporate Conduct: Rewriting the Social Charter* (Westport, CT: Quorum Books, 2000).

10. "Yes, You Can Manage Long Term," *Fortune* (November 21, 1988).

11. Richard Tanner Pascale, *Managing on the Edge* (New York: Touchstone Books, 1990).

12. In *Fortune* (March 18, 1996).

13. Interview in the *Harvard Business Review* (March/April 1991).

About the Authors

Julia Balogun is a lecturer in the strategic management group at Cranfield School of Management in the United Kingdom. Her academic specialties are strategic transformation and the management of organizational change, in particular, culture and managerial cognition during the formulation and implementation of change. As a consultant, Dr. Balogun works with both senior and middle managers on issues of strategy and change in their organizations. Her publications include the book *Exploring Strategic Change* (Englewood Cliffs, NJ: Prentice-Hall, 1999). E-mail: j.balogun@cranfield.ac.uk.

Michael Beer is Cahners-Rabb Professor of Business Administration at the Harvard Business School, where his research and teaching have been in the areas of organization effectiveness, human resource management, and organizational change. Prior to joining the Harvard faculty, Dr. Beer was Director of Organization Research and Development at Corning, Inc. Among the books he has authored is the award-winning *The Critical Path to Corporate Renewal* (Boston: Harvard Business School Press, 1990), written with Russell A. Eisenstat and Bert Spector. Professor Beer consults with many Fortune 500 companies and recently founded, with Russell A. Eisenstat, the Center for Organizational Fitness (orgfitness.com). E-mail: mbeer@hbs.edu.

Barbara Bigelow is Associate Professor of Management at Clark University where she teaches business and corporate strategy. Professor Bigelow, who received her Ph.D. from MIT's Sloan School of Management, conducts research in strategic management in health care. She is coeditor of *Health Care Management Review,* a journal with a wide readership among both healthcare managers and researchers. Recently elected to a five-year leadership position in the Academy of Management's Health Care Division, Professor Bigelow has published in a number of academic and practitioner journals.

H. Kurt Christensen is Visiting Professor of Management at Georgia State University, having previously taught at Northwestern's Kellogg Graduate

School of Management and Purdue's Krannert School. Dr. Christensen's research into the strategic determinants of corporate performance is currently focused on the effective analysis of potentially synergistic strategic decisions and on the managerial implications of a resource-based view of strategy. He has also consulted and taught in executive development programs in the United States, Europe, Latin America, and Asia. E-mail: mgthkc@langate.gsu.edu.

David J. Collis is a visiting associate professor at the Yale University School of Management. Formerly an associate professor in business, government, and competition at the Harvard Graduate School of Business Administration, Professor Collis specializes in corporate strategy and global competition, and is the author of the recent book *Corporate Strategy* (with Professor Cynthia Montgomery). His current research project is an international comparison of the role of the corporate office in large multibusiness corporations. His work has been frequently published in the *Harvard Business Review, Strategic Management Journal, European Management Journal,* and in a number of books including, *Managing the Multibusiness Company, International Competitiveness,* and *Beyond Free Trade.* He is currently a consultant to several large U.S. and European corporations and is on the Advisory Boards of Ocean Spray and WebCT. E-mail: David.Collis@Yale.edu.

George S. Day is the Geoffrey T. Boisi Professor and Director of the Huntsman Center for Global Competition at the Wharton School of the University of Pennsylvania. He was formerly Executive Director of the Marketing Science Institute. His most recent books are *The Market-Driven Organization* (New York: Free Press, 1999) and *Wharton on Managing Emerging Technologies* (New York: John Wiley & Sons, 2000, coeditor with Paul Schoemaker).

Irene M. Duhaime holds the Carl R. Zwerner Chair of Entrepreneurship and Family Business and is Professor of Management in the J. Mack Robinson College of Business at Georgia State University. Dr. Duhaime has extensive experience researching family business, entrepreneurship, and strategic management. She served for three years as a judge for the *Memphis Business Journal's* Entrepreneur of the Year and Small Business of the Year Awards. Other research interests include diversification, acquisition, and divestment of business units, and business turnaround. She has published in *Academy of Management Journal, Academy of Management Review, Strategic Management Journal, Journal of Management,* and others, and presented at the national and international meetings of the Academy of Management and the Strategic Management Society. E-mail: MGTIMD@langate.gsu.edu. Web site: http://www .gsu.edu/~wwwsmg.

Russell A. Eisenstat is the President of the Center for Organizational Fitness (www.orgfitness.com); its mission is to help organizations become fit to compete, a process that aligns their operations with their strategy and increases their capacity for continuous renewal and learning. He is also a Senior Organizational

Fellow at McKinsey & Co. Formerly a member of the faculty of the Harvard Business School, his research and consulting have focused on strategy implementation, the management of large scale organizational change and innovation, strategic human resource management, and the design of complex organizations. He is coauthor, with Michael Beer and Bert Spector, of the award-winning book, *The Critical Path to Corporate Renewal* (Boston: Harvard Business School Press, 1990). E-mail: REisenstat@orgfitness.com.

Liam Fahey, the coeditor of *The Portable MBA in Strategy,* is an adjunct professor of strategic management at Babson College, a visiting professor of strategic management at Cranfield School of Management in the United Kingdom, and a consultant to a number of leading U.S. and European firms. Dr. Fahey has authored or edited eight books on management and over 40 articles and book chapters. His two most recent books are *Learning from the Future* with Robert M. Randall (New York: John Wiley & Sons, 1998) and *Competitors* (New York: John Wiley & Sons, 1999). E-mail: LFahey95@aol.com.

Pankaj Ghemawat is the Jaime and Josefina Chua Tiampo Professor of Business Administration at Harvard University's Graduate School of Business Administration. After receiving his Ph.D. in Business Economics from the university, he was a consultant with McKinsey & Company in London before returning to Harvard where he currently teaches the elective course, Globalization and Strategy. Professor Ghemawat's books include *Commitment* (New York: Free Press, 1991), *Games Businesses Play* (MIT Press, 1997), and *Strategy and the Business Landscape* (Reading, MA: Addison Wesley Longman, 1999). He serves as the Chair of Harvard's Ph.D. program in Business Economics; on the editorial boards of the *Journal of Economics and Management Strategy,* the *Strategic Management Journal,* and the *Journal of Management and Governance;* and on the advisory boards of Enron Corporation and of the Instituto de Altos Estudios Empresariales (Buenos Aires). E-mail: pghemawat@HBS.edu.

John H. Grant, formerly the Robert Kirby Professor of Strategic Management in the Katz School of Business at the University of Pittsburgh, is now developing software and pharmaceutical services for the offices of physicians and related business-to-business e-commerce. Dr. Grant's research interests include the management of diversified firms and the factors that improve organizational learning. He graduated from the Harvard Business School and has served as the chairperson of the Business Policy and Strategy Division of the Academy of Management. His articles have been published in the *Strategic Management Journal, Academy of Management Review,* and *Long Range Planning.* E-mail: GrantJH@aol.com.

Anil K. Gupta is a Distinguished Scholar-Teacher and Professor of Strategy and International Business at the Robert H. Smith School of Business, University of Maryland at College Park. Dr. Gupta is a recipient of the 1991 Glueck

Best Paper Award in Business Policy and Strategy from the Academy of Management and a two-time winner of the Allen J. Krowe Award for Excellence in Teaching from the University of Maryland. During 2000, he is spending his sabbatical at Stanford University as a visiting professor in the Stanford Technology Ventures Program in Palo Alto, California. His coauthored book, *World Wise: Building the Global Corporation of Tomorrow,* will be published by Harvard Business School Press this year. E-mail: agupta@rhsmith.umd.edu.

Ellen R. Hart, a vice president with Gemini Consulting, has consulted for 20 years with hundreds of companies to enable large-scale change. Dr. Hart specializes in organization design, executive team alignment, and change leadership. Along with chapters in quarterlies and books, her articles have appeared in *Executive Excellence, Management Review, Strategic Leadership,* and *Transformation Magazine.* E-mail: ehart@usa.geminiconsulting.com.

Veronica Hope-Hailey is a Senior Lecturer in Strategic Human Resource Management in the Strategic Management Group at Cranfield School of Management, Cranfield University and a Visiting Fellow at London Business School. Dr. Hope-Hailey's areas of special interest are HR strategy and organizational change. She is a founding member of the Research Team for the Leading Edge Forum, a consortium of companies that includes Hewlett-Packard, Glaxo-Wellcome, Citibank, British Telecom, and Philip Morris Corporation. She has published two books *Exploring Strategic Change* (Englewood Cliffs, NJ: Prentice-Hall, 1999) and *Strategic Human Resource Management* (Oxford University Press, 1999). E-mail: v.hope-hailey@cranfield.ac.uk.

Majorie A. Lyles is Professor of International Strategic Management at Indiana University Kelley School of Business and the Kimball Faculty Fellow. In fall 1997, she was the Arthur Andersen Distinguished Visiting Professor at Cambridge University (England). Dr. Lyles consults with government agencies and firms interested in organizational learning, foreign direct investment, joint ventures, technology development, and higher education. She has authored over 70 articles on strategic management, and her research has appeared in such journals as *Administrative Science Quarterly, Academy of Management Review, Strategic Management Journal, Long Range Planning,* and the *Journal of Management Studies.* E-mail: mlyles@iupui.edu.

John F. Mahon is a Professor of Management at Boston University's School of Management and a consultant and executive educator specializing in corporate political strategy. The author or coauthor of over 80 articles and 60 teaching cases, he has won numerous awards for his teaching. E-mail: jmahon@bu.edu.

V.K. Narayanan is the Stubbs Professor of Strategy and Entrepreneurship at Drexel University. His most recent book is *Managing Technology and Innovation for Competitive Advantage* (Prentice-Hall Longman). He is also the author of *Macroenvironmental Analysis* (with Liam Fahey), and *Organization Theory* (with Raghu Nath). His expertise is in macroenvironmental analysis, management of technology, strategic thinking, and strategy implementation. E-mail: vnarayanan@ukans.edu.

Michael E. Porter is the C. Roland Christensen Professor of Business Administration at the Harvard Business School and a leading authority on competitive strategy and international competitiveness. Professor Porter has authored 16 books and over 60 articles. His books on strategy include *Competitive Strategy: Techniques for Analyzing Industries and Competitors* (New York: Free Press, 1980, 53rd printing), *Competitive Advantage: Creating and Sustaining Superior Performance* (New York: Free Press, 1985, 32nd printing), and *On Competition* (Boston, MA: Harvard Business School Press, 1998). His 1990 book, *The Competitive Advantage of Nations* (New York: Free Press, 1990), develops a new theory of how nations, states, and regions compete, and has guided economic policy throughout the world. In 1994, Professor Porter founded the Initiative for a Competitive Inner City, a nonprofit organization formed to catalyze business development in distressed inner cities across the United States. E-mail: mporter@hbs.edu.

C.K. Prahalad, the Harvey C. Fruehauf Professor of Business Administration at the University of Michigan Business School in Ann Arbor, specializes in corporate strategy and the role and value added of top management in large, diversified, multinational corporations. His most recent book, *Competing for the Future* (Boston, MA: Harvard Business School Press, 1994), coauthored with Gary Hamel and printed in fourteen languages, was named the Best Selling Business Book of the Year in 1994. *Harvard Business Review* awarded McKinsey Prizes to Dr. Prahalad for three articles: "The End of Corporate Imperialism," coauthored with Kenneth Lieberthal (1998); "The Core Competence of the Corporation," coauthored with Gary Hamel (1990); and "Strategic Intent," also coauthored with Gary Hamel (1989). Professor Prahalad has consulted with the top management of many leading companies, such as Ahlstrom, AT&T, Cargill, Citicorp, Eastman Chemical, Oracle, Philips, Quantum, Revlon, Steelcase, and Unilever. He serves on the Board of Directors of NCR Corporation.

Nandini Rajagopalan is Associate Professor of Strategy at the Marshall School of Business, University of Southern California. Her research on strategic change, executive compensation, and CEO succession has appeared in several journals including the *Strategic Management Journal, Academy of Management Journal, Academy of Management Review,* and *Advances in Strategic Management.* She is a member of the *Academy of Management Journal* editorial board and participates in executive education programs for the healthcare, utilities, aerospace, telecommunication, and real estate industries. E-mail: nandini.rajagopalan@marshall.usc.edu.

Robert M. Randall is coeditor of both the first and this second edition of *The Portable MBA in Strategy*. Another recent book by Mr. Randall and his coeditor, Dr. Liam Fahey, is *Learning from the Future: Competitive Foresight Scenarios* (New York: John Wiley & Sons, 1998). It is a guide for using scenario planning to ready companies for industry and market discontinuity and new customer needs. With offices in San Francisco and New York, Mr. Randall writes and edits books, articles, and white papers about strategic management. A former Time Inc. writer/editor, he held staff positions in several Fortune 500 companies. E-mail: Randall_Publishing@compuserve.com.

Jeffrey Sampler is Associate Professor of Information Management and Strategy at London Business School. He is currently studying the Internet as a driving force in industry and business reconfiguration.

Ian Wilson, Principal of Wolf Enterprises in San Rafael, California, is a specialist in strategic management and scenario planning. After a 25-year career with General Electric, as a member of the company's strategic planning staff and as a public policy adviser to the chief executive officer, he became a senior management consultant with SRI International working on global strategy and scenario planning projects. A frequent lecturer and writer on management topics, his most recent book is *The New Rules of Corporate Conduct: Rewriting the Social Charter* (Westport, CT: Quorum Books, 2000). E-mail: Jason415xx@aol.com.

Index

403

Lightning Source UK Ltd.
Milton Keynes UK
17 November 2009

146388UK00001B/27/A

9 780471 197089